RUN O' THE MILL BISHOP

The author on the Palace lawns, Wells, 1985

RUN O' THE MILL BISHOP

A *Countryman's Peregrinations*
with the Church

———

JOHN BICKERSTETH

Sometime Bishop of Bath & Wells
and Clerk of the Closet to
Her Majesty the Queen

Cappella Archive

Cappella Archive : 2005

British Library Cataloguing-in-Publication Data
A catalogue record for this book is
available from the British Library

ISBN 1-902918-27-4

A cloth-bound edition of this book is available from:
Cappella Archive : Foley Terrace: Great Malvern : WR14 4RQ
ISBN 1-902918-21-5
Printed and bound by Antony Rowe Ltd, Eastbourne

By the same author
jointly with Robert W. Dunning
Clerks of the Closet in the Royal Household
Alan Sutton 1992

Edited by the author
The Bickersteth Diaries 1914–18
Leo Cooper 1995
2nd edition 1996; 3rd edition 1998

Contents

Preface

My warm gratitude goes to:

Jonathon Porritt, CBE, co-founder and joint director of the charity *Forum for the Future*, for very kindly writing the Foreword. In the ten years we have known each other since I joined the *Forum*, I have been immensely impressed by the religious drive behind his 'sustainability' watchword. A recent hopeful article in *Green Futures*, our magazine, says that maybe right now in thousands of spiritually-minded people the world over we are seeing 'the start of a profound process of connection with sustainable development ideas'. Again: 'vast numbers of those who have faith seek to reflect it in personal action for the benefit of others', or 'their bias to the poor strongly challenges the values of the market and the McDonaldization of both business and society'. Jonathon's vision lies at the heart of all his thinking, and I thank God for him. It is a privilege to print his perceptive words.

Humphrey Stone, book architect and neighbour, without whose editing and designing help this book would not have been brought to bed in the way it has.

Nicholas Smart, Devonshire history don, for encouraging me to start; for reading every word as I sent him the chapters over fifteen months, and returning them with helpful comments and suggestions.

Alan MacDermot, computer-buff *extraordinaire* for coming at the drop of a hat to my study from his home half-a-mile away, and patiently sorting out the computer contortions I create for myself.

Elizabeth Birch, Tisbury resident and Oxford graduate a little senior to me, for her painstaking proof-reading. We discovered to our amazement that we were once fellow teenagers at parties in the early 1930s.

David Byram-Wigfield, the creator and *persona* of Cappella Archive and my publisher. Since I read his letter in *The Times* about 'Book on Demand' publishing, my subsequent contact with his technological skill and phenomenal patience has made the work an eye-opening exercise and great fun into the bargain.

J.M.B.

Foreword

In 1989, I contributed a short Foreword to a marvellous book by Ian Bradley, the Church of Scotland minister, which went by the resounding title of *God is Green*. I hope it's not inappropriate to quote here from that earlier effort on my part to get to grips with my own confusion about the spiritual dimension of today's continuing ecological crisis:

> In any objective analysis of the root causes of today's ecological crisis, there are many who still incline to the opinion that the Christian Church has always been (and still is) part of the problem rather than part of the solution. They feel this despite the fact that many thousands of Christians have been in the vanguard, as individuals, in befriending and defending the Earth.
>
> If it is the destiny of this generation to become stewards of God's Earth (and it had better be, for we are the last generation likely to be given such a choice) then Christianity is going to have to be comprehensively reinterpreted, and its long-suppressed sacramental vision sung out anew. We do not need to invent a new religion, but Christianity assuredly needs to rediscover some of its own very old and resolutely Earth-bound wisdom.

One of those Christians most prominently 'in the vanguard' has been John Bickersteth. He is, by his own enthusiastic account, an up- front, card-carrying flag-waving environmentalist. Though it was only on his 'retirement' in 1987 that conservation as such became the principal focus of his redoubtable energies, there runs a potent green thread through the whole of this very English life, right back to his childhood in the Weald of Kent.

In 1990, he persuaded the Dean of Salisbury Cathedral to let him stage a three-day Creation Festival in that splendid setting. I was invited to speak at it, and spent a whole day there, sitting in on stirring events, uplifted by sculptures, paintings, poems and drama; moved at the transformation of the Cathedral and its Close into a celebration of the natural world, and of the creative purposefulness that informs that natural world.

As a tree-hugging Christian, for whom every life-form is indeed in the words of Meister Eckhart 'a word of God'; a worshipper not of nature herself but of the divine in every facet of the natural world, I'm obviously a real sucker for celebratory festivals of this kind.

These days there are many of them everywhere, but this particular one meant much to me. I was somewhat weighed down by the unyeilding secularism that dominated Friends of the Earth culture; Salisbury that week-end happened to be my final public event as Director, and it was the first time I had met John Bickersteth. His inspirational earthiness went a long way to giving me rather more hope for the future.

As chance would have it, two letters arrived on my desk as I was working, more than twenty years later, on this Foreword. The first provided a transcript of a Lecture given in July 2004 by Archbishop Rowan Williams. In it he was concentrating on 'what the earth can sustain'. Though theologically challenged by his trademark erudition, I couldn't help but write 'Yes' in the margin against this extract:

> Resisting the dominance of secularism is not primarily a political struggle for the rights of religious organisations, but a different sort of political battle; a battle against the reductionism that diminishes both the world and the mind or reason. The Church's contribution has to consist not primarily or exclusively in public lobbying, though that is important, but in its showing forth . . . the truth of creation's relation with the creator and especially the rôle of human work and thought within that.

Hot on the heels of the Archbishop's exhortation to let loose *homo eucharisticus*, that species of human being 'defined by communion rather than consumption' on today's ill-starred *homo economicus*, came a brochure from James Jones, the Bishop of Liverpool, announcing the new Academy of St Francis of Assisi in the heart of the Kensington regeneration area of the city, for children of all faiths and none. Part of the Academy's mission will be 'to develop and encourage a concern and respect for the environment and a sustainable way of living'.

That is of course exactly what we are trying to achieve through Forum for the Future, of which John has been a supporter almost from the start; a fact which makes me all the more delighted that he should have chosen the name of our charity as the title for the final chapter of this book.

I see these things therefore as important and welcome signs of change, long process as it is, on the part of today's church leaders and, if that proves to be the case, I have no doubt that tomorrow's more Earth-bound Christians will look back on the lives of church-men as different from each other as Ian Bradley, John Bickersteth, James Jones, and the then Archbishop of Canterbury, and wonder why it was that more people were not moved by their commitment and wisdom in celebrating God's purpose through creation.

Feast Day of St Francis of Assisi
4th October 2004

Jonathan Porritt

Author's Note

The quotations at the beginning of each chapter have no particular relevance to the text, but everything to do with the beauty and wonder of the natural world. For *New Growth* and *Forum for the Future*, the *alpha* and *omega* of the book, I have gone only to *The Bible*, where suitable passages to choose from are numerous. For the thirteen other chapters in the middle, my second quotations, by kind permission of the executrix of the Nicolson estate, are all from *The Land*, a Virgilian-style poem written in 1926 by Vita Sackville-West of Sissinghurst Castle in the Weald of Kent. I fell in love with the work when I was living in the Weald and it happened to be a set book at school.

I hope these gems will remind the reader that God's creation, the agricultural scene and the round of the seasons are very much at the heart of things for me. By a similar whim, the horticultural headings of the chapters in Part One carry on the idea.

J.M.B.

New Growth

In the beginning God created the heaven and the earth.
Genesis 1.1

Christ is the image of the unseen God, and the firstborn of all creation.
Colossians 1.15

BY 1921 my Bickersteth grandparents had been living for five years in Meister Omers, 16 The Precincts, Canterbury, a large flint and stone 13th century house fifty yards from the east end of the cathedral. At the end of August my mother and father arrived from their London home for her fourth 'confinement'. She loved the house, as we four children later came to; but she was well aware too that, whereas we had one maid and a nanny in London, my grandmother Ella still had her super 'Ninny' (who had been employed for her and Sam's second baby in 1884, and was to stay with the family for sixty years), plus five living-in staff, not to speak of a chauffeur and gardener. It was all a great deal more comfortable a place than our house in London in which to have a baby.

I was born in the Queen Elizabeth Room there on 6 September, and from soon afterwards my grandfather[1] had a framed photograph of me on his desk, changing it every year or so as I grew, and subscribing it very grandly 'John of Canterbury.' It says a lot for my older siblings that they never felt (or at least evinced) any jealousy about the 'title', nor did grandfather ever display any favouritism of which I was aware. He had certainly got it right that for ever after I would think of myself as part of the place. Add to this the fact that, from well before that September day in 1921 right up to my Uncle Burgon's death in the spring of 1979, there were Bickersteths living in Canterbury; and I am fairly sure that for me never a year passed (including the war years, as I shall show) without my going there.

Meister Omers was marvellous for children, with its Long Gallery for hilarious games, the spiral stone staircase, the upstairs passage to which grown-ups never seemed to penetrate because it was where the servants lived, and lots of wonderful nooks and crannies for Hide and Seek. There was also 'cook', always 'cook'; probably there were several in succession, but our treatment from them was

---

1. He was Residentiary Canon and Librarian of Canterbury Cathedral 1916–1936

invariably the same, in that whoever she was delighted in spoiling us ten grandchildren (the three married sons and their children often stayed) with juicy titbits or drinks of ginger beer from big stone jars, on our clandestine kitchen visits. The hall boasted an organ, and at it grandmother played the hymn every weekday for Family Prayers after breakfast. I can see, as if it was yesterday, the servants filing in to sit opposite us; then grandfather, gown and all, would sweep in from the study with Bible and prayer book; his departure from the table a little earlier was obviously the signal to the staff that we had finished eating. To pray, we all turned to kneel at our own chairs, so it was a great game for my brother and me to squint round and see whether any new member of the domestic staff had a specially big bottom, and whether the younger maids were giggling.

Because of grandfather's increasing deafness he disappointingly became a rather remote figure, but I remember his wonderful smile and the great games he used to have with us in his study, where there was a step ladder to reach the top shelves, and the game was to collect as many chocolate drops as we could from their perches on the really high (?dusty) books, with gales of laughter if we did not find them all. My memories of Meister Omers are very happy ones.

The Dean of Canterbury then was George Bell, later Bishop of Chichester; it was he who in 1928 devised, as a way of raising interest in and money for the cathedral, a brand new organisation called 'The Friends of Canterbury Cathedral'. He could not have begun to know then that his initiative would be gradually copied by many thousands of people responsible for churches, historic houses, museums, gardens and so on all over the English-speaking world. For my part, as a seven-year-old, I clearly remember being taken along by grandfather, early on in the infant life of the Friends, maybe even in that year of their foundation, to join the Junior Friends, which I imagine was formed so that local children could become keen about this great House of God on their doorstep. I know I proudly displayed for many years a blue and silver badge, and the subscription was presumably paid by my father until I started taking it out of my pocket money. So I proudly claim that I have been a Friend for nearly eighty years, and no one can gainsay me, as the records were all lost in the Blitz.

We could relate with our blind and very bright grandmother

better than we could with our kindly deaf grandfather. The afflic-
tion hit her in 1928, when I was only seven, and so I do not really
remember her before it. But her mind remained sharper than ever,
and the highlight of those years was their Golden Wedding in 1931,
much more notable an event than these are now, when everyone
lives so much longer. My brother Edward was then sixteen years old
and at Haileybury; he made the speech for the toast, as we sat
round the long oak five-leafed table for lunch, the brothers all in
morning coats. This fine table eventually came to Rosemary and me
in Liverpool and later in Wells, where it worked very hard indeed,
and was bought by the Church Commissioners, when we left, to
remain in the Palace, a final resting-place for it of which the whole
family much approved.

I was back in Canterbury in 1935 for Julian, my first cousin, and
me to be confirmed on April 5th in the Chapel of Our Lady Undercroft in the cathedral. How anyone justified such a private confirmation, just two teenage boys and their families taking up a busy
bishop's time, was not a worry for me; it was simply part of belonging to Canterbury. We were confirmed by the greatly-loved Alfred
Rose who had just been made Bishop of Dover, a post he was to
hold for twenty-seven years; he and his wife Lois became lifelong
friends. Geoffrey Fisher[2] made him the first Bishop to the Forces,
on top of his Canterbury diocesan responsibilities, and he came to
Holland in the bitter winter of 1944 to take confirmations for us in
the British Liberation Army, with whom I was then serving. Our
regimental padre thought he was not very good at it, and against
my better judgment persuaded me, twenty-year-old officer that I
was, to tell the bishop as much. It speaks volumes for Alfred's Christian charity that he took my suggestions seriously, thanked me for
them, and I heard later varied his style effectively right away. Partly
perhaps out of my bad conscience at such cheek, I took to writing to
Alfred on the anniversary of my confirmation, and kept up the
practice until he died nearly thirty years later. When I became a
bishop his generous excitement knew no bounds.

My star 'Canterbury year' was 1941: I lived there on and off for
six months, the only time in my life that I have done more than stay
a few nights in the city. It was the army that did it. I was called to
the colours there during January from my October 1939 enlistment

2. Archbishop of Canterbury 1944–1961

in the Royal Warwickshire Regiment, achieving the transfer I had asked for to the regiment of my choice: The Buffs was one of the famous county regiments, the 3rd of Foot no less, the Royal East Kent Regiment. I had Jelf cousins currently in it; and a Jelf uncle, my mother's brother Gordon, was killed with them in the Great War. As a private soldier I lived in the old Victorian Chaucer Barracks at the top of Military Road for six weeks. From there I was sent to Wiltshire for officer training, and returned to Canterbury on 16th May, extremely proud of myself as a 2nd Lieutenant.

Burgon was there to my great delight, and would often arrange for us to go out together for a meal with one of his friends. These included the aged Cosmo Gordon Lang[3]; sad and frail as I found him, I was mightily impressed to be sitting down to dinner with him in the Old Palace. There were also superb social evenings in St Martin's Priory, the Bishop of Dover's lovely house at the bottom of Sandwich Hill. Every Sunday of the war Lois Rose (mother of four boys, so she knew all about family life, and how much servicemen and women were missing it), invited young officers, pretty WRNSs and VADs, anyone she felt like befriending, for an evening meal, games, and dancing to gramophone records or sometimes to Lois herself at her Steinway Grand; she was a fine pianist. Furthermore her 'meal' was a really good supper conjured up from somewhere for fifteen or more of us; we guessed that the ingredients tended to come from Fortnum and Mason's, as Lois was a Guinness before she was married, so money was no object to this kind and generous woman. I was very glad, twenty years on, that our two small sons were able to experience her hospitality in the house she and Alfred retired to on St Stephen's Green, where they had a gypsy caravan in the garden, the first the boys had ever seen. The Roses were larger than life Canterbury characters, and it was a privilege to know and love them.

Those months were also a unique time for church-going in 'my' city. It was only six years on from my confirmation there, and five from my mother's death which, as I shall show later, 'confirmed' my believing in an indelible way; so I revelled in getting to the cathedral or to the ancient St Martin's. The latter is often claimed to be the site of the oldest church in England, quite simply the place on the edge of the Saxon settlement where St Augustine and his monks

3. Archbishop of Canterbury 1928–1942

stopped on that first journey from their landing place at Reculver in 597 AD. The holy little building was inspiring; and grandfather's grave was and is just outside the east end of the sanctuary, the same plot where the bodies of his wife and two of his sons would later lie, so again my family tie to Canterbury was strengthened whenever I received the sacrament a few yards away.

To hear stimulating sermons I went to the cathedral. Dr Hewlett Johnson, The Red Dean (so-called because of his openly-expressed 'Bolshevik' views) early in the war had the entire nave floor covered with soil four feet deep, brought in by horses and tip-up farm carts; the idea was to lessen the damage when bombs rained in through the roof, but none in fact fell on the main structure; it was the Cathedral Library which was almost demolished. Fire bombs of course in their hundreds hit the building, and (as at St Paul's Cathedral in London) were bravely dealt with by the Cathedral firefighters, or the Local Defence Volunteers. Long before the war had ended the cathedral architect was so concerned about the weight of that damp and by then mouldy earth that he persuaded the Dean to bring all the carts back again to remove it. The Dean was of course vindicated in his extreme and very unpopular pro Soviet stance by the entry of Russia on the Allied side once Hitler invaded it. Very soon after that turning-point, I heard him preach at length on 'The new woman in the new world'.

'He wanted', I spelt out in my diary, "to see every woman get equal wages with men, every woman relieved of the drudgery of the home by having washing and cooking done communally. How enriched our society would be by having all those cultured women free to be themselves, how much finer would be the home where men and women were absolutely equal." It was certainly amazing,' I wrote, 'to hear the Dean of Canterbury propounding these views from the pulpit of Canterbury Cathedral'. But it has to be said that in the Canterbury blitz later on, the Red Dean was invariably at the forefront of the rescue workers digging people out of the wreckage of their homes.

Having gratefully survived both that bombing, more in Dover a few months later, and then the Normandy invasion, I marked my demobilisation leave in August 1945 with a motoring tour (we hired a car), with Mary and 'Ted'; the abbreviation dated from his Oxford years in the 1930s, and stuck He was home on leave from Africa, and had just got engaged to Elspeth Cameron. Of course we included Canterbury in our travels, and I have a happy photograph of grandmother, the 'uncles'[4] and us three outside 5 The Forrens. The Dean and Chapter had made this charming little cottage available for her, when she came home to Canterbury after the war, her Dover Road house having been entirely demolished by a direct hit,with no one in it, back in 1942. No.5 is just off the Green Court, and immediately behind the archdeaconry to which, also in 1942, Julian had moved on his appointment by William Temple[5] to be Archdeacon of Maidstone, and a Residentiary Canon like his father before him.

Grandmother remained consistently interested in us all and our various doings; in fact it seemed perfectly natural to sit down in adult life and write to tell her what we were about; so much so that when forty years later an academic friend, Dr Nicholas Smart, agreed with Ted that he could do some work on the Diary which she had put together in World War 2, he aptly decided (in view of all our letters to her in it) to call the two volumes 'Dear Grandmother'. After the pattern of Victorian matrons, and perhaps also because of the death of her fifth son Morris on the Somme in 1916, she always wore black; I literally never saw her even in a shade of dark grey in the twenty odd years during which I would have noticed such things. But she had a buoyantly cheerful spirit, and after Ninny got too old to be her companion (and indeed to be her eyes), she had several faithful successors who would not have stayed as they did unless they had enjoyed her company.

She died at home late on St Andrew's Day 1954, my father having given her the sacrament that morning, when she was very well and totally *compos mentis*. She was 96. I brought Rosemary to the funeral, she and I having become engaged a fortnight earlier, after which we had agreed a date for us to go to Canterbury so that I could introduce her all round; instead, my fiancée's first experience of her hundreds of new relations was this family gathering for the funeral. But I need not have worried: Rosemary came through it with flying colours, not least due to Uncle Julian being his usual gallant self and taking her under his wing as the daughter of his old House friend

---

4. That was how the grandchildren affectionately described Julian and Burgon, her third and fourth sons.
5. Archbishop of Canterbury 1942–44

and exact contemporary, Dodge Cleveland-Stevens.

After the funeral I took Rosemary for her first visit into Meister Omers, which, since 1936 when my grandparents had left it on retirement, had been a boarding house for the King's School. The housemaster could not have been more welcoming, showed Rosemary the room where I was born, for seventeen years or so already a dormitory for some of his boys. I found it most satisfying that a housemaster, his family, and fifty schoolboys, were now living in the centuries-old building which had been home to one family and its staff when I was young.

Just outside the gate of No 16, we ran into Mr Wood, my grandparents' old chauffeur. It was great to connect again, and I reminded him how one day in the early 1930s when he was giving Mary and me a drive in grandfather's car (we had no car at home, so 'a drive' was a real thrill), we persuaded him to take the Riley up to 72 m.p.h., an event so singular that I can visualize the stretch of road near Bridge now where he achieved it, and that exact top speed, of which Wood was very proud. 'Now Mister John, mind you don't tell the Master', he said as he slowed down from his fastest ever, and no small speed it was for a private car then.

As *The Times* obituary of grandmother mentioned: 'She was one of the last survivors of that small company of little girls who were photographed by Lewis Carroll'. It was the kind of activity which would raise all kinds of questions in today's climate. Dr. Charles Lutwidge Dodgson was a don at Oxford (he lived in Tom Quad, Christ Church), when young Ella's father, Sir Monier Monier-Williams, held the Boden Professorship of Sanskrit. Those photographs came my way in due course, together with a number of 2nd Editions[6] of CLD's work; 'they are of very little value', Burgon pointed out to me in the 1970s, when he decided to pass them on in accordance with his mother's wishes. Twenty-five years later, having tested the waters, we put them up for auction with Phillips of Bond Street, and they netted £25,000, which we had such fun dividing five ways round ourselves and our children.

The second post-war Lambeth Conference was in 1958, and Julian acquired (by sheer nepotism of course) two tickets in the Quire for Rosemary and me to attend the final service, at which, as the

---

6. CLD withdrew the 1st Edition very soon after publication; there are only a handful worldwide

bishops from all over the world processed in to the High Altar, and as the congregation sang:

From earth's wide bounds, from ocean's farthest coast,
Through gates of pearl streams in the countless host

I suddenly got my first real vision of the world-wide Anglican Communion. Julian also wangled us tea in the Green Court afterwards, when we met dozens of overseas bishops, as Julian the senior priest rightly felt that his young priest-nephew would be glad to do.

There have been two other major Canterbury experiences for me. The first was the 1978 Lambeth Conference, which was Donald Coggan's, and so to say 'mine' in that it was the only one during my twelve years as Bishop of Bath & Wells. Donald[7] decided that it would be for the first time totally residential, and the four hundred or so bishops were all of us accommodated in the University of Kent buildings on the edge of Canterbury. The opening service was in the cathedral, with choir and organ of course, but also (imaginatively) with a steel band; and most of the sessions of the conference were within the university campus. I was glad to be in the section on 'The Anglican Communion in the world-wide church'. The prospect of spending three hot summer weeks in theological discussion had not, I must admit, set the pulses racing, but once the eleventh Lambeth Conference began I started reminding myself that taking part in such an event was an amazing opportunity, which thousands of clergy would have welcomed unreservedly. I soon got keen over it all, especially the work in the groups, and the hundreds of informal conversations.

Julian was long dead by then (he had had a stroke at his desk when writing a sermon for St Luke's day in 1962), but this 'Lambeth' took place only a few months before Burgon's death, and he was by then very frail, in a nursing home ('prison really, though the prison officers are wonderful'). But he revelled in my 'feeding' him two Canadian bishops a night; practically all thirty of them knew 'The Warden' from their University of Toronto days, and very moving it was to see this ninety-year-old hero of theirs warming to the stimulus of the occasion, and he to their love and admiration. He had just been made a member of The Order of Canada, and they all wanted to bring him the congratulations of various mutual friends

7. Archbishop of Canterbury 1975–80

from their different corners of that large country. Doing this ferrying of Burgon's devotees, the last time I saw him, made for a lasting memory of this inspiring educationalist and leader of men.

The second memorable Canterbury happening for me in recent years was in the summer of 1982, when Pope John Paul accepted the invitation of the new archbishop Robert Runcie[8] to visit him in Canterbury. It was during General Synod Week, and the entire Synod came down to Canterbury by special train. The bishops robed, and we walked in procession from the Deanery, through the Dark Entry, past Meister Omers itself (I looked up wondering what on earth my grandparents would have made of it; not a lot, I am bound to say; but the anglo-catholic Julian would have been thrilled), and so into the great west door of the Cathedral, with the Archbishop and the Pope bringing up the rear side by side. They prayed together at the site of Becket's martyrdom. In the special service, not a eucharist alas (that must wait for the next visit), the Pope exchanged the kiss of peace with every diocesan bishop.

There was in 2001 what may be for me the last Canterbury Cathedral event that I shall attend robed: we were invited to the installation that spring of the gifted Robert Willis, Rector of Tisbury when we arrived here, as Dean; and then that autumn we stayed with him in the Deanery. Robert gave us both a totally new experience by taking us into the locked cathedral at midnight; we walked in silence, with no lights on, the floodlighting giving us plenty. We knelt in the Corona, the closest part of the cathedral to where I was born, over-awed by the stillness and the borrowed light from outside into this majestic building. How glad I am that grandfather dubbed me on that sequence of desk photographs, sentimental and pretentious as the 'title' was, 'John of Canterbury'; I certainly felt it in the darkness that night.

---

8. Archbishop of Canterbury 1980–1990

Coming On

He laid the foundations of the earth:
that it never should move at any time.
Psalm 104.5.

There is no beginning to a farmer's year,
Only recurrent patterns on a scroll
Unwinding;
The Land: Winter

ALTHOUGH Canterbury was my birthplace, London was my home from that autumn of 1921 until my father accepted a country living in 1935. We lived halfway along the top side of Warwick Square in the Duke of Westminster's Cubitt estate of fine four-story houses. Father had been Secretary of the Jerusalem and the East Mission since 1916, initially commuting up from Cobham, but London itself was obviously the answer for the work to prosper. His office and home were to be in the same building. So two years before I was born, mother gave up the country life she was so much enjoying, and the family moved to London; there was my older sister Ella, (later Kay), Edward (Ted, later on) and Mary (who was later for many of us Mairse).

From then on my rural-orientated mother had to be content with pot plants on a flat roof at the back of the house (it must have been over a single-story extension), and many window boxes, which in due course I enjoyed helping to care for. Mother loved too the visits to St James' Park, and occasionally to Kew Gardens. There were also two episcopal palace gardens where we often went, Lambeth because father had to be there a good deal due to the close links between the Archbishop of Canterbury and the Holy Land; and Fulham, the home then of the Bishop of London, who was ex officio Chairman of the J&EM Council. The unmarried Arthur Foley Winnington-Ingram was the bishop who lived there from 1901-1939; far too long in office. But as a family we all adored him; he had taken father's and mother's wedding, and kept in close touch with us, including tying the knot for my sister Kay in St Mary's Chiddingstone six weeks before the war, when he was a very old man. Those two gardens were still fully-staffed, with maybe six or seven men each; the former was within pram-pushing distance from Warwick Square, with Fulham more of an expedition, but it is that one I remember best, perhaps because it had splendid lawns for making daisy chains.

The Mission's office was on the ground floor and in the basement, in both of which the three secretaries worked; from that small base the Mission literature streamed out to the parishes of England and gradually, as father built up concern for it, all round the world. From a very early age we children folded the Mission leaflets for Good Friday, when father circulated the whole of the Anglican Communion with up-to-date information about the work; and then tied up parcels of the envelopes with which we had filled them, which is why doing up parcels is second nature to me still. He went twice to Palestine, then under the British Mandate, and the second time mother went too, so as to be able to understand better how her husband earned his living.

The whole-day Council meetings about four times a year were always held in the office, and mother gave the eight or ten members lunch upstairs in our dining-room. Not I think until our last year in London, when I was twelve or so, was I allowed to those lunches, but long before that we children would meet the council members on the stairs or wherever, and that was always fun, and I suppose in a kind of way became an important hidden influence in my life, as they were all interesting men and women from the church, education, medicine and the colonial service or Foreign Office; it says a great deal for them collectively that they left such a good impression on a young boy.

With father having no church building of his own, but travelling to other ones three weekends out of four for the Mission, mother was in charge of our churchgoing. We went mostly to the Chapel Royal in St James' Palace, as it was an easy walk, a small enough church not to be forbidding to children, and mother loved its superb music. Matins was invariably the fare; probably my mother had communion at a shortened service afterward; 'are we staying?' was a phrase I grew up with. When father had a Sunday off, we all trooped to St Peter's Ashley Gardens, a barn of a church off Victoria Street; it was badly damaged in the bombing and pulled down after the war. The incumbent was an old college friend of father's named

Schomberg, who had a considerable reputation as a preacher, so the church became something of a preaching house, the material of course far above our heads, and I have the clearest recollection of father, perhaps when I was six or seven years old, taking my hands during the long sermons and tickling them with a delectable circling motion round the palms, each hand in turn, and incredibly more-ish. Our parish church of St Gabriel's Warwick Square where I was baptised on SS Simon & Jude's Day, 28 October 1921 was too 'high church' for mother and father, and still remains a catholic stronghold, or maybe 'weakhold' today. But the Chapel Royal we all enjoyed, partly because the tall box pews, with their deep foot-high hassocks, were splendid places for small children to crawl around in, and remain unseen and mostly unheard.

London then was still subject to 'peasoupers', and while they lasted it was out of the question for us children to go to church, and indeed to leave the house at all. When conditions were right in November, down came this smelly and choking fog (the word 'smog' had not been invented) caused by the millions of coal fires. Visibility went down to a few yards, and we would peer through the nursery windows at the enveloping yellow atmosphere. I suppose we paid our first visits to the famous sights without realizing how very dirty they were.

The capital's great events, too, father and mother took trouble about our witnessing. For instance one of my earliest memories is of getting pushed to the front of the crowd one February day in 1925, a huge guardsman towering over me, and mother's watchful eye two or three rows back, for Queen Alexandra's[9] funeral procession in the snow, on its way to the Abbey along the Mall. The gun carriage for the Queen's coffin rolled silently by a few yards from me. We also went to the museums (boring places then), to Bertram Mills Circus at Olympia (spectacular), and as we got older to several London theatres, to see *Toad of Toad Hall* or *Cavalcade*, or Jean Forbes-Robertson as *Peter Pan*, or our special love in the person of Dame Sybil Thorndike, an old school friend of mother's (both their fathers had been Canons of Rochester together).

On those occasions there was the thrill of a visit backstage to see 'Aunt Sybil' (as we had always called her) in her dressing room; I remember doing this after her wonderful performance as *St. Joan*.

9. King Edward VII's widow

By the time we left London we would have chalked up during the Christmas holidays as many as six or seven West End shows to boast about to our friends, no small achievement on the part of our fairly impecunious parents; I suspect many of these jaunts were Christmas presents from kind relations and friends, as was the regular Christmas crate of Jaffa oranges from the Holy Land, and another every year of Cox's Orange Pippins from our Jelf relations in Kent.

A not so welcome element of the Christmas holidays were children's parties, always seemingly in the houses of people who even at that age we realized had much more money than we had. In retrospect I did not enjoy them much. There was one every Christmas in a big house in Grosvenor Gardens, and to this day if I bus or walk through those gardens near Victoria Station, I get that sinking feeling I used to have as the door was opened by the butler, nanny departed home, and I was being ushered by kind hosts into a huge cleared drawing-room with twenty or more other children I never seemed to know round the walls. There followed an awful succession of games I was bad at, generally including some (horror of horrors), where there was picking up sides, at which in retrospect I was invariably the last one chosen.

School, though, in London I loved. There were two, the first a PNEU[10] establishment for both sexes ten minutes walk from home. I went there for a year in 1927, and recollect only two things about it. One was a production of excerpts from *Alice in Wonderland*, in which I was the caterpillar; I can still feel on my skin the crinkly green 'tube' dress which I wore. I had nothing to say, which was nice; I just sat on my toadstool. Father was asked by the headmistress of the school to tell the audience about our family's link with Lewis Carroll, and mercifully I was too young to be embarrassed. The other thing I enjoyed about my first school was the walk home with mother because it took us past a very good confectioner in Warwick Street, where she would sometimes be extravagant and buy bangs; and 'bangs' were scrumptious pink or white meringues for our nursery tea. The other nursery tea delight I remember was bread and butter spread with brown sugar; or bread and dripping with lots of salt.

The second school, where I was until Easter 1930, was Gibbs's, then quite a famous preparatory school for boys only, at the bottom

10. Parents' National Educational Union

of Sloane Street. We wore red caps; our deadly rivals, Gladstone's, had green ones. Mr Gibbs was very tall, with a commanding genial presence. We seven-year olds thought he was great, and he had collected a good staff, several of whose names I remember now; there was Miss McShea for instance who taught art appreciation, pretty enlightened to do that with such young children (two Vermeers say things to me still); and she also made wonderful sweets, of which you got a packet for good work. Games were a major feature of the place, (to make sure we beat Gladstone's of course), and for them we piled into hired double-decker buses, which drove up to the school door, and we were driven out to playing fields at Barnes. We loved it; I won a running race one year in the school sports, which is no doubt why I remember those seemingly huge grounds.

Gibbs's was a mile or more from home, and for all my two years there father walked Mary and me to school together, north over the railway lines at Ebury Bridge, across Buckingham Palace Road, and into Chelsea where we dropped off Mary at the Francis Holland School in Graham Street; and then it was five minutes on to Gibbs's. Mother always did the return trip, collecting me first, so I had to get in all my school news to her at once before she gave a fair crack of the whip to Mary. Those school walks, of a bit over two miles a day with both parents separately, were important elements in our young lives.

There were also of course proper walks, the daily one with nanny, which I suppose had come to an end by the time I was at Gibbs's. But from babyhood these walks just happened, every day, for hundreds of middle-class London children. We would go to St James' Park to feed the ducks and watch the pelicans; or if Nanny was feeling strong the considerably longer walk to Green Park, going past the sentries outside Buckingham Palace ('They're changing the Guard' etc.), and then into the vast open spaces, as they seemed, of the bigger park. Sometimes our return journey would coincide with a company of the Guards marching back behind their band to Chelsea Barracks along Buckingham Palace Road, and when I was eight or nine the great thrill was to march along the pavement and keep up with them for as long as we were allowed.

One year, when I had graduated to the sort of sit-up-and-beg contraption which passed for a push-chair in those days, nanny had heard of goings-on at the bottom of Bond Street. Sure enough a crowd had gathered by the Ritz, rafts of nannies with prams and push-chairs, but plenty of office girls and others taking time off work for a few minutes. Everyone was waiting to witness the switching on of the very first traffic lights in England; in the world actually, because we had invented them. The traffic was stopped, there was a speech by some bigwig, immediately after which the policeman on Point Duty, as it was called, left for the last time his perilous position right in the middle of Piccadilly facing up Bond Street, and everyone cheered both him and his automatic successor, the red, yellow and green arrangement which we have taken for granted ever since.

Also clearly in my walk-memories are some of the London street scene characters, who have since vanished into history. There was the knife-grinder, who pedalled a trolley round middle-class streets to earn his living. In answer to his distinctive cry, a maid would come rushing out with the household knives that needed sharpening, whereupon he would stop in the gutter, sit on his trike saddle, and pedal away to run the grindstone. It was always a special thrill if we got back from our walk to find him in action outside our front door. Then there was the lamplighter for our part of Pimlico; he would walk his beat every evening along the pavement from one cast-iron lampstand to the next, erecting his short ladder (with the rungs diminishing to a point) against the crossbar of the handsome lamp-pole, and climbing up to pull the foot-long chain, causing a spark to ignite the recalcitrant light. Another character was the organ-grinder and his monkey; there were two or three spots our local one used to favour, and we would try to get nanny to organize our walk to go past him. The unmistakable noise the organ made was surprisingly tuneful, the tunes were often hymn tunes we vaguely recognized, and the trick was to wheedle the operator into letting us work the handle; but one had to be careful that the monkey did not object that his master was being ousted.

But of course the 'Stop-me-and-buy-one' ice-cream man was the person we really enjoyed meeting, except that nanny never had any money, and would no doubt have had a standing order from our parents that a) ices were an unnecessary extravagance and b) they would anyway spoil our tea. But this slowly-pedalling salesman in a white jacket, with *Walls* (in the same writing used by the firm today) sign-written on the yellow sides of his trolley was an immensely familiar figure in every English town and village. He would pull up on a street corner whenever or wherever he was hailed in those traffic-free days; but my recollection is that the local Pimlico one got very little business from either mother or father when they were taking us on our walks at week-ends.

Our parents took great trouble over spotting and using what London uniquely had to offer; for instance there was the Royal Institute in Albemarle Street, where we were enterprisingly taken to the annual science lectures for children. I must have been eight or nine years old by then, and as I was destined to do hardly any science in any school I went to, those enchanting and informative children's occasions have stuck in my mind. Sir Lawrence Bragg gave them one year, I remember, on the moon and the stars, holding us spell-bound in one of those steeply-tiered lecture rooms, as he walked around jotting things down on the blackboard behind him or explaining the gadgets and apparatus immediately in front of us. The Braggs, there was a father and a son, both knighted in their day as top scientists, had lots of links with the family, so we may well have been got in free. It did not of course occur to me what a remarkable feat it was on the part of those lecturers to keep the attention of such a wide range of children, from my age up to fifteen or so. Similarly mother always got us tickets for the Robert Meyer children's concerts in Central Hall Westminster. The supremo for us was Sir Malcolm Sargent; I can hear him now interrupting the entire orchestra, and getting, say, the violins to play again the last twenty bars: 'Now did you hear that, boys and girls? Isn't it exactly like fifty mice rushing across the nursery floor?' Brilliant; we ate out of his hand.

The nursery floor was indeed never far from our thoughts, or rather from our hands and knees. Ours in 12, Warwick Square was made of stripey pink linoleum. In front of the gas fire there was a high fireguard with a brightly polished top rim, where nanny would sometimes let bits of washing scorch. I kept my building bricks in a big red wooden box; and I say 'my' bricks advisedly as they were given to me personally by Bishop Gwynne[11], a great friend of father through his work with the Middle East. I really used those bricks; they were none of them painted, and so wore splendidly; being of

11. Llewellyn Gwynne was the legendary Bishop in Egypt and the Sudan, serving the diocese from 1899–1946

different sizes, they could be used for all manner of nursery activity, and the same ones, still in Mairse's home, are enjoyed by hundreds more of the children who stream in and out there, among them of course, as the years have gone by, our own and our grandchildren.

There was also Meccano, still available I know, but in many respects superseded by today's Lego. You had spanners and nuts and bolts, to make things like cranes and lorries; and sometimes we would persuade nanny to let us take our latest creation perilously downstairs after tea to be admired. My farm was also a great joy; for years a good Christmas present was a farm cart (not a tractor in sight then), or a new cowshed, to augment the collection of animals and 'green-grass' (pieces of painted cardboard six inches square), which you had to have in our nursery, or else the horses and sheep looked stupid on the pink lino. A new acquisition one year was enough grass to have a cricket ground, complete with the village cricket side, eleven fielders, two batsmen, and two umpires. It was an imaginatively-run farm too because it had quite a good zoo, only the giraffes would get their necks knocked off, so matchsticks and glue tended to be the order of the day under father's repairing wizardry; he did the same to the bearskinned heads of my guardsmen.

Father was quite a handyman; we would not call him a DIY fanatic today, he simply got on with whatever repairs to his house or his children's things were needed, and where money could be saved. I have a particular memory of his skill as a cobbler. He had a drawer in his study where he kept all the gear, and we were never allowed to open it because of his ultra-sharp knives. I can smell the leather he bought for soles, in large sheets, to be cut carefully to size. He probably saved a lot of money, and I should have been proud of him for being capable of tackling things like that, but I remember being slightly ashamed of him doing something which none of my friends' fathers did. What a lot of them did not have however was a garden to play in, in the shape of Warwick Square garden immediately outside our house; and as a resident father had a key.

There was grass for ball games, paths for trikes, bushes for hiding in (and how filthy we must have got playing there, right inside them); and when we were older we could use the hard tennis court which took up one end. It was a treat always to go into 'our' garden, and on garden days there was generally no walk. These also of course went by the board if we were 'sickening' for something, or actually ill; making up a bit for being 'under the weather' (a great euphemism of father's) was the lighting in winter-time of the coal fire in one's bedroom, and the comforting flicker of the flames on the ceiling after mother had kissed good-night and one was supposed to be going to sleep.

So were we poor, I find myself pondering, as missionaries' children (to be accurate we were mission secretary's, but the income level would have been much the same) in the not very fashionable part of London that Pimlico was seventy-five years ago? Well of course not, in comparison with the terrible, no-shoes-for-the-children poverty of millions of working-class people then, some of them not a mile from our home. But we were certainly poor by the standard, say, of my godfather, Ralph, an insurance broker in the city, the debonnaire youngest of father's four surviving brothers, with his grand house in Hyde Park Square, a butler, a nanny for their only child Peter, two or three servants right up to the war, plus a car and chauffeur.

Our domestic staff only consisted of a nanny (I have found photographs of several who succeeded each other in the first few years of my life), no living-in maid, but a general factotum in the shape of a cook-housemaid; the one whom I dimly recollect, maybe because she was anything but a neat 'maid' was rather a nice elderly buxom housewife, or possibly widow, Mrs Baron, who came from Peabody Buildings off Victoria Street, which were great blocks of flats replacing some of the appalling Westminster slums (and destined to be pulled down themselves as slums in the 1960s). Mrs Baron did us well and stayed for ages. She was pretty basic, more what used to be called a charwoman; but she was kindly, a good plain cook, immensely reliable presumably, as she was often in charge of us small children if nanny was out or off duty. When I got too old to have a nanny, mother employed on and off for two years or more what would today be called an *au pair* girl, except that she was English and forty. Owen became a great favourite with us all, filling a gap I imagine for mother herself with the departure of the last nanny after fifteen years of them, and also great fun to be with, especially for Mary and me.

On the not-being-well-off issue, I do know that we grasped early on that one must not be extravagant, for example never to leave lights on unnecessarily. But there was the problem that to get up stairs we had to pass, with the top landing light not yet on, a picture on the staircase wall of a forbidding greybearded man, which I always shot past because he was 'scary', as today's child would say. We definitely never pined for things any more than all children do in phases, and we had marvellous presents at birthdays and Christmas. The truth is that Mission salaries, both then and now, have always been modest; and father had no private means. But they managed, without us ever feeling deprived of the essentials; and they had huge amounts of love.

That love came into its own, for children being brought up in the way we were, in the time downstairs after tea. In my memory it was gorgeous. There would always be some music, for mother was a competent pianist, and loved playing to her children, singing with us round the piano, teaching us nursery rhymes and other songs as we got older; there were also games, board games like *Halma* and a bit later *Sorry*; card games like rummy and coon-can; and memory games (*Kim's* was always popular). There was drawing and chalking, and when I got mine wrong, I would fling myself on the floor while mother sorted out the mess, so that the same carpet Mairse has in her sitting-room now still has resonances from my thrashing about on it in a fury under the piano. Stories too: the Arthur Ransome books were so popular that we sometimes had them read to us in the drawing-room, rather than them having to be repeated for two of us separately on our beds at tucking-up time. We would put off bed-going with every ruse under the sun, and I distinctly remember clinging so hard to the solid iron banisters outside the drawing room that Nanny had to hand over to mother to get me prised off them, for going upstairs to my bath. It was indeed a wonderful childhood, made all the more memorable by our family holidays.

It is partly owing to my album that I can recall such a lot about the family holidays which were an important part of my growing up, not least because they were in the country, whereas 'home' was London. 'The album' has been a feature of my life for as long as I can remember. For each of us four siblings, mother began one as soon as we were born, gradually having to acquire more copies of any events or photographs in which several of us had been involved, so as to stick in what she felt best fitted each child. I write 'events' because in a sense these albums of ours are scrap books, not simply photograph albums. But we all felt that use of that word would demean them, giving connotations of a cardboard-backed, cheap-looking, large notebook which one knew would be dumped not all that long after it was full, and particularly when there was a clear-out of the nursery cupboards. But our hard-back albums were in a different league. They were all kept in the drawing room, the entries were only stuck in and written under by mother until we were in our teens and started to do it all ourselves; I bring our current one (the ninth volume) up to date once a year and still thoroughly enjoy doing so.

Looking through my first volume, I detect a very clear pattern which I had not quite realized before, namely that Christmas holidays were mostly in London, but often included an expedition for a few days to my mother's widowed mother (Granny[12] to us) in Westerham; in the Easter holidays we almost invariably went for a week or more to St Margaret's Bay, near Dover, where my other grandparents had a lease on a small terraced house for all their Canterbury time; and summer holidays were in a country rectory or vicarage under 'house for duty' arrangements.

Having the Christmas holidays in London made sense. There were the shows and parties mentioned, and the weather did not make for exploring the countryside. But there was also going to Westerham. I remember perfectly the deep snow there over Christmas 1927, when we were obviously with Granny for the festival itself; being away from home over an important church season was not difficult for father because he had no church of his own. Squerryes Lodge lies just outside Westerham on the Oxted road, and in that December, after heavy falls of snow, it was completely blocked for a while by seven-foot drifts; I can see now (and not just because of the photograph) the walls of snow, with the neat spade marks where workmen, with no bulldozers to help them, had laboured to open a narrow passage for traffic. We had superb tobogganing quite near Granny's house, the extra *frisson* being that the best slope whizzed one down to the very edge of the sizeable river just beside the main road. The freezing water was fast-flowing still; so there was much agitation by our elders and betters, Ted

12. My grandfather, Dr George Edward Jelf (1834–1908), was Residentiary Canon of Rochester before becoming briefly Master of the Charterhouse until his death.

then twelve years old revelling in too many risks for their liking.

Granny's large Georgian house had six foot high sash windows on the ground floor opening out into the garden; there my unmarried Aunt Dorothy presided over a staff of several resident domestic servants. Squerryes was ideal for the young, a particular feature being massive clipped yews abutting the lawns, comfortably big enough inside for passages and rooms that had superb possibilities for hours-on-end games in the summer; and those yews were also a great help over eluding Nanny after tea when one had been summoned for bed several times. The winter evenings meant gatherings round the piano, with granny and mother taking turns at the keys, and us 'singing along'; that generation delighted in drawing-room hymn-singing, and we in those 1920s (children of Victorians, as we were) would ask for all our favourites, especially one that granny, small, plump, rosy-cheeked, always laughing, enjoyed choosing and I have never sang anywhere else, with a fine 'go-ey' tune and a rousing chorus that went: 'We follow, we follow to the Holy Land', which was highly suitable of course for a family where the breadwinner was giving the best years of his life to that part of the world. Very happy vibes therefore float my way whenever we drive past the Squerryes turning, as we seem to most years because of our many links still in Kent.

St Margaret's Bay was quite different: where we stayed was simply an uninteresting little holiday house of my Bickersteth grandparents, what to-day we would call a bolt hole, easily accessible from Canterbury, and no doubt they used it a good deal; but most Easter holidays grandfather gave us the house for a week or more, and we all looked forward to that. Exploring the Kentish countryside in April opened my London eyes to the full beauty of spring.

There was a particular wood, I think of oak trees and coppiced hazel, which was always awash with primroses when we were there, with the result that primroses say 'St Margaret's Bay' to me to this day. There would of course be an expedition to Canterbury to catch up with our grandparents in Meister Omers. There were cliff walks to the Lighthouse and back, quite a long way, often rather hazardous, as the cairn given to my sister Ella (she only became Kay in her twenties) loved rushing dangerously near the edge after the gulls. Lambing-time gave us our first insight, (thanks to a kindly farmer, who let us do the feeding) into how country life ticked. There is not a suspicion of sand on the beaches thereabouts, but rock pools were ideal for shrimp-hunting, and for giving outings to my eighteen-inch-long motor boat, a toy that lasted for years and was very much my pride and joy, partly because Edward had never had one. From the beach or the beach hut we frequently saw the great ocean-going liners of those days steaming majestically by, not far offshore. I had the reverse view in June 1944 on my way from Tilbury to the Normandy beaches, standing with my soldiers on the rails of our heavily-loaded Liberty ship, all of us looking back reflectively at the White Cliffs of Dover opposite us, just to the east of St Margaret's Bay.

But those short holidays at Christmas and Easter, fun as they were, were not our 'proper' holidays: these were reserved for six or seven weeks in July and August, and we had them all over England. I think father and mother must have got out maps (he revelled in maps and map-reading), when they were perusing Church Times advertisements for locums, exactly the same source incidentally as I used in the sixties and Piers in the nineties. Whether or not they deliberately planned what part of England we went to, so as to give us children an overall view of the land we lived in, the fact was that from 1922-1934 the fare was varied from Northumberland to Devon, from Kent to Buckinghamshire, from Suffolk to Gloucestershire, from Shropshire to the Lakes.

We never went to the same place twice, so indeed we were denied the fun of looking up people and places where we had enjoyed ourselves in previous years. But the other side of that coin was the wealth of variety we experienced, and the interesting new things to learn about and see and do, whether it was walking along Hadrian's Wall, climbing the Lakeland Fells, or making outsize castles on those limitless Norfolk sands. We hired our own ponies for a fortnight in Devon (and lost two of them on Dartmoor for six or seven hours, no small anxiety for my poor father, but immensely exciting for his children). In Wiltshire we got up at five to go cubhunting (tea and bread and butter in the September dark of the vicarage kitchen before we set out). There was the corn harvest to 'help get in' in Essex (riding home to the farm on top of the sheaves of wheat, which were piled high on the big wagons behind two straining shire horses). One year we went in a small coaster from the London docks to Newcastle; we were six of only a dozen passengers for the twenty-four hour trip, and had three first-class cabins for good measure. Leafing the pages of the album, I find that the fun and interest of it all floods back.

In the far-off (it seemed to us) country rectory, mother's work would begin, as she bravely sized up what she had only sketchily read about in the advertisement back in February. There were the resident cook and other maids to meet for a start, all *in situ* despite their employers having departed on their own holiday. Falling in with how the parlour-maid served afternoon tea in the drawing-room; hoping for the best that the staff would take to our nanny who early on always came too; wondering whether Cook had any idea what young children liked to eat when normally she had only an elderly (probably) husband and wife to 'do' for, all this must have been extremely difficult for our dear mama, but it was part of the culture of those days. Mother would have simply accepted it, so we did too, even though we were old enough to spot that these rural clergy lived much more grandly than we did in London. The caption under one album photo of a uniformed housemaid reads 'Shall I shut the shutters, m'm?', and with part of me I reckon I can hear that nice country girl saying it; but it shows how the staff tried to fit in with us interlopers. It also reveals that 'the gentry' did not in the nineteen-twenties shut their own shutters, those excellent draught-excluders for houses whose central-heating was still more than a generation ahead.

The houses too were not to-day's mostly much smaller rectories and vicarages. They would have six or more bedrooms, a garden of as many acres, with a gardener and a garden boy; and to go with 'the living' several fields of glebe.[13] These were country parsons' normal homes, which as a diocesan bishop in the 1970-80s it was often my unwelcome task to sign away for ever. In twelve years in Somerset, I probably did the final deed for sixty or more houses, a few of them thoroughly inconvenient and ugly and gladly seen the back of, but the vast majority delightful, or maybe with huge potential; and some of them were nothing less than gems. I used to refuse to sign on the dotted line unless I could see in writing the parish's total agreement, however reluctantly arrived at, that this was the right thing to do.

---

13. Originally the land devoted to the maintenance of the incumbent.

Getting Established

Thou visitest the earth and blessest it
Psalm 65 v.9

The country habit has me by the heart
For he's bewitched for ever who has seen,
Not with his eyes but with his vision, Spring
Flow down the woods and stipple leaves with sun.
The Land: Winter

I WENT off to preparatory school at Lambrook, near Bracknell, in May 1930 when I was eight and a half. The train which the school used on the first day of term with a Lambrook master on it always left from Waterloo's last platform, and so became one that from then on said things to me whenever I was at the station, until it was demolished for the Eurostar Terminus in the '90's. Father took me there in a taxi, and we developed the habit of my having a quick hug and cry in the privacy of it, as we drove through the same tunnel that there is today below the main lines. That meant that I was able to be 'stiff-upper-lippish' on the platform, from which I encouraged father to leave as soon as he had handed me over to the master. This would be several minutes before the train left, so that by the time it did the boys whose parents had stuck around were often at their lowest ebb, whereas I was already looking forward to the new term and feeling fine. We stuck to the same drill all through my five Lambrook years.

In other words I adored home and the holidays, and hated leaving; but I thoroughly enjoyed boarding school from Day 1. There was no question of a long settling-down period, with agonised letters from my mother to the headmaster's wife, followed by the patient standard replies, 'Yes, he's getting on very well and making friends, and coping admirably with the work, my husband says'. The fact as far as I am concerned is that it never occurred to me, nor I am sure to my parents, that I was 'being sent away to boarding school', with the unspoken hint that it was a cruel thing to do to an eight-year-old (and *scilicet* their parents); it may well have been, to both, but I never saw it like that. This was what middle-class chil-

24

dren did if their parents could afford it; mine had not got the wherewithal, but I was heavily subsidised by a bachelor business man who was on the J&EM Council, which as I have mentioned always met at home. I began having a chat with him at council meetings in the holidays for those five years, and he never in any way made me feel beholden to him; I simply substituted for the son he never had. My benefactor's name was Mr Money.

Lambrook, for some years now Lambrook Haileybury, was and is right in the country, on the edge of the village of Winkfield Row, four miles from Bracknell, so all the 'train boys' piled into a hired bus to get out to the school under a couple of staff. The elderly Mr Browne was the priest-headmaster; he was a kind, competent old-style clergyman, whom I do not doubt father and mother had chosen with great care, as they knew that good headmasters are vital to preparatory-school life. That summer term was FDB's last before retirement, and he was handing on to his son-in-law, Guy Cameron, thus keeping the school, after the pattern of those days, within the family to whom it belonged; and my guess is that FDB will have carefully vetted the young brother-officer, Archie Forbes, whom Guy had chosen to be the junior partner with him. The boys all thought of these wartime comrades-in-arms simply as joint headmasters.

Prep. school life was not cushy seventy-five years ago. For my first term under Mr Browne we had cold baths first thing in the morning, and then one lesson before breakfast; we still wore Eton collars and rather scratchy knicker-bockers, (not unlike the breeches I bought for shooting in the 1970s; there is nothing new under the sun). But the fresh regime changed all that, although discipline remained strict, with Stars for good behaviour and Stripes for bad. Stars were on pink slips and you needed four commendations to get one star; whereas stripes were on blue ones and you got a whole stripe at once when you misbehaved or were idle in lessons. Every boy's name was on the Stars and Stripes Board in the main downstairs passage, with them all marked up (or down) every week by the second master; in other words both moral behaviour and slackness in the form-room were very publicly monitored. 'The Path' was also a most effective punishment, given as an alternative to a stripe if the master judged it would fit the crime better; 'it' was simply a length of time, anything from fifteen minutes to an hour, when the

miscreant had to walk up and down a long gravel path in the
grounds, during leisure time, in full view of the rest of the school
who would be enjoying themselves ragging about or kicking a football or whatever. No one could go up and talk to them. Everyone
hated getting 'The Path'.

We were beaten a certain amount, some boys developing a
reputation for being beaten rather a lot, but at a guess most of us
maybe four or five times during our time in the school. I cannot
recall ever reckoning that this punishment was unfair, nor was it administered sadistically by whichever HM you were up before. They
were both charming men, and practically apologised for asking you
to bend over a chair for three or four whacks. Indeed we were very
proud indeed of our two young headmasters, specially on Remembrance Day when they would both sport their MCs. They had been
lucky to survive the appalling toll of subalterns in the trenches, but
Guy had been badly gassed, leaving him with only one lung fully
working, which led to his fairly early death in the 1950s, after which
Archie was still young and fit enough to take the school over entirely. But in the 1930s they played games with us (Guy bowled devilish leg breaks in the nets), there was a lot of music (Archie composed both words and music for the hilarious concerts and plays we
had every year), and they organised winter-term lectures, with
'lantern slides', by well-known people, invited I am sure for their
potential as heroes of Empire. They included men of the calibre of
Grenfell of Labrador, and more controversially as it turned out
'Grey Owl', the 'Red Indian', a fascinating character with some
amazing stories to tell about 'the Wild West'. It was a full five years
later that he was exposed as a failed car salesman from Streatham,
who had enterprisingly used his very hooked nose and sallow com-
plexion to fool thousands of admirers on both sides of the Atlantic.

Guy and Archie had excellent ideas about schoolmastering.
Lessons, which after all were the main object of the exercise, were
fun, and it clearly mattered to them that boys in their charge should
enjoy being at Lambrook. To that end they had gathered, and indeed kept (except when they went off to be HMs elsewhere, which
several did in my time there) a lively staff with the same kind of
ethos, under a strong Christian banner. The chapel was at the
centre of school life: short prayers there every day taken by one of
the HMs, Archie on the organ stool (he had a particular way of

swinging his long legs over it), a choir of robed boys and half a dozen masters for an hour's service on Sundays, with the local parish priest coming to take it, staff families in two or three pews at the back. Along with a sizeable minority of other boys, I had been taught at home that you knelt down by your bed last thing at night to say your prayers, and mother had written out for me a small book of good prayers for nine-year-olds (I have it still, and they are still good); and woe betide any boys who decided to tease (or worse) the ones who stuck to that home teaching; the duty master would be down on them like a ton of bricks.

The class teaching was all geared to winning scholarships (we would get ten or more a year, to go up on the school boards) or at least doing well at Common Entrance, with Eton (close by) a major school we fed, but all the public schools would over the years take Lambrook boys, though I was a bit unusual in hoping to get to Rugby. It was a long way away, but it had been father's school, and both he and I had set our sights on it. I knew from the start I would have to work hard to get there, something of which the school often reminded me, probably because they did not believe I was Rugby scholarship material. In other words I was fairly bright, but not exceptionally so.

Teaching was very traditional, with plenty of learning by rote: I can still recite *a ab absque coram de*, *palam cum* and *ex* and *e* as being prepositions needing the ablative case in Latin. For mental Arithmetic (every weekday) you all left your desks at the end of the lesson, and formed a line in front, so there would be twelve or thirteen of you, changing places up or down as you got the answer off pat or failed to do so; you came out next day in the order you had finished last time, and I rather think you got a quarter of a Star, if you had stayed at the top the whole week. There was a lot of memorising too in other subjects, history for instance, where BROM gives the correct order of Marlborough's four early eighteenth century victories, Blenheim, Ramillies, Oudenarde and Malplaquet; it was to us a most satisfying way of grasping facts and dates, and presumably 1930s schoolteachers believed in a method which would give their successors today apoplexy. Regular tests and termly exams were very much at the heart of the teaching system, with results on the school notice boards at exam. time, and great trouble being taken by us boys drawing up special charts in different colours to take home for the holidays to show our parents. In most subjects it was not a difficulty for me to be in the first two or three, but I was rarely top of the class, partly because I went up the school with a very clever boy named Bridges (I.L. Bridges, I did not know his Christian name, one never did), and he always beat me into second place in the nicest possible, self-deprecating way. He duly collected the top scholarship to Uppingham, and subsequently was on the staff there for many years.

Games were not magnified at all, but the games' masters made jolly sure that we could and did turn out respectable sides, and the excitement was intense if we managed a Star XI or XV (unbeaten, that is). We had a great time going off to away matches in large old upholstered taxis, which had those let-down backward-facing seats in their main part, to play the dozen or so other prep. schools round about; Heatherdown and Sunningdale were our chief rivals. I played for the school in all three main sports, cricket, soccer (Christmas term) and rugger (Easter), but that was really because in your last year most boys in a school of only eighty got a place in the first eleven or fifteen. A new Rugby Fives court was built during my time at Lambrook, and I became sufficiently good at it to find myself a few years later playing for Rugby, the school where it began. Archie Forbes, I remember, was a dab hand with the Fives gloves.

The Forbes' home was a very good, if unusual, element in the place. It was a comfortable Edwardian house beside the cricket field, half a mile from the school buildings. About five senior boys slept there for a term of two towards the end of their time, and we loved the small privileges of living with a family, playing in the garden on summer evenings with the young Forbes girls, and keeping their father sitting on our beds telling stories of his war-time exploits when he was supposed to be shutting us up for the night.

Cubs and Scouts were very much part of the Lambrook scene, with learning how to cook rock buns, mostly very rocky indeed, in a square biscuit tin buried in a mound of earth; and that was where I learnt to lay and light a fire, and also to tie knots which we used to good effect for the contraptions we enjoyed making for the camps we set up for sleeping in overnight during our last year. That introduction to the Scout movement, followed as I say by being a scout at Rugby, taught me enough to run my own troop for all my Bristol curacy days later on; I owe much to Baden Powell's imaginative understanding of boys; and it has been in one way sad to see the appeal of it all fade in recent years. It belonged in the main to the days of empire in which middle-class boys were brought up, right until the start of the second war. They were the days of maps with plenty of red all over them on the class-room walls, and the G.A. Henty novels like *With Kitchener to Khartoum* and *With Wolfe at Quebec* among the favourite books to be taken out of the school library. The Duke of Edinburgh's award scheme has splendidly taken scouting's place for our grandchildren.

As well as Scouts there were wide games, mostly in a big wood with a lake the size of a football pitch in the middle of it. Guy and Archie would invent all manner of outlandish tales to get us interested in why 'the battle' was necessary between the red and blue forces, what tactics would be sensible and so on. If the lake was frozen over, which in January or February it was most years, great vigilance was essential by the staff. Once I remember practically the whole school being on the ice, larking cheerfully about, when there was an urgent but calm shout from Archie, through his megaphone, of: 'Everybody off the lake; forget about being red or blue, simply walk, don't run, to the bank, like the spokes of a wheel, not all in one direction', repeated again and again until he and other staff could see we were none of us still on the ice. The reason of course was that a thaw must have been further on its way than Archie had judged when he had decided it was fine for the game to stray on to it, and one boy (quickly hauled out) had fallen through, near the edge of the lake. Archie's unfussed way of tackling what could have been a crisis made a deep impression on my twelve-year old mind. If ever a headmaster was exercising his responsibilities as being *in loco parentis*, ours at Lambrook certainly was on that cold winter's day.

Parents in those days, apart from keeping up the flow of boys, were not a feature of school life. Only in the summer term was there Parents Day, Mary generally coming with mother and father; to save on a taxi, they always walked the four miles from the station, which used to embarrass me. There were no visits in the winter or spring terms, and because that was how it always had been no one minded. The five years of preparatory school life, interspersed with those great family holidays, passed happily by. At school I had moved on from Sunday nights lying on the HM's drawing room floor as a nine year old, for him to read beautifully to twenty or so of us before bed, to sitting for the Rugby scholarships in February 1935. Mother and I stayed together in the Three Horseshoes just outside the school gates, and I have often wondered since what on earth my beloved mama did for those three days. It was worth it, though, when Mr Cameron called me into his study a few days later to show me the buff-coloured piece of paper in its yellow envelope, which the telegraph boy had delivered to Warwick Square, and father had forwarded on: 'Son awarded £40 scholarship to Rugby School'

There is an album photograph that year in which I left Lambrook of Kay, then twenty three years old, (she had decided Ella was Victorian), leaning nonchalantly with a happy smile on her face against a packing case in the road outside our London home, the removals van in the background. The family is bound for Chiddingstone Rectory, near Edenbridge in Kent, for father is going to be the rector of this long narrow north-south rectangle of West Kent. As was common in those old Wealden parishes, it is maybe eight or nine miles from north to south by only two or three wide, a shape which meant that the farms had some variety from the heavy clay to the much lighter slopes of the North Downs. It had, and still has seventy years later, three or four small hamlets, the biggest where the church is, and that has only a dozen houses besides the rectory; for the rest there are widely-scattered farm houses, with farmworkers' cottages, most of them tile-hung, as are the many distinctive oast houses, for this was hop-garden country.

The Archbishop of Canterbury is the patron[14] of Chiddingstone, so a representative of his presented father to the Bishop of Rochester for institution to the living; anomalous as patronage sounds today, the fact is that in the Church of England it makes for a balance among the clergy of the diocese. Furthermore lay patrons almost invariably take great trouble to find the right person, so in my experience the seemingly strange arrangement works rather well. Cosmo Gordon Lang was archbishop of the Canterbury province in 1935; father had had dealings with him through the Mission for many years, and thirty years earlier the archbishop himself had been a fellow curate with my grandfather. So when father decided it would be good for the Mission and for him and the family to have a change, the wheels were not difficult to set in motion. Whether he was offered any of the other livings the archbishop might have had free, I have no idea.

The choice of Chiddingstone proved a good one for us, and I dare to think for the parish too; father was a fine pastor of his people. Mother too fell quickly into her rôle as the rector's wife she had been in her husband's only other parish on the outskirts of Birmingham twenty years before. She was back at enjoying welcoming parishioners to the rectory, getting out her best china, using the garden for the fête, and playing the organ.

Although a pianist, she cheerfully mastered the basics of managing feet as well as hands, and when I was home, I often worked the bellows, in those days before electricity did the job. I have a particular memory of pumping away while she learnt the magnificent Gustav Holst tune to the stirring words of Sir Cecil Spring-Rice's hymn *I vow to Thee my Country*, which every parish church in England was encouraged to sing for King George V and Queen Mary's Silver Jubilee in 1935.

Father took the Communion Service beautifully; I have a clear recollection of how he would say very personally to each recipient of the cup the last phrase of the words of administration in the Book of Common Prayer: 'and be thankful'; in fact when I had had a minor accident to my foot in the garden which might have been much worse, and I was in church on crutches, I distinctly remember that I thought he had added the phrase specially for me. When as the Sundays went by I took in that it was always there, I began to see gratitude as a vital part both of worship and also of daily living.

As for the garden itself, it was a joy for mother to have one again, instead of making do with pots and window boxes. We took on the existing gardener at £4 per week, but there was great concern as to whether we could afford it when the agricultural wage went up and, in order to keep the differential between labouring and gardening, the £4 had to rise by ten shillings. Mother was marvellous with our rather dour chap, whom she saw from the start was a clever gardener, and she loved planning what went where in the flower beds, what fruit and vegetables to grow and so on. At long last she no longer just had contact with flowers in someone else's vicarage

---

14. Patronage (the *advowson*) grew from the squire owning the parish and acquiring for his church a priest he liked; gradually parishes had colleges, trusts or diocesan bishops as their patrons.

garden, when father was doing a locum, or through pressing wild
ones, when we were on our summer holidays.

Pressing flowers, indeed, was very much a Victorian custom that
was still taught to children: the specimens went between blotting-
paper in thin wooden-backed books, you weighed it down and tied
it up with tape, and when it was dry you transferred the result to
your collection, fixing it to the page with stamp paper. On our
holidays we would bring back to the house various wild flowers we
found, common ones like herb robert or campion or excitingly,
once, on Dartmoor in 1929 some 'Grass of Parnassus'. Over six or
seven summers, I suppose I amassed twenty or thirty specimens,
but despite it being a method employed by hundreds of great
botanists I could never get excited about these poor withered
remains, and it was somehow satisfying to put away my book, never
touch it again, and instead learn about the real thing.

Wild flowers were everywhere in the meadows round the house
(no herbicides to eliminate them then), and in the garden we could
watch their 'tamed' sisters grow, rejoicing in seeing results, discovering the inevitable disappointments, learning how there were
good seasons and bad ones, what did well in one place and badly in
another, making drills for carrots and beetroot, singling young
turnips, digging a celery trench, pricking out cosmea and antir-
rhinum under our gardener's guidance. He had a potting shed attached to the garage, smelling as all proper ones do of sieved earth
and clay pots, and he had rows of his prize certificates from the village horticultural show pinned to the wall above his workbench. It
was all a wonderful new world, in which I have been privileged to
experiment and to revel from that day to this.

All the time too I was learning very fast about just being in the
countryside, and how working people earned a living in it. Whenever I was home on holiday, or later on leave from the army, I went
bicycling along the lanes with father on his continual visiting
rounds; and no doubt I was quietly absorbing a great deal about the
country parson's job, without any conscious thought whatever that I
might one day be following in his footsteps. In fact if anything, like
most clergymen's sons, I probably thought there were many more
exciting things to do in life than being ordained. But I thoroughly
enjoyed from the start sitting with father by the open range in
countless cottage kitchens, listening to these labouring men and

women chatting away; and labour both sexes did, in all weathers and in absolutely basic cottages, for the small wages which along with new machinery was gradually driving working men away from the land. Farms then would still have ten or more 'hands'. Hardly a tractor was yet to be seen, and there would be a fine stable of four or five shire horses, so the carter was a vital member of the farm staff. At harvest-time I often went along to cock up into stooks the sheaves of corn as they fell from the binder, or helped to encircle the diminishing triangle of uncut corn as the rabbits started bolting for the hedge to try and escape the farm-hands' brandishing sticks.

The Rectory household also took our turn on the church bin in the hop-gardens every September. One farmer used only gypsies for hop-picking, but the other nearer one took on village people, and was glad to let church well-wishers man, or mostly 'woman,' a bin for the month-long season. We could make quite a lot of money for St Mary's, and in the process father met dozens of parishioners who were filling their own bins, but probably also giving our bin an hour's picking time to help the church. It was tiring work, and I remember now waiting as patiently as I could at the end of a long day for the cry 'Pull no more bines', which meant that you did not cut the strings of the next 'hill' of four hop bines, but could finish stripping the four that were down. Everyone had to finish as near as possible together, so that the tallyman could do his round of the bins fairly, with his scales to measure in bushel baskets what weight of hops you had picked. Then we helped load the bulging hop pockets on to a wagon behind a cart horse, and would sometimes get a ride back to the oast where the pocket's contents, thousands of yellowy-green hopflowers, were hoisted on to the first floor through an outside opening and spread out to dry with large wooden shovels. As the heat began to seep through from below, there was soon this distinctive strong smell. It was a rural England which was to change out of all recognition after the war, and rectory children were in a unique position in those days to get to know a large number of their father's people by name, through doing things with them, and being welcomed into their homes.

But the family of a country priest also had the privilege of discovering how the squire went about his business. Father had one squire in Chiddingstone itself, and another at the southern end of the parish in Chiddingstone Hoath, both of them with a military background, large houses and gardens, and the broad acres that went with them. One family had two daughters of our age with whom we played tennis on their hard courts, and we could ask them back to our rough and 'sporting' grass one. We often lunched, or when I was rather older I was included in dinners, in both the big houses (butlers and all), and Mairse had the little de Lisle girls from the baronial Penshurst Place, just outside the parish, in her Brownie Pack. On the other side of the parish to the west we had Christmas dinner every year for a decade or more at Hever Castle, and I can see now the charming owner of *The Times*, Major the Hon J. J. Astor, our host there, one of the richest men in England, and surely the most unassuming, as the leading light in post-dinner charades. To all these lovely places we had an easy, almost automatic entrée, and great fun it was.

Because farms needed a lot of men to work them, their cottages had not begun to be redundant and therefore open to being 'gentrified'; and hardly anyone then worked in London and had a second home in the country. One business man who did, Colonel Hugh Francis, was the tenant of father's Glebe House, just across the field from the Rectory, and it was this kindly bachelor who taught me how to shoot. Quite who suggested I bought a gun, my father or his week-end tenant or even I myself, I cannot recall, but a photograph in the album that winter of 1935 shows me in my plus-four suit with a gun tucked, quite professionally, under my arm. It was a four-ten, and I had it for sixty years until IRA scares led to all unlicensed guns being required to be handed in, and I had let my license lapse because I had stopped shooting. The colonel was something of a martinet, a very good trait when instructing in firearms. He would stand beside me in a pit in the sloping glebe field, while his gardener operated the clay trap at the top of the bank above us. We faced the trap and the unfortunate gardener for driven 'birds'; for walked-up ones we two stood beside the trap, as the clay saucer sped away from us after I had called 'Pull'. The colonel would say quietly: 'six feet to the left' or (more often) 'well behind'; he was wonderfully patient, and I soon got the hang of it. From clays I graduated to the rough shoot my mentor had a few miles away, where I would be very much under his guidance, walking round maybe a hundred acres of woods and pasture and ponds, with a couple of his friends, who had been wisely apprised that I was a beginner. We would return with perhaps a duck or a couple of rabbits and sometimes a wild pheasant; and I learnt from the gamekeeper how to pluck and clean a bird for the table, a skill which from time to time has surprised my friends as being within a bishop's remit.

Before long I moved on to a sixteen-bore, and after the war to a twelve. For a time later on I was lent a twenty-bore, so that once or twice, notably on a friend's Scottish grouse moor in the '70s, I was able to take our two older sons shooting with guns from my own 'arsenal'. I gradually during those Chiddingstone years came to an understanding of the lore and the delights of the shooting field: contentment with being out in all weathers and indeed quite happy if you are properly dressed for it; when out shooting with others never swinging dangerously down a line of guns at too low an angle (I was once ticked off for this by a Lancashire host, and never forgot it); observing wild life when you are standing motionless at a peg waiting for birds to come over (a jay perching a few feet over my head, a fox slipping through the brambles a yard away); not talking when you are getting into position before a drive (and trying not to be rude to a fellow gun who is nattering away, and you have never met him before, so it is difficult to shush him); these and many other things which are now unconsciously part of me, I began to absorb during the fifteen years that 'home' was West Kent

After father went to his last parish in 1950 and I began work in Bristol, I did not touch a gun for another twenty years. Probably that long break accounts to some extent for my never shining as a shot. But when I took it up again in the north, I sometimes had rather good days, confounding both my host and myself. Landowners or those in charge of syndicates were immensely generous in asking me back after initial invitations, even though they knew I would not do them proud. Indeed all my shooting has been through the kindness of friends and acquaintances, except for my quiet solo walks round our five-acre garden and wood at Chiddingstone where I bagged the odd rabbit or pigeon. Nevertheless, despite my being anything but a fine shot, and furthermore losing my game book annoyingly a long time ago, I have some wonderful memories of highlights.

I think for instance of snipe shooting in Angus with a Rugby friend before the war, wading through a boggy half mile of marsh when you could never be sure that your foot would not suddenly go in far deeper, the trigger very definitely at 'Safe', and literally dozens of birds jigging away from under our feet, and mostly into the distance; walking up partridges with fellow officers in my regiment over those huge East Anglian fields, in the days when there was always overwintering stubble for the birds to lie out on; shooting seven pheasants at one stand on a very posh day in Devon; a sweltering afternoon on the plains of Central India after peafowl, able to think of very little except when we would next be getting a drink, as my bearer had forgotten to fill up the water bottle; four driven grouse with six shots on the Derbyshire moors, and the cheers from the other guns who had long since foregathered for their picnic by the time I appeared, having picked my two brace without the help of the dogs; a lone very high-flying pigeon thumping to the ground in Somerset beside my rather surprised elderly Lord Lieutenant host, and his quiet, maybe deserved, 'brilliant'; three geese before breakfast, standing in a deep dyke on the North Norfolk coast,[15] after getting out of bed in the dark into the six degrees of an early January frost, and the empty marshes just beginning to show slivers of light, as great skeins of birds came in from the sea.

Vignettes like that are interspersed with recollections of huge shooting lunches, and either missing everything in the afternoon or having an unforgettable couple of hours bringing down almost every bird; of Caspar, the best springer of the seven we have had, being in constant demand from the head keeper of a Lancashire shoot because he was so good at retrieving in water. Every owner of a gundog gets a huge kick out of his one doing well, but there is equal ignominy when on an off-day he (or more likely another one; we had two or three in sequence trained) runs into a covert about to be drawn; I remember an 'it's that so-and-so dog of the bishop's again' of our worst dog one year, and occasionally the beaters would put the expletive in a different place.

I have had many quite deep conversations, walking between drives, with almost unknown men, who were suddenly finding themselves able to tackle a stray bishop about some theological point that has been troubling them; and one shooting day it fell to me to respond to a chap I had never met before whose marriage was

---

15. I refer to this in more detail later.

breaking up and he desperately wanted someone to whom he could unburden himself. Again and again there were these unexpected pastoral opportunities, as men who for the most part did not have much to do with the clergy (let alone, I suppose it should be said, with bishops) found themselves alongside me in the unthreatening surroundings of open fields and woods.

In a different setting, but equally fruitful for worthwhile talking, were the delightful evenings in the great metropolis with the Gunmakers Company, to whom I was chaplain for ten years. There were dinners among the splendours of some Livery Hall in the City of London, of which I became a Freeman. The Gunmakers have no hall of our own, (it was destroyed in the bombing and never rebuilt), so we were fortunate to see the inside of the many others which we hired for our dinners; Ladies Nights were particularly special.

This chaplaincy in my second 'shooting period' (from 1970 until I gave my gun to our eldest son twenty years later) meant that I was coming into contact with a large number of people, who from their various standpoints, both to do with shooting and right outside it, keen churchmen or anything but, all shared a growing anxiety about the need to conserve the British countryside for future generations. Generally-speaking townsmen have no idea that the appearance of the countryside which they like visiting owes so much to both the shooting and the hunting fraternities, who have often planted the woods, bothered about the hedges, and dug or cleared the ponds. 'Nature Conservation' as such, biodiversity and all that goes with it, the delicate balance in the natural world, these things did not swim into my ken (nor if the truth be told into most other people's) until many years later. Even then a lot of my friends reckoned I was pretty far gone to be so concerned about them. That was a common judgement until the last two or three decades, during which the whole notion of caring for our precious and endangered natural heritage, both nationally and internationally, has begun to play an increasingly large part in people's thinking; for me it all started from our moving into the country at an impressionable age, from beginning to enjoy letting soil run through my fingers in a garden of our own, and (I can say without hesitation) from acquiring that four-ten.

Pruning

For nature gives and nature gives again;
Therefore be eager of her liberal hours;
To drought succeeds the flood, to calm the gale,
And winter's frost lays low the summer flowers.
The Land: Summer

A LL these immensely important, as I now see, country matters were a very long way away from my thoughts as a fourteen-year-old, on the day my godfather Uncle Ralph (who was himself at Rugby from 1908-12) put me on the school train out of Euston in the autumn of 1935 for my first term. Ever since I had won my scholarship earlier in the year, father had been looking forward to doing the honours, and taking me himself to the school he had left in 1900.

But earlier in that September, he and mother and I were going home to the rectory from a boys' cricket match I had played in at Cowden, bicycling along a narrow country lane, single file with him in the lead, when he was surprised by a car rounding a bend towards him. There were hardly any cars in the villages round us, and maybe he was not concentrating enough on the corner ahead, but he must have pulled over too sharply when he saw this one coming round the corner. As bad luck would have it, the edge of the metalled road had been worn away by rain at precisely that spot, which made father's front wheel slip off it and drop two or three inches on to the grass verge. The bump off the hard road unsaddled him, throwing his body to the right into the path of the oncoming car, of which thankfully the driver had good control, pulling up a yard or two short of father's motionless body. Mother and I saw it all happen, (as of course did the horrified motorist), and we were off our bikes in a moment and bending over this unconscious figure on the road, the bike undamaged on the grass verge. The car owner was great, and drove off at once to get help, while mother propped his head against her as best she could; she stayed kneeling quietly beside her unconscious husband, while I ran to a cottage nearby for a bowl of water to bathe his wound, which was obviously a nasty one.

The details of the immediate next half hour or indeed of the following few days escape me, for example how soon the ambulance came, what mother and I did or talked about while we waited, how long it was before father came round, and how soon mother knew the extent of the damage. We could see that he had taken the full weight of his body on his head, above the right temple, and the hospital told us that the crash on to the metal road had cracked and dented his outer skull for nearly three inches; after it had healed, wonderfully well, the dent was visible for the remaining forty-one years of his long life. He was very lucky indeed, in that the bang on his head had not affected his inner skull, so his brain was quite undamaged, though mother was not to know that for some time. Once we had been told that he was going to survive, mother was able to take stock, and grasp the unpalatable fact that her husband would be off work for many months, and this at a time when he had not even seen round his first year in the parish.

Father spent several months in the excellent Edenbridge Cottage Hospital, to which he had been taken in the ambulance from the scene of the accident. It was four miles from home, which meant all the problems of visiting, when, like most others then, we had no car; mother often biked to see him. Then there were the frustrating off-work weeks, which continued, with him gradually being allowed to and wanting to do a little, until February after which they then went off together before Easter for a fortnight's convalescence at Lewis Casson and Sybil Thorndike's country estate in North Wales, where they were superbly looked after by her old school friend's staff. This was a lovely bonus from a bad time. I had the thrill of Aunt Sybil writing me a letter to say father really was better; and that Spring he came back to full work in time to take the Holy Week and Easter services, six full months after his accident.

I suppose because of being preoccupied with news from home, I remember very little of the start of my Rugby life. I went into Sheriff House, under 'Johnnie' (even to his wife) Johnson, who was its first and very good housemaster. This new and extra house, built in 1930, had cost £55,000, 'a thousand pounds per boy' people said, 'what gross extravagance'; in fact it was judged so expensive that it was at once christened Vaughan's Folly, the headmaster, W.W. Vaughan, being personally blamed for the extravagance. But he knew his staff well, and Johnnie proved the ideal person for it, starting off with one year's intake of his own choosing, and therefore only achieving a houseful after five years. Sheriff had been well and imaginatively built, but more importantly it had by the time I arrived forged for itself a real sense of identity, and that was largely our splendid Johnnie's doing, together with the hard work of Alice, his always rather detached but immensely kind wife, and the ultra-efficient (but great fun with it) house matron, Nancy Lovett.

Our first Chiddingstone Christmas must have been pretty muted, with father taking none of the services, and having to be kept as quiet as possible in the house. King George V died a few weeks later, to universal mourning. He had been very ill in 1928, and I was among the thousands of all ages who had gone (taken by father presumably) to the Buckingham Palace gates that year to look for the daily bulletins which were posted up there on his health; recovering after a long convalescence, he was never very fit afterwards. But his Silver Jubilee was celebrated enthusiastically in that summer of 1936, and for us in the Rectory it became our first experience of a village fête and sports day, which provided a great opportunity for father to meet his parishioners. I had just stuck a garden fork clean through one of my big toes, and was therefore very disappointed not to be able to take part in anything, but I did hobble about on crutches, feeling very wounded-soldierish. Church services for the King, peals of bells, addresses of congratulation by both Houses of Parliament all ring fairly hollow now, in view of the revelations in recent years about what a repressive and irascible father the king had been. But those were times when the mystique of the monarchy held undisputed sway, so that we knew nothing at all about the royals' private lives. *God save the King* was played before and after every performance in London theatres, and invariably at school concerts, amateur dramatics in village halls and so on. Empire Day was marked with patriotic fervour, and woe betide a schoolboy who could not draw passably well the main pink areas on a world map in the classroom. There was much excitement too over the Prince of Wales now becoming king, not least because he had visited all these areas, and been adulated wherever he had gone. He seemed to be, and most certainly was, much closer to people than his father had been, particularly in his concern for the unemployed. Furthermore around Edward VIII's Accession-time in January, Mrs Simpson was still unheard of by the vast majority of the British public, so the consternation over her increasing hold on our new sovereign was all the greater as rumours began to circulate during the summer.

Father was well enough by April for him and mother to mark their Silver Wedding, and this was the highlight of the Easter holidays. They had laid on a quintet to play in the drawing room (rather an old-fashioned thing to do, I remember thinking), and the party became a very happy one to show that father was fit and well again. My grandparents came over from Canterbury with Ninny (their combined ages we worked out at 222), the last time I was to see grandfather who was just retiring, and died not long afterwards. In view of how the year developed for us, that celebration became a particularly memorable family occasion, with us four children all there, together with some of the wider family, and many friends.

Meanwhile school was going well. I had passed in high enough to begin right away on School Certificate work, and I duly got six subjects towards the end of my first year, collecting also my first school prize on Speech Day. But at the end of the summer term there was suddenly a cloud on the horizon: both parents met me at Euston, instead of only father whom I was expecting, and we went in a taxi to Harley Street, while they explained quite undramatically that before we went to Victoria to catch the train home we were going to a top medical man for him to check mother's health, as a lump had appeared on one of her breasts. Whether or nor they mentioned cancer, I cannot recall, but in any case I doubt if I would have heard of it; the illness was far less on everyone's lips than it is today. I certainly do not remember feeling particularly anxious. I knew anyway that there was no planned summer holiday away, but I was perfectly happy about that as I was looking forward to a home holiday in the countryside I wanted to get to know better.

At the end of August mother had a mastectomy at the same Cottage Hospital which had cared so well for father almost exactly a year earlier, and I began to realize, just by being around both before and after she went into hospital, that she was very unwell. She still struggled down into the drawing-room for part of each day; I remember having hilarious laughter over trying to hump her up

our rather steep front stairs without hurting her; she was to keep
cheerful in a wonderful way all through the three months ahead.
Before I went back to school father told me that if and when she got
worse he would of course bring me home. I am not sure, at this distance of time, whether he explained to me that the operation had
clearly not eradicated the cancer, and that she was dying. The busy
school round stopped me from worrying, and wondering what
might be going to happen. Mother kept on writing to me every
week on Sundays, father on Wednesdays, with ordinary home news.
In the event it was mid-November before father rang Johnnie to ask
for me to come home, and I arrived at the rectory to find I was
sleeping in Edward's room with him, which was a clever idea, as it
both gave me company and also made me feel very grown up to
share a room with a twenty-one-year-old brother. Each morning
father would come in and draw the curtains to say that mother was
still with us. It all seemed very unreal, until after four or five days
father called us four into their bedroom quite late, as the doctor (a
devout churchman incidentally) had just visited, and had felt that
mother was not long for this world. She had been slipping in and
out of consciousness all day. Father was kneeling by her bed; I went
across to sit on her dressing table stool; we were all in the room.

"I said to her' (I quote from father's letter in the Parish Magazine
the following month), 'would you like me to say our evening
prayer?' Immediately she answered, so that we all heard the words
quite clearly, 'Of course, indeed I would'. So the habit of a lifetime
remained with her to the end, and the Guide Who had been with
her daily, filling her whole being with infectious joy and happiness,
was with her over death." Those were fitting words from a priest to
write to his people, and I admire father for them even more now,
nearly seventy years on, than I did then. We did not stay in the
room long, and in fact mother survived the night, by then in a
coma, and we were back there, with me on the stool again, at 11.30
next morning when her breaths got fewer and fewer and then stopped. Father said a prayer, and gave us all a blessing in a steady
voice. No one cried.

I have the most vivid recollection of both the night before, and of
the morning mother died, 2nd December. Many readers could
quote similar experiences; I simply recount mine here because
naturally they have been part of me ever since. After father's bless-

ing I think I got up first, and told Kay as we were leaving the room (because father indicated, thoughtfully for us, that he wanted to be there on his own) that I was going out for a walk by myself. 'Will you be OK?' she asked, and she saw I would be fine. So I went out, down through the dell, past the great oaks at the bottom of the garden, over our stile, and into the fields for half an hour's brisk walking, which made me feel better, as so often a bit of exercise does for many people in a crisis.

For the days up to the funeral, father put me in charge of the flowers that started arriving, a brilliant touch I have often thought since. They poured in, maybe two hundred wreaths and bunches, which I laid out on the brick of the larder floor and passage, where I kept them watered enough for the intervening days, until the Bishop of London, who had married them twenty-five years earlier, and Uncle Julian, came down to take the funeral; of that service I have absolutely no recollection, except that after mother's body had been laid in the (new) churchyard, two hundred yards along the road from the church, and people were gradually dispersing, the squire's wife, Meg Meade-Waldo, called me to come and sit beside her in her chauffeur-driven car (he held the door open for me to get in):

'John my darling, fifteen is very young to have lost your mother; I'll help whenever I can', and we chatted for a bit. Recounted, that may sound very condescending of her, but it was not, remotely. Vague, maddeningly so sometimes, but always loving, she had been close to mother and became indeed, as she had promised, a great help to me. For another fifteen years, until father left Chidding stone, I was in and out of Stonewall Park whenever I was at home, even more so after Edmund, their only son, my best friend in the village, was killed in the war five years after mother's death. When Meg got older she often said that I must at all costs take her funeral, and although Rosemary and I did not see much of her after I was ordained, we gratefully returned to the village to carry out her wishes many years later.

I went back to Rugby a few days after mother's funeral for the end of the winter term, wearing (after the custom of the time) a black armband sewn on a sleeve of my school jacket. It was intended to help people remember one's loss, and perhaps it did; but it should have been removed before the next term, because by Easter

I was being teased for it, as was perfectly natural for boys who rightly felt it was too ostentatious. In those final days, however, of the Christmas Term, the King's Abdication was filling everyone's mind, and in retrospect that traumatic event was an ideal distraction for me. *Omnium consensu capax imperii, nisi imperasset*, I see I wrote rather pretentiously in the album under a photograph of King Edward VIII; Tacitus *Histories*, with a free translation of: 'Everyone thought he would be a very good king, if only he had not ruled.' The gobbet was to prove not all that apposite, so much having come out since about his private life as the Prince of Wales. But how superbly his unwilling brother served our country as King George VI, especially in the crucial war years.

Looking back on mother's death (and Meg M-W was quite right of course that fifteen was very young to lose her), I know that it was my being a communicant that, as it were, raised me up. At my confirmation only eighteen months earlier, I had been encouraged, as many young anglicans were in those days, to go to Holy Communion once a month, though High Church ones began a weekly communion right away. After mother died, I determined at once to keep in touch with her through the sacrament every single Sunday if I could; and that is what I have been doing, if it does not sound too pious to say so, from that day to this. Walking the six or seven minutes from Sheriff House to 'the eight o'clock' each Sunday, generally by myself but every so often with a friend, the service began to mean more and more to me in those three and a half remaining years I was at the school. I know it was absolutely central to my not moping or feeling miserable. I particularly valued the Memorial Chapel, for obvious reasons, and it was used for that service at least once a month. Similarly in our church at home, just across the field from the rectory, the feeling persisted that mother was beside me at the altar, not in a spooky way at all, just comfortingly around, often laughing, interested as ever in how school was going, and what I was planting in the garden. Due to that immensely strengthening week-by-week experience, the fact is that after some bitter crying on the night before the January term at the thought that mother was not going to see my new study, (father stayed by my bed until I had gone to sleep, I realized next morning, because I had been unaware of his slipping out of my bedroom), I never really looked back except with joy and happiness over the great times we had had together. Instead of going on grieving, I found that the phrase from the communion service about 'all the company of heaven' began to ring wonderful bells for me, because with my mother being there, as well as still being close to us here, I felt I had a real stake in the place.

Mairse, only just after leaving school, stepped bravely into mother's shoes. She began to run the house, she formed a Brownie Pack in the village, she helped father choose the hymns, she organised the flower rota for the altar. Furthermore she sewed on my nametapes, and made me a cake for school. On the very evening of the funeral, Doris the cook and Alice the parlour maid gave in their notice to father: 'The new mistress is only eighteen'.

It is intriguing that although in London we latterly had no living-in staff, our parents obviously felt that they could afford this help in the rectory; and moreover that, when those two girls left so precipitously, father and Mairse automatically thought in terms of engaging successors to them. They wisely did not take on two more local young women, but instead advertised for a couple, as a much easier proposition for Mary to cope with. I remember the husband and wife who came being rather good. I can see the man having a roaring coal fire blazing in the dining-room hearth by the time we came down to breakfast, working in the house wearing a green baize apron, and cleaning my shoes if I remembered to put them outside my bedroom door when I went to bed. They lived in the attic, which was very cold and draughty, but it was twice the size of the two maids' bedrooms which had been used by Doris and Alice. All three rooms had missed the decorating that had been done when we arrived, and I have to say that that they were really uninviting.

Servants' rooms were, with the least good furniture in the house, cheap sheets and poor quality blankets that had 'servant' sewn on them; I came across a couple of them years later in our airing cupboard, being used as under blankets because they were so thin. It was not that mother did not care about their welfare, she was an immensely caring person; but mistresses of households treated servants like that, God forgive us, and that was what servants expected, they would have been genuinely embarrassed if they had not had less good amenities than the family.

That first couple left amicably two years later 'to better themselves', and at the time of Munich (September 1938) we took in two delightful and frightened Austrian refugees, for whom even our dreary attic was heaven. When the war began we were afraid they would be interned, but father managed to arrange for the husband (no doubt after careful screening) to join the Pioneer Corps in the land of his adoption, and his wife got work in a munitions factory near where he was posted. Their departure marked the end of our ever again having living-in servants; it was the same with thousands of families, for whom up to the war 'staff' was or were part of the home scene. There were things servants did which you did not do, outrageous (and utterly strange to modern ears) as that sounds. Part of the thinking of course was that the houses with staff gave employment locally; indeed a working-class mother in Chiddingstone, for instance, would expect her daughters as they left school at fourteen to 'go into service'. The village too would have expected the rector to have had a couple of servants, which no doubt was part of father's and mother's thinking in finding the money to pay them the very modest wages of those days. They managed it presumably because Chiddingstone was in the parlance of the time 'a good living', a term used then and dating from before the dioceses began to average the stipends of clergy after the war.

So father started to earn more than he had in London, though there was a problem in that his predecessor in the parish had retired when he resigned from Chiddingstone, and (in the iniquitous way then in the Church of England) this man took with him a quarter of his successor's stipend. I remember how incensed we siblings were about that, and practically started to pray for the old man's speedy demise; but if we did our prayers were not answered for some years, as he took on a new lease of life in his retirement. Father was very saintly about the arrangement, which was simply the way things were handled then; and no wonder clergy mostly stayed in office, getting older and older and dying in harness, because there was only this sketchy plan to encourage them to hang up their cassocks.

Be all that as it may, my remarkable sister, only three years older than me, began in that December of 1936 to do all she could to take mother's place, as father embarked on what turned out to be forty years as a widower. Mairse was perfectly clear that it was what mother would have wanted, and again of course it was the custom of the time for unmarried daughters to tackle what she so gallantly and uncomplainingly undertook; it was a Victorian thing, even though it was father's generation that was Victorian, not ours. She was immediately so busy that she had no time to be, at least outwardly, unhappy; and for his part father never as it were 'hung on' to her. If she had chosen to get married and move away to create her own home, he would have been the first person to rejoice for her. As it was, her life became busier than ever with war work for Red Cross and St John (amalgamated in the war years), and the arrival in the village of scores of evacuees moving out of London to avoid the bombing.

Mairse's salvation, it could be said, and providentially balancing the day-in day-out care of an ageing father, was the discovery early on that she had God-given skills with babies and children of all ages. Friends' children, parishioners' children, cousins' children, godchildren, and (as they began to come along) her brothers' and sister's children, then the children of her 'original' children, all were and are grist to her mill. So much so that I think Mairse sends out now around a hundred and fifty birthday cards each year; and for these nearly thirty years since father died never a fortnight or so goes by without someone from those families blowing in to see her in her Potterne home for a meal or a night. If she has not seen them lately, she rings up for long phone conversations, or drives great distances round England to stay with them.

Sir Maurice Johnston, who with his wife Belinda bought father's house in Worton a month or so after his death, and is a very good friend of us all, told me when he was Lord Lieutenant that he flew the Union Jack on his flagpole when there was a Royal in the county or when he knew that Mary was going to see them. 'She's a saint', he likes saying; 'most of England will come to her funeral.' Hyperbole indeed, and not difficult to refute, and Mairse herself would be in the forefront of demolishing Maurice's case. But not for nothing did she win a year or two ago the silver cup that is awarded annually to the Potterne person 'who has contributed most to the life of our village in the past year'; and apparently the judges had some discussion as to whether to give her the cup outright. So it was she who established two bachelor homes for me after my ordination, one after the other, first in the east end of Bristol, and then a much

more substantial one in rural Surrey, which involved there helping
me choose a housekeeper who would run the parsonage without my
setting tongues wagging. The friendly spinster in her late sixties
whom we engaged proved to be rather a bad cook, and was so deaf
that message-taking for me tended to be a nonsense; but she rose
gallantly to my having to tell her after less than a year that I was getting married, and my conscience was considerably eased by my
elder sister Kay employing her at once.

Bishop Simpson, who took my institution early in 1954, had gazed
at my nice house that night when he came down from Southwark to
authorize me for my exciting task, exciting because the years of
training were at last over and I was on my own with my first 'cure of
souls.' After the service he came over to the house, was charming
with my newly-installed housekeeper, and then sat down in my
study for a helpful chat about the opportunities of the job. When he
got up to go he looked me in the eye and said: 'No house-keeper for
long here, Bickersteth, much too good a building for a bachelor. I
look forward to hearing you are getting married to some lovely
girl'. I obeyed orders, and Rosemary became in the spring of 1955
the first woman in my life, my daily pride and joy for fifty years. But
we both realize from our different viewpoints how much I owe to
the one and only loved and loving Mairse.

Feeding the Soil

Man goeth forth to his work and to his labour: until the evening.
O Lord how manifold are thy works: in wisdom hast Thou made them
all; the earth is full of thy riches.

Ps. 104 v. 23

  There were so many days that I was given,
  But whether of this spring or that? They merge,
  As travelling clouds across my permanent heaven.

The Land: Spring

MENTION 'Rugby' to me (I was there from 1935-40), and a good
mélange of memories easily surges back into my mind, sixty-
five years on. They all centre round Sheriff House, reminding me
how much store a public schoolboy sets by his house. It was the
centre of our school lives; we were not allowed into each other's; we
ate by houses, served by our 'butlers' who were called house blogs,
which sounds very derogatory, but we were fond of ours and got on
well with them; boys always wore house caps except for individuals
who became distinguished in one of the three main games, when
they wore their XV or XI cap for the appropriate term; and it was
only while I was there that houses began to be given names rather
than being called by the initials of their housemasters. All these
things were part of the house identity that was continually fostered.
House matches were passionately fought; I remember our Cock
House Rugger XV being practically idolised the year I surprisingly
played on the right wing in it. Johnnie was immensely proud of the
house he had created, and I can never forget him knocking on my
study door late on the evening of the Officers' Training Corps' annual House Competition. 'Come in' I called, and there was his
ecstatic face, wreathed in smiles and barely able to get out the
words: 'We've won, Bickersteth, we've won.' It was quite a moment
for me, but almost a bigger one for him.

The Corps did indeed gradually begin to take up a lot of time,
particularly in my last year when the war had begun and I was
Senior Under Officer, wearing almost exactly the uniform I would
be in as an officer a few months later. School armouries tended to

employ two retired regular soldiers, both ex warrant-officers, and I had of course worked very closely with them. When I went in to say goodbye at the end of my last term, these two old sweats were waiting for me, to say that they and the CO (who was always a beak in the school, ours at the time was Eric Reynolds[16]) had decided to let me keep my Sam Browne belt, as a thank-you and to wish me luck as a soldier. It was a WWI one, and old ones like it were much prized, I knew. So it was a remarkable gift, probably in fact neither the CO's nor theirs to offer, as it was school property. But of course I said yes, and managed not to cry with pleasure, which would not have been at all right. It was much admired throughout my service, and after my children and grandchildren had used it to dress up in I returned it sixty years later to the school, as a veteran belt of two world wars, and it was gratefully received by the archivist.

Along with most OTC members I thoroughly enjoyed Corps activities, which included the annual camps for the first week of the summer holidays; one year we had, amazing to recall, a full-scale demonstration of a cavalry charge by the 15th/19th Hussars, complete with drawn sabres, (and this in the year of grace 1937); I also shot on the national rifle ranges at Bisley for a few days one Easter holiday (but did not make the Shooting VIII), and both before and after that biked frequently the four or five miles out of Rugby to the school ranges to shoot for the house; we had major Field Days twice a year against another school corps, generally entailing a train journey with a march, which we revelled in behind our band through the town to and from the station; and we took immense trouble over the Annual Inspection on the Close, for which a senior general came down from the War Office. I recall Sir Hereward Wake coming, and Sir Edmund Ironside (names to roll round schoolboy tongues), not to mention the then Major-General Archie Wavell[17]; this unusual soldier had to our fascination lost an eye in WWI, and after his visit we all bought his *Other Men's Flowers*, an anthology of poetry that he allegedly knew entirely by heart.

At the start of the invasion scare in the summer of 1940 all of us who were over eighteen, as well as having joined the army (but being sent back to school) also joined the newly-created Local Defence Volunteers, and took turns at manning look-out posts round

16. Later Headmaster of Stowe
17. Later F.M. Lord Wavell, Viceroy of India

Rugby. Ours was up the Water Tower, a mile out of the town on the Barby Road, to which eight or ten of us senior cadets bicycled as it was getting dark, and remained there on duty in shifts until dawn, before coming back to augmented house breakfast and a full day's work in school, no doubt dozing off at times. What we would have done to German parachutists with our few rounds of .303 ammunition for the WWI Lee Enfield rifles must remain an unanswered question of military conjecture; and that would have applied all over the country where thousands of men between the ages of 18 and 65 became LDVs.[18]

Does all this army talk make it sound as if our lives revolved round what we did in uniform for a few hours a week with the Officers Training Corps? Were we in fact, as the name implies, simply a feeder body for leadership in the three services? Was there much difference between us and the *Hitlerjugend*? The answer of course is that we knew perfectly well that we were at school to study academic subjects, not to have it drummed into us how marvellous England was and how wicked the Germans were. British critical faculties, particularly strong anyway in the young, remained as powerful as ever; boys in OTCs, thousands of us *in toto*, were not remotely belligerent; but belonging to the Corps in wartime all helped to made us think of ourselves as young adults rather than schoolboys, and that in Platonic vein was good for our overall education.

It was quite rightly lessons, not the Corps, with which far and away the majority of our time was taken up. Mine, after School Certificate in July 1936, centred round the Classics. After I was fifteen I did no mathematics, no science, no languages other than dead ones, no geography, only ancient history, and very little English. With adult hindsight, it was all shamefully one-sided although that never occurred to us at the time, except when we were moaning about our third 'copy' (which meant English into Latin or Greek) in two days, yet another 'unseen' (the reverse), or chunks of Herodotus and Virgil homework often on the same night. The B Block (Languages) and the C Block (Science) were probably as tilted towards their subjects as we were in the A Block towards the Classics; but looking back on it I realize that I was not even becoming a proper classical scholar. In other words I never found myself pick-

---

18. The title was changed to Home Guard that autumn

ing up an Aristophanes play to read it for pleasure in his own language, never mastered Greek mythology, only absorbed Latin tags to the extent that the right one for a particular situation does every so often leap into my head.

Years later when I was reading History with the Open University, it really hit me just how blinkered my education had been for four out of my five Rugby years. So I plucked up courage to write to the then Head of Classics there to explain how deprived I felt, fifty years on, of a more general education, and how I hoped that such an imbalance had long since been corrected. In a most helpful letter, he was able to reassure me with specimen curricula, that there was much less early specialization, although he had to point out that in the last couple of years of school (a great deal less than my four) the demands of university examiners had to result in some narrowing of study towards a boy's particular subjects. Indeed that is understandable, but the classical tyranny under which we worked was not necessary, and in my case, not being a top scholar capable of getting totally immersed in it all, it certainly resulted in my often getting bored with the endless Latin and Greek of the typical A Block day. As a result, I was too long in the Lower Bench (or Sixth; only in the A Block did we retain the old term 'Bench', where we actually sat at veteran desks covered with hundred-year-old carved names); and I did not really work hard again until I got into the Upper Bench for my last year in the school.

The other side, of course, to the disgruntlement coin is that into my sub-conscious there undoubtedly went a feel for words, a continuing delight in going to a dictionary to check that I was correctly guessing a linguistic derivation, and a reasonable ability to string sentences together for what was to be fifty years of sermon-writing. It was not the teachers' fault that I was a rather unsatisfactory student. R.R. Timberlake taught me for all my five terms in the Lower Bench; he was the sort of ingenuous scholar that got hopelessly ragged by eye-to-the-main-chance boys. I remember, for example, the form joker deciding one morning when he was bored with Thucydides to liven things up by lighting a fire in his desk, while we all, including RRT, had our heads down. When the smoke had started billowing encouragingly round the room, and the rest of us, knowing the culprit, had all sized up what was happening, the perpetrator calls out urgently: 'Sir, sir, there's a fire in my desk, sir'.

RRT starts up: 'Heavens, Dodsworth, so there is, I'm so sorry, I'll come and help you put it out', and rushes off his podium to tackle the conflagration. RRT, who had a lot going for him in actual fact, went on later to be the highly successful headmaster of Lancaster Grammar School for many years. On the other hand the brilliant R.L. Roberts, who was my Upper Bench Master, became the Head-master of Blundells soon after I left. He was very clever, and you were aware of that all the time; he was also a devout High Church-man, who thought Rugbeian religion left a great deal to be desired. As well as caring for all our classical studies, he took us through several of the Pauline epistles memorably (I have his notes still). Unaccountably in human terms, his headmastership went literally to his head, we eventually heard; he would march up and down his study repeating; 'I'm the headmaster of Blundells, I'm . . . etc'. This eccentricity led to his resignation and the end of his schoolmaster-ing; but the visionary Bishop Philip Loyd of St Albans recognising his qualities, ordained him priest. He joined the staff of *The Church Times* and eventually became the editor who converted the paper from its anglo-catholic stance into one valued by the Anglican Com-munion as a whole. The Crown also appointed him Chaplain of the Savoy Chapel, a post he held for twelve years; he was made a CVO by Her Majesty on his retirement.

In my last year Sheriff held what I believe was the first-ever house dance in the conservative stronghold that Rugby was. Nancy Lovett, our bouncy and delightful matron helped us organize it. She and two or three young housemasters' wives rustled up enough 'suitable girls' (they would have been 'gals' today) to match those of the more senior boys who wanted to be in on this revolutionary venture. Probably about twenty couples, we had records for the dancing, with the house blog getting really keen over producing good eats and (non-alcoholic) drink; we had a super evening, and our en-terprise proved to be something of a prototype. 'Proper' music too at Rugby was always of a very high standard, and my great moment came one term when I, who could not play a note of any musical in-strument, but sang keenly in the school choir and so could read music passably, had to learn how to conduct part of Handel's *Water Music* in the House Music Competition. The reason for this risky request by the Head of Music in Sheriff (David Rossiter, sadly killed a few years later in the RAF) was that every single boy in the house who could play anything wanted to do so (I think about two dozen of them), and none wanted to be detailed to conduct. I got by, finding it an exhilarating exercise of power which I have never indulged in since. It was indeed at Rugby that I learnt to appreciate classical music; top soloists like Solomon came to perform, as did the City of Birmingham Orchestra every other year

It must have been very soon after we arrived in the school in September 1935 that Buchanan, Peters, Ellis (no Christian names then) and I began going for Sunday afternoon walks. We were to keep them up for the winter terms for our entire five years in the school. They were not mammoth treks, probably no more than an hour and a half long, but they quickly developed into a regular 'engagement'. We invariably went south, along the Barby Road outside Sheriff's front door, because that took us into the country at once. Sometimes we would meet an eccentric beak named K.A.R. Sugden, a tall gangly classicist, every bit a bachelor, who if he was feeling like it would humbly ask if he could join us. As he always walked down the white line in the middle of the road, the addition of extra bodies alongside him was not easy, but a great deal more possible in those days of minimal traffic. 'Why do you follow the white lines, Sir?', asked the bold Buchanan once. 'Because, boy, you can be sure not to get lost' came the quick inconsequential reply.

John Buchanan was a Scot, with a beautiful pure Aberdonian accent. Extremely good-looking, he went on after war service as a doctor in the Royal Navy to become a hard-working GP in Kent, and died in the 1990s.

Richard Peters and I had next-door desks the whole way up the school, he having been top Common Entrance boy and I one of the three bottom scholars. He was unassuming and quiet, a fine horn-player, with a puckish sense of humour, and was greatly respected in the house. He joined the Rifle Brigade, and after surviving a dangerous couple of years was killed instantly leading his platoon against unseen Japanese in the jungles of Burma, an example of the kind of cruel casualty of war, that such an unmilitary unintentional soldier should have been carried off by it.

Errington Ellis had gone with John Buchanan to Cambridge to train as a doctor; he joined the RAF once he was qualified and after the war gradually became one of the best-known and best-loved pediatricians in his native Newcastle. In the 50s I was his best man, and Alysoun and he remain our very oldest friends, still seeing a lot of each other.

We four contemporaries loved it when KARS walked with us. I was in his form for two terms before I got into the Sixth. He had the Upper XX, refusing we always gathered to take higher forms because he was only a temporary master, originally taking a vacant post for six months; he said he enjoyed the freedom of remaining 'temporary'; but he stayed nearly twenty years, an inspiring classics master if ever there was one.

'Where do you live, sir?' was a question we loved putting to him, to elicit the invariable reply: 'Wantage, boy, Wantage; you can't miss it, there's a statue of King Alfred there.'

KARS was also one of the beaks who was always in his place in chapel on a Sunday morning, and occasionally he would be glad to discuss the chapel services on our walks, never over-critically, remembering he was on the staff himself, and having therefore a loyalty to the three chaplains, who were respectively a rumbustious rugger player, a fairly dour Mathematics teacher, and a cheerful but rather old Australian housemaster. None were bad at their job, but of course the boys tore them to shreds most of the time.

We had daily prayers in the big chapel before school, and a matins form of sung service on Sundays. Communion of course was voluntary. Those were days long before the young revolted, and there was never any question but that 'chapel' happened; it was part of the place.

The singing was great, under some very fine beaks as organists and choirmasters, who really had us all joining in. I remember years later going to preach at a well-known school just before compulsory chapel began to be phased out, and not a single boy other than those in the choir opened their mouths throughout; how I bled for the youngsters encountering that when they arrived.

Our headmaster, P.H.B. Lyon,was a totally-committed Christian, a wartime poet and hymn-writer, an unobtrusive kind of head; he always wore a grey trilby hat, as never worn by anyone else to watch rugger or cricket matches; but with all that he was a holder of the MC, won shortly before he was made prisoner of war. So he had been through the fire; he was generous and thoughtful, and he preached well. When Hugh was ninety in the 1980s, eight Old Rugbeian bishops gave him dinner in the House of Lords, and that must have been a tremendous thrill for the man who had been HM to us all; we had a great affection for him.

With a man of Hugh's calibre as our headmaster, our particular brand of 'public school religion', derided then as now, was not all bad. For instance I belonged to a small coterie of Sixth Formers, called 'Club', which met in our VIths' private room in School House, and though we were actually there to have bible studies, and that was healthy and fine for boys at the top of the school to fore-gather for, we nevertheless would get bogged down many times in 'What can be done about the chapel services?' John Stott, head of the school my last year, later one of the leading evangelical clergy in England with in time a world-wide reputation, was behind Club, and I think it must have been he who put 'Bash' on to me.

'Bash', the rather apt nickname of the Reverend E.J.H. Nash, was an Anglican clergyman of strong evangelical persuasion, who came to have a remarkable ministry round the public schools in the 30s and 40s, operating from a Christian Union base. One term in 1937 I had a note from Bash asking me to meet him, and we set off round the Close for a talk. I had guessed what it would be about, as he was well-known for these blitz visits. He quickly tackled me over my faith, explaining how he had heard I was a keen member of Club and so on. It was soon obvious that he considered I was not a true believer in the saving power of Christ. But he had actually picked the wrong man, because he was not to know until I told him that my mother's death at the end of 1936, coming on top of confirmation that in itself meant a great deal to me the year before, had between them given me the confidence to be a glad believer in Christ, both in heart and mind.

But Bash took no notice of my trying to explain my firm if still only partly-formed faith in God. He had a one-track mind that only his way was the right one for young minds, and he pressed me hard as we peregrinated once more round the Close; I resisted equally hard. His approach was coming across to me as too cut and dried, too exclusive, too narrow, too, yes, arrogant. I knew deep down that it was not for me. Bash was very put out; clearly most of the boys he walked and talked with responded to his blandishments, and he left me a disappointed man, disappointed in his failure to persuade me to change the way I believed, and disappointed for me and my future as a Christian. John Stott was much more magnanimous and relaxed, when I saw him next. 'Bash is like that', he murmured, 'I am sorry, but I do understand'.

The Rugby experience, therefore, was wide and deep, and after five years it was sadly and somehow unexpectedly over, and I was standing in late July 1940 with the whole school, crowded in below 'The Wall', which is the boundary of the headmaster's garden overlooking The Close. The garden itself is six feet higher than the Close, so the headmaster from Arnold's day on has delivered his end-of-year speech looking down on this large assembly of beaks and boys. He walks out of his house, rain or fine, into the garden, invisibly from the waiting throng; and there he suddenly is above us, standing in a small gap in the hedge (cleared specially by the school gardeners, a yearly task) to address everyone, including of course for the last time the hundred or more leavers. I forget what else my headmaster talked about that summer afternoon, as the main interest of his speech for me was the announcement that I was the winner of one of the two Stovin Leaving Exhibitions.

The value of these exhibitions, presumably funded by an Old Boy of that name, could be claimed from the school whenever the recipient wanted, and were for use at any university. They are awarded most years, for 'services to Rugby School'; I have always thought that my Stovin was a sort of consolation prize for not having won a university scholarship. I perfectly recollect the Upper Bench master saying earlier that year that I could pick up a scholarship at 'some other college', but through persisting in only going for the House, I was unlikely to be successful. I did persist, to RLR's barely-disguised regret, as any Sixth Form master enjoys the *kudos* of his pupils winning scholarships. George Gidney and I went from Sheriff to Oxford together to sit the scholarship exam for two or three days in that last spring we had at school; we enjoyed ourselves, but neither of us was successful. So armed only with my school-leaving award I 'broke up' for the last time, and away I went, not to the university but in the middle of the most momentous year of the century for Great Britain, to join the Colours.

The two years 1940 and 1941 are the only ones in which I have kept a full-page diary, filling it almost every day. 1942's begins well, but peters out. I probably just lost interest. Be that as it may, 1940's begins with the affirmation that 'I think I should have some record of my last two terms at Rugby and what I hope will be my first term at Oxford.' I wonder why I thought I should. It is also interesting that in that 'phoney war' period (as it came to be called), I was still hoping to get up to Oxford in the autumn, as my cousin Tony had in the autumn of 1939. After the war I found plenty of men up who had been there for that 1939-1940 year, but no one from 1940-1941. That will have been because the whole tempo of the war had changed dramatically with Hitler's invasion of the Low Countries and then France on 10th May 1940, followed in June by our complete defeat, but the far from ignominious evacuation of 300,000 men across the Channel.

We heard from Edward (he was Ted by now) in the Sudan early in January that despite the obvious problem of how to get here he was going to be given home leave of the usual three months, which the Political Service had had since anyone could remember in the spring or summer. He was ecstatic at the prospect, glad indeed to be seeing his family and friends, but also clearly determined to persuade the Foreign Office to let him join the army. He was feeling very much left out of things; we could tell from his letters. Sure enough he made it home by the end of April, two or three days only before my last term at school began, so we saw very little of each other.

This perhaps gave enough handle to father's most irregular request to the school that I be allowed some leave in term time, in order to catch up with him properly before he went back to Africa for what would clearly be a long time. Rugby turned up trumps (in these days it is difficult to understand that this was an unheard-of kind of request), and the long weekend Mairse and he and I had in the Lamb at Burford coincided with the end of the Dunkirk evacuation in mid-June, so at times it felt strangely wrong to be enjoying ourselves when these far-reaching things were happening. The fact that Ted's request for indefinite leave of absence in order to join up was categorically refused ('we can't just stop administering the Sudan', said his masters) cast a considerable shadow for him over being on leave at all; but we revelled in being together in that beautiful part of Oxfordshire, where I discovered the delights of good draught bitter.

After the Rugby term had ended a month later, village life in West Kent, which was suddenly Britain's front line, began to feel very different as the weeks passed during the aftermath of the Dunkirk miracle. The Chamberlain government had collapsed as the defence of Europe began to crumble, and Winston Churchill (to rising morale despite the critical situation) had taken over the reins. All the talk was of the coming invasion. The evacuees, as the children who had come down from London's East End as soon as the war had begun were called, stopped trickling home, as they had been doing pretty steadily during the long months of the phoney war. The ones who had stayed were beginning to integrate into their hosts' homes, and were making friends with the village schoolchildren. The Meade-Waldo's home, Stonewall Park, had eight or nine of them, but mostly they were in twos and threes, a total perhaps in our village of thirty or forty of them, some indication of what a major logistic and social enterprise it had been countrywide. Mairse had several in her Cubs and Brownies, and there was one occasion in the air battles of August and September when she had a dangerous time fetching them down from Stonewall's upper floors, where they were having a game as the bombs began to drop. Glass started crashing out of the windows as she rushed round the building getting them all down into the cellar. But it was still safer for these children than facing the blitz in London would have been.

For me personally the weeks stretched into months without my being called up. I heard afterwards that my papers had been mislaid, and it did not help that I wanted to serve not with the Warwicks, with which I had no connection except for the fact that Rugby where I enlisted was in the county, but rather to transfer to The Buffs, which had become very much the Jelf family regiment. My cousin Raymond Grace while serving in a Buffs battalion had just been captured in France, and another cousin Arthur Jelf was with the regiment in the Middle East. Furthermore I had been born in Canterbury. This was the case for transfer that I made with the colonel of the regiment, General Scarlett, when I was summoned to meet him at his London home, the normal drill when anyone wanted to get a commission in a good regiment. All went well with the interview, but still nothing happened; I was learning the hard lesson that waiting is a key part of army (in this case pre-army) life.

There was however never a dull moment, as the sun continued to shine every day out of a cloudless sky. I spent three weeks with Errington Ellis at his Heddon-on-the-Wall home in Northumber-

land, hay-making at the local farm. All over England the farm workers were flocking into the army, though their bosses tried to make a
case for them to be 'reserved occupation.' Both Errington and I had
done quite a lot on farms round Rugby during the spring and early
summer, so it was good to be at it again at once, and to feel one was
doing something towards the war effort. The farmer put up
wonderfully well with our ignorance of how to do things; for example, one day leading in 'my' horse, with a fifteen-foot-high 'pike' of
hay on a tip-up cart in the shafts, I took the turn through the last
gate into the yard too sharply, and the side of the cart banged hard
into the very solid stone gatepost. Over went the entire pike, right
in the gateway; the old horse turned round and gazed at the mess,
as if to say I really need not have done that. It took two of us an
hour to clear and reload all the scattered hay. The farmer's wife saw
it before he did, and rushed out of the house to pour oil. She made
the most delectable Yorkshire pudding, which you have up there as
a separate course with lashings of thick brown gravy, scrumptious
beyond words.

One day her husband let us off at lunchtime and we saddled up
Errington's father's two hunters for a long ride over the
countryside, 'including some grand gallops', and then came in to a
late tea before going out with our guns and bagging several rabbits
for supper. No wartime problems there. The village church, where
I was ten years or so later for Errington's wedding, was packed with
troops on Sundays. The rector, after we had met him once or twice,
and found that he knew of father, asked me if I was thinking of taking Holy Orders; 'You'll see the light one day', he said rather
unhelpfully when I said I wasn't. 'I wonder if I shall!' was my diary
comment.

But Kent proved to be not at all the same as far-off Northumberland, when I got home to realize with a vengeance that what we
came later to know as the Battle of Britain was in full swing above
our heads. The losses of men and planes were much less than we
were told at the time; for example we heard after the war that the
185 German planes shot down by our Spitfires and Hurricanes to
huge acclaim on August 15 should have been only 72, obviously enthusiastic pilots both claiming the same success; and the Germans
did just the same. Although our losses were very serious indeed,
almost catastrophically diminishing our reserves of men and

aircraft, the exaggerations of the German High Command were far greater. We certainly saw and heard many more German planes screeching to the ground than we did ours.

I remember very clearly a Dornier on fire just above our hop garden, while we cowered below a bank; the crew had baled out and were captured a mile away by the Home Guard to their great excitement; but the plane came down in the water meadow just over the hedge. Kay, married as I have mentioned just before the war to Charles Beveridge, a solicitor turned naval officer who was soon serving abroad, was living with her baby on the Isle of Wight, and had the terrifying experience of a Heinkel coming down above her on fire, and missing her house by a few feet, 'the white face of the pilot clearly visible, as Robert and I crouched together in a ditch in the garden' (he was a few months old); 'I'd just pulled him out of his pram on the lawn before I saw the plane. It crashed a hundred feet past the cottage'.

England was bracing itself for the German invasion, and of course in Kent we would have been right in the path of it. All round us the army divisional commanders had pill-boxes built, facing south, and we in the Home Guard had to practise piling in and out of them 'under fire'. Most of us decided we would rather die fighting in the open than cooped up in a twelve-foot-across brick box with a concrete roof, which one well-directed tank shell would have 'brewed up' in an instant. Anyhow the next army commander generally wanted new pill-boxes sited differently, or even facing the other way, so we poor part-time soldiers never quite got the hang of what they were for or how we were meant to use them. Now I believe the few surviving ones are listed buildings.

Certainly Home Guard duty became much more intense in the face of the threat from across the Channel. Father offered us the back regions of the rectory kitchen for the duty patrol; there the off-duty chaps slept as best we could on straw palliasses, tolerably comfy, and of course it was not cold weather. In the small hours we would make cocoa on a primus stove in our scullery. Three of us went on patrol every night round the village and surrounding lanes together, sometimes meeting the 'proper soldiers' patrols for a chat; the boarding school girls in the castle had gone off to Devon when the war began, and we had troops there from then on. In late autumn the farmer at the top of the village invited us to make use of

his oast house, a much better vantage point than the rectory, so at
the end of October Chiddingstone Home Guard moved up there,
and slept on stuffed hop pockets on the oast's wooden floor, and
were quite cosy.

Furthermore when the Germans changed their tactics to the
night bombing of London, we seemed to be right underneath the
hundreds of planes droning unseen above us unless picked up by
searchlights. When there was a moon, the glinting formations of
bombers, perhaps two or three hundred at a time, were an awesome
sight. Many times the ones limping home, after having been hit by
anti-aircraft fire or night fighters, would come back low over us,
frequently lightening their load by letting their bombs go at ran-
dom. There were occasional casualties from the high-explosive
ones; and on Sep 17 I wrote:

> Night duty and very lively; seven or eight bombs pretty close and
> after one double bang I lay down on my face in case there was a
> third. My heart was pounding and I was frightened. Two more
> came down beyond the old oast and made the most lovely orange
> flashes in the sky.

But there were not many nights like that; we more often had
quite a busy time dealing with the incendiaries, beating out the
flames with farm shovels where they landed and burst (they were
only eighteen inches long), and occasionally we had to shin up the
farm ladders and fling them off the roofs of the buildings. All this of
course was very small beer by comparison with what the London
fire-fighters were gallantly doing on a huge scale, notably of course
in saving St Paul's Cathedral night after night for so long.

Meanwhile I was getting impatient with the army for not wanting
me. I got a place at the Home Guard Training School at Osterley
Park, just west of London, and had an astonishing few days under
instruction from Spanish Civil War veterans of a few years earlier.
The head of the school was Tom Wintringham, a legendary left-
wing survivor of that conflict. He and his staff graphically demons-
trated to us greenhorns how a civilian population could wreak
havoc on an invading army of regular troops, provided we were not
at all squeamish about the underhand means we used. It was com-
mando-guerrilla stuff of a high order (indeed did the word *guerrilla*
come from that Spanish war?). One certainly felt that the instructors

had done all these revolting things themselves. I was not brilliant at conveying what I had learned to my rather shocked and unsophisticated Home Guard colleagues back home.

By contrast, keeping up with some Latin and Greek for an hour or two every day, which I decided I ought to try and do, seemed and of course was, totally irrelevant to the topsy-turvy world we were living in. In November I began chasing the War Office, but they were not interested, and said it would all happen in due course. So in desperation I went along to the local office of the Forestry Commission, and on the strength of all the 'wooding' father and I had done together in the garden asked if there was a job going. Fortunately for my morale there was, and I started the following Monday in a fifty-acre wood two miles from home, to which I bicycled every morning for a full day's work, and my first-ever earnings. I loved it from the start. With a drink and sandwiches in my haversack, I set off in the darkness of the seven o'clock morning, passing other labourers doing the same thing, as we exchanged cheery greetings. In the big conifer plantation I began to learn what to do in a clear-felling exercise, and how to produce varying lengths of timber for military use. The foreman was super, soon realizing that I knew how to use a cross-cut saw and swing an axe, and I quickly graduated to managing the horses, with their traces and chains that we used to pull out the heavy stuff. The weather was very hard almost at once, so the fires of brash that were always going were great for us to sit by over 'ten-ses' and lunch. We finished at 4.30, which meant that I got home (as I had left) in the dark, tired out after a strenuous nine-hour day, but immensely fulfilled; and Friday nights, when I had collected my week's pay (£4. 5s. 3d) from the foreman, were bliss.

My biggest black was to break a colleague's finger when I was stacking small stuff (in this case it was 'three by fours', meaning lengths of conifer three feet long by four inches across); the drill was to throw three of them together to the man stacking. With practice the three lengths stayed in one piece for catching, but you had to get the rhythm right, so that the three only arrived just after the stacker had put down the last consignment. An hour of so into it, I must have thrown my three a fraction of a second too soon, and my 'mate' (Snowy Turner; he had very blonde hair) let out a yelp of pain as they landed fair and square on his fingers which were still against the growing log pile. Bless him he made no fuss at all at my careless mistake, but the foreman drove him off at once to hospital for the hand to be x-rayed, and they were back before the end of the day with one broken finger in a splint, and Snowy carried on working with a ready 'It's all fine, don't worry' to my profuse apologies. The amazing sequel to the story is that a full half-century later when we were visiting friends in Chiddingstone, Rosemary and I stopped for petrol at a garage not far from 'our' wood, and who should be filling up there too but Snowy? We recognized each other instantly (1940 to 1995, not bad), and to Snowy's enormous credit had a good laugh about the accident as if it had happened that morning.

It is not surprising that my sheer delight in encountering country people of that calibre since we had left London in 1935, and also enormously enjoying the rural England they lived in, had made me write in the diary in November:

> Told father that I am more and more thinking that some kind of work with the land is what I'ld like if I come through the war. He was fairly non-committal, for which I do not blame him, as it was obviously rather a shock.

As I reflect on that now, more than sixty years on, the conversation brings home to me how father never once made the kind of (well-intentioned) remark of the Heddon-on-the-Wall rector a month or so earlier, about my 'seeing the light' (*sc* of ordination). But without a shadow of doubt father must have kept on praying for many years that I would move towards it of my own free will. That was exemplary parenting, given that he clearly felt any gifts I had might lie that way.

We had a quiet Christmas, and on 6 January I had the call-up papers which I had expected five months earlier. The three of us went straight off for a week's holiday in Herefordshire, staying near Goodrich Court at Ross-on-Wye to which Uncle Julian[19] had evacuated the whole of his school some months before. Then it was home for a last few days in the wood, goodbyes to my forestry friends, and I was catching the train from Penshurst to Canterbury and The Buffs Depot. 'I hated the moment of going, but F and M were very good, which made it easier.' It was 16th January 1941.

---

19. He was Headmaster of Felsted, Essex 1933–1943

On my mother's knee, with Mary (8), Edward (11), and Ella (14) 1926

Father aged 80 in 1963
(Rugby 1896–1900)

At Sheriff House
Rugby 1935–1940

With some of my soldiers, Warwickshire, 1942

Shooting in India, with a Sikh brother officer,
our shikari and driver, 1946

Eights Week at Oxford, Christ Church 2nd VIII, 1947

Outside the Christ Church Boat House, 1948

iii

Best man, Errington Ellis,
Northumberland, 1951

On safari in the Sudan, 1954

iv

Going for a Soldier

The spacious firmament on high,
With all the blue ethereal sky,
And spangled heaven, a shining frame,
Their great Original proclaim.
Joseph Addison 1672–1719

I sing once more
The mild continuous epic of the soil,
Hazel and harvest, tilth and husbandry.
The Land, Winter

I WAS a private soldier in The Buffs at Chaucer Barracks for almost six weeks, enough time to teach me a large number of English swear words; and that was quite a useful acquisition for the five and a half years in the Army which were to come; I also learnt which were the really bad ones that could land anyone who used them in serious trouble from the recipient. Militarily it was not very creative, as I had already covered in the Officers Training Corps most of what we spent our days doing as army recruits. Socially it was fascinating, from barrack room talk with a cross section of trainee infantrymen of my age, only one or two officer-bound like me, to civilised evening and week-end discussion with judges and bishops and retired colonial servants and dear old ladies who were friends of grandmother or the uncles.

There was also the added bonus of Uncle Burgon,[20] back in Canterbury from Canada to which he had returned for duty on 2 September 1939, the eve of the outbreak of war. But now, with Britain under the imminent threat of invasion, he could stand the peaceful life in Canada no longer, and having got indefinite leave of absence from the University, he lost no time in hastening home across the Atlantic, crossing it, as he had gone out, in one of the fast liners which the German U-boats never succeeded in torpedoing. So my off-duty times in that January-February 1941, though occasionally in the pub with the chaps (but against their ability to sink four or five pints without turning a hair, I never managed

20. He was Warden of Hart House, Toronto University 1921–1947

65

really to enjoy more than two), were often with Uncle B, by then an enthusiastic member of the city's Home Guard; or in other charming Canterbury homes enjoying hot baths and gracious company.

To be told therefore one late February morning, with one other private soldier, that we were leaving for officer-training in three days' time brought quite a pang of regret; life in a barrack room had become perfectly manageable, and I was much enjoying Canterbury and everything that it offered. But I was now bound for my next stage of soldiering, 162 Officer Cadet Training Unit at Gordon Barracks Bulford on Salisbury Plain, and it was quite a thrill, as we left Chaucer Barracks for the last time, that the august personage of my Company Sergeant Major, twice my age, with twenty years in the Army, but almost treating us as officers already, helped the two of us get our kit on to the truck for the station. After shopping and a haircut in London (I had been warned about the importance of the latter), we caught a train from Waterloo to Salisbury, where we found ourselves in army trucks as part of an intake of a hundred cadets, all of us *en route* for the very new huts of this rapidly expanding sprawl of military buildings. The entire unit was run by the Coldstream Guards, and one knew it all the time. No doubt the assault training of today is tougher, but what we had to tackle that spring was not a picnic. Yet despite the very hard training, a huge amount of foot-slogging (motorised infantry were not yet around), live firing exercises, and frequent nights in slit trenches on the Plain, I could still write in my diary towards the end of April: 'Today was just like a school Field Day'.

For time-off in the evening there was blanco-ing and equipment cleaning: 'did it in two and a half hours to-night', I noted on 26 February, implying that was something of a record. I was always tired, but seem to have been reasonably content, no doubt partly because of the intensity of it all making boredom impossible. Most evenings various groupings of us would repair to the NAAFI[21] which to its credit supplied much more than the 'cuppa char and a wad, please' of its repute; NAAFIs were important social centres for us all. A concert was generally in preparation, thanks to a lively cadet who had been in show business, and I remember a leading light at each production was a very funny Welshman named Tasker Watkins, who was always coming back drunk at night into our hut,

21. Navy Army and Air force Institute, the services' canteen.

but won a VC in Italy fairly soon afterwards, and is now an extremely senior judge. We all had a great deal of fun along with the
very hard work.

The garrison church at Bulford, where fifty years later I took a
confirmation on behalf of the Bishop of Salisbury, was well attended
voluntarily, as well as the many times when we had to march there
and back on what were then compulsory church parades. On one
such parade, I was unwise enough on a beautiful morning, when
the crocuses were out and I had to agree with myself that it was
(even on Salisbury Plain) positively spring-like, to come drifting out
of church chatting to people as I had been used to doing at home,
when there was a stentorian bellow from the RSM, who had presumably been watching us carefully. I learnt that morning the hard
way that once we had emerged from holy ground, army discipline
took over again with indecent haste: 'Mr Bickersteth sir, come 'ere
sir, please sir' (The RSM had explained to all of us cadets on arrival
that 'you sir me sir, and I sir you sir'); and the outcome of that little
'mistake', to the merciless chaffing of my fellow cadets, was that this
chap who was known to go to church when he did not have to, was
put on a charge for 'not walking smartly out of church' and got
three extra parades for his slip-up. What is more I had a dirty rifle
(which probably meant a minuscule speck of dust somewhere near
the breech block, a notorious spot the sergeant always checked with
special, not to say devilish, care) on the third of my extra evening
ones, and got three more for my pains.

None the less when soon after this incident my Coldstreamer
platoon commander called me in to the Orderly Room to discuss
what regiment I should go for, he said without beating about the
bush: 'Well Bickersteth, I am putting you down for the Brigade'. I
bravely demurred, with lots of 'sir's to soften my challenging his
complimentary remarks. The Buffs was my county regiment, and I
had already been accepted, as I have mentioned, by our Colonel,
General Scarlett. The Guards was too posh for me, and I would not
have been able to pay the mess bills, although I did not put it to my
officer like that probably. Anyhow, down I went for The Buffs, and
many weeks later to my amazement I got a telegram from the previous Colonel of the regiment, General Sir Arthur Lynden Bell:
'Welcome to the regiment, we are delighted you are going to join
us'. He must have been sent a copy of the London Gazette ahead of

my passing successfully out of the OCTU. I had only met him once socially in Canterbury, but how immensely impressive that was, and indicative of what 'the regiment' means to regular soldiers; and indeed how important this family spirit is in making the British Army the finest in the world.

By mid-May I was leaving Bulford for good, to collect my brand-new uniform from Mr Crook himself, friend as he was to so many hundreds of young officers; he was for nearly thirty years the Managing Director of Humphreys and Crook, Military Tailors, of Suffolk Street, near the National Gallery, and he made every client reckon that no one else mattered. I know I walked out into Trafalgar Square as a subaltern in The Buffs with huge pride; and on the Sunday I appeared resplendent at Matins in Chiddingstone Church. But I was back in old clothes very soon after, 'busy with the country things I love', says the diary, including a visit to a young farmer friend a mile away across the fields, 'doing far more for the nation than he would have been as a soldier. He had tried to be released for the army many times, and was kicking his heels at the frustration of his reserved occupation'.

The week's leave went too quickly and I was back in Canterbury, not as I was expecting in Howe Barracks on top of Sandwich Hill, but put up in the Abbots Barton Hotel down in the town; this felt distinctly *infra dig* to the five of us brand-new 2nd Lieutenants, cocky young men that I am sure we were, and mad keen to learn about life in the Officers' Mess.

I had barely moved to the Mess when in early August I was posted to the 11th Battalion, and very pleased I was to get to a proper unit, right in the front line of defence. It was stationed at St Margaret's Bay, of all places, with RHQ actually in my grandfather's house where we had so often stayed in the 1930s. The CO was a charming WWI survivor called Tit (for obvious reasons) Willows, and could not have been more of a contrast to my company commander; he also had WWI ribbons up, but was a former ranker, thoroughly vulgar and uncouth, who drank too much, but with it all he was clearly rather pleased to have this green public schoolboy in his charge. Strangely perhaps I took quite a fancy to him in response; one sensed that he would take charge superbly in a tight corner. But sadly for him, he never got a chance in his second war, as his drinking habits soon landed him in trouble, and by that autumn he was under close arrest, before a court martial sentenced him to be dismissed the service.

Within three days of my arrival the whole battalion was on Exercise 'More Binge'. We were in XII Corps, and the unknown Major-General Montgomery was our energetic commander. Already thought much of, or he would not have been entrusted with the front line of defence in SE England, he was obviously determined to make us get fit and work hard. 'Binge' had apparently been only a month before, and Monty had seen some bad gaps and mistakes in the course of it, so had his Corps out on a repeat performance in double-quick time. The exercise could not have been a better introduction for me to get to know my soldiers, 17 Platoon, with whom I had marched many miles by the time we staggered in again forty-eight hours later, after both nights had been taken up with 'fighting'. Our company commander was not satisfied with how we had done, and almost at once took us out on a company exercise for two more nights.

I found I could 'take' all the marching, which was great, as it enabled the new boy that I was to get established. Before long we left our 'billets' (requisitioned houses) in St Margaret's Bay and went under canvas in Waldershare Park nearer Dover. There we took over stand-to positions from the Royal Sussex Regiment, and suddenly realized that we were the last soldiers on the south coast before you got to the Germans.

Naturally enough we were worked very hard: night operations, more exercises, and a twenty-seven mile route march were interspersed with long days in the harvest field, as the farmers, very short of men, were having to cope with bad weather to get in the harvest as late as the last week in August.

By mid-September we were in billets again, right in Dover; Maison Dieu Road is under the castle, which was Corps HQ and the venue for the first Field Court Martial in which I had been involved; I was to act for a deserter. Many junior officers were detailed to prosecute or defend in courts-martial, before a military judge who was generally a major but always a lawyer by profession. As this prisoner was palpably (and was pleading) guilty, my job was to enter a plea in mitigation. He was quite an intelligent man, and I was able to spend a couple of hours in his cell in the castle, in order to put together my case. Then I wrote out my speech, basing my argument

(I quote from a letter I wrote home to father about it afterwards) on the lines of:

> This man has never had a fair chance in life, nor has he been sympathetically dealt with by the Army; leniency of sentence would show that someone in authority is prepared at last to give him a square deal according to his merits etc etc'. In court I did not feel it went very well. But at the end, the President, who is always a legal man in uniform for the duration of the war, and does nothing but sit like this all over the country and maybe abroad too, asked me to set out for him the main points I had made, and the court would then adjourn for half an hour, after which it would reconvene, but without counsel, so I was kept out. As they were all going in, the President murmured to me: 'That was a very good speech; which were you, a barrister or a solicitor?' Result swollen head for your son. I shall never know whether what I said did in fact have an effect on the severity of the sentence, as of course the details of what they discussed remain private. I am afraid the chap is a bad lot, and is sure to have got 18 months or so.

So that was quite an experience. I did one other court martial, defending someone who had stolen a large chicken from the quartermaster's stores one Christmas Eve 'for his poor starving family', so I am sure I laid on that aspect pretty thick on behalf of a bombardier who ought to have known better. I have no recollection of what transpired, still less whether I had a further accolade. Maybe I would have remembered it if I had; it was after I had stopped keeping a diary.

By October the German night air raids were being stepped up, and Maison Dieu Road became quite a dangerous area, just under the castle as it was. We were often out of bed at night to dig in the rubble of houses for casualties, and it was there that I saw my first dead bodies of the war, as my platoon tried one evening to shift great rafters and lumps of rubble (there were no bulldozers around of course) in our search for casualties. Along with helping the air raid wardens many times, we were flat out every day with training exercises.

Despite it all we still had evenings out in that battered town, either going to 'the flicks', or the pubs, or once I remember having a regimental dance. We all decided that the bombs were easier to cope with than the shelling; you generally heard the aircraft that was going to be a nuisance, and could dive for cover if you were walking back to billets from an evening in the town. But the shells suddenly screamed in without warning; I have an idea Dover was more knocked about by German guns than it was by the bombs of their Dorniers and Heinkels.

But all this ended one morning with the announcement in Regimental Orders that the battalion was to be one of thirty-five others to be transferred to the Royal Artillery. 'The men are delighted', I wrote in my diary, 'as it means different sort of work, and a welcome goodbye to Dover'.

Up and down Britain

Let all things their Creator bless,
And worship Him in thankfulness.
St Francis of Assisi: Canticle of the Sun

Lambs,
Always sturdy, straggle from the flock,
Frisk tails, tug grass tufts, stare at children, prance,
Then panic—stricken scuttle for their dams
The Land: Spring

THE battalion arrived in Yeovil on 27 November 1941, to be met at the station by a Royal Artillery band, which had taken the trouble to learn the regimental march of The Buffs, so we all swung along through the streets to our new home in fine spirits. Someone in authority there had taken lessons in psychology, very necessary we officers were finding, as after the first enthusiasms for 'something new' there was a lot of uncertainty in the air, and a real sense of sadness. We were having to say goodbye to a famous regiment of the line which we had all chosen to join. Now we were being drafted willy-nilly into a vast amorphous crowd, also indeed a very famous regiment, (regular gunners would say the most famous of all), but impersonally large, and what was more without the territorial link, by which all the county regiments set so much store.

After dinner in the Officers' Mess of our new hutted camp, Houndstone Barracks, we argued over the port (no shortage of the essentials) as to why all this had happened to us. In a sense of course we never entirely knew; High Command does not need to explain these decisions of policy to troops on the ground, although it is always a pleasant surprise when they do, in the way for which Monty later became rightly renowned. The best we ever managed to figure out was that urgent representation was coming back from the only theatre of war where British soldiers were in action, the Middle East, that they were desperate for more means of combating enemy tanks and aircraft. In particular of course the Stuka dive bomber, which had done so much damage in the retreat to Dunkirk the previous year, was extremely demoralizing as well as destructive to troops under its attack. 'We don't want more infantry battalions on this narrow front in the Western Desert, we want to be able to inflict maximum damage on aircraft and tanks' was what we reckoned was the message that lay behind this drastic action affecting in the region of 20,000 men.

For the few regular officers and men in the 11th Battalion, the change was very bad news indeed, because a regular is always looking beyond the little matter of a war, (ever optimistic that he will survive it), to his future peacetime career. One old regular of another regiment, who was already established in the Mess that we moved into, went so far as to say quite seriously round that dinner table on our first night that the war was a beastly nuisance, and 'the sooner we all get back to proper peacetime soldiering the better.' Over the following months most of our regulars got themselves posted elsewhere, the War Office, I remember, being very co-operative on their behalf, though we were very sorry to see them go, as they were a good link with our Buffs background. The rest of us just got on with adapting ourselves, with the strong proviso that we would make as sure as we could that we were made a divisional anti-aircraft regiment rather than a static one; for as long as we had been soldiers we had, in unattractively superior fashion, thought of static anti-aircraft units on British defence duty, important as indeed this was, as the lowest of the low.

Among other things that now became clearer to us, we realized at last why, with this sea change in the offing, no successor to our beloved Commanding Officer in the 11th Buffs, 'Tit' Willow, had been drafted in since he left us when we were under canvas in Waldershare Park, as long before as 12 September, on the evening of which I had written in my diary:

> We saw off the CO today in great style. He shook hands with all his officers' (I can see his lovely smile for each of us now), 'after which he was chaired by the warrant-officers to his car, while an accordion played *Auld Lang Syne*. Then we made him sit on the bonnet of his PU' (senior officers had Pick Up cars for their personal use) 'which we officers dragged with ropes across the grass quite a way down to the road, while most of the (600?) men it seemed leant over the fence of the Park and cheered. I hated saying goodbye to him, and I have only been under him for two

months. How he must have loathed leaving the battalion he had formed and led.

On the very first morning in Yeovil we were on parade to meet our new Royal Artillery Commanding Officer. Lt Colonel Bob Cory was a tall elderly-looking Gunner (he had served all through WWI), who had a funny habit of flicking his head to the right as he talked to you; if you were being ticked off, he flicked all the harder. We soon decided he was on his last posting before retirement, but he proved to be none the worse for that. Extremely energetic for his years he was much in evidence from the start, and was most friendly in the mess; a month later I could write: 'I was placed next to him for our Boxing Day dinner, and I like him very much, with the delightful whimsical expression he seems almost always to wear'. He had very powerful glasses, but despite them lost no time in recognizing who his officers were (I was immediately Bick, 'much easier than Bickersteth') and in giving his rather reluctant charges, both officers and men, a sense of pride, rather than resentment, in belonging to a regiment he clearly loved, and indeed to which he had given his working life. We all became fond of this avuncular, faintly Blimpish-looking person, who was anything but Blimpish in welding five or six hundred men into a fighting unit, with its totally unfamiliar fifty or more Bofors anti-aircraft guns replacing all those rifles we had left behind in Kent.

So in a flash (almost literally) we were into courses of every kind, many of us going off to other RA units for them, but we also had plenty of IGs (Instructors in Gunnery) posted to us, so that we could master how these 40mm weapons were operated as soon as possible. Swedish-made, not a very new design, but destined to be standard issue light anti-aircraft guns to the British Army for several years after the war, ours were all made to be towed behind tractors, because we in the 89th were to be, as we had hoped from the start, mobile Divisional Troops, i.e. a division's Light Anti-Aircraft Regiment, as new to our rôle as a former battalion of the Suffolks, also joining the RA and training at Houndstone Barracks, was to be the 'Anti-Tank' one. Within a month we were sewing Polar Bears on to our battle-dresses, the sign of 49th (West Riding) Infantry Division with which we were to go to war. It was not long back from Iceland, which Britain had occupied peacefully in 1940 as a precautionary measure against German invasion.

On Christmas Day I got to Communion in the Garrison Theatre (It was a larger-than-the-rest hut, which was always a feature of any new hutted camp) with 'five or six other Buff officers', and then there was a 'noisy' Church Parade, before we were free, and I took an army push-bike to bicycle five miles to tea in a beautiful house at Tintinhull with a dear school friend of mother's, of whom with her erudite and cultivated husband I saw quite a lot during our time in Yeovil, and found the stimulation of them both sheer delight. That same evening I bicycled on to another family to which I had been introduced, where I had a merry time (there were two Australian Air Force pilots staying), with an excellent meal and party games afterwards until eleven o'clock.

I then cycled back to camp in bright moonlight 'without a lamp of any kind at front or rear. My first Christmas away from home has been a very happy one thanks to the kindness of others.' Actually I became quite notorious in the regiment for, wherever we were in Britain, finding links to look up and have meals or baths with. 'Why not?', I'd comment. 'The people I ring or write to like to be asked, not necessarily because of you but because it gives them a feeling of doing something to help a serviceman away from home, as they hope their son or daughter would be cared for too.' Again and again in those two and a half years of batting up and down the British Isles, I found that was true, because many of the people I bothered told me so.

Two days after Christmas the three troops of 310 Battery, in which I was second-in-command of H Troop, towed our guns to Watchet Camp in West Somerset, where we were to have our first practice firing at a 'sleeve'. This sleeve, which was simply a thirty-foot strip of material, representing an enemy aircraft, was towed on a suitably long rope by a small plane, flying hour after daylight hour specially for us, up and down the southern shores of the Bristol Channel a few hundred yards beyond the cliffs on top of which we had parked the guns. If we scored a direct hit, the damage was visible, but the sleeve flew on; if a shell hit it just where the tow-rope began, the damage could be so dramatic that there was no sleeve left to shoot at, in which case the towing plane returned to base and we all went back early to camp. They never seemed to have a spare sleeve they could pay out to keep us at it, but in my memory direct hits were not all that frequent; the Instructors in Gunnery who stood beside the troop that was firing would tell us how near we were.

It was very cold indeed in the bitter north wind which hit the cliff edge for the next ten days, and the camp was miserable too. Indeed the firing camps we shot from regularly over the next two and a half years were all inevitably (so that the unexploded shells went into the sea) in draughty coastal spots, Morecambe Bay in Lancashire, St Agnes in Cornwall, Clacton on the Essex coast, Manorbier in South Wales and one or two others. It all blurs in my recollection with the tremendous amount of journeying we began to do round Scotland, Wales and England. Father commented at some stage that he reckoned all the restless movement of troops was to stop us thousands of home-based soldiers getting bored; he may well have been partly right, 'but we could do with some of the petrol you eat'. Indeed we must have been in some ways an annoying sight on the very roads which the civilian population could hardly use because of their meagre fuel allowance. But I suppose we were also showing the flag, to encourage everyone that there were lots of stout soldiery defending them.

Early in 1942 Nick Marcy my troop commander went to Regimental HQ to become the adjutant, and I was given command of the troop. Unbelievably our 310 Battery was posted in a hurry to help defend, of all places, the industrial target of Rugby. We were told there was some 'flap' on; this was a word much used throughout the war, to imply that our elders and betters were facing a sudden emergency and did not quite know what to do about it. Our orders were to get deployed quickly round this vulnerable town, so within a day or two we had chosen gun sites all round Rugby and its surrounding villages, not a difficult task for me from my bicycling days thereabouts only two years before. My soldiers were most impressed by the faultless map-reading. It suited me splendidly to be stationed in Newbold Grange, three miles from my old haunts, for six or seven weeks, and I soon got my feet under the table with the new housemaster of Sheriff.

The need for one had sadly come about because very soon after I had left the school a drunken driver had killed dear Johnnie when he was doing Special Constable duty one night just outside the town; it was a grievous loss to Mrs Johnnie, the school, and very many people who loved him. The sadness was a bit lessened for

UP AND DOWN BRITAIN

Sheriff boys by the appointment of the gifted and popular Jim
Bruce to succeed him; JAGB had been my form master in the
Lower Twenty the term mother died, and I never forgot his hitting
exactly the right note of sympathy and understanding when I got
back after the funeral for the last few days of that Christmas Term
of 1936. By the spring of 1942 he had been two years in charge of
Sheriff, and was clearly enjoying himself, as the boys were him. He
was a wise and precise man, never very fit, a keen churchman, and a
schoolmaster who in the class-room saw his task as mainly drawing
everything he could from his boys, never drumming stuff into
them; and of course in that proper process ('e-ducation' in its true
sense) teaching a very great deal. So it was a real joy to get to know
him better; I stayed in the house more than once, had cheerful
evenings with staff and senior boys there, went to school chapel, and
even helped umpire a Corps Field Day. Furthermore I must have
persuaded my Battery Commander (I have found the invitation), to
throw a party for various people, mainly to do with the school, who
had welcomed us to the neighbourhood.

We only left because there was a fresh 'flap', this time at Cowes on
the Isle of Wight. It was either just before or just after the abortive
Dieppe Raid, which cost the lives of too many Canadians, but did
teach valuable lessons for the main invasion. I wrote to grandmother afterwards:

> I came back from the Isle of Wight just over a week ago, after
> eight days of the most perfect weather in Cowes and Yarmouth.
> We all enjoyed it immensely, not least because we saw our first
> action when the Germans bombed Cowes on the night of 4-5
> May. Of course the men were very pleased to have been the first
> in the regiment to fire their guns in anger. There were two raids,
> both fierce ones, and both starting with the dropping of flares
> and incendiaries. The barrage was the heaviest I've heard, since
> our four guns were by no means the only AA defence of the town
> and the ship-building yards. Our men did extremely well, put-
> ting out dozens of incendiaries, as well as keeping their guns in
> action all the time.
>
> Three men from one of my crews rowed across the river, a
> good 150 yards wide there, to free a barge from a blazing wharf;
> and the same men earned a recommendation from the railway
> company for putting out incendiaries which fell in showers (liter-

ally) on goods wagons and coal dumps. Another gun crew were exceptionally lucky in having a 1000lb bomb fall ten yards away, but as it did not go off on impact it might have had a delayed action fuse. They moved the gun at once; and when the bomb did go off 36 hours later, it became clear that there would have been 50% casualties' (very definite of me) 'if the thing had gone off right away.

Early in the raid some Guardsmen and I managed to get an injured old man out of a house that we watched getting a direct hit, and take him to hospital in one of our trucks, but we were sorry to hear later that he had died that night. The town's firemen worked wonderfully well; and all night the ferry-bridge across the river, the only connection with East Cowes, kept going while the docks were blazing near their landing stage on both sides of the river.

The little town that thousands of yachtsmen must have known in peacetime days was a sorry sight next morning, and 162 people were buried in Cowes two days later.

We went through much the same thing in the docks at Southampton not long after, but thereafter a kaleidoscope of places and names takes over. We were in the huge Victorian pile of Llanion Barracks, Pembroke Dock for a month or so, and from there I had a trip in a Sunderland flying boat; Coastal Command operated from Milford Haven Sound just below the barracks, and a beautiful sight these great lumbering seaplanes were, taking off after a long run along the Sound, and later after their Atlantic patrol touching gracefully down again. My genuine excuse for the trip was that I wanted to see how well we were camouflaging our gunsites when we were out of barracks on exercise.

One January we did combined operations training at Inveraray on Loch Fyne, actually in the icy water quite a lot, as the mechanics were practising their waterproofing for vehicles landing on an enemy beach, often having to be hauled out by other tractors after getting stuck in the rocks that litter the loch floor. It was midwinter, and I had to take thirty guns over the Rest and Be Thankful Pass (the old road is still visible below you, as you sweep along the beautifully-contoured 1970's one). A violent snow storm was blowing, as my sergeant-major and I leading the column on our motorbikes got off them at the top of the pass to count the vehicles past us.

It was a nasty moment, given the weather conditions and that treacherous road, to find that we were a gun and towing-tractor short. I decided to send the sergeant-major back to look for it, with my heart in my mouth in view of the precipice on one side of the road. Mercifully the tractor-driver and his gun had skidded to the right, into the ditch against the mountain, rather than to the left and over the edge. Troop Sergeant-Major Brunton told me afterwards that he had practically hugged him, and then remembered he was really there to dress the driver down for carelessness, poor chap, in allowing the skid; he would have ticked him off charmingly, being rather an unsergeant-majorish wartime soldier.

At a different time of year I can see myself sleeping under the stars one May near Llandilo in South Wales and listening to the nightingales, much the finest chorus of them I have heard anywhere, before or since. Another spring I did a gas course based in the commandeered Ullswater Hotel, right on the lake. 'Are you interested in gas, Bick'? asked the CO one day in the Mess; 'not particularly, sir', I truthfully replied. 'Well, you know the Lakes; the Ullswater used to be a damned good hotel, and I'm sure you'll make the most of it. Off you go'.

So I did, and got a distinction, which pleased Bob Cory inordinately. A group of us went up Helvellyn by the Striding Edge route, new to three of them, and we were rewarded with superb views, a day to reinforce my love of the Lake District, in which I have indulged on and off since our first family holiday in a vicarage under Saddleback in 1933.

There were several good leaves, either 'forty-eights' or seven days, interspersed with all this continuing mixture of training and operations, the latter of course being necessary because the *Luftwaffe* was still very active, particularly over the south of England, and there were not enough static anti-aircraft guns to cover the country when there were 'flaps'. I was home a good deal, seeing friends there (of both sexes), going up to town for shows and concerts, all of which kept going throughout the many months after London had become the prime German target, once they had given up on attempting an invasion of the south coast. For my twenty-first birthday I got some leave (I came up a few days before on the night train from Truro) and was treated to a magnificent party, fourteen strong, in the West End, first seeing Jack Hulbert and Cicely

Courtneidge in *Full Swing*, and then repairing to the Mayfair to eat and dance till 12.30 when all London's restaurants had to close; 'I simply could not stop dancing', I wrote in the diary, 'and enjoyed every minute of it.'

After a final trek for a few weeks to Milngavie near Glasgow, where several of us officers had a wonderful day's shooting with the local laird, we came south from the last of our prolonged travels, and by the autumn of 1943 were in East Anglia which was to prove the forming-up area for the division in the final preparations for D Day. First there was more farming to do, in our case helping short-handed farmers lift their sugar-beet harvest, round March and Wisbech, and then we were on the North Norfolk coast at Sheringham and East Runton. Thanks to a Rugby connection, it was there that I first met Lilias Rider Haggard, daughter of the author of *King Solomon's Mines* and other romantic tales from South Africa, which I had devoured at Lambrook; Lilias was by then a middle-aged spinster, with a lovely cottage on the Haggard estate at Ditchingham. She and her neighbour Margaret Spurrell became firm friends for the next twenty-five years; I bought one of Lilias' yellow labrador puppies after the war. The two friends introduced me to two Norwich artists, taking me to their studios, and helping me acquire my first-ever paintings, a great thrill; they were water colours by Gerald Ackerman and Jack Harrison; the Harrison which I chose (partly because our own division, the 49th, had just come back from there) was of *Whooper Swans at the Vatnajokul, Iceland*, and the Ackerman of *The Old Bridge Blakeney* on the North Norfolk coast, which I was getting to know well; the drawings are still treasured possessions.

As well as many of us in the 89th making individual friends in Norfolk, we also enjoyed for the first time as a regiment the pleasure of meeting large numbers of Wrens (Women's Royal Naval Service), both officers and ratings. We had parties for them, they were ideal as the essential female element at regimental dances, they came to drinks after church parade on Sundays, and so on. It was suddenly a new dimension for us all, strange to relate when we had been to so many places where we might have had similar experiences. My handsome Old Haileyburian friend, Roger Keane, who had joined the 11th Battalion a month before me, fell seriously in love with one of the girls, and I found myself being Best Man at his wedding in Yorkshire, both of us in uniform, when the war was hardly over in August 1945.

His bride-to-be's best friend took quite a penchant to me, and so there developed during the six months prior to D Day my first love affair, and great fun it was while it lasted. But I began to realize that she was a lot keener on me than I on her, so before we were due to leave for the invasion I decided that I must tell this affectionate girl, who had only just penned a poem in my honour, that I had so much enjoyed our friendship, but that I felt it would not survive our separation and it was better to say good bye, as I would not be writing to her. As I expected, there were passionate pleas that we could keep up, and floods of tears. I stuck out the sobs, feeling a brute of the first order, but I knew all the more as the agony was going on that it was right for me to desist for both our good. I was very glad to hear much later from the Keanes that she was happily married not long after the war.

As anticipation mounted during that spring of 1944, we were inspected as a division by both The King and Monty, the latter home from his triumphs in the Western Desert and Italy in order to command 'Overlord', the code name for the invasion of Europe (maybe we did not know that name then). For Monty's visit the rain tipped down, as seven or eight thousand men foregathered in the grounds of Somerleyton Hall outside Lowestoft. I remember we looked thoroughly unmilitary, draped in our unbecoming gas capes, which were what soldiers had then against the rain. We formed up in a huge square in the park, (very difficult to look smart on the grass, with no stamping possible), and the great man drove up in his Jeep, these brilliant little US open-sided vehicles which were fast replacing PUs for officers' use. He stood on a milk crate and at once told us all to break ranks and crowd round him; I remember commenting to another officer that it was a good thing that there were no *Messerschmitt 109*s in the area, or the invasion would have been a division short, and maybe missing a C-in-C too. In five minutes Monty got it across to every single man present, with that already famous strong rasping voice of his through the megaphone, that we were about to 'knock the Boches for six'. I believe that in that April and May the King and the General saw every division, the gallant assault ones of course, which Monty had brought home from Italy specially for the purpose, but also the back-up ones like ours that would arrive a few days after them, by which time it was confidently expected that they would have established the bridgehead.

I did not see Monty again until we had been in France a week or two, and suddenly his Jeep had pulled up at one of my gun sites when I happened to be visiting it. Out he gets. 'Now all of you come round and take a look', and seven or eight men are in position in a jiffy, as their general spreads out his map on the bonnet: 'Here's the present Boche line; here's your division, with the 15th Scottish on your right and the 43rd Wessex on your left; this is what we've got to do!' and then a quick resumé of the allied plan, without of course giving anything vital away which could find its way into the chaps' letters and get missed by our censoring. After his driver had given out English newspapers and several packets of cigarettes, off he goes with a word of encouragement as he shook hands all round. He was indeed the soldiers' general *par excellence*.

By contrast the King's visit to us, on a gorgeous May morning only three weeks before the 'Off', was low key. He walked slowly down the drawn-up lines looking each one of us in the eye, and talking with a few, before the Divisional Commander led us in Three Cheers for him. It was quite a moment. I remember being shocked at how made-up he appeared to be; it was much too early in the summer for him to have been so brown. He was never a fit man of course, so our guess could well have been right. But if ever a sovereign cared for his subjects, King George VI did, thrust into the limelight as he had unwillingly been only two and a half years earlier. I did not see the King again until 1946, when he and the Queen, a first-ever university occasion for the Sovereign's consort, came to dinner in Christ Church Hall, to mark the 400th anniversary of our Foundation. For such a notable event in post-war austerity Oxford, we undergraduates had all been carefully rehearsed by the cathedral's organist and choirmaster, Dr Thomas Armstrong, to sing the Restoration piece written for Charles II 'Here's a health unto His Majesty'; we were to watch Tommy's surreptitious conducting like a knife. It was a memorable evening. But in the very different setting of that May 1944 we were about to give him the best we could in return for his wonderful and greatly admired devotion to duty.

Owing to a couple of officers leaving shortly before the invasion, the CO had to do some reshuffling, and to my dismay I found myself posted one morning in Regimental Orders away from my beloved H Troop in 310 Battery to command F Troop in 309. I asked at once to see Bob Cory. 'What's the problem, Bick?' he asked considerately enough. I launched into my complaint, that I knew all my soldiers very well, and quite a few of their families too, that we had trained hard together for so long, and now I was to be posted away from them just as we were going to put it all to the test. I have never forgotten how Bob handled it. 'Thank you for explaining it all to me, Bick. I promise you there are good reasons for what I am doing. You'll damned well start tomorrow'. So I saluted with a rather surprised 'Sir', marched out, and proceeded to do what I was told. Our CO simply did not like his orders questioned, and I knew in a second that I had met my match. We remained firm friends.

It was suddenly early June. I was to leave my new troop to cross the channel after me, and myself go on a small advance party of four or five of us travelling with 185 Field Regiment to which, when it arrived, my troop would be attached as its own air defence unit. I knew the 185 officers a bit, and (what was just as important) my batman knew some of their officers' batmen. Mine, whom I made sure came on the advance party, was William Clark, who had joined The Buffs a little after me, coming from a job as 'gentleman's gentleman', which was how he liked to describe himself, in a big house near Hythe.

Clark was a valet to the manner born, and I was very fortunate indeed to have him as my servant for four years. It seems absurd now that he cleaned my shoes every day, polished my buttons, and pressed my best uniform; and when I was in battledress he brushed the mud off it, and dug my slit trench as well as his own. In the field he was ingenuity itself, always thinking of little comforts (for us both, I'm bound to say), for example discovering whether the hens in a French farmyard close by were in lay (German officers had probably benefited from them a few days earlier). Ultra-polite, quiet, fastidious, intensely loyal, always immaculate, he was probably in today's terminology gay. Given, I guessed, by his master in Saltwood a lovely pair of ivory-backed hair brushes, when he left for the war, he presented them to me for my 21st birthday, and I use them to this day sixty years later. Batmen are not quite replicated in the other two services (where 'stewards' are the nearest equivalent), but certainly in the British Army they were, and perhaps still are, a key element in an officer's life. When I landed up later in India, feeling I would never have a batman to match Clark, I was again lucky in that a smiley Hindu, Nanta Ram, took the place which Clark had so splendidly filled while I was soldiering in Britain and on the continent. I became very fond of them both.

By dawn on 5th June the sea front at Great Yarmouth was packed tight with guns and vehicles. My troop sergeant-major was coming with me, but my second-in-command, an actor in civilian life named Hugh Paddick, (later to reach 'the lights' outside several West End shows; he was a brilliant Dr. Pickering in *My Fair Lady*), got up early to wish us luck, along with dozens of heartbroken Wrens. We moved off on time to cheers and tears, ran into huge delays from meeting other military stuff making for London, but before dark were bedding down in a Purfleet warehouse beside Tilbury Docks for our last night on English soil. It was D minus one.

The Normandy Invasion

Genesis 1

I sing the tillage of my country's year
I sing the tillage, and the reaping sing.
The Land: Winter

'REVEILLE at 5, breakfast at 6, loading starts 7'; so ran 185's Regimental Orders for 6 June 1944, cyclostyled out after we had arrived at the dockside. Word had also got round from the padre that there would be Communion in the warehouse office at 7, so it was easy for me to be there (along with eight or ten others), as I had no loading responsibilities. We prayed for the souls of the brave men killed on the beaches three hours before and during our communion service. Roy Jenkins in his *Churchill* (2001) says there were 3000 dead among the casualties, much less than had been feared likely; and probably three-quarters of them were American, as they had a terrible time on 'Omaha' beach towards the Cherbourg Peninsula.

Our guns and vehicles were to be hoisted into Liberty ships, of which several were alongside, and others were hove-to out in the river. These were smallish cargo vessels given us by the US, the arrangement dating from before they came into the war, in answer to urgent requests from Churchill for a gesture to make up for the U-boat toll of merchant vessels in the Atlantic. I think the original gift was of fifty of them. The two holds were not all that big, and we needed two ships to get the regiment and its equipment loaded up; this was done by each individual 25-pounder and every vehicle being hoisted by crane from the quayside and down into the holds, a laborious business. There were also delays through the dockers going on strike for overtime pay because they were kept loading during their mid-morning break, such miserable behaviour provoking torrents of scorn, and worse, from our soldiers. But by one o'clock we were all on board, the tugs started to ease us out into the river, and there began one of the most exhilarating hours of my life.

Because it was lunch hour the factory and office workers were all out and about, and they had climbed on to and into everything they could, including other ships alongside other quaysides, to see what was going on, and to shout and cheer us on our way. I should imagine that to our astonished gaze there must have been approaching several thousand people, crammed on to every conceivable vantage point. The invasion was on, they had all heard about it that morning on the wireless, and this was their chance to be as much in it as they could, and to wish us luck. Ships and boats and ferries sounded their foghorns, and factories their hooters, to the Victory V. We all lined the rails to wave back our gratitude, and indeed in the men's case (before we got too far out for it) to throw messages, weighted by something, on to the quayside asking for delivery to a nearby relation.

The idea had caught on because the night before one of the soldiers had actually seen his mother walk down their street, as we were crawling slowly through the crowded dockland where several of the 185 Field Regt gunners came from; I wonder if any of those scribbled notes got home, they might well have done, but anyhow the notion was great and an extra boost to the high morale everyone was experiencing with all this cheering. The soldiers also began disposing of the remains of their English money, 'hurling coppers and sixpences on to the quayside below, where a crowd of small boys scrambled for them', I wrote in a long description of it all to father later on. Now under our own steam (the tugs had cast off) we chugged slowly downstream in the hot June sunshine, past more docks, more factories (the ones that had not been burnt out by bombing), and more and more Londoners to take up the cheering, as long as we were near enough to the shore. It was very moving. We stayed lining the rails until the river got too wide.

Before long our two ships, joined *en route* by others, were right down in the Thames Estuary, not far from Southend Pier, where we were to anchor to await the formation of a convoy to take us down channel. It proved a tedious three-day period of inactivity, while the number of ships built up to whatever quantity was considered the optimum. Keeping the men's spirits up, in crowded conditions as they were, was difficult. The ship's officers had very kindly given us officers their quarters, not palatial because four or five of us crowded into their double cabins, but we were still better off than the troops on the open deck. Endless games of housey-housey (the same as the bingo of post-war generations) were the order of the day, plus a great deal of PE (or was it still called PT?); and that was not easy because of the lack of any free space.

Eventually this great armada, mostly Liberty ships like ours, got on the move early on D+4 and were formed up by several destroyers; there were three or four rows of us in line astern, quite a way apart from each other, each row of about ten ships, so this large flotilla was of not less than thirty to forty ships. What a vulnerable target, we who had been trained to look up in the sky all the time, thought; but we soon began to discover the first great secret of the success of 'Overlord', that the RAF had beforehand, by bombing all the airfields along the French coast, largely immobilized the *Luftwaffe*.

During that whole day of stately progress down-channel, not one attack from the air materialized, as we steamed at the speed of the slowest ship fairly close to our shoreline. This lack of air attack was a foretaste of what we would all be finding later, and already an encouragement to a pretty apprehensive and green bunch of men, as we began to appreciate how stupendously good all the preparations had been. The weather was fine; it had of course been rough on 4th June, which had made Eisenhower, the supreme commander, take the very big decision to postpone everything from 5th to 6th June. We all enjoyed picking out the familiar landmarks, in my case particularly St Margaret's Bay, with its holiday memories.

We went to bed when it got dark, so were not on deck to see ourselves arriving off the beaches about three in the morning, with the tricky business of just how each ship slipped into its place in the offshore jigsaw. But we were up with first light of course, and anyhow a battleship, HMS *Ramillies* we were told, a mile away woke us by beginning to fire its huge shells. And the jigsaw? It really is the only way to describe the unbelievable sight which greeted us as we stood in crowded awe on the deck of that well-named 'Liberty' ship. This vast assembly of vessels, no doubt every single one precisely in its allotted space, which was bringing ashore the British Liberation Army, stretched for hundreds of acres all round us; I remember giving up counting when I had reached a total of two hundred ships of every kind.

After a quick last meal on board (the cooks had done a great job for four days with their petrol-operated field cookers in among the men on deck), vehicles and guns were soon being swung over the rails by the ship's cranes into the LCTs.[22] Officers and men clambered down ropes slung over the side. I recorded in my album a year later that 'I stepped on to French soil at 1300 hrs on D+5. Above that slightly pretentious note is a *Times* photograph which father had cut out, dated 12 June, of 'the centre beach', wherever that was (deliberately vague, no doubt), showing very much what we had seen, with men in tin hats in the sunshine on the beach or in the dunes, some looking seawards incredulously as we had been, wreckage on the waterline, several landing ships anchored offshore, and prominently in the foreground, where children had made sand castles in happier times, a manned Bofors gun exactly like ours deployed for action, and obviously belonging to a regiment which had landed earlier. The actual beach where we went ashore was in front of the smashed-up village of La Valette, just west of Courseulles.

From then on my mind has a confused jumble of bridgehead memories. I imagine my small contingent went inland with the HQ of the Field Regiment to see where it was deploying its guns. Generally speaking, gun positions for obvious reasons are a mile or two behind the infantry, which enables me to say (looking back years later at those eleven months I had in forward fighting areas) what an enormous admiration gunners quickly develop for the 'Poor Bloody Infantry'. No wonder indeed that it is they who are exposed to fear far more often, who sustain much higher casualties, who understandably have many more 'bomb-happy' cases than the artillery do, and who are always terribly short of sleep when they are in the line. Gunners may, we often did, feel a bit envious of a battalion that was passing back through us for a rest after having been relieved by a fresh one, but not a single artilleryman would have challenged their right to it.

My troop was due to land a couple of days after our advance party, so I went back on my motor bike the six or seven miles to the coast as an old hand to welcome them, and we began to sort out deployment of men and equipment. That same week a gun detachment of ours brought down a *Me. 109*, meriting a little snippet ten days later in the *Chatham Rochester and Gillingham News* under the

22. Landing Craft Tanks.

heading 'Local Gunners Take Toll':

> Although Allied air superiority is still undisputed in Normandy, a few German fighters have attempted machine-gun attacks, especially when there has been cloud cover. A Kentish Light A.A. detachment took the opportunity it had been waiting for, and bagged one and severely damaged another.

The article then mentioned to their great pride the names of several of the lads in the regiment, all old Buffs and therefore likely to be familiar to many readers of that local paper. The 89th incidentally never had more than about a third of our total strength who had never been Buffs, but were artillery intake. It was pleasing that the new men became proud of the unit's origins.

For several weeks the British line was only fifteen to twenty miles deep. That precarious bridgehead had been quite rapidly achieved in the initial surprise of the D Day landings, against mostly second-rate German troops, as Rommel had expected the invasion much higher up the coast. But resistance stiffened markedly with the post-haste arrival of the Panzer divisions, and neither our tanks nor infantry were able to make the hoped-for headway. The virtual stale-mate even caused Churchill, we heard long after the war, to have a terrible foreboding that trench warfare was about to develop. At one of the worst sticking-points just south of the village of Audrieu, our 49 Div. War Memorial was eventually built; Rosemary and I visited it in the late 50's. It stands in close bocage country, with small fields and thick hedges, much easier for defence than attack. In that June 1944 bloated and stinking dead cows, killed in large numbers by shellfire in their formerly peaceful meadows (the smell sat per-manently in our nostrils), lay in their hundreds higgledy-piggledy on the grass with their legs in the air.

I vividly recall too, very early on, driving carefully (because of the danger of mines) to site a new gun position, that my driver and I came across the body of a Tynesider from 50 Div. (one of the assault divisions the week before) lying in the track in front of me. I had been warned what to do: tie a rope very gingerly round the dead man's ankle, retreat into the ditch, having moved the Jeep back, and ease the body slowly towards you. This procedure was necess-ary because it had been discovered the hard way by stretcher-bearers that the enemy was leaving many dead British soldiers where they fell, and booby-trapping them as they retreated. But this one was untouched, and the two of us lifted the body reverently into the back of the jeep, took it to the field outside the nearest Advanced Dressing Station, and notified the Medical Officer in charge that we had checked it for explosive devices.

Having taken over from an assault division, 49 Div. had only been in action for a week, or less even, when my troop had an unnerving experience. Clark had dug me a fine slit trench to sleep in, or indeed get into quick in the daytime if necessary, and I had climbed late on to my sleeping bag, dressed of course, with my boots on, when very soon there began as it got dark a great many crumps and bangs to our front, and I got up at once. Troop Sergeant Major Standish (who was proving every bit as good as my TSM Brunton had been in 310 Battery) reckoned they were coming from a mile or two away where the front line was, as we knew from our maps. The noise got no closer after half an hour or so, we both tried for 'a kip' again; the soldiers did too, as best they could with that background of bangs. These continued on and off, mostly it seemed to us 'on', for all the hours of darkness, after which the noise petered out. The troop 'stood to' at first light, as we always did.

We soon began to spot them: in the grey dawn British soldiers were trickling back towards us by ones and twos, wild-eyed and terrified, some were 'walking wounded', with bloody bandages tied roughly on to their arms and legs. They had been staggering past our by now very surprised chaps for a few minutes before one of my sergeants who had WWI service behind him realized before I did what was happening: 'they are on the run, sir', he came over to say to me quietly; 'we must stop them'. Grasping that he was absolutely right, I quickly got a dozen of our men to take them individually by the arm as they trailed past, saying at the sergeant-major's suggestion: 'hallo mate, our cook has got the tea going, so have a sit-down for a moment or two, and we'll get some of the hot stuff inside you' (every officer had rum rations for emergencies). It worked brilliantly, and I was so grateful for this old sweat, who had actually often been a great nuisance. Within a quarter of an hour we had fifteen or twenty men from the battalion which had been in front of us sitting quietly drinking their tea, thankful to be alive, and making no attempt to go any further. I had meanwhile loaded my pistol, uncomfortably recalling from the training manuals that officers must be prepared to shoot deserters. Mercifully the flow of shattered infantrymen stopped quite suddenly with the arrival of a lone subaltern, very shaken himself, not wounded, and well aware of what was happening to his unit.

He gladly stopped too for some rum-laced tea, and began to blurt out the situation. His company had dug in along the forward edge of and indeed all over a ten or twelve acre wood, when this heavy mortaring began as it got dark. The enemy were only about a quarter of a mile ahead, and the company commander decided, rightly or wrongly (probably the latter; he had had only five days experience), not to pull back from the wood under cover of darkness so that he could review the situation in the morning. His orders therefore to the company (and maybe they had come from battalion HQ, I did not ask) were that they must stick it out. Mortars make an awful noise anyway, I knew. 'But', this young officer said, 'when they hit the very tops of the trees and therefore burst above you the row is deafening, and the damage dreadful; and on and on it went hour after hour with more and more of my men being hit, and our stretcher-bearers being killed too, whenever they ventured out with casualties at the back of the wood into the bocage.'

So the sad story poured out, as I thankfully unloaded my pistol when no one was looking. Once everyone had had some of our tea, the subaltern got his men into some sort of order to march them off behind us and look for more of his unit; 'I think the wood is empty except for our dead', he said pathetically through his understandable tears of shame and frustration and disappointment for himself and his famous regiment. Over the field telephone to me came the welcome information that the gap had been plugged, and we were not to move; the stark truth reaching me over the wire was that several hundred yards ahead of us those men who had been left alive and unhurt at first light, or able to move with only superficial wounds, had simply scrambled out of their slit trenches and made off, no doubt shot at in the growing light as they fled from the jubilant enemy. These were the broken men we had had trickling past us. As for the hapless battalion to which that particular company belonged, we were told within a day or so that *pour discourager les autres*, (if the French negative is permissible), Monty had ordered it back to the UK, and asked for and got an immediate replacement. The battalion had been in France for under a week.

With two subalterns to help me care for the troop, I was able to do a little 'swanning around', as we called getting time off to see what else was going on or just for a break. I successfully ran a Chiddingstone major, Dick Streatfeild to earth, and another whose regiment had been billeted in the Castle adjoining the village. My attempt to look up Robert Bickersteth, a cousin whom I knew was a captain in the Seaforth Highlanders in 15th Scottish Div. next to us sadly failed, as he had been killed on the morning of the day I found his battalion. He had been taking shelter behind one of our tanks during a brief lull, talking with its commander standing up in his turret, when an 88m German shell hit the British tank, came out intact the other side without having touched the commander, and killed Robert instantly. So all I could do was write to Penelope, who had only married this delightful schoolmaster a few months before. In happier times he had been a very knowledgeable bird-watcher, and after the war Pen kept in touch with us, and gave me his field-glasses; so I often remember him. She outlived him, as so many war-widows did, by fifty years; I looked her up last in the Chiswick nursing-home that saw her devotedly through altzheimers, and took her funeral in the city church where she and Robert had been married.

Another 'swan' that June 1944 was to join the padre on a visit to Bayeux Cathedral, where I had been only six months before the war. I was thrilled to find it quite undamaged, following only minimal street fighting, I think on D+2. Our padre, who had already been with us for a couple of years, was Angus Inglis. He was excellent at getting round the various batteries and troops, and one never knew when or where he was going to turn up, which was great. I often chose a place for him to have communion in the field, perhaps in the open air, or if it was wet in part of a shelled barn or abandoned cottage, where I could put together four ammunition boxes to make a table, and he would bring a clean white cloth and a cross with his travelling communion set; and half a dozen of us would try to be free to share a short service with him. There was no time for conversations in any depth with Angus in those hard-pressed days, but we were most certainly glad to see him constantly around

In early July 185 Field Regiment, we in the 89th still with them, was moved a bit to the west, nearer Caen. The bridgehead was still no bigger. We were near the remains of a village called Demouville,

in much more open country, mostly hundreds of acres of what had
been ripening corn, but of course now trampled down by tanks and
vehicles. The weather continued peerless, so there were clouds of
dust whenever vehicles moved; and it was the dust that the German
gunners went for. Our military police on point duty at dusty 'cross
roads' in the flattened corn fields were therefore particularly
vulnerable, and we all found ourselves seeing these brave redcaps in
quite another light from their usual rôle of enforcing discipline, or
marching unfortunate defaulters into the Guard Room.

On one beautiful morning (after my Jeep had created dust, I
remember reflecting later; but officers had to get round our detach-
ments) I had asked my driver to stop beside a three-strong signals
unit, which was mending the telephone line to one of our guns,
when I had quite a close shave from an exploding shell. The bang,
uncomfortably close by, made my driver and me jump a mile out of
our seats. As the smoke and dust cleared, I saw one of the signal-
men lying a yard or two away with a great gash in his back, and one
of my gunners was clutching his head. There was also a lot of wild
shouting, and I realized at once that it was coming from perhaps my
most respected sergeant, who had gone completely bomb-happy,
and was rushing around bellowing his head off, and in the process
demoralizing everyone else. The poor chap had been obeying the
demands of nature when a shell from the same German salvo
landed on the hard ground a yard beside him, and did not explode.
The experience had so unnerved this quiet former city librarian, a
man less suited than most of us to soldiering, that we never saw him
back; he had to be invalided home. Stretcher bearers materialized
from nowhere (they always did, they were courageous men), and
collected all three, my sergeant not without a struggle.

The shell wounds were mortal for the two who had been hit. The
signalman died before they got him to the ADS near the beachhead,
and Gnr Tribley in it, as the medical boys had classed him as badly
wounded, but fit for evacuation by the hospital ship, which went
home every day with casualties. I found the wooden cross above his
grave in the sand dunes, where there was a temporary cemetery.
His death quite shook me, as the wound had looked superficial, and
I had gone back in the hope of seeing him sitting up perkily in a
bed in the tent, as he was a very perky sort of chap, always quick
with a joke when the going was bad, and a great morale-booster in

consequence. I asked the RAMC corporal there about him: 'had the wound been more serious than they had first thought?' He was busy and unhelpful: 'men get killed in war, you know sir, I can't remember his case I'm afraid.' So I had to go matter-of-factly on my way, to write that night to his widow. Looking back on it now, and recalling that in my troop of sixty men no one else was killed in those eleven months of fighting, (I think there were two dozen fatal casualties, with forty or so wounded, in the whole of the 89th), I ponder again what dangers infantry soldiers face by comparison with us in all other arms; for example probably twenty-five had been killed in a few hours during that terrible night of the mortaring of the company that ran away in front of us. Several other front-line units suffered big casualties during the two long months we were unable to make progress, the Germans always mounting successful counter-attacks against any small advance of ours, and even the fighting experience of the three battle-hardened assault divisions (7th Armoured, 50th Tyne Tees and 51st Highland) was not enough to drive them inland.

But at last: 'We started moving east from the Caen bulge on 16th August, and went fast to the Seine which we crossed on 2nd September', reads my album under a *Times* photograph of huge piles of burnt-out German equipment by the riverbank at Rouen. It must have been taken close to where we ourselves crossed the river on a Bailey Bridge, the permanent bridges having all been blown by the retreating Germans. The crisis for the latter had come when the Americans broke through on the west side of the Cherbourg peninsula, swept on south very fast and then swung east to batter their way through the Falaise Gap, as it came to be called. The position of the thousands of enemy who were containing the British suddenly became very precarious indeed; the Americans were swarming eastwards behind them, so they had to get out quick to avoid encirclement, leaving behind masses of equipment which cluttered up the roads and were easy prey for our aircraft. There was suddenly nothing less than a German rout; and we all had an exhilarating chase after them. I was able to write to father: 'we nightly pitch our moving tents a day's march nearer home,' which was exactly what we did, except that there was no time to pitch any tents. 49 Div. had a brief hold-up because of being ordered to capture Le

Havre, so after crossing the Seine we turned west to do so, and our guns were used with tracer shells, ground to ground instead of ground to air, in order to guide the infantry for a night attack on the town.

My battery was not involved, but I could not resist going along to the operation's gunlines to see what was happening, and an amazing sight it was to watch six of our guns belting away for all they were worth, with the bright light of every sixth shell I think it was streaking through the night air like a rocket. It was not actually a very sensible ploy by our superiors, as of course the German gunners were able fairly easily (because of the tracer) to pin-point precisely where the firing was coming from, and soon began counter-battery fire, fortunately for me against the other concentration of our regiment from the one I was visiting. One of our officers and two men were killed, before the advancing infantry had signalled back to stop firing as the Germans were surrendering fast, coming out of their gun-emplacements with gear packed to be taken prisoner. The town fell that night after feeble resistance; but not alas before this very popular officer, 'Queenie' Garman, a Dunkirk veteran, had met his death, going to the help of a wounded sergeant in his gunpit, a moment before a second shell landed.

Le Havre duly captured, we swept on east through the largely undamaged French towns and villages along the coast, getting a great welcome as we went. That was when my troop's association with 185 Field Regiment ended, and we were back with the 89th. This was the period of the advance when officers' jeeps would be found queueing outside cheese factories and wine cellars; *Camembert* and *Benedictine* sales must have kept up well, by our taking over from the Germans with hardly a break. The *Benedictine* was a lot less damaging than the lethal Normandy *Calvados* had been. That really did incapacitate our soldiers whenever they responded overmuch to the kindnesses showered upon 'our liberators'; the enthusiastic French people lining the roads had handed up glass after glass of the stuff to our unsuspecting soldiers.

We crossed the frontier into Belgium in mid-September just as the ill-fated operation 'Market Garden' was being launched by air from England in a bid to capture Arnhem, well ahead of where the leading British troops had reached. Hundreds and hundreds of gliders and airborne troop-carriers sailed majestically, but as it

turned out tragically, over us in the sunshine to unload their human
cargoes seventy miles or so away, over the town they had hoped to
capture in that gallant 'Bridge too far' failed operation. The 'chase'
halted; if our leading units were held up, everyone was. Furthermore anti-aircraft guns, it was quite clear by now, were largely
redundant; the *Luftwaffe* never recovered from its virtual elimina-
tion before the invasion was launched. So divisional and corps commanders had to think of ways to use the light anti-aircraft regiments, consisting of several thousand soldiers, whom the generals
were not at all keen to leave idle and using up supplies of food and
petrol for no work. Nor were we, of course. Various solutions were
tried, and I only know about our own: we virtually reverted to being
infantry.

Most of the 89th became Bobforce, named thus because our CO,
Colonel Bob Cory, was given the command of it, with other units
added, including parts of a Reconnaissance Regiment, and some
Free Netherlanders. Others of us were for a time called 49 Div. RA
Bn (Buffs), and my troop was in that cumbersomely-named unit in
the early autumn, when a patrol I was leading captured a German
one in some flat open country. My soldiers, equipped of course
again (after two and a half years) with rifles, had wounded two of
theirs, and I could see through my glasses that no more than half a
dozen of them were lying in this wet ditch, either waiting to surrender rather than leaving the two we believed we had wounded, or
on the other hand devilishly ready to fire on us if we moved up
across the open. How we got to them I cannot remember, but when
we did, it turned out that the last thing they wanted was to do any
more fighting. I can see myself now bending over a badly wounded
very young (?14 year-old) German soldier with some water, who was
muttering '*Kaput, Kaput*', and feeling sorry enough for him to mut-
ter encouragingly, I hoped, in reply: '*Nichts kaput, nein*'; but I
reckon he probably succumbed later.

Early in November my troop had orders to collect our guns again
and move north of Nijmegen, into the 'island' between the Rhine
and the Maas, take over a large old pre-Victorian fort just east of
the bridge, and be ready to fire upstream, ground to ground again,
at any suspicious objects flowing down the Maas that might be
mines intended to blow up the bridge. It was a strange assignment,
but it was obviously vital for any spring offensive that the bridge

(damaged already in the September battle) remained sufficiently serviceable to be ready to carry large quantities of troops and materials. So there sixty or so of us were for all that very cold winter of '44-'45, with the troop sleeping when off duty in this superbly constructed brick fort, as dry as a bone; we could indeed have been much worse off. In fact for Christmas dinner I had everyone not on duty seated at greenhouse staging 'scrounged', or to put it bluntly borrowed, yes temporarily stolen from a deserted nursery very close, where there were also dozens of cyclamen in their pots, all ready for decorating our underground abode.

The gunners' task was a bit nebulous, because it was almost impossible to recognize what was what floating downstream, but we fired thousands and thousands of rounds during those many weeks, and every now and then there were some quite satisfactory bangs in the water, but thankfully none against the bridge a few hundred yards past us. We had of course carefully checked that any rounds that ricocheted or failed to explode sailed on into enemy-held territory. For a week or so we put up in the fort a gentle war artist named Thomas Hennell. He was intrigued enough with what we were doing to draw a fine watercolour of the gun positions, and I had prints of it done for the troop Christmas card that year. After the war I handed over the original (with which Thomas was not sufficiently pleased to include in his 'quota' of paintings, so had kindly given to me) to the Imperial War Museum, which received it gratefully, as our delightful guest had been killed painting in Java not long after he had been with us, and the museum had not got much of his work. I learnt years later that he was the only war artist to meet his death in any theatre of war.

I got a short Paris leave in March, staying with a brother officer in the Salvation Army British Officers' leave centre in the Rue St Honore, and very central and comfortable it was too. I had home leave too that winter, which was specially good because during it my only niece Sarah, Kay's second child, was baptized at Chiddingstone. Her father in the RNVR was stationed in Ceylon, so could not be there, but Ted was home again from the Sudan, so that was a lovely reunion, very precious events in wartime as these were. Before Christmas three of us officers from the 89th also had an Antwerp leave for 48 hours, a week-end that became famous or infamous for my only sight of the inside of a brothel. We had gone into what looked like a perfectly harmless-looking, rather smart, restaurant for a drink and a meal; it was a big place, crowded with other officers and friendly local girls, which did not strike us as untoward because of the welcome which Belgians were giving British troops everywhere. After half an hour or so, Nick Marcy, the only married one of us three, and ten years older (he could well have had a fairly chequered past in his bachelor days) spotted, as indeed all three of us had, some of these girls climbing on to the laps of British officers who were sitting and having their drinks. The atmosphere was thick with cigarette smoke as restaurants invariably were in those days, and you could not see properly across the room. 'Come on, Bick', he suddenly said, 'some of these chaps are going upstairs with their girls, this place is a brothel; out we all go in double-quick time'. He had obviously been observing things which were passing by us 'innocents abroad.' So we did just that, and uncommonly glad we both were to have been rescued, before Madame had latched on to her newcomers, and walked over from where she presided in the bar to fix the three of us up with an appropriate member of the oldest profession in the world.

49 Div. had by now become part of 1 Canadian Corps, but it made no difference to us on the ground for many weeks, as we stayed put in our fort. The snow, and the mud after it, would anyhow have put paid to any advance, and we began to share the great disappointment of the high command at not having pulled off Operation Market Garden, which would have shortened the war by six or seven months. Nothing much happened at East Fort, as January heralded the sixth year of the war. The men all got some home leave, with resigned 'still here, then's, when they returned to find nothing changed. The weather improved a bit in March, and my battery commander told me to go and liaise with the battalion in front of us (it was 4th Lincs), to make sure we knew what to do if the Germans had a final fling in our direction. People had got a bit jittery after Rundstedt's devastating attack in the Ardennes in December, in which there had been 10,000 American casualties after a major break through into the Allied line, which only ended on Christmas Eve when the enemy suddenly ran out of steam. But the 4th Lincs company commander sent me packing: 'No need for a plan' he said, 'tell your battery commander not to be defeatist; everything's fine'. As he was a major, and I merely a captain, I retired hurt.

After four fairly boring months in one place, everything started happening the whole way along the line. The Rhine crossings to the east of us had signalled the beginning of the end in March, while on our front the Germans pulled out of Arnhem in early April without much resistance to make off home while the going was good; the stuffing had gone out of them. 49 Div got a great welcome from the town's battered citizens, most of whose houses, systematically looted by the Germans after their defeat of the British, had not been repaired much since the September battle. They were pathetically grateful that this time we had come to stay. I buried (the padre was very busy) the decayed bodies of several Airborne Div soldiers which had not been found six months earlier by the German stretcher-bearers in the dense gardens of suburban Arnhem.

After a few days the division started to move westwards into the countryside to deal with the many thousands of enemy troops still in Holland; we were a single British division in the Canadian Corps, and therefore the only British troops to end the war in friendly territory. It was a very privileged situation for us which the men kept remarking on, as spring flowers were heaped on to our guns and vehicles by happy laughing and crying roadside Hollanders (they did not like being called Dutchmen, it sounded too much like Deutsch-men).

One balmy evening early in May our BSM Bushell stuck his nose into my tent as I was lying on my tummy writing home: 'A patrol has just come in, sir, to report Germans singing in a barn they had been watching. I reckon the Boches are packing it in'. He was right. Next day, 5th May, 120,000 German troops in the Western Netherlands surrendered to our Canadian GOC. The following morning we mustered, at splendidly short notice, a large contingent for a Victory Church Parade; several hundred British soldiers had an exhilarating march, heads held high, through cheering crowds in the streets of Ede, to a service in the Dutch Reformed Church. The campaign in North-West Europe was over; very many ordinary serving men like us had lost their lives, and we were glad that our senior commanders felt that it was important to remember them in a church service. There was no sense of crowing; it was just so wonderful that the fighting had stopped, and we were alive to tell the tale.

Holland, Germany, and India

Christ is the image of the unseen God, and the first—born of all creation.
Colossians 1.15

Strange lovers man and earth, their love and hate
Braided in mutual need, and of their strife
A tired contentment born.
The Land: Winter

'**T**HE glorious weather continues', I wrote to father in mid-May:
'the only trouble is that it makes us all lazy just when we are
working harder than we have done for months, rounding up these
Boches and Dutch SS. The first two nights up here, we (that is 89
Company as we now call ourselves) spent in Doorn, where the
Kaiser[23] had lived and died in exile. We were sent for at midnight
on the first night as a local burgomaster reported trouble with
Dutch SS in his district. You see an entire Boche division was still at
large in the area, and all armed. The patriot or Dutch Resistance
forces, also armed, want nothing better than to shoot up Dutch SS,
who of course are all traitors and, knowing as they do that there is
not much future for them, the SS are fairly keen to keep fighting,
whereas the Germans are not, particularly as their General
Blaskowitz surrendered a fortnight ago, and all they want now is to
get protection by the British from the Dutch. It must be a typical instance of the muddle and internal strife common to all Europe at
this strange time.

On Thursday our Company moved to this village of Elst. Here a
vast cage has been constructed by our Sappers; it is simply a three-
strand barbed-wire fence in open country, marked with white tape
forming the perimeter; the cage itself, we have worked out from our
maps, is one and a half miles long by three quarters of a mile wide.
At a large country house a few miles away, an SS Battery was on
parade ready to receive us, just under three hundred men. Their
guns and ammunition, their small arms, their personal kit and food,
were all laid out. It really was an amazing sensation to witness the
CO, a typical top-booted Nazi, coming up complete with Alsatian

---

23. Wilhelm II 1859–1941, third and last German Emperor.

hound, to salute me and report and that the battery was ready and awaiting my orders.

Search parties started on the men. All Germans smell, and these were no exception, so we had reliefs laid on. Personal kit was searched for obvious loot, of which there was plenty, while I got other men going through the food, mostly mouldy bread. I had made fifteen sacks of potatoes turned out on to the grass, to demonstrate to me that they did actually contain potatoes and nothing else. Others of my soldiers supervised the central dumping of all small arms and general equipment.

By the afternoon all the stuff they were being allowed to keep was ready to be loaded on to their carts; I say 'their' but all the carts are looted, as well as the bulk of the horses, which is of course another reason why the civilians are inclined to cause trouble; and who can blame them? But the orders for the moment are that the Boches keep all horse and carts, and even cattle which they have acquired, as they can be slaughtered to help feed them when the great trek to Germany begins next week.

I had to lead the column down to the cage. We set off with me sitting on top of my Jeep, then there was a Bren Gun carrier with armed men on board, then the German CO, still with his hound, then his marching troops; and after that about thirty horse-drawn carts, with another carrier bringing up the rear of the column. For miles around in the spring sunshine you could see other columns moving along the farm tracks towards the symbol of their defeat, this huge barbed-wire cage; and they are a defeated lot too, no question of 'unbeaten in the field' which I believe is what the Germans tried to plug after the last war.

The next day the medicine was repeated when we dealt with a Flak battery of the *Luftwaffe*, a smart unit, and I fancy very proud of the fact that they were nothing to do either with the Wehrmacht or with the Dutch SS. The monotony of the march to the cage was relieved by the excitement caused when a horse bolted, and brought its wagon (with five Boches on top, as white as sheets) galloping up the column on the wrong side of the road absolutely flat out. The carrier overtook the cart, and managed to slow it down but not before a violent swerve had flung one German into the ditch

All incoming parties have to be checked and counted; other small bodies of men had to be taken out under escort for work on dumps;

various stragglers were admitted, including two Armenians and an Italian. These three are so scared of what the Germans might do them that they never let our soldiers out of their sight. The two Armenians have been in the underground movement for over a year, so it is hard on them to be in there at all, and they keep on appealing to be allowed out. But they are in German uniform, and there is no one to prove their story, so they have to wait and see for the time being.

Last night we were relieved of the perimeter guard defence, and tonight Roger Keane and I are going into Doorn to 'sightsee' round the Kaiser's old home, and then into Utrecht to have a look round there. Tomorrow my troop provides a 'ceremonial' guard for the German Divisional HQ (can you beat the British race, ceremonial indeed) and I have to sleep there as liaison officer, which might be rather interesting.'

I cannot recall anything about the Kaiser's house, but I do remember the slow creaky scraping noise made on the pave of Utrecht's streets by hundreds and hundreds of its citizens bicycling along, without rubber tyres on the wheels. No small inconvenience like a wartime shortage of rubber was obviously going to keep the Dutch off their bicycles; one wonders how long the rims lasted under treatment like that. The ceremonial guard I only remember for the query I had with myself as to whether I, a mere captain, should salute a defeated general; I decided there would be no harm in it, and if it gave him pleasure, why not, he had had his humiliation. He had commanded the 34th SS Division, 'so he was not small fry', my album tells me. I was rather disappointed when he simply acknowledged my salute unsmilingly, just as if I had been one of his own officers a month earlier; but why should he have smiled?

Several of us found ourselves staying where some of his officers had certainly been a little earlier. This was the Hotel Ittman at Nunspeet on the Ijsselmeer (we used to call it the Zuyder Zee), which was operative almost at once as a leave centre for British officers after a quick turn-round by the Dutch staff, very quick actually as I was on leave there for three days by 18th May. It was a luxurious place on the sea, with its own stables, from which several of us rode every morning, and it had the equivalent of Mirror dinghies with which we had a lot of fun on and in the shallow waters; shallow is the right word, as of course the whole *meer* is barely above sea level, and when we capsized in a squall about a mile from the shore, all we had to do was to wade in the sea up to just above our knees to right them. I was lucky enough to come in for a posh dinner at the Ittman, as on the night I arrived our GOC had invited Prince Bernhardt of the Netherlands to dine there with him and a cross-section of his senior officers in the division., and the twenty or so of us captains and subalterns who happened to be on leave that night in this idyllic spot were included in quite a historic dinner party, sixty strong, to mark the successful end of hostilities. Already by then the Ittman, says the menu, was '49th Div Officers' Hotel', not bad going only thirteen days after the capitulation in Holland.

We loved being with such friendly people as the Dutch were, and realized how lucky we were not to have had to endure the sullen stares and roadside spitting at the first British troops advancing on to German soil. Despite such an unpleasant 'welcome', the British soldier thoroughly disliked the 'no-fraternisation' rule issued by Monty immediately after the cease-fire. Not to share a bar of chocolate with a hungry German child seemed totally unnatural and indeed wrong to him, and the 'no-fratting' order (though not I think ever officially rescinded) quietly lapsed, without the officers having to jump on the men for disobeying it. But that of course was after we as a regiment had got to Germany. Before we left friendly territory my happy memory of those charming Hollanders in early May 1945 has ever since been epitomised for me by a letter to *The Times* that summer. It reads:

Sir, We are a Dutch family in Amsterdam, man woman and one child, four years old. We had a bad season this winter. We had no bread, no potatoes, no butter or fat. We had no gas to cook and no electricity. We had nothing. Just one thing we had here: that was the Germans. They are called here 'Mofs'.

So it was six weeks ago. And now this Sunday morning, it was a fine breakfast, bread and butter and cheese, and a cup of milk for the boy. We are so grateful, and my wife says to me: "We must tell the English people how grateful we are." Will you do it for us in your newspaper? And will you say we will never forget it?

Always yours, F. J. Schroder, wife and child,
Maurestraat, 48.11, Amsterdam 17 June'.

As we left Holland for Germany I was made Regimental Education Officer, which would mean leaving the battery for Regimental Headquarters. Although it was an honour to be asked to fill this new peacetime-soldiering job, it meant that I must leave the fighting units and the officers and men with whom I had shared everything for the four years since I joined 11th Buffs in Waldershare Park outside Dover. But everything was different now that we were all waiting for our demobilisation papers, and I was excited to be tackling work that had come under Burgon, the British Army's Director of Education until the war ended and he returned to Canada. While he held the post, he had been responsible from 1942 onwards for initiating and publishing both the *Army Bureau of Current Affairs* leaflets and their successors *The British Way* and *Purpose* ones. We regimental officers all had to use these pamphlets with our soldiers as often as duties allowed, and very good they were, particularly the first series, the *ABCA* ones. Burgon I know came in for some criticism that the ethos of both sets of leaflets was to some degree slanted in a socialist direction, and there were those who said that they had some influence with the troops in their voting at the General Election of that summer of 1945, which saw Churchill's coalition government fall. I remember teasing Burgon about the charge. 'Yes, probably', he would say, 'it was my job to make the troops think about what would be best for Britain after the war, and maybe my own inclinations crept in a bit too much.

I was only in Germany for two months, but very interesting months they were. Our first billets were in a pleasant country house four miles south of 'what was Dortmund', in the Ruhr. It rapidly became clear to me as the new Education Officer, and thankfully to the CO too, that everyone was far too busy looking after 10,000 local DPs[24] to give any time to a comprehensive education scheme, and anyhow the books and manuals I needed were not going to be available for many weeks. Instead I got deeply involved in Field Security, which meant in effect screening Germans for jobs under the allied administration of the whole area. 'Nazi types' had to be rounded up under pretty clear rules as to who came within the 'automatic arrest' category. That included most ranks of the SS, and many more who we knew from detailed lists we acquired had belonged to Nazi organisations. But there was also all the detailed

24. Displaced Persons, the term then for the refugees all over Europe.

'informing' that inevitably began at once, and sifting that was a considerable undertaking too, as of course there was a great deal of hopeful 'feathering of nests'. Suspects in their hundreds went to the internment camps that were being set up.

Then there was the vetting of every German who had been or was being put by the military government into a position of authority in the new administration. They all had forms to fill in, and extremely comprehensive they were, so that it was not easy to cheat, nor worth while if the applicant was serious about wanting a) to get work and b) to help rebuild his country. Once the big fish, the Burgomaster and heads of departments, had been through interrogation which was based on their forms and been passed as untainted with Nazism, it was then for them to get on with 'de-Nazifying' the minor official posts under them. We were soon encouraged that the system, which of course we were basically inventing as we went along, was going fairly well; it helped that we encountered maximum co-operation all down the line. I remember going to see the Burgomaster of Dortmund, working away in a few rooms of the burnt-out Town Hall, and realizing what a mystery it was as to where all the people of the city lived amid that devastation. They were either, he told me, in the cellars of their houses, or if they were lucky in one or two ground-floor rooms they had made habitable. Room for one line of traffic in the streets had been cleared of rubble, so cars and horse-drawn vehicles (mostly the latter) picked their way between these thirty to forty feet high piles of rubble which stretched as far as the eye could see, out to the less-damaged suburbs. The trams had begun running, as electricity came through again; there was water to most of the town, and quite a lot of telephone communication. 'These Germans are certainly making the most of things and working incredibly hard', I commented in a letter to father.

Our own living conditions in the Mess were superb by comparison. The garden of this big house was full of vegetables, and the strawberries were just ripening. From my bedroom, with a desk in the window, I looked out on to green fields beyond the mown lawns, 'with only the odd slag heap visible', which was amazing when we were actually in the middle of the German coalfield. Our two Boches men-servants did their work well; and as I was PMC[25] I

25. President of the Mess Committee

was soon calling on the town's wine merchants, whom I recorded as having large stocks of 'champagne, hock and moselle, but facing the major problem that their cellars had all been flooded to four feet or more when the town's water mains were destroyed by bombing and the labels were almost entirely washed off. For recreation there were lots of horses to ride at nearby racing stables, which in fact made us tend to bite off more than we could chew, as these animals were very under-exercised. When we got them out into the country they went like the wind; negotiating bomb craters all over the grass fields we were riding in added a considerable extra hazard, and one or two officers came to grief when their horses diverted at speed to avoid a hole.

Quite suddenly for me this not uncongenial existence ended, because I and another Buffs officer, Teddy Edwards, still sixty years later a firm friend, were posted home in early August to do a Field Gunnery course at Catterick in Yorkshire. So, goodbyes quickly and sadly done after such a long time together, and with the Education Officer task not even begun, he and I were off home. It was the end of an era for me. Much as I had naturally got to know the officers more intimately than the men, I knew as soon as Teddy and I had left that it was the men I would miss most: their names still come tumbling out of my head, Sgt Major Bushell, Sgt Magenty, Gnr Gibbs (my faithful driver), Gnr Clark (my even more faithful batman), I could go on and on, with stories about them (and they of me, no doubt). I remembered Sgt Ford (him of the early morning in Normandy when we were faced by those deserters) one bitter evening in the Brecon Beacons two or three years before, leaning with me on a five-barred gate as the cooks were preparing a meal; we were overlooking the farm where I had managed to get the whole troop (sixty men) bedded down overnight in the hay barn. My townsman sergeant, with twenty-five years' service behind him, turned to me and said ruminatively as the sun went down in a spectacular sky: 'Well, sir, you always seem to go for a good smell of manure, but we've certainly got a very contented lot of men in there out of the weather, so thank you very much, sir'.

I remembered too cocking up stooks of wheat with them in the harvest fields just outside Dover, when I knew I still had to tell them that we would be up till 4 a.m. on a night defence exercise, without mentioning that the German invasion could begin next day; I remembered the anxiety of caring for them all in the Normandy bridgehead, with the gunsites scattered over a wide area and wondering when I got into my slit-trench for the night whether the six crews would still be all right when I did my rounds of them next morning; I remembered the excitement when the August breakthrough sent us chasing across Europe with the feeling that we might be home at any moment; but then the long cold 1944-1945 winter in that hundred-year-old fort on the Rhine. All these unlikely wartime soldiers, with among them a tiny smattering of professionals who were actually a wonderful backbone to what we had to do, had become part of my life. They had been my close companions since 1941, and now in July 1945 I was realizing that I would never see most of them again. It took a lot of getting used to, but was helped a little by the fact that for three or four years after the war I had the fun of organizing regimental re-unions; we had them in a Lambeth pub., and they drew together the first time eighty or more officers and men for an evening of reminiscences. By 1950 or so numbers were dropping off badly, the ambience of where we had known each other so well had melted away, and we had started going on our civilian ways for too long; so there was mutual agreement that we stopped. I owe them all so much. Imagine the thrill then, in December 2003, of a Christmas card, with unrecognized writing on the envelope, and on the card besides the printed seasonal message these words from two men I had not seen or heard of for fifty-eight years: 'Best wishes, sir, we hope you keep well, from Gnr Russell and Gnr White. We had some good times together.'

On the ferry which took Teddy and me back to England, leaving the only theatre of war in which I got personally involved, I had reopened the letter father had given me just before the invasion. I had read it first, as he had asked I should if possible, on D Day, after we had had that memorable down-river trip from Tilbury to the Thames Estuary, and were waiting for our convoy to get up to full complement and move off for the beaches. The letter has resonances of the one, in reverse as it were, which my uncle Morris wrote to his father and mother on the night before the Battle of the Somme, on the first day of which he was killed within minutes of leading his men over the top; I remembered, as I read what father was saying to me, how in his letter Morris had wondered so much whether he would let his men down. Father's to me brings in my mother, by then eight years in heaven, and he would often do that on birthdays, and I loved him for it. This is word for word what father wrote to me on 12th May 1944:

My dear son, Though written days, perhaps two or three weeks before you start for the continent, you must have a letter from me when you actually sail. You will be very busy and very thrilled that the day has come at last. The army has done its best to train you, short of letting you experience active service. But in this want you are like hundreds more. Being a Bickersteth you will be a little anxious as to whether you will come up to scratch when the test comes, spiritually, mentally, and physically. Do not let this thought be more than a passing one, drive it out with a little prayer: 'Lord I shall be very busy, if I forget Thee, do not Thou forget me'. You are in God's hands on the sea, and on the land, and He rules both, and your destiny. Also your father has complete confidence that you will acquit yourself worthily and unselfishly. In the background of your mind will be this thought: 'God has never failed me yet and though I pass through the valley of the shadow of death I will fear no evil, for Thou art with me, Thy rod (to guide) and Thy staff (to protect) and comfort (strengthen) me'. Love of God and love of the family is no new experience for you, that love surrounds you, as your love reaches out to embrace it, and is not confined by space, for we know how darling Mother's love surrounds us perpetually. Neither of us can foresee what experiences will be yours, but you have always made the most of your opportunities and will naturally do so now; and though your letters will be able to tell us little, there will be all the more to tell when you come home; and one day we will visit the scenes of your adventures (treat them as adventures) together, and you shall point out the tight corners. I could write on all the morning, putting in different ways my love and confidence, my thanks for all you have been and are to Mother and me, my hopes for you in the future. God bless you until we meet again, Your proud and devoted Father.

I have no means of knowing whether other young men heard like that from their fathers to launch them on the biggest seaborne invasion in history, but I am quite certain that no one had a letter he valued more than I did mine. It sums up and reveals so movingly the calibre of man, indeed of priest in the Church of God, that my Victorian father was.

Teddy and I had barely unpacked in Catterick when the atom bombs were dropped on Hiroshima and Nagasaki, and Japan capitulated two days later. I can see myself now in the Mess discussing over drinks before dinner what would happen next. The main topic of conversation of course was how soon we could get out of the army in order to start, or for older men to continue with, normal living. It was soon explained to us that this would not be in a matter of weeks; for the younger men like me it could well be a year; The gargantuan task of demobilisation, we heard and indeed were more or less expecting, had to be staggered, and it would be the older men who could go first. Everyone got a number, the smallest the first to go; mine was 36, for which the forecast was 'early to mid-summer 1946'.

Having to stay on in the army was hard for many thousands of us wartime servicemen. There seemed very little point for example in learning (on a gunnery course) the calibration and bracketing and maintenance of twenty-five-pounder field guns (all of these things simply extensions and enlargements of what I knew anyway), when it was obvious that none of this knowledge would now be of the slightest use to me or to the nation. At the same time we could see perfectly well, as we argued away about it during that summer in Yorkshire, that the civilian population could not possibly take a huge influx of men and women all abandoning their uniform together, and lining up at the same time for work in the poverty-stricken country that England was when the war ended. So we simply had to put up with the frustration of it, and I was only so glad that I was not a married man longing to get back to his wife and children. We were kept as happy as possible with plenty of leave. I was frequently at home during the autumn, and the army found further courses for us; for instance when Catterick was over, I had an interesting three-week one on international relations at Ashford, which of course was very handy for both Canterbury and Chiddingstone. At home father had the satisfying pleasure of employing an ex-soldier from his son's regiment as his gardener. Gunner John Wood was a quiet reliable person, whom I had known for four years, and when I asked him in Germany whether he would like to get back to gardening he had jumped at the idea. He was ten years older than me and therefore in a much earlier demob. group; father invited him to the Rectory, he and Mary liked him, and they engaged him at once. So he was ensconced in the parish's tied cottage on Somerden Green, half-a-mile away across the fields, by the time I came home. We rebuilt the almost derelict greenhouse together, a sort of symbol that things were back to normal, for there was no danger of the glass being blown out again.

Then suddenly the opportunity came to finish my army service on a staff job in India, retaining my captain's rank, which was a help as I was trying to save hard. I jumped at it, to sail just after Christmas, and left Southampton on 28th December in the P&O liner-turned-troopship *Strathnaver*; she had two thousand service personnel on board, and a hundred or so civilians, the latter mostly civil service wives who had been separated from their husbands for the duration of the war; but we all shook down happily for the three-week voyage, across the Bay of Biscay (a first for me; it was quite calm), through the Straits of Gibraltar (near enough to the Rock to see the apes in our field glasses), along the Suez Canal ('get your knees brown, then', well-justified ribaldry from soldiers on the canal banks, who could well have been there for four or five years), and across to Bombay, which like two hundred-years-worth of British troops before us we smelt a long way offshore. In fact there cannot be a port anywhere in the world where you are so dramatically introduced to a totally different way of life. We lined the *Strathnaver's* rails spellbound by what we saw, from the bumboats to the minarets, and the hundreds and hundreds of people swarming everywhere.

I was bound for Jhansi in the United Provinces, to work in GHQ 2nd Echelon, right in the middle of India, and a very hot area indeed. I got there by train from Bombay, and found I had quite a nice brick hut to myself, only five minutes walk across the cantonment from the Mess, which was the social centre for around sixty officers. What everyone else did I never really discovered, but I soon got the measure of my department's task, which amounted to clearing up administrative matters in that Indian and Malay and Burmese theatre of war. We were part of South East Asia Command, under Lord Louis Mountbatten, who had been chosen to lead the entire campaign against the Japanese. With their capitulation in mid-August 1945, everyone and everything changed gear of course; our tiny contribution in 2nd Echelon to the running-down exercise was tackling claims of many different kinds from local populations over a huge area, and also dealing with the personal effects of our casualties in that theatre of war. This was poignant work, often involving moving correspondence with relatives, but it had to be done. We were very busy, so boredom was not a problem.

We heard it was the C-in-C's personal directive that we young officers who had been in Normandy, as well as his own who had been in SEAC some time but still had high demob. numbers, were to have the opportunity of generous local leave. I was in India for less than six months, but I had a 48 hrs in February, another in March, and just under six weeks in April-May. In order to plan whatever leave did come my way (not knowing of course in January how much that would be) I took the train the short distance to New Delhi to stay a night with my cousin Lawrence Monier-Williams; he was a Gurkha Brigadier on his last job, and at once started to work out the best way to use the ample time off which he was sure, rightly as it happened, I would be given. 'The Taj Mahal for a start', he said, so I got through to Teddy Edwards who after we had left the 89th together had arrived in India before me, and was serving in a Sikh Mountain Battery RA up north; he wangled a short leave to coincide with mine, and we had a fabulous time in Agra, from our base in the Cecil Hotel, one of the best old colonial ones in British India, exploring with a delightful guide, and without a tourist in sight, the wonders of the Taj.

For March's leave I stayed in Lawrence's palatial home in New Delhi. With thirty years in the Indian Army behind him, this very experienced Gurkha officer and his nice wife Dorothy knew the sub-continent backwards, and became good friends back in England over the next twenty years. They took me round all the famous sites of British imperial power, and in fact we were able to see the whole Lutyens 'plant' used magnificently on the second day I was there for nothing less than WWII's Victory Parade. Lawrence was personally involved, but Dorothy and I had superb seats near the Viceroy as he took the salute from thousands of men and women marching through the Arch. I had last seen the Viceroy, Field Marshal Wavell, when as a major-general he inspected my contingent at Tidworth Pennings OTC Camp in the summer of 1939. This great

parade was an amazing spectacle for a new boy to India. But Lawrence also made sure I saw the other side of things by taking me to
the Red Fort, of Indian Mutiny fame, and then through the
Chandri Chowk bazaar in Old Delhi, where we called at Bickersteth
House, named after my great uncle Edward who helped to found
and then lived with the Cambridge Mission to Delhi in the 1870s;
two English and several Indian members of the Community of the
Ascension gave us a great welcome.

My third and longest leave was to the North West Frontier. My
bearer obviously expected to come with me, and very glad I was
again and again in those weeks to have his presence and his counsel.
He was, as I have mentioned, a charming Hindu, named Nanta
Ram, and no one could have looked after this total newcomer to the
East better than he did. For instance on the two-day train journey to
Peshawar in the growing April heat, he would get out at stations
and miraculously bring a meal for me, or stagger back with a huge
ice block he could hardly carry, to put in the tin bath he had sensibly brought with our kit. Very welcome that cooled air coming off
the ice block was, in days when air conditioning was unheard of;
and he knew just when to tip the sloshing water out at unscheduled
stops (hundreds of those) before it spilt all over the carriage when
the train lurched.

I stayed in Dean's Hotel, again one of the great old hotels; Nanta
would just disappear round the back regions, and be on parade
next morning with a large grin on his face. In Peshawar Lawrence
had organised an Indian officer to come with me on the short run
to the Afghan border. We saw the regimental crests carved in the
hillside rock face by generations of British troops right up the Khyber Pass near Landi Khotal, and I stood on the frontier at Landi
Karna beside a Khyber Rifles sentry for the traditional 'one-foot-
into-Afghanistan' photograph. One night my new officer friend
drove me up the Malakand Pass on the road north from Nowshera;
and my best uniform had been specially brought from Jhansi by
Nanta because Lawrence had organized dinner for me in the
Guides Cavalry mess, an unforgettable occasion. Every kind of hal-
lowed mess tradition was observed, including the loyal toast to the
King Emperor. I was also proudly regaled with the (true) fact that
the young Winston Churchill ('who has just won this war', I was
confidently informed) first made a name for himself when he

reported for the *Daily Telegraph* on the Malakand Field Force's 1897 expedition commanded by Sir Bindon Blood. I had to prick myself to be sure I really was the only white face round that candle-lit table, less than fifty miles from the border of a country which still said to me G.A. Henty's *Kabul to Kandahar*.

From Peshawar Nanta and I went by train the two hundred and fifty miles to Rawalpindi, where Teddy met me in his Jeep and we drove up into the Murree Hills together, for me to spend Easter 1946 with him and his Sikhs in the remote Kayhra Gali Camp. One clear morning we were rewarded with a fine view of the 26,000 ft Nanga Parbat; more than fifty years later I saw the 28,000 peak of Everest at the other end of the Himalayan range, when we were staying with Sam in Kathmandu. Both times the long and deep line of snow-covered mountains, which at first sight seem to be clouds because they are so far up into the sky, constituted a unique and totally breathtaking experience. On Easter Day we went into Murree itself for communion in a packed little church, though where everyone came from to fill it I do not know. The battery's guns were all mule-drawn, and there were some fine chargers too for the British and Sikh officers, so we had several good rides, for which I was lent a handsome grey; riding her was sometimes a bit hairy because of the narrow mountain tracks on the steep sides of the craggy hills.

I left Teddy after a fascinating four days with his charming Sikhs. Nanta and I were making for the final destination of my long leave which was Srinagar in Kashmir. I stayed in Nedou's Hotel but spent a lot of time with Canon and Mrs Tyndale-Biscoe. He was the almost legendary, and by then 84-year-old, Principal of the CMS schools; he had gone out to a temporary post and was still there sixty years later. One of his party tricks was to do school fire drill for his visitors. I was the Canon's only guest that week, so all these scores of boys, when the clanging fire bells began one evening when they had all been in bed about half an hour, slid down the fire-station-type brass poles and dived into the Jhelum River fifty yards away 'in case their pyjamas were smouldering'. The story behind that little extra in my honour was that the superstition, when he had joined the staff, was that the river was infested with crocodiles, but T-B having carefully established that there were no crocodiles ever in the Jhelum dived in on his second day as headmaster, with all his boys lined up along the banks to watch him being gobbled up before their eyes. His 'miraculous' survival was the moment for an immediate order to follow his example. History did not relate how long it actually took to break down the crocodile tale, but many years before I arrived the boys had become renowned for their swimming prowess.

Indeed the whole set-up, as was the case all round the British Empire, was geared to the English public school and 'varsity traditions. Everyone in Srinagar knew the Canon; wherever you were, you simply had to say to the tonga driver (the pony taximan): 'Tyndale-Biscoe Sahib ko', and off he would go to deliver you home. The Canon had a 'cutter' (he called it) on Nagin Bagh, the beautiful lake quite close to Srinagar, which was full of house boats for Raj visitors to hire for holidays, and I had some exciting surf-board riding behind motor-boats. I read recently that through neglect during these long Kashmir troubles, the Bagh is entirely swamped with hyacinth weed, and not a boat can move on it.

Looking back gratefully, as I often have to my short stay in that vast, then undivided, sub-continent I realize what a tremendous privilege it was to spend a little time there before the Raj came dramatically to an end; in 1946 that way of life was still in full swing as if it would last for ever. In fact I came to the view that five years of war around its eastern borders had made very little difference to how things had been done in British India since the great shake-up of the Mutiny ninety years earlier. Although of course the work of Gandhi and others was beginning to come to fruition, it was never expected to do so anything like as quickly as it did, and no wonder that our April 1947 division of India, with the creation of Pakistan, led to such massive slaughter.

After that memorable leave I had no sooner got back to Jhansi than I succumbed to a bad go of jaundice, so spent most of my remaining six weeks in the country under the care of the Royal Army Medical Corps. Fellow officers were extremely kind over coming into the hospital to cheer me up, and I appreciated their helping to pass the time, even though I soon rumbled a major reason for their solicitude: the hospital was the only building in the cantonment that had fans, and the Indian plains were heating up in a big way. From recollection my sailing date for demobilisation came through while I was ill, and there was indeed some question as to whether I was going to be fit enough to travel. But all was well, and I duly left Jhansi without much regret for a few days at the Deolali base outside Bombay, notorious for how beastly it was for generations of servicemen. But being homeward-bound made it perfectly bearable for a few days, and off I went in the trooping liner *Highland Princess* on 24th June, for the three week voyage. The journey was enlivened by our breaking down in the Mediterranean, to the extent that we had to limp into Malta, whereupon every soul on board had to disembark and transfer to another ship. But we still docked more or less on time in Tilbury, a few hundred yards as it happened from where our Liberty ship had sailed for the Normandy invasion just over two years earlier.

Our part of the large demobilisation contingent on board, twenty or so officers, had to report to that *fons et origo* of all things military, which actually I had never set foot in before: Aldershot, and it did us well for our last night in the Army. We were even driven in style the few hundred yards to the demob. centre next morning, and I can hear now one officer we did not know (so we were a new audience for him), who was added on to our India crowd, expatiating during the three minute trip on what a very sad day this was for us all. It was a conversation we had had many times in the bar on board ship, so we let him prattle on. He was right that there was more than an element of sadness in what we were about to do, ending the matchless comradeship every soldier experiences. But, lucky enough to have survived the war, we had all become quite clear that the freedom to get on with our own lives and values would make up many times over for everything to which we were about to say goodbye.

I can only record, with a real sense of gratitude, that I enormously enjoyed being a soldier. Again and again in my life since, what I learnt in those years has been invaluable: I have been so glad to know 'the language', I have gone on making contacts which would never have been possible otherwise, I have been helped to understand how and why people think and act as they do.

Having 'debussed' for the last time on arrival at the centre, we were marched up individually to a senior officer at a barrack table, saluted smartly, were thanked (I think), given our discharge papers on to the Reserve, and shunted into the clothes store. There I chose a brown herring-bone suit and a trilby hat, and they both lasted me for years. We got completely, if simply, kitted out, assisted by considerate civilians from the outfitting trade. We signed for everything, and walked out to the buses taking us to the station. My service with the Colours was over, although I remained on the Reserve of Officers for some years; it was 16th July 1946, five and a half years to the day since I had arrived as a private soldier at Chaucer Barracks Canterbury.

Oxford and Wells

Holy, holy, holy Lord, God of power and might,
Heaven and earth are full of your glory
Sanctus, Holy Communion, *Common Worship*

All craftsmen share a knowledge, they have held
Reality down-fluttering to a bench
The Land: Summer

TED was in England again, to my delight, when I got home back to Chiddingstone as a twenty-five year-old civilian ready to take up my deferred university place, six academic years after I would normally expected to have got to Oxford. It was great to be able to discuss it all with Ted (Ch. Ch. 1933-36) as well as father (Ch. Ch.1900-03).

'Holiday, first', said Ted; so he and Mairse and I hired a car for a week to go for an expedition looking up family and friends in Devon and Somerset and Dorset. It was a sturdy Morris 10, and I proudly recorded that we did 700 miles in her, so perhaps that seemed quite a lot. We shared the not very arduous driving on the empty roads of those days, and stayed in no hotels thanks to generous hosts at our stopping places. I had passed my test in 1940 in Tunbridge Wells on a Standard 8, owned by the London family friends, the Matthews, who lodged with us for the first two of the war years; but of course I had driven all manner of vehicles in the Army, as indeed Ted had for ten years or more in the Middle East. Mairse had driven extensively round Kent on her Red Cross and St John work, but always in the cars of other people who had special petrol allocation for her duties. So in 1946 the Bickersteths, uniquely among our friends, had still never owned a car, for the simple reason that father was quite sure he could not afford one.

But the following year a bachelor great-uncle of ours (Uncle Bob, almost the last of the Bishop of Exeter's sixteen children) died, and Bob had made a lot of money in business. I remember him as every inch a Bickersteth, rugged, not to say red-faced, with white beetling eyebrows; and he left his money to his brother Sam's two eldest sons, Monier and Geoffrey, judging correctly that the other three surviving boys had no particular need of unexpected windfalls. Suddenly, then, Father who was sixty-five that year and had never had any private means whatever all the time he was bringing up children, received a handsome legacy of shares in his old uncle's firm, and typically used some of his new income to buy a motor car for his younger daughter, who was giving up her life to help him. He never learnt to drive it, but 'kept' Mairse in her own transport for the thirty more years until his death. The new capital did not in any way change the lifestyle of father or daughter beyond their enjoying the many benefits of becoming car-owners; but he would also delight in giving us four an occasional hundred pounds when he knew that a gift out of the blue would be useful.

I came home from the family tour to the pleasing contemplation of Oxford. What should I read there? I had taken some of my classics texts out to India with me, and tried not very successfully to do some work on them. Herodotus for some reason went better than Thucydides, but I was not picking up Plato's *Republic* for pleasure and I knew in my bones that those Upper Bench years had not made a classical scholar of me. It seemed obvious, however, to the two old Oxford men that Father and Ted were, as well as to me, and also to some Rugby beaks I talked with, to go in hope for the two year shortened Greats course, shortened that is specially for men returning from the services; the plain truth was that I had no background in anything else. Once I got into the work that autumn, I frequently wished I was reading history, but to change in midstream, when the course was so short anyway, would have been absurd. So I had to wait fifty years for a serious study of history, in the Open University after retirement, and I loved it.

However, the bonus was that reading Ancient History at Christ Church brought me into contact both with the legendary figure of R.H. Dundas, and also the gentle cultivated Michael Foster for the Greek and Latin texts. RHD had already had Lewis Carroll's rooms in Tom Quad for many years, so I soon found myself sitting in an arm chair for his tutorials in the very room where (because it had been Lewis Carroll's) my grandmother had often spent time in the 1860s, being photographed. Robin Dundas was far and away our senior Student (the House word for Fellow), and was especially kind to men like me from the army, having served in the Black Watch himself in WWI. One of his small idiosyncrasies in about February was to pin up on an ancient black beam at the bottom of his staircase the same piece of yellowing notepaper which he had used for the last two decades or more, so it was indescribably messy, which simply read: 'The *Iris reticulata* in the College Garden are at their best and well worth a visit'. Robin Dundas really was Ch. Ch. in that period of the House's life; I was very glad to have rooms on the staircase next to his for my last year.

Michael Foster had served in the war in the Intelligence Corps, and most of the time was far more intelligent than I could rise to, partly because he was painfully shy, and therefore not a good communicator to the indifferent student that I was. He had the most wonderful smile. I never knew how to handle the long silences in tutorials, not at all sure whether I should break into them or not; but he was always the very soul of kindness and consideration. In fact he would tend to take the undergraduate view if a potential clash with the college authorities was looming, as for instance there would have been for me over a very good invitation I got to shoot partridges one October day at the beginning of my second year. RHD was away, so I only had MF to consult over a minor moral dilemma: it was whether or not to accept the invitation and cut Collections, which was the college test at the end of the long vac., and I was due to sit for them on the same day. There was only the briefest of pauses while he considered my extremely cheeky request; then 'Have a good day's shooting', said Michael, to my naughty delight; it was the sort of humane ruling which would not be given in a month of Sundays these days. So I never did Collections, in the only year when I should have done. He was a sensitive and devout Christian, and unlike RHD, who only turned up in the cathedral for special college occasions, was invariably in his place on Sunday mornings. It was therefore all the more sad to hear two or three years after I had gone down that Michael's death recorded in the Christ Church Report was due to suicide.

Because of the post-war shortened course I was doing, I only came in for one long vac., that of 1947 and I spent a month of it with Brian Edwards, my fellow Buff for four years (Teddy was only what the army called him). A competent water-colour artist, he was even then beginning to exhibit and sell his work. We had already had a painting holiday in Pembrokeshire together, and 1947's was a more ambitious one in Denmark and Norway.

Oslo provided us with a wonderful example of how grateful Norway was to Britain, and still is (witness their Christmas Tree in Trafalgar Square every year now since) for our vain attempt to stop the Germans over-running their country in 1940. In a restaurant in Copenhagen we had got talking to two Norwegian brothers on their way to England for a holiday. 'Well we are on our way to your country for the same reason,' we said. 'Then you must stay in our house in Oslo', they said. Despite our protestations about the nuisance we would cause with their home being all locked up and so on, they gave us their address, and even told us where the front-door key was. So thinking we ought at least to make a gesture of thanks for the invitation, we took the tram out to the suburbs and found their beautiful house. While we were scribbling a note to put in the letterbox to say how much we had enjoyed meeting the two brothers, a husband and wife appeared from next door, and asked if we were the English boys their neighbours had rung them up about. Yes, we said, whereupon they unlocked the door (the key had indeed been precisely where we had been told it would be), took us in, showed us our room with the beds all made up, toured the kitchen cupboard with us and insisted that as well as staying we must eat as much as we liked, and to ask them if we were short of anything we needed. So, unbelievably, that house was our base for a couple of nights, a quite astonishing example of international friendship and hospitality.

That summer of 1947 the fine weather went on and on. I had a week with several other House friends staffing a camp on the river at Sutton Courtenay for some of the boys from the East End of London who belonged to the Christ Church Club there. That was a time when most of the public schools and Oxbridge colleges had clubs in poor parts of our great cities. The Victorian idea of fortunate boys helping the less so sounds very paternalistic to our 21st century ears, but in fact both givers and receivers enjoyed the contacts enormously, and that week under canvas together was no exception. I happened to be the only non-Etonian from the Oxford end, but the others seemed to suffer that all right, and for both 'sides' it was a learning experience as well as a lot of fun.

In the college itself there was almost inevitably a bit of a division between us older men who had come up several years late and the immediate ex-schoolboys. This cannot have been at all easy for the latter, but at a Gaudy years later I sat next to a 1946 eighteen-year-old, and he was kind enough to say they never felt we were stand-offish. Among our ex-service crowd was my fourth cousin and slightly younger namesake, John 'of Ashburnham' as we later came to call him within the family. We had lived in neighbouring villages in Kent before the war, so were quite up to having some fun at each other's expense when we found ourselves up at the House together. We would sometimes tend mistakenly to open each other's mail, correctly addressed to 'John Bickersteth, Christ Church, Oxford'. 'Is this a girl you know at all?', one would say to the other across the breakfast table in Hall, 'because I don't think she is one of mine'. John inherited the Ashburnham estate in 1958 after he had been ordained, and his life's work became to begin, develop and lead the Christian centre that he made it. I revelled in keeping up with that saintly man until his death in 1991.

When we were undergraduates together, the older and younger men met socially for meals in hall if not for much else, and a certain camaraderie developed when we had to apologise for accidentally knocking into each other on the Hall stairs when we were both carrying our week's butter ration back to our respective rooms, and squashing it irrevocably underfoot. The whole country was on rations for all manner of things for my Oxford time and beyond. My demobilisation 'outfit' itself was 'utility'; everything 'utility' had a distinguishing mark, meaning that for instance the tweed of the suit I was given was of a material that did not infringe manufacturing regulations. In the college, rationing made itself felt for example over that butter; one collected a week's supply (an eighth of a pound from memory) from, appropriately enough, the Buttery every Monday morning, and took it on an increasingly empty plate to one's rooms and back for the next seven days. That first winter I was up was a very cold one, with frost persisting from December to March, so there was the extra hazard of both Tom and Peckwater Quads being slippery. Many of us began too going further afield with a chunk of our butter because of the founding of the Oxford Committee for Famine Relief just before Christmas that year.

It was launched at the end of a memorable and packed meeting in Oxford Town Hall, with the main speaker being Victor Gollancz, the distinguished publisher and anglicised Jew; he gave us a terrible first-hand account of the plight of Europe's Displaced Persons, and had a wrapt audience hanging on his every word. Within a few days the infant Oxfam had been presented with a spare shop in the Broad, and believe it or not we could take our butter portions there for these untidy bits to be sold to undergraduates wanting to supplement their own, and so swell Oxfam's very first funds. Students tend to care about the underdog, and that post-war generation was no exception.

I rowed. 'You'll meet nice men rowing', said father vaguely, having never rowed himself. I was a bit doubtful, not having been at a rowing school, but he was absolutely right and the Rugby background proved to be no disadvantage. I revelled in the daily walk down through the Meadows with rowing companions, and the strenuous afternoon exercise. The bitter frosts of Hilary Term 1947 meant that we were able to go on rowing while the football fields were unusable for many weeks; on the river our blades skidded on ice floes when the thaw began, so that my moustache, which I sported briefly then, regularly got frozen solid from the splashes. The Isis was just clear enough of ice flows in time for Torpids, and I rowed in the House Second, but also briefly in the First because of someone being ill; for Eights Week the following term I was in the Second VIII, which made a bump every single night, and we felt very pleased with ourselves, and even more so for George Harris, the House waterman who cared for the pavilion and our boats. George was a great favourite with us all; he really purred that year, as the First VIII too did well with three bumps, so he felt at last that the war was over.

In fact all the college staff became friends, as so many men before us had experienced. Scouts looked after only one staircase then, and ours on Peck V was a winner, always the first, we soon discovered, with the early tea and the hot water jug he brought into our rooms for shaving, however cold the morning; and he also cleverly eked out his staircase coal ration. This got dumped by the outside staff into the original eighteenth century large wooden trunks for the purpose on each landing, so that we could have an open fire in our otherwise unheated rooms. The porters too, invariably put themselves out to help. Club dinners must have been rather a trial to them. One evening after a *Twenty Club* meeting, a very old college Debating Society which tackled important issues like: 'This House agrees with Henry Ford that history is bunk', four or five of us who had particularly enjoyed the Christ Church cellar that night thought it would be fun to have the traditional, but as we knew not yet revived post-war dip in Mercury, the shallow ornamental pond in the middle of Tom Quad. It was a lovely mid-June evening and I was almost undressed beside the pond when I spied the familiar and awesome figure of the Head Porter striding across Peck from the lodge under Tom Tower. 'I'm afraid there will be trouble', I murmured to my friends. 'Good evening, sir', said the great man to little me, 'you'll be wanting me to take your watch'. These loyal and delightful servants of the House were part of our traditions; they loved them as much as we did, and I do not doubt still do, in their familiar uniform of black jacket and bowler hat.

I began to value the worship in the Cathedral, with its unobtrusive entrance off Tom Quad, where I was proud to walk in past the carved names on the war memorials, including on the left (for WWI) my uncle Stanley Morris Bickersteth, killed on the Somme in 1916, and on the right (for WWII) my first cousin Julian Dunlop Bickersteth, with whom I had been confirmed in Canterbury twelve years earlier, killed in Greece in 1945. Christ Church Cathedral was the first of the four cathedrals where I have been privileged to savour, regularly over a period, top quality choral singing; Wells came next, then Liverpool, Wells again and finally Salisbury. John Lowe, a shy Canadian, was our Dean; I never set foot in the Deanery during my two years. Francis Dashwood, brilliant with the trumpet, once organized an impromptu band and choir to greet him when, very unusually for those days, he landed in a helicopter one evening, right outside his front door in Tom Quad, and Francis struck up with we hoped disarming irreverence the Advent hymn 'Lo, he comes with clouds descending'; but sadly Dean Lowe was not amused. The most eccentric canon was the immensely learned Claude Jenkins, then Professor of Ecclesiastical History at the House; I was once invited in for tea, as he had known grandfather well, so I experienced the mountains of books which covered every available space, with ten-book-high piles all the way up the stairs. Jenkins had a huge regard for Edward Bouverie Pusey (1800-1882), one of the leaders of the Oxford Movement, so much so that when he moved in procession up the aisle past us undergraduates on a Sunday morning he would always, very deliberately, skirt round Pusey's memorial stone in the nave floor.

There were also, to add to the agreeable social scene, the long-established Christ Church Beagles, kennelled at Garsington under the watchful eye of the kennel-huntsman Walter Clinkard and his son Gordon. Gordon came out with hounds much more than his elderly father, and was busy in those immediate post-war years getting to know the country, which is to the east of Oxford, learning the care of the pack, and the intricacies of the hunting field, so as to help and advise the succession of undergraduates who provided the Master and whippers-in. Luckily there were generally some enthusiasts in the college from the schools which had packs, Etonians and Radleians, plus an occasional boy from Ampleforth. I had been out for many years with the Bolebroke Beagles, all round Chiddingstone, so it was not long in that first Christmas Term before I had dug out my corduroy breeches (they had been father's) and got a lift to a meet. It might even have been at Tetsworth, where the parish priest was a keen hunt supporter, and could be counted on to slip in an appropriate word to the notices at morning service: 'Good morning, everyone; the Mothers' Union foregathers at the Rectory on Wednesday, and on Thursday hounds meet at *The Three Pigeons* here in the village, so mind you're all there.'

Gordon Klinkard very much took me under his wing, as he could see I knew a bit about it all, and I was in consequence never all that far behind the Master, even if hounds might be several fields ahead of both of us. Bill Birch-Reynardson was Master that first season, and I began going often to his lovely home at Adwell, and getting to know his family and friends. Sumptuous teas were a notable feature of beagling days; we were treated to them, after five or six strenuous hours in the hunting field, by the kind owner of the big house where we had met. With only 7 couple of hounds we did not kill many hares, but watching a line worked by the pack, and following it over the countryside was what delighted me about the whole activity, with the making and meeting-up of good friends a great part of the day's pleasure. When my second season began, the new Master, Bobby Manners, asked me to whip-in to him, which was a delightful surprise. As I had decided not to row again (for work's sake), regular exercise still was all the more important, so I accepted the honour, and hardly missed a meet all season. Whippers-in have to learn the whole pack well, not all that easy, but very pleasing it was to be able to call out with an air of authority (and 'don't anyone dare to challenge me' implied): 'Come on, Lively' or whatever, the whippers-in vying with each other on knowing the names of twelve or thirteen couple of hounds.

Another reason why I so much enjoyed beagling days was because I had fallen in love, and the girl in question was a fellow enthusiast. This was for me a far more serious affair than with my first flame in Norfolk three years earlier, where the girl had anyhow made all the running. We started seeing a lot of each other, had many friends in common, went to dances and shows together, and wrote to each other in the long vac. of 1947. Both of us left Oxford in June 1948 determined to keep up, at least until I had begun getting further along the road towards earning a living, and therefore more able to contemplate asking someone to marry me. The deep joy of being in love for all the later part of my Oxford time added immeasurably to what was for me a milestone period anyway; I suppose, though, it militated a bit against hard work.

Justification for the milestone phrase lies in the fact that during the Christmas holidays of 1947, I found myself talking with father for the first time about being ordained. I had discussed the possibility, almost against myself, with friends, back in the last part of Rugby days, before the powerful impact of army life. But always I had come up with the wish that had been growing, since very soon after we had arrived in Chiddingstone in 1935 from living in London, to tackle a job to do with the country. A major drawback, I quite realized, was the lack of any money to start me off in farming itself, but a landagent's life had its attractions. I had even gone so far in my leanings towards a country life as to buy the puppy (already mentioned) from Lilias Rider Haggard; she incidentally was quite sure I was going to settle for the rural life, but 'probably as a country parson.'

All this time, however, nothing at all obvious had struck me as the right way forward, despite many conversations, like the recurring one with Lilias. Angus Inglis, my regimental padre, who had remained a good friend after he had gone on to parish life, was probably the one who was most definite that I should test the waters by offering for ordination. 'After all,' he said more than once, while we were still serving together and afterwards, 'going for an ordinands' selection conference is a very different thing from actually making up your mind that you want to kneel in front of a bishop and be ordained. I think you should get yourself on to a selection conference. The actual process will clarify things for you.'. This was what father had never said, determined as he was not to press me on it, he told me years later, though I am sure he had prayed about his hopes for a long time; he had however never raised it until I did that Christmas, and then he made a comment I have never forgotten: 'You enjoy people, and that is a wonderful start in any call to be ordained'. He did not talk about saving souls; if he had, I think I should have called off the whole idea.

Where to train? I had liked Wells on our demob. leave visit with Ted and Mairse; it was father's and Uncle Julian's college, and they had often talked about how much they loved their time there. Very soon, therefore, after that discussion with father, who had played the whole thing so wonderfully over the years in which we had both of us been pondering the idea without either saying so, I set the ball rolling both for a conference I needed to be sponsored for, and for a college to apply for, if I was accepted for training.

In the end it was the Rochester diocese, because that was where my home address was, that arranged for me to go to an ordinands' Selection Conference. I spent three days with a dozen or so other hopefuls, plus the staff of three or four, in Lichfield Theological College, just before the start of Hilary Term 1948 at Oxford. A few days earlier I had gone down to Wells for the day by train (the smallest City in England had two railway stations then, both of them misguidedly victims of the Beeching cuts in the 1960s), to have an interview with Canon Salmon, the Principal of the Theological College there.

All that I can remember of the Lichfield Conference is that I found on that sculpture-adorned west front of the cathedral the figure of my cousin Edward Bickersteth,[26] ('one of the most useful ecclesiastics in England', *Vanity Fair* 1889); he had himself carved life-size holding a 2 ft high model of the cathedral against his ample frame, because it was he that had restored the building from its previous dilapidated state, and the Chapter, maybe he too, wanted to record the fact for posterity. Apparently his efforts at Lichfield led to the cathedrals of England organizing their own badly-needed face-lifts, after the eighteenth century years of neglect; so he had a part in putting these great buildings on the map again. The good

26. Dean of Lichfield 1875-1892

news fifty years on, for his young fifth-cousin-twice-removed, was hearing a few days after he had got home that he had been accepted for training for the priesthood. Of the vetting visit to Wells I recollect no detail of any kind, which is odd when I later came to love the place so much; but what mattered was that the Principal would have me in the college for the August term.

So quite suddenly my immediate future had been arranged by the appropriate departments of Church of England, with me (as it were) tagging along behind, still pretty hazy as to why I had set the whole thing in motion. But in a strange way I warmed to the idea of what I had done to myself, particularly when friends started asking me what I was going to do when I went down, and no one appearing in the least surprised when I told them. The college chaplain Eric Mascall had certainly done some work for me behind the scenes, and implied when he kindly asked me round to his rooms for a chat that he had known all along that I would be ordained, clairvoyance indeed when I had not known myself until a fortnight earlier.

On the strength of now being an ordinand, I was invited to go to Swanwick for a week-end that summer to meet some of the bishops who were over for the first Lambeth Conference since the war. I see from the photograph in my album that nearly twenty bishops attending Lambeth were prepared to give the extra time, after the considerable rigours of a three-week conference, to come and inspire English clergy of the future with the concept of our world-wide Anglican Communion; and they must have been greatly encouraged, as I was, to find over two hundred men there, either already in a theological college or booked for training at one. Those three days together were a wonderful eye-opener for me, even though I had had the good fortune to be brought up in a missionary atmosphere. The bishops pitched what they had to say about the many Christian opportunities throughout the world absolutely right for priests in training. I had to be careful, not for the last time, to keep fairly quiet among my peers about my knowing a good deal already about the Communion. That visit was the first of many more I had over the next forty years to the Mecca for church conferences that Swanwick is.

The two years training at Wells began in that August of 1948, during which I also received the unwelcome letter that I had been ploughed in my Finals; I had got by in Ancient History ('let's be thankful for small mercies' said RHD, who had after all tutored me on it), but the main Classics element defeated me. I knew all along that I was not going to do it brilliantly, but I had hoped the result would not be so disastrous, as it was among others for my first cousin Tony who was also up at the House; but he never knew what had happened to him, 14th Army veteran that he was, because a fortnight after term ended he was killed instantly by lightning when walking in the French Alps with his two sisters. It was a particularly bitter blow to his parents, my Uncle Geoff and Aunt Jean, because of Tony's brother Julian having been killed three years earlier in Greece.

For me there was nothing for it but to begin at once to read for a Pass Degree alongside my ordination studies at Wells, and that was not as complicated or detrimental to the ordinands' course as I initially feared it would be. It meant that spare time was at a premium, but I still played tennis a good deal, of which a pleasant feature was the occasional friendly match against local villages. I have a photograph of our 1949 Tennis VI, which includes John Waller,[27] to whom a few years on I was best man; and now, more than half a century later our homes are close enough to each other for us often to put the Church of England to rights over cheerful foursome lunches. The extra work (successfully completed in my first year in Wells) did not in any way spoil my enjoyment of college life, worshipping in the Close Chapel and the Cathedral, learning from my fifty or so fellow students, appreciating the music accompanying the services in both places, and above all beginning to master the tools of my trade: prayer and bible study and doctrine, church history and pastoral concern, all of them taught with the aim of deepening one's own faith, and so becoming more able to share it with others.

Canon Salmon, who had accepted me for the college, had been made an archdeacon by the time I arrived, and the new Principal was Kenneth Haworth, whom every Wells student of his years in office came to love deeply. Prayerful, smiling, never ruffled, diffident, always appearing interested in each of us, he led his disparate staff team, unchanged in my two years there, with what behind the scenes must have been consummate skill. There were three of them: the scholarly Welshman Lewis Clarke tended to be outshone by

27. Bishop of Stafford 1979–87

John Robinson and Kenneth Skelton, both of whom later became bishops; Kenneth, our quiet musical tutor, after two incumbencies, accepted the challenge to be consecrated Bishop of Matabeleland, where he developed rapidly into a brave protagonist of the Zimbabwean people, incurring the wrath of Mr Smith of UDI fame (or infamy) and leading to his eventual expulsion; or possibly he decided to resign in order not to make things more difficult for his black colleagues in the diocese.

The Chaplain, John Robinson, was later the Bishop of Woolwich who wrote *Honest to God*. John and I had played on the lawn of Meister Omers in the Canterbury Precincts in the 1920s, because his father and my grandfather were both Residentiary Canons of the cathedral, John having been born when his father was in his sixties. The Robinsons lived the other side of the War Memorial Garden from the Bickersteths. So a full twenty-five years later we two Johns connected again, and he became a godfather to our daughter ten years after I had left Wells. But when I arrived there as a student, JATR had just joined the staff from being a curate of Mervyn Stockwood, twenty miles away in Bristol. Where Kenneth was traditional, John was radical and innovative, a contrast which of course thoroughly suited students. Inevitably we tended to divide ourselves into followers of the one or the other, but we were mature enough, almost all of us older because of the war, to realize what a blessing it was to sit at the feet of two such contrasting and able men. The huge repercussions of *Honest to God* were still a dozen or more years ahead; we simply enjoyed from those four Wells lecturers stimulating and splendidly different contributions to the sum of what we were learning.

All our mentors took turns at being the speaker in what we irreverently (theological students are an irreverent lot, rather wisely; it debunks piety) called 'Flash' Compline; on Fridays Compline included an address; hence 'flash' or special. It was the teaching highlight of the week. John tended to be the most controversial, but Kenneth Skelton could be too. The Principal was the most devotional, for we had at the head of the college a deeply spiritual man. Two other such were R.H. Lightfoot, who had retired from his New Testament chair in Cambridge, but came to us memorably as an occasional lecturer on St John; and Fr Algy Robertson SSF who loved Wells, and introduced those of us who were new to them to the Anglican Franciscans from Hilfield in Dorset, where I had stayed with them in my Rugby days. This puckish holy man of God was in huge demand in the '40s and '50s to speak at church and school gatherings and retreats all over the country. One very cold winter term Algy spent the three or four days of his college visit in our house, No.16, and we were initiated into the mystery of how, to help him keep his constant internal pains under control, he had a hot water bottle which you could hear sloshing about on his tummy, held in by the girdle of his Franciscan habit.

The Dean of Wells then was the Victorian R.H. Malden, one of the last deans to live in the historic deanery on Cathedral Green, and out of another age to us students. Every Sunday of his life, perhaps uniquely among the deans of England in the year of grace 1950, he wore his square frock coat and gaiters and top hat to the cathedral. I recall him once being beadled by his verger across from the Deanery two or three minutes late for the main eucharist of the College Triennial; coming in through the North Door to find me as cross-bearer already leading the two hundred-strong procession westwards down the north aisle, he bellowed: 'Stop, Bickersteth, stop'.

Taught in the army to obey the last order, I did so at once, while RHM went very deliberately into his vestry, robed and then appeared in his rightful place at the rear of the procession. Spectacular stuff indeed, alleviated later that day as he sent for me to apologize, and we had a most amicable talk, the only personal contact I had with him during the two years I was in Wells. This was unsurprising, as the dean's job is with the running of the cathedral; it was for the bishop, then William Bradfield, not the dean to relate with the ordinands in the college. RHM wanted to reminisce about his time on my grandfather's staff at Leeds Parish Church (where there were always ten or more curates); and years later I found in family papers some letters which his curate-turned-naval-chaplain had written to grandfather, while serving with the Grand Fleet at the Battle of Jutland, in which he was mentioned in dispatches.

Two doors east of the deanery was the former archdeaconry which had been adapted as the college library and lecture rooms when the college started in 1847. It was and is a good building, which has been used for many years now as the Music School for Wells Cathedral School; so Rosemary who taught there for nineteen years was in and out of it a great deal, much later on. It was our social as well as our teaching centre, with occasional sherry parties, and productions of college plays, notably a very good one (I watched rather than acted, because it fell in my 'extra-study-year' for Oxford) of *Trial by Jury*. In the following year I was an unlikely angel in a production of part of the York Mystery Plays in St Cuthbert's Church down in the town; that performance 'in public' was very much in tune with a quite deliberate policy whereby the theological students tried to interact with the local community.

This mainly made itself felt through every student being allocated to one of three or four chapels-of-ease or daughter churches near Wells. I belonged to Dulcote, and there in a little church which is now a private house we took services (other than eucharistic ones) under the guidance of a member of staff every Sunday. We also ran the Sunday School, with twenty or more children, visited the homes in that part of the parish of St Cuthbert's Wells, and generally began to get the feel of what it would be like to be a parish priest. The gallant parishioners in those little villages round the city must have been the most 'visited' men and women anywhere in the kingdom, but they seemed to take it on the chin, and it was of course superb training for us. For my last year I was 'Bishop of Dulcote', each hamlet having its designated student head. Thirty years on, I never took our dogs out into the Bishop's Park without remembering that lovely walk over the fields to do my two afternoons a week round the homes of the village.

In the houses of the Close, built in 1348 (it is the oldest inhabited complete street in Europe) we were looked after by landladies, in fours or fives or more according to the size of house. I was in the largest, No.16, the only one with a 'modern' façade, as the house was burnt down and rebuilt in the 17th century. Eight of us lived there, presided over in my time by the formidable Mrs McEwen; at least that was the reputation she had among the other students and their landladies, but in fact she was kind and efficient with us, and a very good cook into the bargain. Her husband served at table and did the heavy housework; he was fairly hen-pecked, so we used to try to prop him up. I had no difficulty over staying on the right side of Mrs Mc., as I kept her supplied with fresh rabbits, from a rough shooting arrangement I had with a farmer a couple of miles outside Wells on Launcherly Hill. Mrs Mc's rabbit pies became quite famous. I could also shoot on another bit of land at Milton, rented by the land agent who occasionally had my Labrador bitch to stay. Vicars' Close was a very special place indeed in which to live, and successive Wells ordinands loved it for more than a hundred years.

Daily compline in the Close Chapel was so much at the heart of our college life that when the triennials came round, we still had the service there last thing at night, even though there was only room inside for about thirty really ancient 'old students' who needed to sit down; the rest of us, scores of clergy and any wives who were down for the reunion, stood in the paved street facing up towards the chapel for the amplified service, and recited the age-old and wonderful words from memory, if we were not too moved to say them at all. Ask any old Wells man what is his main memory of the college, and he is almost sure to say: 'Compline in the Close at Triennials'; with the possible alternative of our singing 'Hail the day that sees Him rise' on top of Vicars' Hall tower on Ascension Day morning.

Every August, while the cathedral choir was on holiday, and also for a week after Easter, the college took over the quire stalls and sang the Sunday services. We were trained by Kenneth Skelton, who cast off his shyness and really came into his musical own over it. Kenneth was a rigorous conductor when he was not playing the organ, never fussy, and constantly reminding us that we were there to enjoy ourselves to the Glory of God. As a result we made a passable show at times of year when the cathedral was very busy, although there were not the thousands of tourists and pilgrims that wear out the flag stones of our cathedrals to-day. So for the first time in my protestant experience I was sharing in Sung Eucharists, mastering *Merbecke*, many anthems, and various settings of the canticles at matins and evensong, all very new to someone like me who was used to a village church with one stalwart old man and an even older soprano in the choir stalls at Chiddingstone. To this day I cannot join each spring in Darke's *This joyful Eastertide* without happily recalling my introduction to it under Kenneth in Wells Cathedral. The Lady Chapel was where as a college we said Matins and Evensong every day (because we could not all fit into the Close Chapel), so the Cathedral's east end became a focal point for me in a building which was the first cathedral I had regularly attended over a longish period; and it was also in the late 1980s the last. I grew to value tremendously the cathedral's 'sermons in stones'. The whole place spoke of the numinous, one of the many new elements of faith to which I was being introduced.

Six months or so before I was due to leave the college, the Principal called me into his house to talk about where I should 'serve my title', the arcane phrase which the Church of England uses for an ordinand's first job. So it was an important interview, and I was glad to see John Robinson in the study too, because he was my personal tutor. I had no ideas whatever as to where I might go, except that I would prefer to be in the southern half of England, so that father and Mairse were reasonably accessible. I knew this would be a minor black mark against me, because obedience to a 'Go north, young man' tradition had grown up among ordinands at that time: 'you ought to go north, among the teeming millions,' was what college principals allegedly said,' if you are really serious about becoming a priest'. A few men, indeed, had arrived at college two years earlier knowing they had a particular job to go to 'in the north'. But most of us were wide open to suggestions.

'I wonder whether my old boss would have you, John', mused JATR. 'Do you think that is John at all?' the Principal asked John immediately, and he turned to me: 'how does the idea strike you, John?'. We had all heard of Mervyn Stockwood of St Matthew Moorfields, Bristol, already a controversial Church of England incumbent. Most of us students had crossed the Mendips once or twice as part of our training to experience worship in St Matthew's, which he had been transforming into a famous (notorious in some eyes) parish over the past dozen years. 'Not sure' I replied guardedly, 'and anyhow I doubt if he would have me. I would not be catholic enough for him, it had never occurred to me even to think of it', which was the plain truth. St Matthew's was all a bit *avant garde*, I felt, for me, and I said so there and then. 'I don't know, John' mused JATR, 'I somehow think you'ld be a better priest after a spell with Mervyn. He would de-Bickersteth you a bit'; and we all fell about. But when we had got over that one, I had become converted to the idea, to the extent at least of letting John ask Mervyn to see me; there could be no harm, I felt, as over the selection process two years earlier, in testing the waters. JATR agreed to sow the seeds, and within a week I was going over in the bus to East Bristol.

I met various people on Mervyn's staff, looked round the

unattractive streets a little, had only ten minutes or so with the great man himself, and went back over the Mendips quite drawn, to my surprise, to what I had seen and heard, but feeling sure that the whole thing was very unlikely to come off. But almost at once I had a friendly letter with a Bristol postmark, and it was Mervyn offering to have me for my title, at the standard curate's salary for that time of £82 a quarter. I knew it was right to accept; after discussing the offer with the Principal and John, I wrote to say so.

What then about my girl-friend, who was on an extended visit to 'the empire,' a post-university ploy in those days for a great many 'gals' of independent means. She had done some social work first in Oxford for eighteen months, and after New Year 1950 had headed off for a tour to look up family and friends, and see the world a bit. We had corresponded every week since both of us had gone down, and she wrote super letters about what she was up to; I would emerge from my study, after the postman had been to No 16, to look down over the banisters to see if there was a blue airmail envelope on the hall table. I knew I must tell her at once about the plunge having been taken, with a definite job organized. The reason was that my future as a priest had been a bit of a grey area between us, with me consistently taking the line that she would be a marvellous parson's wife; but I had begun to realize that she was fairly uncertain about the prospect and not all that willing to talk about it. It was essential therefore to put her fully in the picture right away, and I waited with my heart in my mouth to hear what she would say.

The answer did not come for four weeks, because I had caught her on the move. In a loving letter, when it eventually came to relieve me of my terrible uncertainty, she broke the news to me that she felt sure she must pull out of our relationship. Christian believer though she was, she simply could not see herself as the wife of a clergyman. It was a bitter blow, though I had half steeled myself to hear that answer. As I read and re-read the letter, I realized that I had made most of the running for the last three years or more, quite unlike my first love affair. This time, five years on, it was I that was the more enthusiastic one, whereas in Norfolk it had been my Wren girl-friend. From the affectionate but quite definite line I read in this letter, I knew I would not be able to change her mind.

Somehow or other I penned a reply. My family and friends were nearly as devastated as I was; for a long time they had assumed we would get there in the end. My brother Ted wrote to commiserate from the Sudan: 'Elspeth and I' (he had been married to Elspeth Cameron in 1947) 'were really looking forward to having her as our sister-in-law, but good luck old boy as you pick yourself up from a corker like this', or words to that effect. Gradually the news got around that our love affair was over. The silver lining for both of us took a long time to emerge from very heavy cloud. My erstwhile flame did not get married for some years, but when she did it was to a delightful man who gave her two or three children, and we have all met happily every now and then at weddings and funerals over the years. For myself the immediate silver element was that I was able to tackle my curacy fancy-free, which was an enormous advantage, given what incredibly hard work it turned out to be; courting time, let alone a proper start to married life, would have been very difficult, to put it mildly. Longer term, it was almost exactly four years before I met Rosemary, so 'silver lining' when it came was and is an inadequate description, with an April 2005 Golden Wedding.

A final reflection on Wells days can be semi-frivolous. Soon after arriving in Somerset, and missing the regular exercise I got from my Oxford beagling, I went up the hill on the Bristol bus one day to Downside Abbey, in order to connect with the Master of their long-established pack of hounds. As at Christ Church with the undergraduates, he turned out to be a senior boy, but the staff member in charge of the beagles was a monk in the person of the genial Fr O'Hara. 'Could some of us Wells students join the Downside staff and boys hunting on the Mendips?', I ventured. 'I'll ask the Master', he said enthusiastically, 'I'm sure he'll say Yes', which he did at once with equal delight. So with the Abbey only a few miles away, Fr O'Hara, his boys and his hound trailer became a frequent *rendezvous* for several of us from the college, and a few from the city as well, at the pub. meets round Wells. Thus began an ecumenical activity of an agreeable kind, which was appreciated on both sides of what theologically was then a huge divide. Vatican II was still an age away, but the hunting horn echoed cheerfully round the Mendip Hills to unite young Anglicans and Roman Catholics, happily disporting ourselves together in the chase, without any hang-ups over the celibacy of the priesthood or the infallibility of the Pope.

Country Layman to Town Priest

The sower went forth to sow his seed
Luke 8. 5

Ancient as man on earth, man turns to wine
Or bread earth's produce, seeks escape or need;
Release, necessity, the alternating creed;
Necessity, release; food, anodyne.
The Land: Autumn

IT was a considerable culture shock for me to set up house in a dull little terraced house in a back street of the east end of a large city. John Maclean had been there for three months. He had survived a tough infantry war serving with his fellow-New Zealanders in the Middle East and had won a Military Medal at the Battle of El Alamein. Having him show me the ropes of a curate's job under Mervyn Stockwood was a great help; we got on well from the start.

St Matthew Moorfields was quite unlike any 'sacred space' in which I had worshipped before. There had been five main ones: Lambrook Chapel, St Mary's Chiddingstone, Rugby Chapel, and the two cathedrals of Christ Church and Wells. The cathedrals were catholic; the others were what was called then Low Church, not evangelical for there was none of the evangelicals' all-embracing and passionate devotion to the person of Jesus. In fact to be perfectly honest there was no passion at all, no excitement whatever about the whole idea of being a Christian. The faithful simply went to church, and full marks to them for keeping on doing so without much at all to inspire them. The cathedrals, which I only experienced when I was that much older, with their superb full-time choirs, thundering organs, and grand occasions had introduced me to a whole new dimension of worship, which I was fast coming to value greatly.

Furthermore in Wells I had been discovering, through reading and endlessly discussing, the central thrust of a book by Hebert called *Liturgy and Society*, in which the author expounded the proper centrality of the Lord's Supper, the Holy Communion, the Mass, call it what you will, in the life of every Christian and every church.

This was nothing to do with 'high' or 'low', evangelical or catholic, but with what Christians should be up to in church if we were to be true to our Master's command. For here, argued Hebert, in the breaking of the bread and the pouring out of the wine was expressed in visual terms man's labour and his recreation, the pleasure of wine or the misery of drunkenness, his entire *persona*, and all the joys and trials and opportunities of the world he lived in. In other words Jesus had never told his disciples to remember him by having Matins and Evensong, good as those offices later became to emphasize the importance of scripture; rather had he simply said 'Do This '.

There were other books too of course, some from France, which helped to unpack a theme which has had such a huge effect on the Church of England in the post-war years. For me personally, St. Matthew's, and all that it stood for round that basic 'Do This,' burst almost literally upon my scene in that autumn of 1950, to demonstrate to me as a newly-ordained minister how under good leadership obedience to Christ's command could so dramatically affect the whole life of what had been, I soon gathered, before Mervyn arrived early in the war, first as curate and then as vicar, a very ordinary anglo-catholic parish.

For a new boy to go into the clergy vestry twenty minutes before the Parish Communion was to feel a buzz that had been entirely beyond my ken. The Master of Ceremonies was busy organizing his servers and thurifer and boatboy, the churchwardens were getting cheerfully in the way because they wanted to ask the vicar about something as soon as he arrived, the sacristan was making sure the vessels and vestments were ready, and the curates were doing their best not to interfere while quietly ensuring that, when the vicar did sweep in to be the celebrant five minutes before the start of the service, we were all set to begin exactly on time. Punctuality was an absolute must for Mervyn; that was a useful lesson for a new curate to get hold of for a start. After his vestry prayer, out would go the clergy to pray with the choir over the road; the choir had no boys in it on purpose, as Mervyn recruited them for servers rather than as choirboys, leaving the composition of the choir to adults only, 'they are much less trouble'; and while we processed up the aisle from the west end, the altar party, some six or seven strong, came in from the clergy vestry to the south of the sanctuary, and we were away.

There was this indefinable feeling of excitement that everyone, back-pew types every bit as much as incumbent, was about to embark upon something of immense significance because of Christ's command (it seemed totally personal to all of us in church) to 'Do This'. I had reached the age of thirty without experiencing anything remotely like this before.

It is not easy to pin-point what the secret was, not just for me coming from a 'Low Church' background, but for the scores of people who packed that Parish Communion Sunday by Sunday, with rarely an empty seat. Maybe it was the continual freshness of what was happening; it was never a routine, never just the same ceremonial that everyone had experienced before. The very fact that Mervyn never used the term 'Sung Eucharist' but always 'Parish Communion' made a difference in itself, as the latter dispensed at once with the 'High Church' connotations of the former. It might have been also because people really came to that service expecting to be (and almost always being) inspired; or it was possibly because the congregation knew in their bones that what was happening in front of their eyes, what they themselves were 'doing', was the climax, the weekly climax, of all that went on for God in and around this dull-looking Victorian building, which was becoming so well-known in Bristol and far beyond.

After the service, practically the entire company of two hundred and fifty or so strolled in animated conversation fifty yards up the conveniently dead end street to the parish hall for coffee and chat, an unheard-of thing to do in those days. Most congregations all over England simply went home after church, 'the coffee hour' together not yet having reached us from across the Atlantic. Meeting socially the people who had just been in the pews was quite a new idea to me; congregations I had belonged to by and large chatted for a few minutes on the church path if it was not raining, and then went home.

Not so in St Matthew Moorfields: in the capacious church hall there would almost certainly be something the vicar wanted to stand on a chair and talk about (generally hilariously); the secretary of the social committee had notices about the parish dance; the lay reader who handled the sick communion rota could be told by the street visitors (there were twenty or more of them) of new names needing to be added to his list; the drama producer had the chance to press her cast about slack attendance at rehearsals, the organiser of the coming Bank Holiday outing told everyone there were two empty seats still on the thirty-seater coach etc etc etc; I had never known anything like it, this was 'church' such as I never imagined existed anywhere, least of all in a parish where the church building had no sense of the holy at all, no architectural merit, so dull-looking from the outside that thirty years later it was fair game for the redundancy and demolition that was its fate in the 1980s.

But St Matthew's in my day was full twice a Sunday, the morning congregation almost entirely from the parish; those Bristol Eastenders had come to trust, and above all to understand, this down-to-earth vicar, now into his fourteenth year there. 'Outsiders', of whom there never very many, mostly came for the evening service; they were schoolmasters, lawyers, business men, university lecturers, and often their families who had left their own church, or maybe not belonged to it or had already drifted away from any church at all, in favour of ours because of Mervyn's preaching. It was him that people came to hear, but they frequently sat under other people, partly because Mervyn by those early 1950s was in such country-wide demand that he was often away, but also because he took infinite trouble over giving his curates experience in the pulpit.

There was a steady flow of first-class visiting clergy and laymen: I remember Sir Walter Monckton, the distinguished Conservative politician; Dr. George Macleod, founder of the Iona Community in the Church of Scotland; Sir Stafford Cripps, at that time Chancellor of the Exchequer in the Labour Government and a great friend of Mervyn, and George Reindorp,[28] not long out of his naval chaplaincy.

In the week before it was a curate's turn to preach, the regular submission to the vicar of our sermons for either service, in advance of preaching them, led more often than not to their return with a lot of red pencil. I recall ingenuously beginning one sermon in an Old Testament course, chosen as always by Mervyn, with the first verse of Exodus Chapter 3: 'Now Moses was keeping the flock of Jethro his father-in-law', and I must have gone on to develop the lowly job of the future great leader of the Israelites. Back came my effort:

---

28. Later Bishop of Guildford and then of Salisbury.

This may become interesting later on, but I haven't bothered to read it because I switched off after the first sentence like everyone else will. Holy Moses is a swear word they rather like round here, and as for the Jethro bit they would probably think it's the name of a pub they don't happen to know. Sorry. Please have another go. The key thing is to remember you've got predominantly working-class listeners, and you need to grab them in those first few seconds or you'll never get them back.

Mervyn was a past master at doing just that, grabbing his congregation at once; he continued all his life to write out every sermon in full, maybe boring reading in a hundred years' time, but as delivered they were superb examples of a preacher's craft: funny, topical, only moderately exegetic, full of passion when the occasion called for it, and never too protracted. In fact one of his cracks, when pressed sometimes on where exactly he stood in the churchmanship stakes, was that he was never quite sure if he was High or Low, but he knew that he was not Long.

Part of the preparation for Sunday was Benediction on the Saturday night, attended by twenty to thirty local working-class people, mostly elderly; none of the professional members of the Sunday congregations would have dreamed of coming. Mervyn always wore his biretta for it, and invited me (once I was priested) to buy one and do the same, which I declined; John Maclean said No too. Ralph Scrine the senior curate was more than a little shocked at our not accepting this St Matthew's custom, but Mervyn did not worry about it. Although the service would have brought about apoplexy in my evangelical forebears, I came to value this short act of devotion. One of the clergy took it in the Lady Chapel, which was simply a side aisle where the Blessed Sacrament was reserved on the altar. None of this aumbry arrangement, namely a cupboard on the side wall for keeping the sacrament; Mervyn, I am sure without permission, followed the Roman practice of having the consecrated Host in a box in the middle of the Lady Altar. In our form of Benediction we had the exposition but not the elevation of the Host. It was of course totally outside the *Book of Common Prayer*, but allowed in some dioceses. Our bishop, George Cockin, was marvellous with Mervyn; even we curates realized he had long decided to accept any number of irregularities, for to his eternal credit Bishop George saw that the Gospel was reaching people through this maverick priest's ways, and that was what mattered.

The curates also took their turn on Sunday nights at the inter-denominational Youth Club two hundred yards up Redfield Road in the Methodist Church Hall. This was exhausting on top of a full day's work. Anything up to a hundred youngsters would be playing table tennis or darts or just rushing about, and our job was to chat them up and try to establish relationships. I always enjoyed that part, but it was the last bit that was terrifying, as I knew that when the youth leader, for much of my time a super Methodist sister, decided to end the evening I had to give the assembled company (as they stood round the walls of the games room) a five-minute epilogue which I had painstakingly prepared; and then pray with these unwilling teenagers. I suppose perhaps once in six months it went really well and I felt I had got somewhere.

The St Matthew's Scouts however, which I took over in that first autumn, were a very different matter, and great fun; there were three patrols, and I remembered enough of the basics of Scouting for me to look after my twenty-five boys happily. I came to love tak-ing them off to the local countryside for the Whit week-end, and then for a week further afield in the summer. I had inherited the splendid help of Michael Lane, housemaster of School House, Clif-ton, who faithfully came across town on scout evenings, generally with two or three boys from his house, to give me a hand. The Lanes soon became great friends, and it was not long before I had persuaded Michael's wife Patricia to start a Young Mums' Group in the parish. Today this husband and wife's involvement, leaving aff-luent Clifton to help an East-end parish, would smack of a patronis-ing approach. But, mother of five children, Patricia was as natural with the mothers and babies as her husband was with their older boys. 'Using' a handy public school like this was of course in the same mode as the school missions, started during Victorian times in the slums of our great cities. They were all part of middle-class ap-proach to the working-class until well after WWII. St Matthew's had for many years had the Blundell's School Mission, and I became Missioner for my last eighteen months with Mervyn.

The Blundell's experience was very satisfying. At least once a term I rode the seventy miles on my motor-bike down through Somerset into the heart of Devon, to stay a couple of nights in one or other of the school houses, meet some of the older boys who might be interested in coming up to help us in Bristol, preach in chapel on the Sunday morning to update them about the Mission, lunch with the headmaster or other members of staff, and thank them all for the giving of their time and money. Again my recollection is that no one in Bristol resented the link, and that was not just because St Matthew's scored by being given sports equipment, for example, or good second-hand clothes (they were always far better than jumble, I hasten to say), and in other *ad hoc* ways. The climate was still right for this relationship, widely the practice all over England, whereby one part of our society learnt that another part was human and interesting to be with; and it also taught mutual respect.

There was another vital part of the life of St Matthew's, which proved over the years to have been a most important part of my training in the priesthood: namely the bond Mervyn had established between the denominations in our part of East Bristol. It was called the Redfield United Front, and it functioned on what had become known as the Lund principle (the name came after a conference had been held just after WWII in a town of that name in Sweden) whereby 'the churches did together whatever they did not need conscientiously to do separately'. There was in those days no conceivable chance of the Roman Catholics being part of such a demonstration of the basic unity of all Christian people; 1950s Anglicans were quite simply not proper Christians in Rome's eyes; and it was to be another ten years before Pope John XXIII appeared so wonderfully on the scene. But despite RC absence the RUF was still immensely worthwhile, consisting as it did of a Congregational Church, the Anglican Church up the road from us (dedicated to St Leonard), two Methodist Churches, one of which before their act of union in the 1920s had been Wesleyan (High) and one Primitive (Low), and ourselves. In my last year I edited the *Redfield Review*, which Mervyn had started as a monthly magazine for these five churches, a totally innovative idea; he told me once to invite the Archbishop of Canterbury to write for it, and he kindly did.

The ministers moved round our churches for communion together every week on a Tuesday, before having breakfast in a church hall kitchen; it was always rather too hard-boiled eggs. We got to know each other very well, and it was completely natural therefore for us all to receive the sacrament, no doubt variously interpreting what we were doing, as happens anyway within a single congregation all over the non-Roman Catholic world. Any tender Anglican consciences were quietened by the fact that we all said the words of consecration together. Once again Mervyn was far ahead of his time, doing it as he did long before the word 'ecumenical' had become part of ecclesiastical jargon, and grasping the truth that in the working-class area of a large city it must make sense to work with other churches, if any kind of witness to the things of the spirit was to be made. He passionately believed that what we were attempting locally could lead to greater things on the wider scene.

Meanwhile he continued to be much in demand, many of his absences due to engagements in the public schools; and when he could not accept invitations because he was already booked to do other things, I was generally the one who stood in for him. It must have been infuriating for keen admirers of Mervyn who had asked him to come and do this or that, to get the reply that he was 'sorry to be engaged then, but John Bickersteth would gladly come instead'. I went to several schools as a poor substitute, and also became much caught up with a middle-class Christian movement called the Wives Fellowship, who mostly had their meetings in gorgeous country houses in Gloucestershire, frequently with a pretty girl or two hovering around.

My New Zealand colleague was a good deal more conscientious than me, and a demon for work; he was the sort of eager young clergyman who would never take time off, something which was never a problem for me. He had a cheeky habit of wandering into my study sometimes to ask how my visiting tally was going. The tally was what we called the guideline that we were expected to follow of twenty-one visits to homes in the parish every week. To keep up an average of three a day as part of all the other regular events and activities, not to speak of unbargained-for extras like funerals and so on, was hard going, to say the least. We had to submit to the parish office every Monday the list of where we had been the previous week, together with any comments on personal troubles we had met and been expected to deal with; there was no question of running to Mum (alias Mervyn) for help, unless the problem was particularly dire. But the visiting itself was superb training, and immensely enjoyable in ninety-nine cases out of a hundred. That St Matthew's

period of my life, on top of what I had done with father in Chiddingstone, led me to love visiting, together with its necessary ad-
junct, which is the gentle art of disengagement. You have to learn
when to leave unhurriedly, for example never to look at your watch
during a visit until maybe very near the end of your stay. I used to
make a point of drifting towards the sink in case there was some
washing-up to do, a simple ploy people loved and will remind you
of years later if you happen to meet them again.

The curates got about locally by bicycle. I only used the motor
bike in order to be able to cover the Tiverton run, and also the fifty
miles home to Orcheston on my day off. I generally managed, especially in good weather, to leave Bristol late on Sunday, so as to wake
up in my own bed at home next morning. Father had become
Rector of the Orchestons on Salisbury Plain the same year that I
arrived in Bristol.

He rightly encouraged me to get a crash helmet, but literally the
only motor-bike riders who had helmets then were the police, so as
the local policemen were all friends of ours on the staff, I asked
whether I could buy one of theirs. 'Buy one, vicar?', said the in-
spector (everyone in a dog collar was 'vicar' I had realized by then,
but I purred none the less), 'you'll do no such thing; here's one with
our compliments'. So I became the proud possessor of a black
peaked hard hat, standard police issue; and probably the only
motor-cycle owner in Bristol with a hard hat of any kind, as they did
not become law for another ten years at least.

But the push bicycle was ideal otherwise; you saw someone you
knew on the pavement, diverted into the gutter, and with one foot
on the curb stayed in the saddle for a conversation. In a motor car
you would have had to drive straight past. Once I was having a
pavement gossip with someone a hundred yards up Redfield Road
from St Matthew's itself when I saw a hearse with two or three
funeral cars behind draw up at the west door. 'Who's taking that
one?', I wondered idly, while the person I was with did the talking.
'Heavens it's me,' I broke in rudely; 'I saw the family yesterday',
and shot off down the road, in at the side door, robed, breathed
deeply as I walked sedately down the aisle between the assembled
company, and was reasonably ready to greet the funeral party
whom the undertaker had been lining up outside. That was a lucky
one.

Another time, on a winter's day in February 1952, I was biking back to the house about five o'clock, after a happy afternoon on the job, when I saw in the bright lights of a newsagent a poster on the pavement reading in large letters: KING DEAD. There had been some photos a few days earlier of this much-loved man standing on the tarmac at the airport waving goodbye, with sad and haggard face, to his elder daughter and her husband flying off for their holiday in Treetops Wildlife Camp in Kenya. Most of us had no idea he was so ill, and it was a huge shock to the nation that King George VI's gallant reign was suddenly over, gallant because he rose so wonderfully to the challenge of being unexpectedly made king after his brother's abdication. Next day there was a poignant photo of the Prime Minister, the old man Winston Churchill, waiting at the bottom of the gangway to greet his young sovereign, as she bravely stepped off the aircraft to begin her new life.

Twice a month I bicycled the three miles into the centre of the city for Post Ordination Training. The ride into town took me right through the ruins from war-time bombing; Britain was broke after the war, and none of the repairs really began anywhere until the very late fifties, more than ten years after the war had ended. So for nearly the last mile of my route there were great piles of rubble or gaunt wrecked buildings on either side, where the houses had been, and hundreds of yards of white tape on iron posts driven into the edge of the wasteland to stop pedestrians straying off the pavements at night; it reminded me of seeing what we had done to Dortmund, which was still fresh in my memory from serving there only four or five years earlier. Great clumps of buddleia twelve feet high blossomed in the devastation, a cheerful hope for eventual recovery, as yet another summer came round with nothing started.

I suppose there were about fifteen of us who came in from our parishes to sit under Canon John Peacey, who was on the staff of the cathedral where I was deaconed and a year later priested; he organized lectures and seminars for us, read and commented on the essays he set, and saw us through both the ordination retreats. We all enjoyed foregathering, with lots of opportunities to compare notes and tell scurrilous stories about our incumbents; and we also came to love JRP, whose ministry was a model, I realized much later, of what cathedral ministry can so usefully be. He showed a personal interest in each of his young men, helping us at that important time in our development not to take ourselves too seriously. Full of faith and fun as he was himself, he also expressed his faith in hymn-writing, with no less than five of his in *100 Hymns for Today* (*A&M* 1969), including 'Awake, awake, fling off the night', which goes so well to *Grenoble*.

For my last year in Bristol I moved down to the senior curate's abode at the daughter church in the heart of the slums, where the housewives still painted and polished their front door steps with cardinal red paint, wore pinafores, kept their hair in curlers all day, and had rows of children. Within a flash of arriving, indeed, I was acting as a godfather to a Mrs Fussell's tenth, having discovered that Mervyn was godfather of her second, his first curate of her fifth, and John Robinson of her seventh; so I made a quick decision that any scruples about being unlikely to keep up with my new godson's well-being must be disregarded for the sake of good relations with the vast Fussell tribe all over East Bristol. Those people of St Saviour's, which was the dedication of our Mission Church there (long since pulled down, together with hundreds of the homes around it) were the salt of the earth. Mervyn had put a bath into the vestry, and I had a bedsitting-room above the Welfare Clinic attached to the church-cum-Hall; a fairly primitive place to live, but the army had been a good school for adapting to what was available, and I loved it all.

A saint named Mrs Pocock looked after me; I later introduced Rosemary to her, and we went on seeing Mrs P. and her family with I think mutual delight until she died. Her house was the other side of the back alley behind the Mission, and in all weathers she carried my midday meal on a plate out of her back door, down the strip of garden, across the alley, through my bathroom-vestry and up into my bed-sitting-room. No wonder that I developed quite bad tummy trouble, a combination of odd eating arrangements and overwork; but those hospital sorties meant that I got to know the inside of the Bristol Royal Infirmary at its receiving end, and this helped when I was regularly doing the rounds of St Matthew's people who landed up there as patients.

I really had very few one-to-one conversations with Mervyn; he did not manage his staff like that. But those discussions were enough (and the subject does not call for more than brief comment here) for me to know that the over-emphasis on his sexuality in the late Michael de la Noy's biography (*A Lonely Life*, Mowbray 1996) is misplaced. True enough that he was happier in the company of men than women, but then so are thousands of other bachelors. Mervyn could not have begun to achieve all that he did in Bristol and beyond if he had had a wife and children to care for; nor would he have bothered to nurture his marriage. There was simply too much to do, too many interesting people to meet and spend time with, if the coming of God's Kingdom was to be properly addressed. Without question Mervyn Stockwood has an honourable place in the noble company of homosexually-orientated men who continue to contribute so much to the life of the Church of England, particularly in our big cities. Celibate as he was; self-centred showman, possessed with a wonderful flair for creating a sense of occasion, enormous fun to be with, and the life and soul of any party whose composition appealed to him, especially if a few of the good and the great were thrown in, Mervyn was also the disciplined, imaginative, hard-working catholic priest, whom I knew and loved both as my vicar, later as my bishop in Southwark and finally as a retired bishop living 'under' me in Somerset. I shall always regard having been trained by him as a very great privilege.

Whether or not he had much luck in de-Bickerstething me, as John Robinson had suggested, well, heaven only knows; I remember him saying once rather despairingly: 'I shall never make a catholic of you, John'. Nor I suppose did he, in his fairly extreme sense. He had been brought up at All Saints' Clifton, far and away the 'Highest' church in Bristol. But I learned so much about the breadth of the Church of England that I could probably have acquired nowhere else in the country, incidentally stopping an in-built distrust of incense and all that went with it.

He and I chatted on and off during that spring of 1953 about my next move, and he took a lot of trouble about putting out some feelers. The patron (whom I knew) of a charming village church in Gloucestershire wrote with a warm suggestion that he should present me to it. The very high-powered rector of a large parish in the Potteries had me up to meet him, and offered me a job in charge of a daughter church; but it simply did not feel right, and he was fairly cross when I refused, which made me very glad I had; I suspect he was the sort of man who did not expect potential curates to do anything other than accept with alacrity. But he was the catalyst for my deciding that at the age of 32, with some responsible leadership posts in the Army behind me, I wanted a sizeable parish of my own, and Mervyn totally agreed.

It was actually my old principal at Wells, Kenneth Haworth, who rang him to say that the Bishop of Southwark was after a young priest to begin a Conventional District. That term has long since dropped out of Church of England use, but it was in vogue then to describe a geographical area being carved out of an existing parish because of growing population. This one was to be hived off the ancient parish of Oxted in East Surrey, and Kenneth felt it sounded about right for me: a big new housing estate had been added on to a part of the parish, which since 1912 had had a good permanent church building and a parsonage house. There were rising two thousand parishioners, whose houses would be put into this new District, and the priest appointed would have sole charge. It was on the edge of the countryside, without being an 'attractive country parish', which Kenneth and Mervyn and I knew would not be for me for many years, if at all (it never was). The new District was to be called St John's Hurst Green. Mervyn felt it had possibilities, and was sure I should go to see and be seen. I took the train to London, and went down on the East Grinstead line to Hurst Green Halt, getting out at the tiny platform which at that time was mostly made of railway sleepers; I saw only two hundred yards away the flint and stone tower of St John's as soon as I left the station, and in a very few minutes I was at the attractive brick house which was to be my home for the next eight years.

'I've been praying for you to come' was the wonderful greeting I got from a smiling old man as I walked up the brick path to the Parsonage. He was the priest-in-charge, Arthur Norton, formerly of the China Inland Mission, who six or seven years earlier had been offered this 'house for duty' post by the Rector of Oxted after the CIM missionaries were all herded out of the country at the Cultural Revolution. Arthur did not of course mean that he had prayed for me personally, since we had never met; he was simply telling me encouragingly that he had been praying for a young man to come to St John's, where he could tackle the needs of what he knew would be a growing parish.

So this shy and charming former missionary showed me round the house, and took me over to the church, unfinished at its west end, which was simply a brick wall, neatly rendered outside and plastered in, against the day when it might be completed. At Arthur's suggestion we prayed together at the altar rail, and then talked hard in the parsonage before walking together to the station for me to go back to London to meet the bishop. I was conscious that I had spent a couple of hours with a holy man of God, as indeed I experienced again at once in the person of the Bishop of Southwark, whose home was then off Kennington Park Road. Bertram Simpson had another four years to run before retirement, so he was a very senior man, probably rising forty years older than I was. I warmed to the job he was outlining; and we also very happily sorted out Church and State together as if we were close contemporaries. By the end of the interview he had offered me the post almost without my noticing it, and I must have said Yes, because he dug out his diary and fixed a commissioning service three months or so ahead; it had to be well after Christmas so that Mervyn could find another curate, and for Arthur Norton (with no money as far as I could tell) to make a plan for retirement. I caught the last train back to Bristol a very excited chap.

In my last few weeks at St Matthew's I was on the boards as Major Sergius Saranoff in Bernard Shaw's *Arms and the Man*; amateur dramatics were quite a feature of our church life, and I took part in several ambitious productions. After the last night one of the churchwardens sagely observed, with ten years of experiencing Mervyn's ministry behind him: 'Every priest has to be to some extent an actor both in and out of church, and you've done rather well', which was high praise from a man so devoted to the vicar that passing curates did not count for much. The only present that I remember when I left was a useful set of kitchen utensils, and another of table knives, which my very good friends the nurses in the Welfare Clinic under my bedsitting-room kindly gave me: 'Surely one of these days you'll have a kitchen of your own, instead of your hopeless arrangements here', they laughed; and most of what they gave me is still in use fifty years on.

I flew abroad on December 8th 1953 for a long holiday. I went in a Viking, which could carry so little fuel that we had to have a night stop in Malta, then on another few hundred miles south to Mersa Matruh for a final refill to get us to Khartoum. There I was based

for a month with Ted and Elspeth, then in his last job in the Sudan
Political Service as a Deputy Governor. They lived in the Mogren,
which were a pleasant group of executives' houses almost on the
White Nile. My godson Michael was five and Tony was three, so we
had a lovely Christmas together, and lots of parties with other expatriates, all of whom knew that their days there were numbered,
because of the run-up to Independence.

On New Year's Day I watched the impressive parade for the
Opening of Parliament by Ted's boss, Sir Robert Howe, who drove
through streets lined with crowds to the Government buildings in a
red Rolls Royce with a cavalry escort; in those days a Rolls was the
standard car for every Governor-General throughout the British
Empire. Ted or Elspeth showed me all the sights: we went to a
reception in HE's Palace on the Nile, where General 'Chinese' Gordon, a G.A. Henty hero of mine, had been murdered in 1885 by the
forces of the Mahdi; the site of the Battle of Omdurman, avenging
his death a full thirteen years later, when Winston Churchill as a
young subaltern had taken part in the famous cavalry charge by the
21st Lancers (although he was a Hussar); and the Gordon statue at
the confluence of Khartoum's main streets, which had been laid out
in the shape of a Union Jack after the subjugation of the country.
Years later I preached at the Gordon Boys' School Annual Service
in Guildford Cathedral, and there on the main lawn of the school
was the transplanted Gordon statue, aptly acquired after Independence. It was also fascinating, when Ted had to go out into the surrounding countryside (read 'desert', to be honest) to share in
several day trips with him, and to learn a little about his work.

I took part in several Cathedral services, and preached at one
Evensong ('absurd of the Provost not to ask you for Matins, and use
you more', expostulated Ted to me), and saw quite a bit of the cathedral staff, who, *pace* my beloved brother, could not have been more
welcoming to the young and inexperienced priest I was. The
diocesan bishop was no longer our unique family friend Llewellyn
Gwynne, who gave more than half a century of service to Egypt and
the Sudan. Bishop Gwynne had a profound influence for good in
my life, visiting us at home every year because father was his com-
missary and so responsible for helping him find clergy for work in
the diocese; to me he was the personification of an uncomplicated,
caring, prayerful bishop.

With all his links after fifteen years in the job, Ted fixed up a good trip away from Khartoum for me, so as to see something of the bush, and more important to go into the villages in order to understand a little about how these fine tribal people lived. So I spent a memorable ten days in the Nuba Mountains; I preached in St Paul's Wad Medani, and St Peter's El Obeid, and I prayed with the men who staffed both Katcha and Kadugli churches, staying mostly with Ted's friends, the District or Assistant District Commissioners, practically all of them graduates of Oxford or Cambridge, where incidentally many had been distinguished sportsmen; hence the crack which had more than a little truth in it about the Sudan being a country of blacks ruled over by blues. Most of those in the Political Service were devout churchmen, some were also Lay Readers; I so much enjoyed taking services with them in the little mud-walled thatched churches.

At one of them I caused mild trouble, as towards the end of my sermon a single drum began to beat very loudly outside the church door; as it was quite clear that no one on the benches could any longer hear what I was saying, I finished quickly, we sang the last hymn competing with the drum beats which were getting more and more urgent outside, and I gave the final blessing. Outside there was a crowd of stark naked Nuba tribesmen laughing away, I very soon discovered at my expense, because I had preached a few minutes too long, so that the English-speaking service had run over into the time for the Nuba one. It was a salutary reminder of something Mervyn had been very strict about, the importance of not running over time; I have heard those drumbeats in my head many times since, over the years.

By mid-January I was on my way, really glad to have seen a little more, on top of my months in India, of the way the British Empire functioned. Strictly-speaking the Sudan was a Condominium with Egypt, but the Administration took good care to keep Egyptian officials away from the south of the country where with slave-trade memories any Arab would have been *persona non grata*; so only British officials were in charge south of Khartoum. I remember asking Ted when I got back to the city the naïve question as to why we were leaving: 'Simply because the rapidly-changing political climate all over Africa means that we can do no other', he replied, disconsolately enough, as he loved the country and its people.

It will no doubt be a century or more before the two hundred odd years of the British Empire will be properly written up without bias either way. At the risk of course of a straight Colonel Blimp charge, I can only say that the 1920s child that I am saw for myself in 1946 British India and in 1953 Anglo-Egyptian (mostly Anglo, I am bound to say) Sudan some indication of the overwhelming amount of unselfish goodness shown by hundreds of thousands of British administrators in that passing phenomenon of an empire 'on which the sun never sets'. Perhaps the former colonial territories had to go through the misery of these last forty years of upheaval, and it must be right for them now to be free at last; but in the long march of history I believe that despite initially bloody conquests, the appalling blot of occasions like the Amritsar massacre, our inhumanities in the Boer War, a great deal of fortune-making, and plenty of brazen exploitation, the legacy we left behind us, as the *Pax Britannica* fades into the past, has been positive and helpful and just plain good.

Two nights on the Nile steamer to take me north again was a pleasing introduction to the wonders of Luxor and Karnak and Thebes. The Abu Simbel temple was still right on the banks of the river, so the ship's captain, after finding out that three of his passengers wanted to see it, (even though we would be getting there at 11.30 p.m), simply waved a hurricane lantern to and fro on deck when we were nearly opposite the temple, until he got an acknowledging signal from the shore, then pulled the helm hard over, headed straight for the sandy bank and rammed it hard enough for the bows to get stuck in the mud. A Sudanese advocate, a Greek doctor and yours truly were helped to step rather gingerly on to the nine-foot gangplank that the crew put out over the rails, and we were being greeted on the desert sand by a couple of guides with more hurricane lamps. They were not put out by the lateness of the hour (our *baksheesh* after the tour must have made up for it), and it was an unforgettable experience to walk round this astonishing monument, as the lamps' shadows played on the soaring statues. With slave labour all those centuries ago on a massive scale, those ancient Egyptians certainly worked miracles of construction: for instance the fallen figure at the Ramassaeum in Luxor, which we saw next day, weighs a thousand tons (there were four others still standing), and they had all been floated down the Nile on barges. At the end of our visit, we three edged our way back up the gangplank, the engines went noisily into reverse (we felt a bit guilty over waking up the other passengers), and the steamer was sucked out satisfactorily into mid-stream for the voyage to continue while we turned in on our bunks.

At the Assouan Dam I made friends with a party of twenty Egyptian schoolmasters, and we had a merry conducted tour of this major engineering achievement. I remembered them two years later when HMG made its ill-advised attack on their country (I find people tend to call it, derogatively, just 'Suez 1956' these days), and hoped they survived and did not begin thinking that every Englishman was a born pirate; they were a very bright bunch of men. In Cairo I stayed a few days with Bishop and Mrs Johnston in their lovely house beside the Cathedral, and both he and the Provost and his wife (the Freemans were much nearer my age) gave a lot of their time to show me round the famous sights, including of course the Pyramids and Tutankamen's treasures in the Cairo Museum. With the Egyptian archdeacon Adeeb Shammas I had the privilege of a visit to the 5th century Hanging Church in Old Cairo. The title arose because it was built on stilts to avoid the ravages of Nile flooding. Bishop and Provost had both been 'head-hunted' (though the term was not yet in use) by father, so their kindness to me was pleasantly vicarious. Thanks to them too, I had talks with several Coptic priests, including one super old man who cared, rather badly, I gathered, for the church of St Sergius, a 12th century building in a back street that I would never have found by myself.

My next stop was Jordan, where again I was fortunate enough to stay for a week in Jerusalem with the Bishop. The Stewarts lived in St George's Close under the shadow of the cathedral, so I woke every morning to look out on its tower, modelled very accurately on that of Magdalen Tower in Oxford, and to look forward to another absorbing day following in the steps of Our Lord. I had after all 'lived with' Jerusalem for as long as I could remember, not only from beginning to know the Bible, but also from folding Mission papers and filling envelopes with them from a very early age.

More importantly I had met over the years a great many people concerned with the Jerusalem Archbishopric, as it had become by then. Father had recently been given an honorary canonry in the cathedral, so it was a particular joy for me, as the stall he was given in the Quire was that of Cana, to find my way (soon after I had gone on from Jordan to Israel) to the village of Cana in Galilee, and sit down outside his church with the Greek Orthodox priest. We read together at my suggestion, in Greek, mine just not too rusty, the passage in St John's Gospel about the wedding feast. Whenever I read or hear it again, I think of that moving inter-church setting.

In those early days after the end of the Mandate in 1948 there was a hundred yard strip of barbed wire in Jerusalem between Israel and Jordan, and I knew well before leaving England that to cross it I needed two passports, one for each country. So I solemnly had my Arab-visa passport stamped at the frontier, put it in my pocket, walked a hundred yards through the wire, and produced my Israeli-visa one, for all the world as if I had dropped from heaven to get there. Leaving Jordan meant saying goodbye to Stewart Per-owne (OBE, FSA, FRSA etc), the orientalist and historian, who was at that time advising the archbishop on how best to help Arab refugees. These had poured into the new state after the Mandate ended and Israel had been created, and both Mrs Stewart and Stewart Perowne were trying to help them. They each took me out on several of their working tours round the camps and new villages. We delivered fir seedlings and young plum trees, called on feeding centres, and looked doubtfully over the border from frontier homes. Stewart was a fund of knowledge on Arab affairs, and had fired up his bishop's wife to care for these displaced people.

Stewart knew the archaeologist Kathleen Kenyon well, and arranged for us both to visit her 'dig' in the excavated part of old Jericho. So we climbed rather perilously down thirty baked-earth steps to well below the level of the city that Joshua had captured, and were introduced to her little labels stuck with strong spikes into the dried mud walls, labels which read things like 'first century level' or 'not later than third century BC'. She was probably the greatest living guide at that time to the 2000 years of history tower-ing above us.

Once I had arrived in Israel there was plenty more to experience. I sat by Jacob's Well at Sychar, and I climbed Sebastiya, the old Hill of Samaria, from a good base for two or three nights with the then renowned missionary Doctor Bathgate at the Edinburgh Medical Mission Hospital, in Nazareth. I was particularly glad to come in for Church of Scotland hospitality there after the Anglican kind in

Jordan. Then I travelled by sea via Cyprus to Piraeus for a week-end in Greece with Trevor Watson, an Oxford friend, on my way home. He was working there for BP, and knew the country well.

We drove one very cold day 150 miles to Delphi, where we two were the only visitors to the theatre and temple; we also saw the ruins of Mycenae, looked down on ships navigating the Corinth Canal and had a drive into the hills of the Peloponnese. Just as the Holy Land had made the Bible come alive in a new way, so even this short time in Greece gave new significance to all those years of classical study which I had behind me. I also made a point of visiting the grave of my cousin Julian who had been killed in Athens, as I have mentioned, while serving with the 60th Rifles only three months before the war ended.

My two months of travel and education and holiday were almost over, as I went by sea again via a stop in Corfu, where there is still the quite unspoilt English cricket ground from the days when it belonged to the Empire; then across the Adriatic to Brindisi, and so home by train and cross-channel ferry. The trip had included an interesting mixture of ways of getting about, which would be most unlikely today, given the speed and convenience of modern air travel; but the variety and lack of hurry then made for a real feeling that one was doing something quite different from the everyday. So many kind people of many nationalities, and so many famous natural or man-made sights left me with abiding memories of the wonders of God's world.

I arrived home ten days before the start of the Hurst Green adventure.

Commuter-Belt to the Medway Towns

Some of the seed fell on good soil
Luke 8.8

The orange harvest moon, like a dull sun,
Rolls silent up the east above the hill;
Earth like a sleeper breathes, and all is still.
The Land: Autumn

I HAD transferred all my belongings from Bristol to Surrey before leaving for the two months abroad; and equally necessarily I had engaged, with Mairse's help, a 66-year-old (safe age, we reckoned) spinster named Edith Fort as my housekeeper. Miss Fort and I arrived in Hurst Green within a few hours of each other, so I was at once in business, with just time to prepare for my licensing in St John's by the Bishop of Southwark on 27th February 1954. The night before, I made a kennel for Tessa, my new yellow labrador puppy. Four years earlier in Wells, I had left behind my then labrador Judy, also yellow, to live in a farm just outside the city, with the land agent who had begun by simply housing her when I was at the college; but I gave her to him as a thank-you when I moved into city streets.

Excitingly there was almost everything to do. For a start I needed a Parochial Church Council, so I spent several weeks visiting the homes of churchgoers in order to accumulate enough faces and names for an election at the Annual Meeting, which conveniently was then as it is still during April. In the event we had a most amusing evening, with me attempting a thumb-nail sketch of each of the thirty or so people, of varying ages and backgrounds, who had told me on my rounds that they would be willing to stand. Everyone had a good laugh at my expense, as I gave the assembled company my impressions of the candidates, from knowing them for all of six weeks; but by the end of the meeting we had two churchwardens. In those days there was a Vicar's Warden and a People's Warden, the first traditionally middle-class, so I nominated a retired Major, Humphrey Prideaux, whom I knew had been a staunch ally to Arthur Norton and became one from the start to me; and the second was Alfred Sharp, elected by everyone present; he was a highly respected local shopkeeper. All this, of course, was quite terrible class-distinction, but it simply harked back to the feudal society in which the Church of England was embedded; mercifully the custom of centuries was eradicated not long after, so that for the last thirty years congregations have elected both their Churchwardens. But as well as the two wardens and, almost equally important for the fledgling community we were, we had a Parochial Church Council of eighteen or so who were raring to go.

This was therefore the perfect wicket for experimenting with a brand-new act of worship every week. By Easter we were able to hold the first Family Service, which young marrieds on the Church Council had promised to back, and one of them kindly agreed to play the hymns at it, as the organ would be too 'heavy'; it got off splendidly to its 9.50 a.m. start ('they'll never turn up so early,' warned the 11 o'clock diehards). with a congregation of two or three dozen. Within six months St John's was bursting for that service, with thirty- and forty-year-olds who wanted to bring up their young in the Christian faith, but had till then voted with their feet against traditional church services A marvellous atmosphere soon developed, as word got around that the families who were coming were enjoying themselves.

With what had been the main morning service at 11 o'clock, I had no difficulty in starting an alternative Matins and Communion plan, instead of only having one communion a month. Looking back, half a century on, at the many changes I made early on in my time in the parish, I realize what a huge help it was a) that I was new and young and energetic; practically everyone connected, or prepared to begin being connected, with St John's wished me well, and wanted to support me, b) that despite Arthur Norton's sheer goodness the whole set-up at St John's had been for several years plain dull, and the majority of 'the faithful few', very few actually, maybe thirty of them if every soul who went to church was included, were bored enough with their church-going to be prepared for a new look, and c) in those first two decades after the war there was all over the country a steadily increasing number of people in every walk of life who were either drifting back to church or ready to discover for the first time if the Church had anything to offer. In other words I was fortunate to arrive at Hurst Green on a rising tide of enthusiasm for the things of the Spirit, which I believe as a matter of history reached its peak in England early in the 1960s. However I was not aware of much of this in those fulfilling months when our church, so everyone round about was saying, was taking off; and I was much too busy for it to go my head.

I wanted with the new alternative Communion and Matins to emphasize visually the difference between the two, so I wore for Communion a plain chasuble over an alb, instead of my only using 'choir robes' which were and still are standard clerical dress for both Matins and Evensong; I had said nothing beforehand about vestments; if I had, there would certainly have been some opposition to the idea 'because it is too high church'. Instead, on Communion Sundays I just put them on in my vestry, as I had done for the past four years in St Matthew's, except that there the colour of the chasuble varied with the church's seasons. One thing at a time seemed sensible, and bright colours would have been much more obvious.

So when the one and only church bell stopped being rung, I processed in with a server behind the small choir. I doubt if people knew what the server was for, but they recognised this particular one because he was the reserve cross-bearer, so that made them happy. Hardly anyone noticed what I was wearing, but one or two who did (I heard long afterwards) thought that it was simply what the new vicar had dreamed up to make the service special. After I had left in 1962, my successor had no difficulty in introducing coloured vestments; by then I guess that the congregation just thought that each priest wore what he preferred. I am not denigrating the ecclesial knowledge of every church-goer on the finer points of what priests dress up in; most people in the pew are not remotely fussed by its vagaries. For myself I still like to wear something special for worship in church, but having said that I am not worried by evangelical clergy wearing simply a suit; these things cannot be important to God.

We had the usual headaches every parish priest experiences over the music, but two or three organists in turn built up a fairly good choir of seven or eight boys (girls would have been unheard of) and another dozen men and women. Thanks too to Penelope Owen, the wife of my Oxford friend John, who travelled from London to help, religious drama became quite a regular feature of our church life, with a fine production one year by a visiting company of T.S. Eliot's *Murder in the Cathedral*; and Penelope at other times produced Henri Gheon's *Way of the Cross* and Dorothy Sayers' *Man born to be King*, all of them to justified acclaim. St John's was beginning to be a church that people who might or might not be church-goers came to for extras like that, which was exactly what I hoped for. The plays undoubtedly helped put the Church of England locally much more on the map, because they were talked about, to the Gospel's good. Furthermore as a result of them and of the links developing too among churchgoers I found myself being invited out to meals, which was an agreeable change from the Bristol scene, where that was not the order of things. So I began making personal friends through the privilege of being welcomed in scores of homes. It was these pleasing encounters which led to by far the most important happening of the Hurst Green years to me personally: I met Rosemary Cleveland-Stevens.

Rosemary's church was actually St Peter's Limpsfield two miles away; she had been at school in Manor House next door, was confirmed in St Peter's, and even though her parents worshipped in St John's, where her father had been church treasurer at one time, Rosemary went on going to Limpsfield. But he must have bullied her into the odd visit to their church soon after I had arrived, if only in order to see this young man on the job. One day when I was on my bicycling rounds I paid a return visit, making my way unannounced up the imposing drive of Gaines in Ice House Wood, one of the Oxted roads north of St John's designated as part of the new district. In other words I was not poaching in the next parish, and anyhow her parents were 'my' churchgoers, both of which were etiquettes scrupulously kept in those far-off days. I spotted Rosemary in the garden with her father, and walked across to talk to them; they were at opposite ends of a cross-cut saw in the oak wood, by the ice-house. It must have been in March or very early April before the bluebells, or they would not have been wooding, and trampling on them. After I had mentally noted with quiet approval that Rosemary knew how a cross-cut needed invariably to be pulled rather than pushed, they stopped for a cup of tea back at the house, where her mother fished out the silver teapot; I only discovered later that she never used anything else. That afternoon was the start of an exhilarating courtship.

Father and Mary and I had the second of our motoring tours that summer. The first had been in Ireland the year before; we went to Glendalough and Bantry Bay and the Ring of Kerry, not to speak of Donegal and Galway, wonderful, in a serviceable hired Ford 10 in which we did 1300 miles and felt very proud of ourselves. This time we took off for Scotland, of which the highlight was my first visit to the numinous island of Iona, off the south-west tip of Mull. Memorable also in my book was the fact that, quite unplanned, Rosemary and I exchanged holiday postcards, she from Switzerland, I from the Braemar Games. This, we delightedly realized years later, had never happened to either of us before. From then on, time whizzed happily by, via the first-ever St John's fête; 'the date of the fête is September 8' was the successful slogan, and the bye-product there was that Rosemary won the hare that a gamekeeper friend from Chiddingstone had given to the cause.

Through the autumn I was frequently up at Gaines, where Dodge and Muriel, Rosemary's parents, were increasingly kind. Dodge had been up at Christ Church with the uncles, which was a bonus for a start; they maintained that Dodge were much the most handsome man in the college at the time. Married a few months before the first war ended, the Cleveland-Stevens began their married life in Palace Gardens Terrace, Kensington, but soon after Heather and then Rosemary had been born they moved to Oxted, and Dodge started forty years of London commuting to Great Tower Street in the City, where he became Secretary of Harrison and Crossfield, Tea and Rubber Importers. The office was near All Hallows on Tower Hill, so he picked up on his wartime friendship with Prebendary Tubby Clayton, of Toc H fame, by then the indefatigable and long-serving Rector. Dodge soon became Tubby's Church-warden at St Dunstan in the East, part of All Hallows; I learnt before long that my father-in-law-to-be said his own Evensong every day.

This second daughter of theirs, I had been discovering, was a professional pianist of no mean order: trained at the Royal Academy of Music after very fine grounding in the piano at Manor House School, Limpsfield, she had gone on travelling to college in London and back every day through the last half of the blitz, including of course the V1s and V2s. After the war she did two Wigmore Hall recitals, and also played in Livery Halls and an embassy in Belgrave Square. Rosemary's musical skills were a huge extra attraction for me; I could remember my mother at the piano, but although she was a competent musician and I still have happy memories of her playing Chopin beautifully, I was fast realizing that the girl I was falling in love with was in a very different musical league indeed. She earned a modest living teaching the piano at a prep. school in East Grinstead, and began helping me by being the courier for the monthly *Hurst Green News*, which I had started at Easter and found a good printer for, conveniently close to that East Grinstead school. This was another useful and quite frequent (what with proofs and so on) opportunity for meeting, so the contacts grew pleasurably during the autumn, with a dance or two, and an increasing number of (very good) meals at Gaines.

Finally, on 22nd November, St Cecilia's Day the Patron Saint of Music, when Rosemary had been out at an Oxted Musical Society evening, she called in at the Parsonage on the way home (which it was far from being); I asked her to marry me, and she said Yes. She went home on a high, and I had to refrain from waking up my housekeeper to tell her about it; Miss Fort was probably the only person in the parish who had guessed what was in the wind, and she was very generous about it next day, realizing, as of course I had long since, that it would mean the end of her job.

So it was a pretty euphoric Christmas for us both, shared between Orcheston and Hurst Green, where of course I had a load of work up to the festival itself; but after midday on December 25 10,000 clergy stand down for a break. Alas, Ted knew at once that he would not get home for a spring wedding, 'but don't you go postponing things for me, Johnnie, at your advanced age' was his typically kind observation. Apart from that real regret we had fun working away at the guest list, with the added problem, which every vicar experiences over getting married in his own church, of whom to include from the parish; in the end we settled for churchwardens and PCC members, which worked well. In those days most couples fixed their weddings for a date just before the end of March, so as to beat the tax man; I would have maybe ten sets of banns to read out in church on Sundays. I sandwiched mine in the middle of them, and kept reading pretty fast, but I could see churchgoers enjoying a smile over my unsuccessful ploy to try and wrap up my own banns in amongst the eight or more others.

On April 20 father, whose own wedding day it was in 1911, gave a merry lunch just before the service to thirty or more of my relations in a Westerham hotel; we have often thought since what fun it would have been if etiquette, and the little matter of getting ready for the day, had allowed Rosemary to be there too. But more importantly we had met early for Holy Communion in St John's. The Bishop of Salisbury, Bill Anderson, very kindly came to marry us; as a family we had become very fond of him when he was Bishop of Croydon in the war years, and had regularly taken his day off to sketch in Chiddingstone so as to get out of London's bombing for a bit. Sitting incognito with his drawing board on his knees, the bishop could not conceal his identity all that long, and both families became lasting friends. We have one of his attractive watercolours at the top of our stairs now.

Rosemary chose Sarah Boas, Kay's twelve-year-old, and the six-year-old Eiluned, the elder daughter of David and Helen Pugh, one of her best friends at the Academy, as bridesmaids; and we asked Stuart Laing, her doctor's eldest son, who was six and her piano pupil, to be page, for which he wore his tartan kilt; he is now at Ambassador level in the Foreign and Commonwealth Office. My best man was Edmund Haviland, also a priest and a great friend from Wells days; we both revel in close contact still. Father was in excellent form, wearing as he had for both Kay and Ted's weddings the frock coat, rather green if the truth be told, in which he was married to mother. Everyone sang their heads off, the whole service went well, and the village gave us a boisterous welcome as we emerged into the sunlight.

Up at Gaines there was a marquee on the lawn, where our health was cleverly proposed by Uncle Bob, alias William Cleveland-Stevens QC, Dodge's brother; and we drove away when the April light was fading in the 1936 Morris 8 which Rosemary had used for several years and had been generously given to her that morning by her parents. We spent that night at The Compleat Angler at Marlowe, (roast duck and green peas for dinner), and next morning caught our flight at Heath Row by a whisker, as there was fog to contend with all the way to London. Our honeymoon at Paguera in Majorca was ideal, despite the hotel being extended all round us, with the hot water pipes in our bathroom running salt water from time to time; and despite also bumping the second day into (of all people) none other than my old boss Mervyn Stockwood, who was holidaying on the island. But he had us to a very good meal in a Palma restaurant, and was, as they say, no trouble at all.

So began real living. We had four children in six years, all delivered in the Parsonage by our doctor, Denys Laing, except for the last, for whom Denys decided he would rather have Rosemary in Oxted Cottage Hospital for a few hours. He was a reassuring family doctor, always quickly at hand ('Heavens, I've not put any trousers on', he laughed to me before one of the births on a very cold February night, as he ran upstairs to Rosemary at 2 a.m.). Thanks to a dear friend's anonymous generosity, Rosemary had the luxury of a maternity nurse for all the babies in turn, staying for a month and greatly helping us ignorant parents to start in the way that we should go.

Within two or three years we were beginning to have the fun of sand castle-building with our growing children, by my doing three-week holiday locums during August at Appledore on Romney Marsh, and going down from there to the fine beaches at Camber and Littlestone. Thanks too to father and Mairse having our young in Orcheston Rectory several times, Rosemary and I had some splendid holidays on our own: Normandy (including the 1944 battlefields, Rosemary very patient over my reminiscing) and Brittany (it was *Pardon* time in the villages, so everyone was in their colourful traditional dress) in 1957; walking in delectable Housman country one year; and going to Austria and Germany for the 1960 Oberammergau Passion Play, surely the experience of a lifetime. In the Parsonage we began gradually to have a bit of help with the children in the shape of Daisy Bell, who kept house nearby for her carpenter-brother (both of them keen church-goers). Daisy became very much part of the family, and a great favourite of both Piers and Julian, who greeted her with shrieks of delight when she arrived to take them out for walks.

There was one sizeable factory in the parish, making electrical parts for industry; it was a good employer of labour for men and women in Hurst Green, and I often blew in to see office staff, but it was impossible to get into the factory itself for safety reasons, quite apart from noise ruling out any conversation. But I had an idea arising from theological college study and discussion a few years earlier, when many of us had become interested in the Worker

Priest Movement in France (Abbe Michonneau *et al*). The thought struck me that it might be a help to the Kingdom for me to see what it was like, as a minister as well as a factory hand, to work from 8 to 5 at a bench, and meet other employees on their own ground. So I put it to the management, who were mystified but helpful, and agreed to take me on for a month; my bishop gave me leave of absence, and the Rural Dean organised cover of the regular services, presumably by the gallant local clergy doing a bit extra each. I drew the standard wage for unskilled labour, and arranged with Inter-Church Aid as it was then, the precursor of Christian Aid, to have my stipend for four weeks.

My heart was in my mouth as I clocked in one Monday morning with my packed 'ten-ses' and lunch. I need not have worried, because the few people I knew had tipped others the wink that 'a reverend' was joining them, and those of the two hundred strong workforce who realized what was happening could not have been nicer. There was certainly everything to learn about their way of life and outlook, although having been a soldier, and a private soldier at that for some weeks, helped me to grasp the ethos (and the language) pretty quickly. For almost the entire month I was in a shop which cut up different thicknesses of copper piping, joints and so on. One week I did nothing but half-inch piping for plumbers. There was too much noise to talk.

I found the experience absolutely deadly, relieved only by the breaks. I discovered almost the first day how one watches the clock for this tyranny of dullness to end. The breaks, which were longed-for of course by everyone, were specially good for my purposes as the chaps really wanted to talk: why I was doing it; what did it feel like when surely I normally only worked on Sundays; and what the church thought about this or that current issue. I really valued all our conversations in the breaks, but by half-way through the month I was praying for it to end, for me to be released from this soul-destroying activity. I did my best to look at it all positively, but there seemed no sign of my being used to bring a new soul to Christ. 'Cast your bread upon the waters, and it will return to you after many days' became an over-used text in my head, as I tried to keep reasonably sane through the monotony of totally unskilled labour. The whole hands-on four weeks made me reflect (really for the first time, God forgive me) what the Industrial Revolution, with all its vast benefits to mankind, had done by creating these thousands of mind-numbing jobs, which are essential for the economy, but which men do solely for the sake of the money at the end of yet another indescribably boring week. Only the comradeship of the factory floor and the regular pay packet must save millions from utter despair. After that venture into industry, I sent an article on the off-chance about my experiences to the editor of *Theology*, and he rather surprisingly published it (January 1959).

It was sheer joy to be back on the job in the parish, where things had been humming along very happily without me. Then one Sunday morning not long after, when I was talking with the congregation outside after church, a rather crusty old widower looked up at the rendered wall of the uncompleted west end of the building (a stark contrast for the past forty-five years to the pleasing flint and sandstone of the rest of the church), and said to my amazement: 'You know, Vicar, we are big enough now to set about completing this church of ours'. One or two others heard him say it, and voiced their enthusiastic agreement; it had not occurred to me as a priority, but the suggestion having been raised it was quickly on the agenda of the next PCC. A feasibility study came up with the estimated cost of £25,000 of which, said financial advisers in diocese and parish, we would be well-advised to have three-quarters in the bank before we started to build. Amid mounting excitement through the winter of 1958, we got a plan together which we called 'Extending our Church', with the *double entendre* of the people and the building needing extending, and we were able to recruit sixty men as Church Builders, *double entendre* again, to begin tackling the task by Easter. They did very well on both counts: the congregations grew, and the money was raised.

Dove Brothers, who were then in the country's first rank of ecclesiastical work, won the contract, and fascinating it was to see the sandstone and flint structure creep up from below ground level. Of particular interest was a rose window for the west end, to be filled with stained glass in honour of St John the Evangelist, our patron saint; it is of strong colours in eight lights round the central one, and was designed and fixed by a husband and wife team, Jasper and Molly Kettlewell, an amusing and gifted couple who became firm friends. Jasper had been in Royal Navy torpedo boats in the war and had to have a leg amputated after being seriously wounded off the North Norfolk coast; 'extremely careless of me to lose my leg in the Wash' was one of his fund of quips, and to see this man hopping up and down ladders despite his disability was astonishing. The whole construction took about a year, and as always on these occasions we were getting rather nervous as to whether it would be finished for the bishop to dedicate it all in July 1962. We decided to make the first Sunday of that month into our Patronal Festival, marking this first one with a production of Benjamin Britten's *Noye's Fludde*. A cast of seventy, including a lot of children (Piers, at 6, was a cuckoo); Rosemary as continuo, in itself no small achievement, as she had to take a week off at a crucial stage in March to give birth to Sam; two Coldstream Guards trumpeters from Caterham; a fifty-strong orchestra; and a roomy ark in front of the screen — all these things were making parish life hum considerably.

Adding to the pressure that spring was the sad death of Rosemary's beloved father in early May, just after I had succumbed to mumps, an illness not to be recommended for adults; so I was unfortunately bed-bound for the funeral. To have a Memorial Service later appealed to the family; and with Mama's warm approval I invited Tubby Clayton to come and preach. 'Of course I will, my dear boy' was the immediate response, 'as long as you write the sermon.' How could I, a very junior priest negotiating with an internationally-known figure, reply other than that of course I would? So I did, and sent it up to London for him to mull over and play about with as he wanted.

Down to Hurst Green came the great man, duly preached to everyone's admiration and gratitude, and not a syllable of my offering to him had been altered. My final happy memory of him is his comment in the vestry, as we were disrobing: 'Thank you so much, John, that was a great help; I really enjoyed preaching your sermon and remembering my old friend; I'll keep it if I may, as it could well come in useful'.

There was yet a further major complication. Just after Easter I had had an invitation from the Bishop of Rochester to become the Vicar of St Stephen's Chatham, in the Medway Towns, and Rosemary and I had decided to say Yes; but obviously at such a time of parish celebration in St John's it was right to say nothing to anyone until after these great events were over.

Noye's Fludde proved to be nothing short of terrific. I can hear as if it was yesterday the singing of those majestic words of Joseph Addison, set to the haunting Tallis tune:

> *The spacious firmament on high*
> *With all the blue ethereal sky*
> *And spangled heavens, a shining frame*
> *Their great original proclaim,*

sing Noah's children. Then the sun appears (a two-foot golden ball rises slowly backstage), and Noah and Mrs Noah join in a metrical version of Psalm 19:

> *Th'unwearied sun from day to day*
> *Doth his Creator's power display,*
> *And publishes to every land*
> *The works of an almighty hand.*

I was intensely moved when I watched and heard all that on production night, the culmination of so much rehearsal, all of it from my personal viewpoint at the emotional time anyway of the last part of Rosemary's pregnancy and the birth of our fourth child; and there was his mother sitting at the grand piano (on long loan to St John's as a result of a *Times* advertisement), playing her vital part in something which had drawn in so many people of the parish which I was serving, enthusing them with belonging to the church they were filling with tumultuous sound. The large orchestra, the seventy actors on stage, and the entire audience were joining in for the hymn; and here too in the audience were the very people who were actively helping to 'extend our church', all mixed up with the people they were visiting in the cause of Church Extension. Furthermore Addison (1672-1719), classical scholar, poet and politician, was expressing in his hymn a major component of the countryman priest that I was and am. Moreover the performance of Britten's masterpiece complemented unforgettably for me and Rosemary the bishop's act of 'hallowing', we called it, of the new west end of the building. Mervyn had come down, as he had promised; it was all televised by ATV, with fanfares by trumpeters of my old regiment, and attended by four hundred parishioners, nearly half of them in a marquee on the church lawn to which the service was relayed.

So why were we leaving all this, for goodness' sake? On the face of it the very idea sounds crazy. But we were both very sure that it made sense to hand on now to a fresh mind a going concern. The church building itself had become vastly more useful, in that the extension included a large meeting room (which could be incorporated into the church for big occasions), a kitchen and a lavatory (both unheard of in a church then), and a roomy porch for notices and chat. What is more it had all been paid for, with about a week to spare. From my personal ministry angle, I needed after the fast-learning curve of Hurst Green, to spread my wings. The children were beginning to be of school age, and we were after much more educational choice than there was locally. Then there was the strong attractiveness of this particular invitation into the beloved Kent of my birthplace, to a parish in the Rochester diocese where father had served as a rector and was an honorary canon, where my Jelf grandfather had been a residentiary canon and held country incumbencies, and where the bishop, David Say, knew me slightly through father, and was the patron.

But inevitably we felt rather traitor-like when we told St John's what we were going to do. 'We hoped you would be here to start us off in the new set-up', said one of my churchwardens rather reproachfully, and I did not blame him for it. The prevailing mood, however, was generous and understanding, which made it much easier to uproot ourselves from Rosemary's old home area, from the place where we had met, married and had all our children, and from where I had cut my teeth in sole charge of a parish. To go and live in the Medway Towns was hardly a prospect to stir the blood, but we set out like Abraham (Genesis 12. 1 & 4), said goodbye to St John's at the end of September, and had a week's holiday in the Lake District in gorgeous autumn weather.

Westmorland, as it was then, was all new country to Rosemary; we explored Tarn Hows, Saddleback, Derwent Water, Cartmel Fell, where father had done the duty for the summer holidays of 1934, and many other lovely places which I remembered. To have, from then on, a wife as keen on the Lakes as her husband meant that we took our children there for two holidays in National Trust cottages in the Langdale valley, and moreover at a charge of five guineas a week, which really was very little money even then. Now to our delight Piers takes his own young there, generally to cottages he has been lent by kind parishioners. Liverpool business men often had second homes there, and were equally generous to Rosemary and me in the 1970s.

That year that we left Hurst Green, father received the OBE at the Queen's hand, Mairse going with him proudly to the Buckingham Palace investiture; as a family we were all so pleased that his forty years' work for Jerusalem and the Middle East was recognized in this way. To offset our delight at that came the sudden death at his desk in mid-October of my beloved uncle Julian. Rosemary too had got very fond of this courteous man, a catholic priest to his fingertips, and it was a sadness to her as much as me that we could not go to his funeral as it clashed with the date of my Institution to St Stephen's. Julian's notable headmastership of St Peter's Adelaide, and then of Felsted here in England has meant that all my life I have run into boys who were under him; and for our Julian in Australia the family's name has opened many doors, over the twenty or more years now in which he has made his home in Sydney. Uncle Julian was passionately devoted to his younger brother Burgon, with whom he had summer holidays on the continent for more than forty years; they timed their holidays from Canada and Australia to coincide. In the 1990s it was a wonderful surprise to be invited by the Oxford University Press to write, as one of the 10,000 contributors to their *Dictionary of National Biography*, a piece on 'Julian, co-subject Burgon'; and my modest twelve hundred words found a place among the sixty million, in sixty volumes, put together into this magnum opus, far and away the biggest printing enterprise ever embarked upon by any British publisher. The uncles would have enjoyed the pairing up by the OUP sub-editor who had approached me.

So I set about before Christmas 1962 getting into my stride as the vicar of a heavily populated neighbourhood, where green fields were at a premium, to serve a church which was already very much of a going concern. There was not the scope, or more accurately I did not discern the scope, for many new initiatives; my predecessor, David Halsey, who left St Stephen's to become Bishop of Tonbridge, had already done so many of the sort of things I had started at St John's. But we soon began enjoying ourselves in the Medway Towns. That first winter was one of the coldest on record, with frost in the ground from Boxing Day to the end of March. We found magnificent tobogganing slopes, as there were eighteen inches of snow on the ground for weeks on end. The boys began at a fine dame school in Watts Avenue Rochester, and that made for another source of friends for them and us, on top of church ones. I inherited an outstanding choir of rising forty men and boys under the inspired leadership of Keith Miller, a former music scholar of King's College Cambridge; he and Edna his wife, also very musical, became probably our greatest friends in the parish.

I am reminded by an article I wrote for the *Rochester Diocesan News* in July 1965 that our lives in St Stephen's, with St Alban's which was then a flourishing daughter church at the southern end of the parish on Bluebell Hill, were far from dull. I called the piece:

ON THE JOB

House Communion 6.45 a.m. (Saint's Day). Nine of us sitting round a living-room for fifteen minutes. Bread and cup passed from hand to hand. 'Marvellous start to the day', commented a commuter, rushing off. 7.30 a.m. Matins and silence (45 minutes) in church. Crescendo of cars outside gives point to prayers for the world.

9 a.m. Secretary arrives and we tackle morning mail, including (a) Hospital Matron asking for comments on an applicant for Nurses' Training; (b) Local Mayor's request for Progress Report on a Charity Appeal; (c) Priest in Kenya sounding out the possibility of a job on the staff here; (d) Doctor in Nigeria who has written an article for the parish paper-plus a number of other letters. We then press on with invitations to street representatives for their half-yearly consultation (forty to coffee at the vicarage). Get down, amid phone calls, to prepare speech at Roman Catholic Laymen's Dinner, and also a talk at withdrawal class for nine-year-olds in local primary school. Time for twenty minutes on John Robinson's *The New Reformation?* before driving to twelve o'clock cremation 9 miles away.

2.15 p.m. Appointment with architect at church hall, considering gloomy surveyor's report. 3 p.m. Teach in school. Reflected on great good fortune of having really co-operative headmaster. 3.50 p.m. Two Baptism visits to fix times when dads would be at home for going through the service. Call on an arthritic 60-year-old (her cheerfulness a tonic as usual), to arrange communion there next week. Visit a factory worker home after a head injury. 4.45 p.m. Tea with the family. Girl having a ghastly time with mock G.C.Es, so quick ten minutes on the French Revolution. Get in two rows of carrots before biking to church for junior Confirmation class. Disturbing half-hour on 'What the Church is For' according to eleven local young.

6.15 p.m. Evensong; two confirmation girls stay for it. 7.15 p.m. Supper early, wife (thanks to our liver-in) bound for committee meeting. Self to church for wedding interview, then on to a chap to talk over a personal problem, listen till ten and fix a further visit. Return to a refreshing ballet on I.T.V., my wife and I relax with a cuppa.

This is the parish priest's job. Bitty, intensely personal, requiring self-discipline, very much what you make of it, productive of deep friendship, exhausting yet utterly invigorating at one and the same time. Vital as other patterns of ministry are, industrial, hospital, school, university, or whatever, I remain completely convinced of the value of the parochial one.

HAPPY INCUMBENT

It was a joy too to have the cathedral on our doorstep; my mother had grown up beside it in Minor Canon Row, and the Lady Chapel has several Jelf and Chenevix-Trench memorials. There was great music of course, and Rosemary learnt the organ from Jo Levett, the assistant organist, who had the distinction of harbouring a large organ, with the pipes all on their sides behind louvres, in his drawing-room. In the Old Deanery, Canon Stuart Blanch was the gifted Principal of Rochester Theological College, where he began asking me to address his students from time to time; and another canon, Ross Hook, was married to my cousin Ruth, whose mother was a Bickersteth from the Devonshire branch of the family; and these links led to happy entrées to two homes next to the cathedral. As a family we regularly got out of town into the Kentish countryside, especially when the soft fruit ripened; in fact Rosemary was so quick at raspberry-picking that one farmer wanted to take her on his temporary staff. A succession of lodgers brought in some useful income; we generally had foreign students, so as to contribute in a tiny way towards solving the housing problems they often had, but also in order to introduce our growing children to the wider world. Two or three Nigerians and an Israeli became good friends, and we kept up with them all for some years after they had left college.

Internationally it was, as ever, a time of turmoil, and we got very mixed up with the Freedom from Hunger Campaign in the mid to late sixties. Rosemary took on the Secretaryship of Christian Aid for the whole of the Medway Towns, and we handled that as part of the Campaign, which worked admirably as people were finding it difficult to sort out priorities in concern for the developing world. So 70,000+ Christian Aid Week envelopes arrived at our door every May, for distribution round scores of helpers in the four towns. One particular CMS agricultural missionary in Uganda, Stephen Carr, became linked to St Stephen's through these various ecumenical endeavours; he was beginning in a very small way with clearing bush on the foothills of the Ruwenzori Mountains, the place name still tripping off the tongue as if I knew it well, but I never got there. On this virgin soil he planted tea bushes, and the enterprise flourished so much that Stephen was able in his retirement forty years later to publish a book which he called *Surprised by Laughter*, a welcome title amid the gloom and doom stories, often alas true, of bloodshed and corruption in the former British colonies. He generously acknowledges in it that the Medway Towns' £60k input all those years earlier, modest enough we always thought from a conurbation as big as we were, was what really got them going. Whenever Stephen is back in the UK from his Malawi home, he always delivers some Nyakashaka tea to us.

Much of the success of all that we were able to do by way of outreach was due to a remarkable person named Marjorie Pettitt, from the Bluebell Hill end of the parish; she was and is a shining example of a dedicated Christian who consistently looks wider than the local church. 'Overseas' does not mean for her something miles away; it is simply a word meaning 'the extended parish'. When I suggested importing our 'Overseas Week-end' idea, which had gone well in Hurst Green, she jumped at it, and we had some memorable occasions, each time with forty or more London-based men and women from various parts of the world. For most of our congregation these week-ends led to radically fresh thinking about their wider Christian responsibility, in fact of the then very new word 'ecumenism'. For neither that word itself nor what it meant and entailed had yet reached most English parishes. I was lucky in that respect: I had been a Student Christian Movement member at Oxford; I had had the eye-opening experience of the Redfield United Front in East Bristol for four years, and that was followed by significant co-operation with a lively congregational minister of my age in Oxted. Only with the Roman Catholics was there no movement for anyone anywhere, until suddenly Pope John XXIII burst upon the world scene in 1964, and through his charismatic love for all Christians the 'great new fact of our time' was that Anglican and RC relations could from then on only get better.

That same year I found myself at the British Council of Churches' Conference in Nottingham University, quite a major event in the post-war Church of England because it was when the evangelicals began to come in from the cold, not least through the leadership of John Stott. In 1966 my own church education was much enlarged, by being invited (with Rosemary, which made it much more fun), to undertake a three-week preaching tour on the eastern seaboard of the United States. It was very generously arranged through an Episcopalian priest-friend of the Bishop of Rochester, a great anglophile named John Harper, and I mean generously because one gets paid for preaching in the Episcopal Church, and I remember feeling rather a fraud over collecting a hundred dollars for an indifferent sermon, and arriving home barely out-of-pocket after a huge amount of travelling. We finished up in Canada to meet some of the people who had worked with Uncle Burgon for so long between the wars. So the wider scene, which I had known in my heart for some time was becoming important for me, started really to open up.

In our part of the Medway Towns there was fortunately a go-ahead minister of my age at St Luke's Methodist Church in City Way, which was the western boundary of our parish; he and I did a good deal together in 1967-8 under the auspices of an *ad hoc* organisation named Towards Anglican Methodist Unity. We went as a pair to deaneries and 'circuits' to talk about the official scheme then on the stocks for the reunion of our two churches after nearly two hundred years. It was a great disappointment to us both, as to so many in and out of the churches, when the Church of England turned down the draft plan after the Methodists had approved it, which made it all the more shaming. Uncle Burgon told me that the Archbishop of Canterbury, then Michael Ramsey, to whom Burgon was very close, had buried his face in his hands to hide his sadness over the adverse vote in the Church Assembly; locally I could only ring up my opposite number in St Luke's and persuade him against all his teetotal principles to join me in the pub; we had a pint and some orange juice to drown our sorrows.

In the autumn of 1967 Rosemary and I had a rather disturbing, and as it proved quite unnecessary jolt: the Bishop of London, Robert Stopford, asked me to go and see him, which I was glad to do; he was *ex officio* father's chairman in J&EM, so we had often passed the time of day. His question was: 'Would you please consider becoming Bishop of Stepney?' Then almost as an afterthought: 'I had hoped to persuade Trevor Huddleston to fill the vacancy when he comes home from Tanzania, but it doesn't look likely now that he is going to be available, and everyone tells me that you etc etc.'. It was a gratifying suggestion, especially as I knew very well that I was not remotely in Fr Trevor's league. So off trundled Rosemary and I, fairly inconveniently at a very busy time for me, and young children needing a plan for the day made for them, in order to 'walk round the streets a bit' says the bishop, 'and get an idea of what it might all be like.' The then Bishop of Stepney was still around, hence the frustrating secrecy. The tied house for the job was in St John's Road, in lawyer country behind Gray's Inn. This pavement-peering proved to be as we expected a totally fruitless exercise. We paced up and down gazing at the imposing nineteenth century terraced house, and trying to contemplate a town upbringing for our children, with no garden, new school arrangements, and so on, without knowing how serious the bishop was over the whole invitation.

Mercifully we were not kept waiting long. My own bishop David Say had rung me about it, since of course out of courtesy the two bishops had discussed the offer; and the day after Rosemary and I had been up to view our possible home, he rang again: 'I've told Robert he should see you again at once as there are developments'. Next day I got a call from the secretary in London for another interview; and exactly a fortnight after the original one the bishop was explaining to me that unexpectedly Fr Trevor would after all be available, so his suggestion to me fell to the ground. We did not mind too much, as we were so thankful not to be making for London E1, where Bishop Trevor was to have a widely-renowned ministry, of a class to which I could not possibly have aspired. We later discovered he had been within a whisker of being deported by the Tanzanian government

It was all the more exciting therefore to hear very shortly afterwards that I had been nominated to be one of the dozen Church of England delegates to the 4th Assembly of the World Council of Churches, due to meet at Uppsala in Sweden during July 1968. Maybe partly on the strength of the honour that it was, David Say made me just before the conference an Honorary Canon of his cathedral church, as father had been until leaving the diocese ten years earlier. That offer really did delight me. My sister Kay quite rightly put me in my place when she heard about it, with the healthy sibling comment: 'Well done you, but surely you are not anything like old enough'.

That conference at Uppsala University was a mind-changing experience for me. Old hands noticed at once that there were many more Orthodox this time than there had been in New Delhi fifteen years earlier. These Russians, Greeks, Armenians, Serbians and so on actually constituted the largest 'confessional' group among the participants. It was sometimes difficult to understand what they wanted to say, not so much because of their different languages (in the plenaries there were already the beginnings of simultaneous translation), but because of their thought-forms. For instance I vividly recall the worship group I was in wrestling with the need to work away at church services which were more relevant to today's world, particularly for younger Christians, with the use of art and drama and music and modern translations, when a Rumanian patriarch asked if he could speak. Our New Zealand chairman said 'Yes of course', and the bearded black-habited figure simply said with a smile: 'What about the angels?'

In addition to such pungent Orthodox contributions (anything but orthodox as they generally were), there was the youth element. Among the two thousand or so 'extras', there were scores of young men and women from all over the world, many of whom had paid for themselves to attend as observers, making themselves felt, often very effectively, at every stage of the proceedings. They published a provocative newspaper every two or three days, and woe betide the delegates if we did not acknowledge that we had at least skimmed through what radical offerings they were quite rightly shoving under our noses. A third major factor was the continuing pressure to us from the West, by delegates who came from the developing world, reminding us that their countries existed; and furthermore that they frequently had quite different agenda from ours. The rest of us were not allowed for a moment to indulge in dividing Christians' socio-political-economic responsibilities from the evangelistic ones; it became an issue that sank in deep for me.

To mark the end of the conference, delegates were invited to Stockholm for an open-air lunch in the sunshine (just) in the City Hall quadrangle as guests of the municipality, and then we all stumped along in the rain that had taken over, behind a Salvation Army band, for a rather damp but boisterous service in the new shopping centre. This was a good idea, as it stopped any notion that these Christians were operating in some sort of ghetto and were much keener on the church than the world; as it was, many of the shoppers found themselves laughing away with us across language barriers, and joining in the hymns. From Stockholm I went by boat with a small group of new friends to Gottland, where we stayed the week-end in the homes of young Swedish clergy and explored the old city of Visby, with its broken-down mediaeval walls, met the Lutheran bishop, and worshipped with them in their modern church. Their Synod had recently voted to ordain women, more than twenty years before we did; the bishop was keen about it, the clergymen we met not at all.

At Uppsala I met some of the best-known leaders in the World Church: among them was the charismatic Roman Catholic Barbara Ward, who was technically an observer, D.T. Niles of Ceylon, Visser t'Hooft of the Netherlands, Bishop Lesslie Newbigin of the Church of South India, Ernest Payne of the Baptists, Norman Goodall of the Congregationalists, and many others. These were encounters in a remarkable setting not to be repeated on the same scale in one time and place for most of us including me; and as usual with conferences it was the informal discussions we had with each other that were often more useful than the official 'conferring'. It was not a time when Churches were pinning all their hopes on the formal reunion of Christians the world over, any more than we do now. But that conference taught me so much about the hugely-varied

make-up of the Church of God throughout the inhabited earth, and
that it is more important to build up friendships and respect
between Christians of different traditions than to aim for wholesale
amalgamations, with the inevitable loss they could cause to individual insights and emphases, and the strong likelihood of fresh rifts
soon developing. I also learnt, in this dramatically-visual way that a
major international conference affords, that it was both impossible
and wrong for any one group of Christians to claim that we or they
had all the late-twentieth century answers to the church's mission.

That new understanding of Mission must have encouraged me to
put pen to paper again for the *Rochester Diocesan News*, and this time
(Nov. 1969) I wrote:

THAT LITTLE 'S'

Not for nothing has that doyen of ecumenical journals the
International Review of Missions just dropped the final 's' from its
title. This modest but welcome change leads to encouraging
thoughts for the local scene:

1. May the phrase 'For Foreign Missions' now be for ever ex-
punged as a block heading from those hymnbooks where it sur-
vives, with its smug implication of 'enlightened we' to 'benighted
them'. There is and always has been One Mission from the One
God to the world He created, redeemed and inspires. We are all
at the receiving end.

2. Are there still parishes which allocate money 'For Missions'?
Convenient short-hand phrase it may be, but its (perhaps unconscious) effect on most of those who read it will be clean contrary
to the spirit of mutual responsibility and interdependence in a
common task. Far better to take a little more space in the
accounts to spell out 'Towards a priest's salary in Sabah', or 'For
Christian literature in Malawi'. . .

3. Do any of us still describe the daughter (?sister) church in
the parish (if we have one) as 'the Mission'? Bad enough for us to
imply that at the Parish Church we are past the mission stage;
but I found that in the United States they have whole 'missionary
dioceses'. I got rather excited about this until I discovered that,
as soon as these dioceses become self-supporting financially, they
cease to be called missionary. Thus the scandal is that both here
and in too many parts of the world, we Christians are only 'miss-

ionary' or a 'mission church' for as long as we depend on outside help; once we can balance the books we become established, permanent, unchanging, instead of always being flexible, footloose, intent on mission.

A Russian priest I got friendly with in Sweden last year often talked about 'the dynamic of the Church's Mission'. These seem to me some of the small but significant ways in which congregations can be helped to share, dynamically, in God's 'Mission in all six continents'.

J.M. BICKERSTETH

I wrote that with The World Council of Churches in mind, but there was still of course one major church which did not belong to it, that of Rome. My most reassuring link with Roman Catholics came a few years later, when I had become a suffragan bishop and we had taken the family on holiday from Liverpool to a village in Austria, and I was looking after the Anglican church locally for three weeks. On one Sunday my service was in the evening, so I was free to go to morning Mass in the village church. I called on the priest and asked him whether I could receive the sacrament. 'Of course', he replied in excellent English, 'and would you please read the Gospel? We like to practise our English'.

In the last hymn he wandered across to where we six were sitting: 'That was fine' he commented on the two major things I had done, in both Word and Sacrament, 'would you very kindly give the blessing?' When I queried whether his people (it was a full church) would be happy with this, as well as himself, he said: 'Of course, you are a bishop, they will value this as much as I shall'. So much for Pope John Paul II's continuing directions to his priests that the growing practice of giving communion to 'non-catholics' should be discontinued forthwith; my guess is that (despite the Holy Father's disapproval) occasional sharing like this has come to stay, to the great good of the universal church. I mentioned the incident to my local Roman Catholic bishop, a good friend, when I got home: 'Ah', he said, 'yes I suppose they are a bit ahead of us'.

Uppsala had been my longest time away from the family yet, and I was longing to see everyone again, so there was a great home-coming at the very start of the summer holidays. We were soon off to Cornwall, our second summer there out of four. The sailing lessons in Padstow estuary of the previous year meant that the older boys were straight into it again. Those Cornish Augusts (1967-70) were absolutely right for the stage the family had reached, following as they did the Norfolk ones (1963-6) which again had been ideal. In East Anglia I had done a locum just outside Cromer for an old Rugby friend, Gilbert Spurrell; there the mixture of sandy beaches and the Broads, of visiting lovely places like Blickling Hall and Blakeney Point; of tennis on Gilbert's grass court which most of the rectories and vicarages of those days had, and games in his huge garden; of following the binder in the cornfields and stooking the sheaves as they fell on the new stubble (I lost my signet ring stooking once, and found it again a methodical hour's hunt later); of innumerable joint picnics and extensive parties with new and old friends.

All these things added up to two splendid quartets of holidays after the Camber Sands ones (1959-1962) with which we began when the children were very young. In Norfolk, to our distress, Gilbert himself, a bachelor who to accommodate us had only moved ten miles away to stay with his mother, died there unexpectedly at the very end of our three weeks in his home; so I took his funeral, surely a unique thing for a *locum tenens* to find himself doing for an old friend.

Meanwhile in the Medway Towns I began not only talking around on the Uppsala experience, but more importantly (someone has said 'conferences can be felt but not tellt', a very true aphorism) I had been made chairman of a new Missionary and Ecumenical Council for the Rochester Diocese. As I was also by then on the national council with the same name in the Church Assembly in London, I had plenty of opportunities to meet and pick the brains of church leaders of all traditions in England, on top of having been able to do this on a wider scale through the WCC, and I began to realize the deep distrust there was at local level of 'Geneva', the WCC's home. Parishes in the shires were convinced it was a very left-wing organisation, and therefore anathema in the current climate of paranoia over the Soviet Union.

This view came to a head shortly after the Church Assembly was replaced in 1970 by the General Synod; and in protest against the stance which many of us ecumenical enthusiasts (we were, partly derisively and partly affectionately, called 'ecumaniacs') were taking about the evils of *apartheid*, the fledgling GS withheld a token £1000 from its annual grant to the WCC. The main reason for this reactionary move was the unpopularity of its Programme to Combat Racism (the PCR); some representatives on the central bodies of the Church of England sincerely believed that the WCC was subsidising terrorism in South Africa by helping the illegal African National Congress's humanitarian work. It was a charge that was not easy to refute, particularly as the apartheid regime was officially supported by the British Government, albeit with many reservations by far-seeing souls.

However enough of us believed that the denial of this small sum to those who were committed to work for a more just society in South Africa sent all the wrong signals both to the beleaguered black South African people and also to the free world at large. So a small committee got itself organized, and within a month, despite some irritation in London, we had satisfactorily and with little difficulty raised the shortfall from well-wishers, and dispatched it, for onward transmission to the ANC's medical department, to WCC headquarters in Geneva. The incident helped me to learn how hard it often is to trust Christian bodies in the developing world, or indeed anywhere else, to do what they say they will with charitably-raised funds. To deny that trust is hugely damaging, as well as being plain wrong, even though the consequence may be that otherwise good people sometimes let you down.

A year or so before that 'little local difficulty',[29] Rosemary and I were in Geneva ourselves on much more agreeable business, namely an Easter holiday tour with the St Stephen's Choir. Piers and Julian were choirboys by then, and Rosemary was asked to be the organist. Such tours were in their infancy then for cathedral choirs, let alone parish church ones, but that was no deterrent to Keith Miller. He arranged for us to sing and stay in three or four places, all reached on our German coach the whole way from Chatham. After a night stop in Luxemburg, we reached Geneva where Rosemary and I were put up by our Sam's godmother who had a house there, but the choir slept in the crypt of Holy Trinity, the English church, where they were to sing next day. In Grenoble the choir was in action in St Mark's Ecumenical Centre, from there we went on to Lyons and sang in the RC cathedral, and thence to Taizé in Burgundy, to sing in the almost new *Eglise de la*

---

29. Harold Macmillan, asked by the press in S. Africa about a crisis at home

Reconciliation of the Taizé Community. This last was the highlight of the tour.

Taizé was not new to us both, as we had made a point of going there on a holiday in France a few years earlier. God had blessed from the start the 1946 brain-child of Roger Schulz, and by the time of this second visit of ours there were thirty or forty brothers of various nationalities, and they had so outgrown the little Romanesque village church that they had built a striking new one. St Stephen's Chatham Parish Church Choir was having the distinction of being the first English choir to sing in it. We gave a concert there for Taizé funds. Playing for it when the organ was one side of the church and the choir had to sit on the other was quite a test for Rosemary's skills, but needless to say she managed very well, and the large audience gave their visitors rapturous applause.

But the best part of the visit for the whole choir was undoubtedly attendance at the half-hour-long Office or Daily Worship. To be present was not an obligation in any way; but the magnetism of these robed figures at prayer in the central part of the church, much of the time in silence but also singing the simple and beautiful Taizé chants, drew this international crowd together, whether normally churchgoers or not. Community members come silently and swiftly in, as the two or three hundred holidaying campers are arriving in church, leaving for the brothers their rectangular praying space. Rosemary and I revel still, with a great lift of the spirit, in any opportunity to join again in the Taizé chants, some of which have found their way into our hymn and song books in the Church of England.

Looking back now at our years in St Stephen's, I realize that so many of the most special moments I recall from them did in fact happen outside the parish boundaries. This is not to say that we did not also enjoy ourselves greatly in the parish itself. Having that superb choir (even Sam, at 7, was invited by Keith Miller to join for a few months before we left), and the delightful dreamy musician-schoolmaster Arnold Coulson as the organist (so dreamy that he sadly slipped into altzheimers in his sixties), meant that it was only the fault of myself, a succession of good curates and two fine readers, if the services were not imaginative and inspiring. I had three curates in turn, David (later Canon) Knight, Michael Dunn and Bill Penney, who with their respective families, each very differently contributed much to the liveliness of the place; they worked hard, they were cheerful company, we valued praying and planning together; we laughed a lot, and between them they added to our lives this extra 'curate-dimension' which we had not known in Hurst Green days. But the truth is that neither Rosemary nor I managed to get so utterly caught up in the parish life of St Stephen's as we had of St John's. In the former we inherited an up-and-running 'show'; in the latter we had had to start everything, so it was hardly surprising that the 'first fine careless rapture' of St John's, where there had been both that exciting feel to the start of a brand-new parish, and also the gorgeous 1955 upheaval in our lives of marrying, establishing our home, and producing children, could not in the nature of things be repeated.

It was, I was sure therefore, good for the parish, as well as for me as a priest and us as a family that, following the strange episode of the London suffragan bishopric, various other invitations began to come my way. I was sounded out about the possibility of taking on the Directorship of Christian Aid; but it would have meant a major disruption to family life, and anyhow I doubted whether I would have been up to it (for example I had not got fluent French). Moreover I was not drawn to a mainly office job, however interestingly it would have also taken me round the world's trouble spots, so I stifled that flattering suggestion at a fairly early stage. But two diocesan bishops wrote to me almost simultaneously during that summer of 1969 about much bigger jobs than I was doing, one for the living of St Mary's Portsea, and the other for St Mary's Southampton. We went to see them of course, but were not all that attracted.

Two days after the Southampton visit I heard from Stuart Blanch. He had been Bishop of Liverpool since mid-1966; I remembered bumping into him in the SPCK Bookshop beside Rochester Cathedral on the morning his appointment was announced. 'Sad for us, but hooray for lucky Liverpool', I said and meant it profoundly, because Stuart's creation from scratch of Rochester Theological College had been truly inspirational, with his unique mixture of scholarship and simplicity and fun; not surprisingly the students were devastated to see him go. 'Well John', he replied typically on that day in Rochester, 'they're scraping the barrel now all right'. They were doing nothing of the sort of course, and Liverpool, I knew, had taken him to their hearts. Now eighteen months after we had spent those three weeks at Uppsala together, this lovable man was asking me to join him for lunch in the familiar surroundings of the Royal Commonwealth Society in Northumberland Avenue, where we were both members. As soon as we sat down he came to the point: would I be prepared to succeed Laurie Brown, who was leaving the suffragan see of Warrington to be Bishop of Birmingham? It proved to be quite a lunch.

Rosemary and I went privately to Liverpool to see the house in which we might find ourselves living. It was in Elm Avenue, Crosby, a fine building put up by an Aintree punter whose luck had been in on an outsider for the Grand National twenty years before. Bishop Laurie, who was a very wise financier among more obvious talents for high office in the church, had bought the house for the diocese quite recently; and Rosemary and I fell in love with it at once. Wellbuilt in the local brick (that punter had taken good advice over an architect), and being two hundred yards off the main road out of Liverpool towards Formby it was quiet and safe for children, with an acre of garden, and parkland immediately behind, contrasting with the twelve solid miles of streets which there were in the other direction to the centre of Liverpool and out on the Hale side. Conveniently accessible to the sprawling towns and the small number of villages I would need to get to know north of the city by means of the East Lancs Road, Crosby would be only half an hour from my office in diocesan headquarters.

So how would the children's schooling be affected? Piers was just starting at Marlborough, Julian was nearly through his prep-school years at Hildersham House, Broadstairs; Janie, a day girl in Chatham, could change to Merseyside without difficulty; Sam newly at Hildersham could move to a prep-school near Crosby. All fours' education was being paid for through a trust funded by 'the uncles' (when Uncle Julian had died I was his residuary legatee, and Uncle Burgon kept on generously adding to the Trust), so the only extra expense for us would be over travel, not to speak of wear and tear for Rosemary in mostly doing the long journeys at the beginning and end of term. Leaving St Stephen's? It is rarely, if ever, the perfect moment for a priest to move on, unless he has been such a disaster that parishioners are glad to see the last of him. No particular venture within the parish was in our sights, which is not to say (maintaining the analogy) that I felt I had shot my last St Stephen's bolt. But the offers beginning to come my way were leading to the view that not only Rosemary and I but also other people, whose opinion I valued, thought it was about time I moved. So I knew it was right to 'listen' to what was going on; yet the big parishes I was being asked to consider were not enthusing me. The Bishop of Rochester, a perceptive and wise father-in-God if ever there was one, was convinced that we ought to look very seriously at this sea-change to consecration as a bishop. All these factors were helping us to make up our minds; I have never been a person for great blinding flashes to light up that well-worn track to Damascus.

We stayed that night with Stuart and Brenda in their Woolton home, where slowly, almost imperceptibly, after much talk and laughter and prayer all mixed up, I found myself (after affirmative glances between Rosemary and me) saying before we all went to bed: 'Thank you Stuart for this unbelievable invitation. If you really think I might be able to do the job, I'm going to say Yes.'

After a wedding in
St John's Hurst Green, 1961

Overseas weekend,
St Stephen's Chatham, 1963

Down the Haydock coalmine, Lancashire, 1972

Planting a *Malus tschonoskii* with the Mayor of Wells and Men of the Trees
Palace Arboretum, 1977

Visiting the Royal Naval Air Station, Yeovilton, 1978

With Rosemary and the Diocesan Staff, the Palace, Wells, 1980

Dedication of memorials to 'the uncles' by Donald Coggan,
Greyfriars, Canterbury, 1981

With Rosemary by the Palace moat, 1982

Bishop of Warrington

The unwearied sun from day to day
Does his Creator's power display
Joseph Addison *op.cit.*

For as earth
Rolls on her journey, so her little fields
Ripen or sleep, and the necessities of seasons
Match the planetary law.
The Land: Winter

MY consecration in Liverpool Cathedral on 7th April 1970 was certainly irregular and probably illegal. I suppose the Dean was the technical offender, but the Archbishop of York was without doubt an accessory before the fact. That spring the nave of York Minster was out of action, because all the floor was up, so that any major service like a consecration was out of the question. Obviously therefore the normal arrangement whereby the bishop or bishops to be consecrated stayed, with their wives and families, in the archbishop's home, Bishopthorpe, the night before the service fell to the ground; there would be no point in everyone having to set off after breakfast for another cathedral. 'Could we come to Liverpool?' asked the archbishop, and Edward Patey, then the creative dean of the cathedral, agreed at once. There had not been a consecration there since 1948.

So Edward, in that autumn of 1969, immediately set about thinking how best to do it, and (being who he was) lit upon the Liturgical Commission's draft Ordinal, only just out, which was the first major re-ordering of the service for consecrating bishops since the *Book of Common Prayer* in 1662. 'Are you happy to use it,' asks the dean of the archbishop, 'it seems rather good to me?'

'Excellent', replies Donald Coggan, never one to be very aware of bureaucratic niceties like central bodies in the Church of England, not to speak of Parliament, needing to approve draft documents before they could be authorised for public use, 'I like the look of it too.' So we used the brand-new Ordinal.

Only some time after the whole occasion had been superbly

carried through (for Liverpool Cathedral knows how big events should be run) did some pundits from Church House in Westminster start making noises to the effect that the General Synod had had no chance to consider the new ordinal yet. 'What did Liverpool think it was doing jumping the gun?'. By then it was much too late to unscramble everything; very few people ever knew there was a problem, but enough of them in Liverpool and London saw that beginning all over again was not a starter. Possibly there was a bit of rapping over the knuckles, but I was not told, and only heard years afterwards in casual conversation with Brian Hanson, the senior lawyer in Church House and a good friend; whereupon we had a good laugh, and agreed that I seemed to be very happy masquerading as an illegally-consecrated bishop.

The family therefore never stayed at Bishopthorpe, a minor disappointment to Rosemary and me, but Brenda Blanch turned up trumps, and gallantly had all our family of six to Bishop's House in Woolton. It was incidentally a pleasing coincidence that Dick Watson (who was to become Bishop of Burnley) and I were to be consecrated at the same time. We were Old Rugbeians of almost the same vintage; so it was fun (in exercising the customary right of priests to be consecrated whereby they nominate the preacher) to recommend to the dean that he asked a third contemporary of ours at Rugby, Patrick Rodger, at the time Provost of Edinburgh Cathedral; he gladly fell in with the idea, knowing privately (what he could not possibly tell us) that his name was going forward for the See of Manchester. 'I loved coming' he told Dick and me later, 'it gave me a good idea of what I was in for'.

The service in Liverpool Cathedral was a memorable evening for our first taste of that vast building in resplendent use, with quire and nave full of people right back to the bridge. Noel Rawsthorne was at the great organ, and Ronald Woan directed the large choir of men and boys. It was nothing short of wonderful to revel in Orlando Gibbons and Gustav Holst, in Tallis and Gabrieli and Bach, in such an incomparable setting, even if Rosemary was in a fitter state to be aware of the magic than I was. But the archbishop was not remotely intimidating, and once we had started I began to enjoy myself, and get caught up in the spirit of it all. David Say, who had played such a large part in helping me to get to this point in my ministry, came up from Rochester to be the other presenting bishop with Stuart, who had been a member of his cathedral staff in Rochester, as I have mentioned. There were some fine hymns: 'God of Grace and God of Glory', to *Regent Square*; 'Christ is made the sure Foundation', to *Westminster Abbey*, and others.

In interesting contrast to what would happen to-day a rubric declared in bold print: 'it is emphasized that, following the normal practice, this service is not a general communion'. Instead Stuart Blanch and I, and Dick and his new diocesan, Charles Claxton (as it happened, the bishop who had last been consecrated in Liverpool in 1948) simply 'administered Holy Communion to such of the Bishops, and of their personal friends and family who desired to partake'. That accurately reflects the fact that in 1970 the Church of England was far less of a sacramentally-centred church than we are now. A ruling like that would not even be contemplated now; instead an army of stewards would have moved into the aisles to guide the congregation to various stations throughout the building, where maybe twenty priests or lay administrators would share the giving of communion, taking at the most ten to fifteen minutes to complete it, while the choir would have sung anthems or motets. That would all have seemed very odd indeed only thirty years ago; present practice undoubtedly makes these big occasions far more the concern of every worshipper.

Along with a splendid turn-out of near relations, I was glad that the hundred-and-fifty year-old family connection with the city and cathedral of Liverpool was kept up that evening by my fourth cousins Ailsa and Arthur Bickersteth coming from the Lake District, where brother and sister (then in their late sixties) lived at Borwick Fold near Hawkshead. This little fell cottage, with some land still where Ailsa had her ponies, was all that was left then of the large estate round about. Their father was the last of the three generations of Robert Bickersteths who were surgeons to the Liverpool Royal Infirmary, and the middle one ('arguably in his day the best surgeon in England', says an article I have about him) figures in the medical window on the north side of the cathedral nave, just west of the bridge. Although I was pleased that 'the Liverpool Bicks', as they were known in the family, were represented, it was sad that Ted woke in the middle of the previous night with an acute attack of his recurring bronchitis, and could not possibly contemplate crossing the Pennines from their home in Hull. This was wretched for us both, because having been abroad for so many family events he had counted on being with us; but Elspeth brought their fourteen-year-old Peter in his place. Many friends gallantly made the journey from Rugby, the Army and Oxford, from Hurst Green and Chatham, from both Limpsfield and Chiddingstone

Afterwards we embarrassingly heard that Willie Gladstone,[30] with whom I had rowed at Christ Church, had his car broken into in the Cathedral 'car park', one of three vandalized that night while the service was going on. The owners were all very good about this maddening inconvenience, not having realized beforehand that this was a regular occurrence in that part of the city. The waste ground of those days, where worshippers tended to park cars just to the south of the cathedral, has since been imaginatively developed residentially. To Rosemary and me, moreover, the local culture was still strange enough for neither of us to appreciate that it was not wise for her to be the unaccompanied driver of the last car away from the cathedral, with four children under fifteen on board, in the dark, at ten o'clock at night. Dick Watson and I were scooped up by our respective bishops after the vast building had emptied and we had finished greeting people at the west end, where queues had formed to speak to us; but to my shame I had not checked carefully beforehand what would then happen to Rosemary and our four. She had to get tired children out into the empty car park, with one steward thankfully helping her (he was horrified that she was by herself), and then drive through hardly-known streets two or three miles to Woolton. However we all got in one piece to Bishop's House, where the Blanchs could not have been more welcoming, and made staying there a great experience for our four as well as Rosemary and me.

The next morning we six headed off on holiday to the village of Askham near Ullswater, where we had very kindly been lent a cottage, for a lovely week together, before Rosemary and the children went south; it was cold but sunny, the boys sailed the 'cadet' on Ullswater, we climbed the fells, and it was a thrill to see that the pull of the Lake District was beginning to get hold of our two eldest sons. The timing of the change of schools was too complicated for us all to move together into Martinsfield, and anyhow the house was being done up, so Rosemary went south to hold the fort in Chatham while

---

30. Now Sir William Gladstone Bt. KG, of Hawarden Castle, Clwyd.

I lodged for the summer term in Grassendale with the Cottons. Vere was a famous Liverpool figure then, with a stint as Lord Mayor behind him, an elder statesman with an unparalleled knowledge of the city. Every Saturday he would plan a tour for us to take together in my car: it might be to the Walker Art Gallery, or the University, or the Cathedral itself, he was an expert in so many fields. These conducted tours were a superb introduction to the totally new environment in which I found myself. During the week he would always wait up until I was in at night, rarely before 10.30 p.m., when he would have ready for me the unlikely mixture of beer and Dundee cake, which he was convinced was exactly what I needed as a pick-me-up, and I was too scared of this fairly formidable eighty-year-old to say him nay. He and Elfreda (equally formidable, but like Vere with a heart of gold) could not have been kinder to this upstart of a young bishop, their junior by a generation, and I shall for ever be grateful for the way they rose to Stuart's inspired suggestion that they should put me up for this initiation period. I was glad to be able to get back to Liverpool some years later to take part in Elfreda's funeral, by which time she had passed her hundredth birthday; less than a year after that, and much more sadly, we were in the cathedral again for the funeral of their eldest son Henry, who was diagnosed with terminal cancer just as he was getting into his stride as Her Majesty's Lord Lieutenant for Merseyside.

My first confirmation was before the end of the month, at Mossley Hill, and my first ordination in St Helen's in May. Whatever I was doing the faithful went out of their way to make this southerner ('with that funny accent', I overheard someone call it at a reception quite early on) feel at home; Merseysiders are a warm people, and I felt happy in the parishes from the start, despite that BBC pronunciation of mine. My office in Hanover Street was in Diocesan Headquarters, half an hour from home through Bootle; but my inherited secretary, Margaret Boyd, a motherly laughing widow, whose home was in Formby, often came to me in Martinsfield to save me going into town if I knew I was later bound for the parishes to the north.

So where best to head for over the novel question of family church-going? Every new married bishop has that one to sort out, more particularly if he is a suffragan; diocesan bishops' wives for the most part have a cathedral on their doorstep. But for the first time in fifteen years of married life, Rosemary did not have the obvious solution of taking our growing family to my church, for the simple reason that I had not got one. We made an immediate decision that it would be quite wrong, for the children's sake, to go with Rosemary and me to a different church every Sunday. Instead (after a little bit of shopping around, with good music an important criterion in our search) we opted for Holy Trinity Southport, a convenient twenty minutes away to the north of Martinsfield. There was an outstanding parish church choir of men and boys, a fine organist, and a flourishing congregation. The incumbent of whom we became very fond was John Davidson, formerly a regular soldier, commanding a battalion of the Border Regiment in action. His thinking had moved during the war, very much as mine had, towards ordination as a practical way of saying thank-you to God for survival, and as a tiny contribution to helping to build a saner God-centred world. Holy Trinity is a large Victorian building with a moderate catholic tradition, and Canon John, as he became during our time there, was absolutely right for it. Before we left, Janie had been prepared for confirmation by him, and while Julian had been confirmed by Stuart in Bickerstaff (a planned choice of church through me), I confirmed Janie in Holy Trinity. Rosemary and the children were very happy there, and we kept up with John in retirement near Penrith, his old regiment's recruiting area, until his death.

Almost equally as easy to reach as Southport was Woolton, where the bishops of Liverpool had lived from the creation of the see. One of my first ordeals that summer of 1970 was the meeting of Rural Deans in Stuart's home. Stuart and both the very good archdeacons, Eric Corbett for Liverpool and John Lawton for Warrington, set enormous store, I was swiftly grasping, by the Rural Deans. Never having been one myself was a distinct disadvantage. To watch Stuart and his archdeacons handle RD's Meetings was therefore important for me, and I learnt much. Thirty years on I could write a longish paragraph on each of those Rural Deans without difficulty. As the new suffragan, it was my privilege then to join in the day's work; hear how things were going in the two archdeaconries, share any new diocesan or Lambeth-led policy, listen to suggestions and try to help over problems. I grew to look forward to those meetings, which went on for five hours or more, including much informal talk over elevenses and at a sit-down lunch laid on by Brenda. The RDs themselves thoroughly enjoyed coming, I soon realized. It was a pattern Rosemary and I were to copy gratefully in Somerset, with the addition (where they were free) of the Lay Chairmen of each deanery, who were by then playing an increasingly large part in the life of the church.

Meanwhile it was very satisfactory that the twenty years of having found parish visiting such a marvellous part of a priest's life merged, almost without my noticing it, into experiencing the same thing, less concentratedly, in the two hundred parishes of a small diocese. I say 'small' because Bath & Wells has three times as many parishes as Liverpool, so in Somerset a bishop's visiting is less concentrated still. The task of a suffragan, as I began to see it, is very much to mind the shop, since the diocesan is frequently away on central affairs of church and state, and also in Stuart's case because he was so much in demand to speak in other parts of the country. I was glad too to be a solo suffragan, because it meant that I acquired some knowledge of the whole of the diocese, together with its parishes and clergy and people, in a way that two or more suffragans can never do. 'You'll find it a rotten job being a suffragan' was the not all that encouraging comment I had from a disgruntled specimen of the breed soon after my appointment, 'you are neither one thing or the other'. That was never how the job struck me, nor I hope and believe the two successive Bishops of Taunton whom I appointed for Bath & Wells later on. A diocesan and a suffragan can work together in harness, the junior one perfectly and comfortingly aware that the buck ultimately stops with his boss, but free to take his own initiatives, make up his own diary, and try to help in parish or personal crises; often incidentally too to make mistakes that can be avoided in the future.

An attractive extra way of meeting people leapt to mind while I was studying the one-inch map one evening. I saw that the Leeds-Liverpool Canal lay through fifteen or more of our parishes. 'I'll walk it over five or six days,' I exclaimed to Rosemary, 'coming home each night, not doing it consecutively, wearing a cassock, carrying my staff, and taking the dog; and I will invite clergy, churchwardens, anyone who would like, to meet me on the towpath as we cross into their parish boundary and walk their patch with me. Nor need they stop off when the towpath takes me on into the next parish, the more the merrier and there'll be some worth-while inter-parish fertilization.' That is exactly how it worked out: we were never more than a dozen or so men women and children (plus dogs), and we either brought a haversack lunch or sampled the beer in the old bargees' pubs. The little 'reception committee', as we hove into sight on the tow-path towards the next parish boundary, was such fun and always different in its make-up; old friendships were renewed, and I had a great chance for informal conversation with probably a hundred people all told. The local press loved it of course.

Indeed it began to amaze me how bishops are news. It is almost as though cub reporters want to help spread the Gospel. Some I know do. More realistically of course most men and women of the Press simply find it intriguing that these men who live in palaces actually do some work, and I have always found reporters' general attitude friendly, especially if you take the trouble to ring them up from time to time to tell them what is going on. Some journalists of course only want the salacious stuff, but the best of them are genuinely keen to cover senior churchmen going about their business. Those tow-path walks were ideal for them; they would get some scribbles for the notebook as well as a good picture or two.

Ecumenical (or, as it tended then to be called, interdenominational) activity began taking up more of my time. To initiate a means of getting to know the Methodists after the Church of England had snubbed their readiness to come together in a formal reunion, I decided to ask the Methodist Chairman, a delightful Manxman named Rex Kissack, if I could join a Circuit or two, and thereby simply be notified (as visiting ministers and local preachers are) as to which church I was going to on a Sunday two or three months ahead, and (so important for Methodists) to choose the hymns. It was generous of the Chairman, roughly the bishop, to agree, and I carried the plan out once a quarter for five years. It was a fascinating honour to be in charge of a Methodist Church service, not it needs to be said in total charge because the preacher has to recognize the key function of the lay deacon, who prays lengthily in the vestry before the service, welcomes the preacher, gives out the notices and generally emphasizes, simply by being there, that this movement begun by the anglican Wesley brothers is primarily a lay one. I loved those occasions; often pressed to come more frequently, I had to remind my Free Church friends that I was actually being paid to be a Church of England bishop.

Only once was I temporarily floored. I had prepared a twenty-minute sermon, longer that the ones I preached in our own churches, so when sermon-time came (mostly the deacon sits beside the preacher in those capacious pulpits) I duly preached it, felt I had held the faithful reasonably well, and sat down. There was a long pause. Then the deacon who should have been giving out the next hymn rose slowly, and I suddenly sensed ominously, to his feet and said: 'That was a very interesting introduction by the bishop. Thank you most sincerely for it', and he smiled in my direction, so I smiled back. But he went on: 'The text my friends is . . .' and proceeded to give those long-suffering souls twenty minutes more of the best. I went red with embarrassment, as I noticed quite a few of the people in the pews did; but afterwards in the vestry and at the church door nobody referred to the debacle, though one or two went out of their way to be more effusive than ever in their gratitude for my visit.

But that one incident in no way detracted from my enjoyment of the five-year-long experience. In particular I came to appreciate how much of Methodism is bound up with hymn-singing; only those boisterous and devout congregations do justice to for instance the great hymns of the Wesley brothers and of Isaac Watts, who between them account for a quarter of the eight hundred in the *Methodist Hymn Book*; and as for 'O for a thousand tongues to sing My great Redeemer's praise' sung to *Lyngham* (which was actually composed by a Baptist), where in the third line everyone sallies forth in different directions, but miraculously foregathers in the last bar of each verse, I never fail almost to take off with Wesleyan fervour myself. I can only say that, ever since all that work in the Redfield United Front in 1950s Bristol, I have loved 'doing church' with 'the people called methodists', and I treasure the MHB I was given on leaving Somerset in the 1980's, with the charming inscription 'in recognition of your excellent church leadership in our area'.

At the other end of the churches' spectrum I saw an increasing amount of the Roman Catholics. I had arrived in staunchly RC Liverpool only a few years after Pope John XXIII's momentous reign, and even in Liverpool the welcome thaw was beginning. The saintly Archbishop Beck was their leader, and Bishop Stuart asked me to respond to an invitation to Archbishop's House to open up the dialogue on what more we could do together; in fact more simply on what we could do, because we were not doing anything much. I shall never forget being ushered into the study of this holy and very traditional old man, well over 70 to my 50. 'Please sit down my dear bishop, I'm so glad you have come, because the Holy Father has told us we have got to be ecumenical, and I want you to advise me how we might perhaps start.' I nearly cried. That was the moving introduction to much fruitful endeavour, the most spectacular of which was the amalgamation of the two main teacher-training colleges, ours of St Katherine's (of which I was chairman) and theirs of Notre Dame, with Bishop Gus Harris as its chairman. The two diocesan bishops (Stuart for the Church of England, not I, as he had far more knowledge of the educational scene than I had) and the two Principals did many hours of negotiating, as this completely revolutionary idea was not easily achieved; but the four of them persevered, mostly due to Stuart's eirenic approach. It happened in the end, after a couple of years' work, and he and the archbishop led a memorable act of rededication.

After the formalities the top brass of clerics and students repaired together into the newly-furbished Junior Common Room bar for the first ecumenical drink. 'We thought' said the (student, of course) President of JCR, 'that it would be great if the Auxiliary Bishop (Gus Harris) and the Bishop of Warrington, our two former chairmen, both sank the first two pints', pause, 'in one gulp each'. Gus guffawed cheerfully, his ample frame revealing that a good deal of beer was not unfamiliar to him; I had always enjoyed a drink or two, but had never attempted a one-gulp pint, that is with no pause for breath. But we were both clearly on our mettle, so 'Yes' had to be the reply, and 'Yes' we did it, mine a little after Gus's, but both, said our laughing and critical audience, passing muster at the challenge. We were thereupon presented with inscribed silver tankards to record, not the one-gulp feat (in case we had not done it), but a lot more significantly the new era that was dawning that night. Hope Street, the road running between the RC and the Anglican cathedrals, lived up to its name that evening, which proved to be the catalyst for co-operation in a wide variety of ways.

For example our home in Great Crosby was only half a mile

across the fields from Little Crosby, which has been a village of 'the old religion' ever since the Reformation. In other words Queen Elizabeth I's troops never penetrated 'the mosses' thereabouts, so to this day the church is an RC one, in the presbytery next door lives the local RC priest, the squire belongs to the very old catholic family of the Blundells, and all his houses in the village are let to catholics. Rosemary and I became great friends of Brian and Hester in the Hall, and I had some good days' shooting with him and his syndicate of friends, out on those self-same 'mosses'.

At Martinsfield itself, Stuart came early on to dedicate our eight-seater chapel of St Martin, which we had created out of an unwanted coal-hole. When we needed extra seating we overflowed into the covered yard, off which the chapel was. On one occasion we got twenty people in for the confirmation of Brigadier Sir Douglas Crawford, a leading but unassuming figure on Merseyside (again a splendid shooting host; I often tramped his woods and fields within sight of the great tower blocks of Liverpool only fifteen miles away). We got to know Douglas and his sister Mrs Jessie Little, a devout anglican, who kept house for him, very well. He had been chairman of Crawford's Biscuits, and was our widely-admired Lord Lieutenant, a lifelong member of the Church of Scotland, and a keen Territorial Army soldier. His regimental padre in the war I knew had been Eric Treacey, who by then, thirty years on, was Bishop of Wakefield.

When Douglas told me he had decided he would like to be confirmed in the Church of England, (partly so that he could honourably behave like the Queen, who is Church of England in England, but Church of Scotland north of the Border), he asked me if his old friend Eric might confirm him. I rang Eric, to get a characteristically robust reply: 'You ask if I would cross the Pennines to confirm Douglas; I can only say that I would cross the world for my old Commanding Officer'. So to Douglas's intense pleasure his wartime brother-officer made the easy journey across the Pennines one Saturday morning; Eric confirmed, Stuart celebrated Holy Communion, and I assisted. We were a bit cramped, but bursting with joy in that tiny special place, for what was certainly the chapel's most significant event in our time; small and unheralded, the confirmation meant a great deal to all concerned. Afterwards Rosemary and I gave a celebratory lunch for Crawford friends and relations.

I soon settled for Matins only in our little St Martin's Chapel, after more than twenty years of saying both the offices in church. I found it made sense to give up Evensong, as my new life meant that I was more times than not on the road by six o'clock in the evening for a confirmation somewhere, not to be home again until well after ten if I was lucky. So I reckoned the confirmation was my praying for the evening, especially as Rosemary and I were continuing our long-established practice of reading the Bible Reading Fellowship passage and (generally) its notes, in bed before turning the light out. More disciplined bishop-contemporaries somehow or other fit in evensong as well as their parish church engagement, often I think in the car if they are chauffeur-driven (which I was not). I love the office of evensong, so very anglican as it is, and it was always a delight when I met it on my rounds.

Since my job was to get round parishes, I was not in the cathedral much, but always loved it when I did take part in what was continually being organized in that huge space. I preached there several times a year, and soon appreciated Edward Patey's gifted leadership. He had inherited from Dean Dwelly the most unusual and greatly-admired Cross Guild, whereby former choristers join the Guild and so go on taking part in the life of the cathedral. Robed in striking gowns of varying hue (Dwelly was an expert in fabrics, and design of every kind), a dozen or more of the guild move purposefully about the cathedral for the Sunday services, acting as vergers or beadles or lay chaplains. Their unobtrusive presence is a much remarked-on feature of Cathedral life; and I do not know another cathedral that parallels the Cross Guild exactly; I certainly found nothing approaching it in Wells a little later on.

One year the Diocesan Youth Chaplain booked the cathedral for an all-night Vigil for World Peace, and invited me to look in, as I was getting mixed up in peace concerns, being by then chairman of a Peace Forum in the British Council of Churches. The occasion attracted hundreds of teenagers who, with their sleeping bags and thermos flasks and Bibles and notebooks, camped out all over the building. The Dean asked me to give the blessing to round it all off. I wondered if I could do this from the Bridge, half-way down the nave, and one of the more striking features in Gilbert Scott's massive project; I gathered it had hardly been used liturgically over the fifty odd years since that part was built. So I said to Edward that I liked the idea of blessing the assembly from the Bridge instead of doing so as a tiny remote figure right up at the High Altar. 'Great idea', he replied, 'but no one will hear it. There are no technicians around' (it was 6 a.m.) 'to fix up a mike there. Do have a go though.'

So I climbed the thirty or more steps with the Youth Chaplain, who had never been on the Bridge before. We stood there for a moment, gazing down at the praying, arguing, laughing, breakfasting or snoozing youngsters below. I interrupted them by clanging a bell for a couple of minutes, and began to see these scores of white faces looking up at us, wondering what on earth was happening, as nothing at all like this was in their carefully-crafted programme. I cupped my hands and shouted, very slowly: 'We are packing up. Well done to have spent last night arguing and praying about this funny old world God has put us in. Keep on at home what we have been doing together. Let's stand for God's Blessing'.

I repeated the gist of this, facing in four different directions, as the huge crowd started to cotton on to a good deal of what I was saying, and staggered wearily to their feet. The Youth Chaplain stood behind me so that he could cup his hands on either side of my mouth. With my shepherd's staff in my left hand and my right raised in blessing (a visual aid, in other words), I bellowed a blessing, again in four directions. There was a great cheer from everyone, which we heard afterwards meant that most of them had got the hang of what I was doing. Certainly many times in the next few weeks, as I moved around the parishes, that blessing from the bridge was mentioned, which more than made up for my sore throat.

Quite another group of young with whom I became much involved was through being chairman of St Elphin's School in Darley Dale on the other side of the Pennines. The reason for such an out-of-Lancashire activity was simply that this girls' school had been founded in Victorian times under the shadow of the magnificent spire of St Elphin's Church Warrington, to be a boarding establishment for the daughters of anglican clergy. The Rector of Warrington for historical reasons was still *ex officio* one of the governors, and the chairman, similarly, was the bishop, even though, once the growing town of Warrington began to be considered insufficiently genteel an environment for the education of these girls, it had moved lock stock and barrel to a large former spa hotel eighty miles away in Derbyshire. It was a situation which I challenged when I arrived, as it seemed to me crazy to have to flog off there several times a year, not to speak of having to shoulder responsibility for management. Stuart however gently asked me to take this on from my predecessors, at least to the extent of giving it a go for a year: 'I think you might come to enjoy this different kind of task', he sagely observed.

He proved absolutely right. Chairing governors' meetings, preaching regularly, taking RI lessons for the senior girls, discussing staff and policy matters with Miss Robinson, the brilliant headmistress, getting to know the other governors and considering possible new members, I soon began to enjoy myself. What is more, Rosemary came in for special occasions when VIPs were visiting, or for a black tie dinner, when the school would generously put us up overnight in the famous Pheasant Inn at Rowsley, near the top of the dale. St Elphin's soon became a valued part of my job.

Meanwhile, back in Liverpool from my forays into Derbyshire, I continued my growing links with the Roman Catholics, preaching in 1973 in 'Paddy's Wigwam', as Scousers affectionately call the catholic cathedral. That is an experience in itself, because except for a small segment where there are no benches directly behind the altar and sanctuary, the congregation sits all round you, so you have to try and bring everyone in by turning your head a good deal, without throwing the amplification system too much; this was of course before the days of clip-on microphones. I was there in connection with a major evangelistic drive, which the whole northern province held that year and named 'Call to the North': 'We want to speak the Word of God to this generation', ran our 'Call to the North' poster that Lent, 'and we want to do it together'. The new feel in inter-church relations, engendered world-wide in the first place by Pope John XXIII, and followed up in this traditionally-divided city of Liverpool by the Bishop of Liverpool and the Archbishop, became almost tangible in the mid-1970s. 'You're Better Together' was some years later the cry directed at Bishop David Sheppard and Archbishop Derek Warlock, as they were walking up to an official tape-cutting for some new flats which they were jointly opening; and they subsequently used it as the title for one of their books. But the beginnings, after four centuries of often bloody distrust, were made under Stuart Blanch and Andrew Beck, as David and Derek were always later acknowledging.

Ecumenical endeavour and actual progress were very much happening at parish church level too. One Good Friday I was asked to lead a great Procession of Witness in Walton in north Liverpool. Columns of the faithful (and you have to be faithful to do such a thing) wound their way from different starting points at the various churches, Methodist, Salvation Army, Roman Catholic, to foregather at St Mary's Anglican Church, where (thankfully in a fine Easter week-end) we were too many to get into the large quire and nave and galleries (would the latter give way through never being used? They held). Loud speakers had been installed in faith outside.

I was so moved by it all that, as the buzzing assembly quietened down, I did something which suddenly came to me: I gave, robustly over the amplifying system, 'Three Cheers for God', paused for people to grasp the rather unusual idea (to me as well as everyone else), and ventured 'Hip, Hip,' whereupon to my relief hundreds of people came thundering in with their 'Hoorays', which was a stout effort as they were not exactly expecting it. After a stirring service led by the various priests and ministers, a Salvation Army major asked if he could have a word with me. I feared the worst: 'I thought that start of yours was quite terrible ', he said, 'but by the last resounding Hooray I was joining in as loud as everyone else. Thank you so much'.

But most of the time of course I was confirming, or celebrating renewal of baptism vows, or blessing church extensions (once it was just a new floor and some lavatories), or sharing in a Patronal Festival or other special services where the Rector thought a bishop's *imprimatur* would be a good thing. These parish visits would be to the tune of two or three a week, and twice on Sundays. I loved them, high, low, middle-of-the-road. Before long I was asked to conduct prayer and planning week-ends for parishes, for which we went off to a conference centre in the Lake District.; a particularly happy one was for St Michael's Aughton, near Ormskirk. In the churchyards of both those fine parish churches many of my Lancashire forebears lie buried, so it was pleasing to lead congregations of Christians three hundred years later in the worship of God, and working out together how we could serve Him better.

I was never invited as a bishop to take a full-scale three-or-four-day silent retreat. I doubt if I have ever been holy enough. The only

one I have conducted was in November 1963; it was in St Gabriel's
Retreat House Westgate-on-Sea. The warden of it at the time had I
suspect been encouraged by Uncle Julian to ask me, and I rashly,
probably rather flattered, agreed. It was a general retreat for the
Canterbury diocese for twenty-five to thirty lay people, who mostly
did not know each other. We talked over supper on the first evening, as is the normal custom, and then after my first address the
company went into silence. The following morning everyone was
just going into (silent, of course) lunch, when the warden called me
aside: 'I think, Mr Bickersteth (never John in those days, strangely
to today's ears) you should know that President Kennedy has just
been assassinated. Ought we to tell the retreatants?' 'I'll come into
your office after lunch if I may' was how I played for time. We settled down half-an-hour later to mull over this world-shattering
event. We were sure that if we told them everyone would at once
want very naturally to talk about it, and some would head straight
for home; if we did not tell them we should be accused of missing an
opportunity for this dreadful happening to be prayed about for
three days by a group of Christians. We were totally at one in deciding not to tell them until our first 'talking' meal, namely breakfast
on the third day. As we expected there were then some pretty violent reactions, from 'How dare you treat us like small children?' via
'You never even brought it into your talks and prayers' to the
minority 'Absolutely right, thank you for a brave decision'. I
returned gratefully to parish life.

I was finding one important part of my new job as a bishop very
difficult: this sudden proliferation of preaching four or five times a
week, instead of only on Sundays for the last twenty years, was becoming a considerable strain. Then a friend passed on to me something I found immediately helpful, namely the advice of the
archbishop (then Michael Ramsey) that bishops would do well in
their sermons to work at a biblical theme for a couple of weeks, and
play around with it to suit the occasion. This proved my salvation,
and as a result the vital preaching and teaching element of a
bishop's task began to be very rewarding, instead of the relentless
burden it had fast been becoming in those early months. I started
doing what the archbishop recommended, choosing a text, writing
my sermon and delivering it, and then varying the same script to
the need of the next church I was to address, altering the illustra-

tions if necessary. I would then play around with the basic structure perhaps ten or more times until I got bored with hearing what I was saying, when I would scrap it and write a fresh sermon, sometimes even returning to the earlier one, if it seemed rather good. I believe John Wesley said sermons were generally better at the tenth delivering.

Only once was I caught out by an almost straight repetition, but that was in Bath & Wells days. There were two communion services fifty miles apart on the same Sunday, for which I had prepared a sermon on the gospel for the day, so I could use it perfectly well in both churches. The morning one was on the Mendips, and after lunch back at home I had driven forty miles to a small Exmoor church, where I repeated my message, very nearly word for word. Only as people moved to the altar to receive the sacrament did the penny drop that there was one man there who had been sitting under me in church eight hours earlier. We both came clean in the churchyard after the service, over a good laugh; 'I make this journey quite often', he said, 'as my aged mother lives here and it was my turn this week-end to come and look her up; so when I had said goodbye I dropped in to her church on my way home, not realizing you were going to be here. I'm so glad I did, as your sermon was much better the second time round.' That was really kind of him and the sort of personal encounter which make a bishop's job (in a rural diocese perhaps especially), so rewarding. I drove home a happy man, enjoying more than ever after a typically long day the sudden beauty of Wells Cathedral, as I rounded the particular bend on the Glastonbury road where I knew it would come into sight.

From Liverpool I was increasingly going to London; whenever I did, the five hours on the train from Lime Street Station and back were ideal for catching up with reading. Nor did I only go for work. Two London dining clubs were a delight: the first to which I was elected was the *Noblemen and Gentlemen's Round Catch and Glee Club* which met twice a year in the House of Lords, so I had eaten there occasionally for some years long before I sat on the red benches. After dinner we sang together, as the name implies, but we also by long tradition had the benefit of singing members, who belonged to the St Paul's or Abbey choirs; so they provided a professional touch to our making music more melodiously. Our president would invite one of us to choose a glee, or whatever, from one of the three or four ancient tomes put out in our places by the secretary; these had belonged to the club for two centuries or more. We had some wonderfully civilized evenings, especially the Ladies Nights, when Rosemary was in her musical element, in full alto voice with these top singing men from the choirs. The other club I was nominated for about then (and I still belong to it as a supernumerary, which means younger members are not kept out) is also of eighteenth century origin: *Nobody's Friends*, the name deriving its title from the modest name by which our founder called himself. He was a Mr Stevens, who 'unswervingly advocated sound religious and political principles', and the society he started has consisted from the start of an equal number of clergy and laity. We dine in the Guard Room in Lambeth Palace, and only make a speech on election to the club, when we have to 'justify our presence as a nobody', or later make a brief acknowledgement if we are greeted on receiving some honour or award. After all-male membership for two hundred years the first two women to be elected, after a major revision of the rules, justified themselves memorably in November 2004.

Martinsfield was proving ideal for our own entertaining. We gave dinner parties for twelve or more, and had buffet suppers for twenty-five to thirty clergy and their wives. In the summer everyone would spill out on to the terrace to eat and drink, in the winter we had fires in the three reception rooms where there was plenty of space for sitting around. More often than not, I would end those evenings with Compline in chapel, cramming into the covered yard as well as St Martin's itself. This was generally a new experience for some of our guests, particularly the wives; most of the priests had got to love this late evening service in their theological colleges. Two or more garden parties each year enabled us too to invite larger groups from the community; we had a specially happy one for all the Guiders on Merseyside, most of them saying they had never had such a thing happen to them before. Another year we got the four or five industrial chaplains for whom I was responsible to invite on our behalf men and women from both shop-floor and management in 'their' businesses; this was far more a venture into the secular world than the Guiders had been. Industrial chaplaincy was started in Liverpool during my time, under the leadership of a fine parish priest in Warrington, Canon David Stephens, who was also incid-

entally one of the best fly-fishermen I have known. He suggested
that Brother Ronald of the Society of St Francis was probably the
man to launch it, and he was right. I was able to acquire funds, and
we took on a house in Wavertree for Ronald to have as a base.

'Would you feel a Franciscan friar could come into your works
every so often,' I had asked several managing directors of big
Merseyside firms, 'to meet people and maybe help them with practical problems from a Christian perspective?'. Without exception
the bosses were very doubtful indeed, but because I had brought
Ronald with me for the appointment, and he had such an immensely attractive personality, they all agreed, from the MD of
Littlewoods downwards, provided it was not more than once a
month. So into these bleak factories (I recalled my brief foray into
the engineering works in Hurst Green) goes this eccentric, deeply
spiritual layman, wearing his brown habit, totally unabashed at the
challenge.

After a bit I began to get phone calls: 'Bishop, you remember my
agreeing to allow this Franciscan to come into the works not more
than once a month, if my foremen were happy about it?' 'Ye-e-es', I
replied, feeling my way. 'Well, the foremen are all saying could he
come more often. Shall we say once a week?' So there indeed in the
making was a good garden party list, almost entirely made up of
people who had no connection with any church anywhere.

Work in London gradually proliferated. My first major involvement in the central affairs of the Church of England was in 1972,
when I was asked to serve on a Working Group of the House of
Bishops to 'advise them on the formulation of a scheme for the
fairer distribution of manpower'. Our brief was nothing less than
the re-deployment of the clergy, a revolutionary idea arising from
the need to bring to an end the free-for-all recruiting by the forty-
three dioceses of the diminishing number of ordained men; inevitably for many years the richer dioceses and livelier bishops amassed
more clergy. Gordon Fallows was invited by the archbishop to chair
the Working Group; he was Bishop of Sheffield, so according to
custom the name of his diocese was attached to our final report.
There were also in the group one other more senior bishop, three
clergy, one layman and one lay woman, plus two very good full-time
secretaries seconded from their central church work.

It took us eighteen months from December 1972 to produce 'The

Sheffield Report', and none of us could have guessed how that single word 'Sheffield' would go on reverberating through the deliberations of the hierarchy up and down the country from that day to this: 'No,' says the Archdeacon of Somewhere, at a staff meeting in the Diocese of Hereabouts, 'if we go and appoint this priest to the Longish Team of parishes, we shall exceed Sheffield. We must forget it, unless we stop having a full-time man in Smalltown and save one clergyman or woman there'. That was how things began to go in 1974, and so they go on thirty years later. It still amazes me that our little ten-some started this major change in the way the Church of England works; but the nettle simply had to be grasped, as two examples from the dioceses I know best can easily show: thickly-populated urban-dominated Liverpool had 316 clergy in 1973, and we recommended that it only dropped five (down to 311), while sparsely-populated mostly-country Bath & Wells with 374 clergy in 1973 had to set itself to lose one hundred and nine men (down to 265). Because this was such unpopular stuff, the triumph of Gordon in carrying the recommendations through the General Synod in May 1974 was all the greater. We had much enjoyed working with him; and for me there were strong family vibes as I walked in to Lambeth Palace through Morton's (15th C.) Tower for every meeting. Father had known the archbishop's London home extremely well in the early 1920s, which was when, as I have mentioned earlier, I often came with my mother to play on the great lawns at the back; father was frequently in and out then, on Jerusalem matters, when Randall Davidson was Chairman of the Mission. What he and other of my various bishop forebears[31] would have thought of that same building being the scene of the ruthless drawing up of a deliberate plan to share out fairly the many fewer clergy, when they had all had a seemingly endless supply, can only be guessed at, but I like to think that they would have approved of the eirenic acceptance by both provinces of the Church of England of what we ten representatives of the bishops and clergy, on a 'beggars can't be choosers' principle, were recommending more than a hundred years on.

Meanwhile my own work under Bishop Stuart was beginning to draw to a close, in that when he and Brenda got back from their 1974 holiday they had a letter from No 10 Downing Street inviting

31. Robert (Ripon) 1870s, Edward H. (Exeter) 1880s, Edward (South Tokyo) 1890s

Stuart to leave the diocese of Liverpool for the Archbishopric of York. He was well aware of the strong (and basically correct) rumours that three or four men had already refused the offer to succeed Donald Coggan in charge of the northern province; Donald's long reign there was over, as he had just been called to Canterbury after Michael Ramsey retired. Being the person Stuart was, with a simple creed that you listened to God's call, mediated through fallible men and women, but none the less frequently discernible as the real thing after you had humbly prayed about it, he and Brenda said their prayers.

It cannot have been easy to leave a diocese where they had I am sure realized that in eight years Liverpudlians had taken them both completely to their hearts; everyone ate out of Stuart's hand, from the crusty but immensely able chairman of the Diocesan Board of Finance to the street kids of Liverpool 8, past whom he bicycled down hill every morning to their welcome shouts (and his chauffeur collapsed the bike into the back of the official car for Stuart to be driven back to Bishopscourt). But now, still at the height of his powers, he felt because he had been asked to that it would be right to use them more widely, and his decision to go to York was bound to affect me, because I knew that his successor, whoever it was, would want sooner rather than later to choose his own suffragan, as Stuart had chosen me

David Sheppard,[32] at that time Bishop of Woolwich, was to be Stuart's successor, and it fell to me to introduce him to Liverpool at a great service in the cathedral during the summer, almost immediately after which I left England for my first overseas assignment as a bishop. I was sent to a Partners in Mission Conference in Malawi, and very excited I was at the prospect, though the whole idea was considerably marred by the conference falling in the middle of the summer holidays, to Rosemary's and the children's undisguised dismay; 'but of course you must go'.

The idea of P.i.M. arose out of Lambeth 1968, and in essence it was that we should try to break away from the paternalistic approach to 'Foreign Missions' by expressing the truth that at home or abroad we were all partners in helping to spread the good news of Christ. To that end English dioceses began to be linked up in 'Mutual Responsibility and Interdependence' with the younger ones,

32. Later Lord Sheppard of Liverpool, of West Kirby, in the County of Merseyside.

which they had mostly founded round the world. It was a great thrill for me to make my first visit to Central Africa, a long way further south in that vast continent than I had been on my Sudanese preaching tour twenty years earlier. Transported from Inverness Airport (the family was on our holiday in Wester Ross, so flying from and back to Inverness meant the least interruption to it), I was ensconced in a flash in Chilema Conference Centre, not far from Lake Malawi, for what was the start of an enthralling three weeks. One Sunday, conference members had a memorable day off on and around the lake itself, lunching on the shore among the fishing boats at Malindi, after bathing first in what the locals still called Livingstone's Lake; later two or three of us were strolling along the water's edge when who should emerge from a thatched mud hut but Susan Varah,[33] who was then in office as the vivacious worldwide President of the Mothers' Union, and so was in Africa on a different exercise from us. Such encounters are great fun, I have found many times since. We all kissed, to the huge hilarity of the small crowd of fishermen: 'so you know each other then?', they laughed through our interpreter, and were very surprised that all English people seemed to be friends.

A carload of us also had the unusual chance of diverting off the route back to Malindi to take John Undulu, a young highly-educated African on our conference, to see his aged great grandmother. We bumped across the bush, not on a road, for three or four miles in order to reach John's home village, and on arrival were invited to bend down and enter the dark hut where the old lady lay on her wood-and-string bed, sick, toothless, but smiling as Africans generally are. We talked through John for a few minutes. Outside, we stood in the scorching sunshine on the dusty area between the ten or twelve huts of this typical small village; he had played on the neatly-swept baked mud there, when he was still at the mission school, whence he had got to university. John must have suddenly become conscious, not I am sure for the first time, of the unbelievable gap between his neat grey-suited figure and the traditional home where he had been born in that timeless village. 'If you like' he said to me confidently, eyeing my camera,' you could take a photograph of me outside my birthplace, and give it the caption De-

---

33. Susan's husband Prebendary Chad Varah was Rector of St Stephen's Walbrook, (1954-2004) and Founder of the Samaritans.

vclopment'.

'Are you sure that's all right with you?' I asked, because I dreaded any feeling that he might regard this as a condescending thing to do, even though he had suggested it.

'I would like you to', he said, 'my great grandmother has never met a white man before, and she is really excited, so you must send me two copies'.

This of course I did, and I have never forgotten John's humility in sharing with us that telling example of the colossal change which formerly subject people have been through, in at the most two generations. We were a thoughtful carload as we lurched the ten minutes back to rejoin the 'main' road.

From Malawi I flew up to Zambia to stay with a missionary doctor friend in Lusaka, where I celebrated Holy Communion in the modern Cathedral at the invitation of the (still white) dean whom I knew slightly. My host, at lunch the morning I arrived, asked me when it came to dessert whether I would like a banana. 'No thanks very much' I said, seeing there were none in the fruit bowl. 'O come on' he replied, 'I'm longing to show off', so we went into his small garden where he put his foot against the green trunk of a ten-foot high tree, and pushed hard, whereupon the whole tree fell over and he cut a bunch of bananas from near the top of it. 'They grow so quickly here,'he explained,. 'there's the young tree beside it, and with the parent now out of the way I'll be picking fruit from that in a year or so.'

From there I went on by air to see Ian Bickersteth, a sixth cousin, and indeed head of the Bickersteth family, in Southern Rhodesia, and stay for a few nights in his and Pat's home in Salisbury (today's Harare); he was a District Commissioner in the colonial service, as Ted had been back in the Sudan of the 1950s; and it was disturbing to hear how fearful they were of the inevitability of change. Not long afterwards he was having to fight in the so-called Liberation War, where there were no less than 30,000 black and white casualties, a little-known figure among the astronomical war statistics of our generation.

From the Jumbo back to Heath Row, I transferred to a Scottish aircraft, which dropped me down from my eye-opening African trip on to the grass runway at Inverness, where I spotted Rosemary waiting for me as we taxi-ed in among the rabbits to the portacabin 'terminal'. We did not draw breath on the 50 mile drive to Poolewe, where we made for the same beach from which I had said goodbye to the family three weeks earlier; there were our four 'messing about in boats' (they were 18 years old then, down to 12) and we had a wonderful reunion, after I had lost out on a considerable part of our summer holiday.

Before I left England I had been booked by Derek Pattinson,[34] to tell the House of Bishops about the Central Africa Conference. It was most unusual for a suffragan to join the diocesans at any occasion other than once a year in October, when every serving bishop is invited by the archbishop to come to Lambeth for morning and afternoon meetings, with a merry lunch in the middle. I discovered from Derek that Michael Ramsey wanted to hear at first-hand how this particular PiM Conference had gone; so as Donald Arden, the Archbishop of Central Africa who had been the able chairman of it, did not want to cost his province the expense of flying him home specially, I was deputed to stand in. I was nervous at being welcomed to the diocesan bishops' gathering in Church House, with the archbishop in the chair kindly motioning me to sit beside him, as I was ushered in by Derek to face this sea of senior faces. I gave my spiel and then answered questions from the assembled company, all of whom were soon (how soon neither they nor I knew) to become my much closer colleagues.

Holidays had switched from the west country to Scotland after that 1970's one in Cornwall which had been arranged before we knew we were bound for Liverpool. In Scotland we began our series of holidays there (as with Kent and Norfolk and Cornwall, there turned out to be four of them) by renting a rather damp house at Aros Mains on the Isle of Mull. For three Sundays that first year I did the duty at the island's episcopal church in Gruline, where deck chairs had to be brought in from the big house to seat everyone, not a conducive aid to the parson as he tried to keep the congregation awake during the sermon. Michael and Judy Colman were the summer tenants of that house, having been introduced to us by Ted, who worked for Reckitt & Colman as their overseas director

---

34. Secretary-General of the General Synod 1970–1990
35. Later Sir Michael Colman, Bt., First Estates Commissioner, Church Commissioners.

for twenty years after leaving the Sudan. Michael[35] and Judy and our two families became friends, and we later stayed with them more than once in Perthshire where they bought a house, and invited us to shoot there.

After Aros Mains we had two or three holidays in what had been the butler's quarters at Glengorm Castle, right at the northern end of Mull, by then having upgraded our dinghy to Jeronimo, a Kestrel, which did the young proud for a decade, surviving many towings up and down motorways and innumerable launching places.

During the latter part of 1974 Piers, who had left Marlborough that July, began to work on the Glengorm Estate (we left him on Mull at the end of our holiday), and next year he moved to the Colman's farm at Malshanger near Basingstoke, where he further developed his skills in country ways. That summer of 1975 he applied for a place at Cirencester Agricultural College, which led to a very happy three years there. Julian had followed him to Marlborough, where he eventually became joint senior prefect; Janie was doing well at Merchant Taylors in Crosby, and Sam was at Holmwood, a Formby preparatory school one station up the Southport line from Blundellsands; he began as a dayboy, but later boarded as the headmaster wanted him to be head boy. Rosemary, with a bit more time on her hands, added to her regular commitment teaching the piano at Padgate Teacher Training College near Warrington and in Merchant Taylors by joining the team at the local Citizens' Advice Bureau. We were all therefore well settled, in our varied ways, by the time Stuart handed over to David Sheppard.

A fortnight after David took office in July 1975, I heard from Harold Wilson, who was then at No 10 Downing Street, with the nomination of me to be the next Bishop of Bath & Wells. I was enjoying myself greatly on Merseyside, but the idea of becoming number one undeniably appealed. Moreover I knew and loved Wells. Rosemary and I drove down together a few days later, and when we got back to Liverpool I wrote to the Prime Minister to accept the challenge.

Bishop of Bath & Wells

Before anything was created, He existed;
and He holds all things in unity.
Jerusalem Bible: Col 1.17

September mornings, when the sun's yet low,
And dew upon the leas
Makes brambles glisten and the mushrooms grow.
The Land: Autumn

'I KNOW who you are', this from a smiling stranger after church in the west of Scotland (it is mid-August 1975), 'you are our new bishop'. He had guessed right from seeing our photographs in the Somerset papers the week before, after which his family as well as ours had headed 500 miles (for him, less for us from Liverpool) north to the top of Loch Maree, whence we had all gone on the first Sunday of our respective holidays to the Episcopal church in Poolewe; there, in response to a last minute request from the churchwarden ('is there a priest in mufti here?') I had offered to take a chalice and help administer the sacrament. We could not deny the charge, and so it was that I met my first priest from the Diocese of Bath & Wells since the announcement of my nomination. It was a delightfully informal start to the considerable task of getting to know more than three hundred of them.

'Three hundred' that August meant for me the number of letters of good wishes which needed an answer. I did it before we got back to Merseyside, rationing myself to fifteen or twenty a day, so as not to spoil the holiday with overmuch letter-writing. In fact it was very much a labour of love, with the memories tumbling over each other from all the varying ways in which these kind congratulations were expressed, as they cascaded in from the astonished bicycling postman's bag. Everyone who had taken the trouble to pick up a pen to write to me was either a member of our large tribe, or a friend from one or other of my or our incarnations over the previous forty years, so the problem was not in finding enough to put into a thank-you note, but rather how on earth to stop writing a screed each time. Rosemary and our four would say that that still remains

difficult for me, and of course they are right because as my professor son-in-law charmingly, and I admit correctly, articulates from
time to time, I am a compulsive letter-writer.

We had quite exceptionally good weather that year for the north-
west coast of Scotland. Sailing, bathing, fishing, climbing, walking
the two springers and our game little long-haired dachshund blur
happily in both our recollections. It was our first family holiday
without our eldest, quite a break for any family, but we made a
point of having friends of Piers' siblings to stay, and we also looked
up other families we knew who were holiday-making up there for
huge joint picnics, so there was plenty going on. We came back to a
very good first visit to our new home *en famille*. Jock Henderson, the
fine bishop whom I was to succeed, was there in the Palace porch
with his wife Hester, to give us six a wonderful welcome. 'We can
only hope you come to love this place as much as we do', said the
bishop, 'I can hardly bear it that we are tearing ourselves away after
these wonderful fifteen years'.

By the beginning of September I was back at work in Liverpool,
embarking on that never easy period when you know you are leaving one job and, however hard you try, are half living in the next
one. David Sheppard was taking up the reins in the diocese he was
to serve for more than twenty years, and from the start he could not
have been kinder to me, as I grappled with my 'half-life'. I can only
say that I tried my best to go on working hard in those three
months, and indeed for much of the time I was so busy that I almost
forgot we were on the move so soon. But I shall always remember
DSS having the kindness to stand me down from the diocesan synod
in early December, as soon as the generous farewells and presentations to Rosemary and me were over. These had been arranged for
the very beginning of the day's work, in the school where synod was
meeting. After all the speeches David simply murmured in my ear
on the platform: 'Why don't you leave when Rosemary does?
There's no point in your ploughing through the next five hours
when we'll be tackling things which you won't be here for'. So we
gratefully left together, to (if it may be said) very movingly-
prolonged applause. That was my last contact with the clergy and
laity of the Liverpool Diocese, for whom I had developed a huge
regard, among whom I had made many friends, and from and with
whom I learned so much by trial and error as to how to be a bishop.

'I love that necklace', said the girl we knew well at our local Crosby garage one morning as I was filling up the car shortly before we left; she was looking intently at my pectoral cross as she operated the pump, and she added: 'can I get one anywhere?' In a profoundly new way on top of my twenty-year parish priest experience, I know that I 'got' from Liverpool, and I owe to Merseysiders, very much of my present understanding of the meaning and significance of the agony and the triumph of the Cross, constant evidence of the Resurrection in parish and diocesan life, and the continuing eruption of the Spirit in the life of both city and Church. I thank God for those warm-hearted Scousers, whose company we revelled in for five and a half years.

In the sometimes arcane ways of the Church of England, election follows the nomination of a new diocesan bishop. 'Election' is what the Dean and Chapter of the receiving diocese have to do, without even having been allowed the chance of giving a once-over of their new father-in-God; I hope this quaint and frankly dishonest procedure will bite the dust for ever during Dr Williams' tenure of the Archbishopric. The election duly over, I faced the ecclesiastical lawyers, to be 'confirmed'. This makes a lot more sense than the 'election' by the Dean and Chapter, for since the Church of England is by law established, and bishops have expressly to safeguard that law ourselves, and also to articulate it every time we put a new priest into his parish, it is clearly right for us to be reminded in our 'confirmation' that we are under that law ourselves. Traditionally bishops have for centuries been confirmed in the Church of St Mary-le-Bow in the City of London, but for me (just as with York Minster five years earlier) it was sadly out of use because of repairs, so the ceremony was arranged in the more mundane setting of the Chapel of Church House in Dean's Yard. Donald Coggan, the quite newly enthroned archbishop presided, as happily he had done in 1970 when he was still in charge of the Northern Province. But this time there were only six or seven people present, mainly wigged and gowned lawyers, and it only took ten minutes, after which I leapt into a taxi for the final hurdle, that of Homage to Her Majesty the Queen.

I happen to be the last bishop in the Church of England appointed in the old way, which I tend to call the 'lunch in the Athenaeum' arrangement. There used to be in other words a discussion among three or four key Church of England people (always men, and led by the archbishop of the province concerned) around two or three likely names, as a result of which the name they agreed on went to the Prime Minister for forwarding to the sovereign. That way of doing things had lasted on during the considerable innovation of there having been, since the 1920s, Prime Minister's and later the Church's own ecclesiastical secretaries. These two men, keeping careful lists of episcopal possibles, gradually came to exercise a sufficiently influential rôle to prevent the choice of diocesan bishops being solely just the Queen's and the Prime Minister's; for instance many of the Victorian appointments had been known as 'Gladstone bishops', while some were widely known to have been Queen Victoria's personal choices.

In my case, having become a diocesan bishop in mid-December 1975 I had lifelong tenure by about a fortnight, as after 31st December the ruling made two or three years before by the infant General Synod began to diminish extensively the key rôle of the ecclesiastical secretaries in favour of the brand-new fifteen or so strong Crown Appointments Commission. From 1st January 1976 the commission recommended bishops to the Queen, via the Prime Minister; and these new bishops along with all clergy had to retire at 70. Therefore in this year of grace 2005 I could still, perish the thought, be in harness.

From Homage on, I was the Bishop of Bath & Wells, so it was better to leave Merseyside where I now no longer belonged. On 16th December 1975 we drove away from Crosby, very happy home as it had been, to stay at the Priory in Wells for two nights while some semblance of order emerged at the Palace. This thirteenth century house at the bottom end of the town had recently been bought and done up by Liverpool friends of ours, Tim and Elizabeth Gregson, against Tim's pending retirement from the Royal Insurance Company. The Gregsons' typical (as we later came to see) generosity was quite marvellous, especially as it went down to filling their larder and refrigerator for the six of us for two whole days' stay, a really kind gesture which alleviated tre- mendously all the inevitable upheavals of a two-hundred-mile move, buying food to keep us going, and furniture-placing in a very different kind of house. So we did not lay our heads beyond the drawbridge until 18th December, with a large dinner party only four nights later for two families of old friends who could not wait to see where on earth we had landed up; Rosemary in other words was beginning as she meant to go on, filling that great house with visitors; we had an uproarious evening, as the guests included several friends of our young.

No responsibilities would come my way for another month, so after an acclimatising and carefree Christmas holiday, Rosemary and I headed off to Crete. We had had another between-jobs overseas holiday when we left Chatham for the North; that was to Tenerife, where we stayed in Puerto de la Cruz. This time we were also in a holy-named place, Aghios Nicolaos, and again we explored around by bus and on foot. The Minoan remains in Crete were fascinating, in particular Cnossos and Heraklion, and we had a trip by local bus through the high plateau of windmills in the middle of the island to the old Venetian port of Ierapetra, the most southerly town in Europe. It was a good unwinding week.

PALACE, CATHEDRAL, PARISHES, AND LONDON

I asked the seventy-five-year-old Prebendary Herbert Barnett, whom I remembered as Vicar of St Cuthbert's Wells when I was a student at the college, and my fifth cousin David Bickersteth, the youngest Bickersteth priest, who was twenty-five and had been made deacon the previous summer, to be my chaplains for the enthronement, on the bitterly cold eve of St Paul's Day 1976. The moving lay spirit behind the faultless organising of it all was a fine old soldier named Major Peter Henfrey, who handled the correspondence with parishes, the seating details in the cathedral, and the introductions to sixty people or more on my walk-about with Frank West, the Bishop of Taunton, which Peter put after the blessing and during the singing of Vaughan-Williams *Te Deum*. The Dean, Patrick Mitchell, later Dean of Windsor, was three years into his sixteen at Wells, during which he was to be for a whole decade the driving force behind the great task of restoring the Cathedral's West Front. I inherited George Newsom QC as my Chancellor ('I can't tell you how to behave, but nor can you tell me. We are pari passu' was how he neatly encapsulated our official relationship), so he and Bernard Pawley as Archdeacon of Canterbury, at the time quite one of the funniest priests in the Church of England, were in charge of the legalities. That archdeacon is the archbishop's representative throughout England for the installing of every diocesan bishop, and I was particularly glad that Bernard was then in office as he was a great friend of Burgon, and therefore brought in ideally my Canterbury background. As so many Wells bishops had done before me, I swore the oath of fidelity to the cathedral statutes on the book of the Gospels from the 15th Century Bishop Bekyngton's Bible, now in the possession of New College Oxford and brought from there specially for the occasion.

We had great music: Parry's 'I was glad,' the first of many times I was to hear the choir sing it in the cathedral, perhaps the most memorable for us being at Janie's wedding in 1985; the hymn 'Christ is the King' written by Bishop George Bell, one of my heroes, Vaughan Williams arrangement of the *Old Hundredth* for 'All People that on earth do dwell' (with of course Bishop Ken's Doxology; he was 57th bishop, Bekyngton 38th, myself 74th); Cyril Alington's 'Ye that know the Lord is gracious' to *Abbot's Leigh*, composed by Canon Cyril Taylor, again a Canterbury and Royal School of Church Music link which I much valued; 'Ye Holy Angels Bright' which I was to choose again for one of my farewell services in 1987, and Charles Wesley's 'Forth in Thy Name O Lord I go', to the haunting Orlando Gibbons tune, which I also chose in 1987 for the other farewell. Both those last two incidentally are also in the frame for our funerals.[36] Add to that enthronement feast the Herald Trumpeters of the Royal Artillery, which a member of the cathedral congregation, hearing of my Gunner connections, had kindly mustered to play fanfares at suitable points (was that a touch triumphalist, I have wondered since? I doubt if anyone regarded it as more than a stirring extra to the whole occasion); the Lords Lieutenant of Somerset and Avon, (the latter county then a short time into its brief existence), a dozen or more bishop friends (nothing to the twenty or thirty who turn out nowadays for these occasions), and last but not least the presence of ninety-three-year-old father, whom I made for, unscheduled, in the walk-about, to kiss to everyone's delight. He appropriately headed up all the members of the family; and as my cousin and dear friend Oliver Grace, who came with his wife Marjorie to the service, said afterwards; 'If ever there was a suitable moment for anyone's *Nunc Dimittis*, surely this is Cousin Monier's'. Father died in his own bed that July, and I shall

---

36. Rosemary and I revise these services every Remembrancetide

always be thankful that he lived to be in Wells that day and knew exactly what was going on. His cup must have been full that evening, as indeed Rosemary's and mine were.

Having preached in the cathedral then, I stood for the first time in the pulpit of Bath Abbey at Matins the following day, led up the aisle by the two churchwardens in morning dress, a gracious sartorial habit from the past which was only to last a few more years. Then I was in at the deep end right away: two nights in London for Bishops' Meetings, next day my first meeting of the trustees who ran the more public part of the palace; the following one, being introduced in the Palace to the sixteen Rural Deans; next morning eight days away at St George's House Windsor for the senior church staff course, booked long before but there could not have been a better moment to be on it; straight back to Diocesan Staff Meeting the following morning, with Rosemary presiding for the first of many such twelve-strong lunches; and that night my first institution of a priest to his new parish, with next morning the first of my whole-day parish visits.

It was to prove a not untypical two and a half weeks of diary, in which of course I leave out of account the twenty or more letters a day arriving in the post (against the half-dozen I used to get as a suffragan), together with the multitudinous phone calls and actual callers with which or with whom my two secretaries, both new, did their best to cope. The much bigger mail was something I initially found very difficult. Trained, and anyhow inclined, to answer letters by return, the large increase in the number and complexity of them was a major jolt. I soon gave up writing detailed replies; if one was really needed, I learned early on how to pass the query or the problem to an examining chaplain or an archdeacon. Where it was clearly proper for me to reply myself, a ten-line answer soon became the form, unwillingly but necessarily, so that the mail could be swiftly dealt with.

Every new diocesan plays in his own way the important task of getting to know the parishes and his clergy. Somerset, in which Wells sits not at all centrally, has nearly six hundred churches, and in 1975 the clergy serving them were responsible for two or at the most three, not the twelve or more which some are today. So the grouping of them for my visiting was much more a matter of going to meet the priest and his taking me to his church, or two or three churches; and the obvious way to handle that was by deaneries, with the Rural Dean working out my itinerary. There were twenty-three to get round; my first all-day visiting was on 11th February and my last on 9th July; so it took me five months, and I reflected after the last one that I had glibly reckoned to complete the whole thing in three. There were just too many other happenings to fill up the diary.

I loved those visiting days, which began with my driving out of the Palace at 8.30 a.m. and finished with my return by 7 o'clock, never with an evening engagement. I only drove myself to the first vicarage or rectory, thereafter following the RD's plan and being taken round entirely by each parish priest giving me an hour or two and then delivering me on to the next one. I made a point of praying with him in one at least of his churches, as well as talking with him in his study, and in two or three cases every day having coffee or a meal with his wife, until maybe 5.30 or 6.0 p.m. when the last priest would get me back to my car for the run home. It was exhausting but a lot of fun too, and over the years ahead I or they would often find ourselves referring to what we had done on one of those days. I asked them in advance not to call into their homes their key people, because this was an exercise to meet the clergy; but none the less I inevitably bumped in to a few churchwardens, church cleaners (a gallant breed, generally voluntary), flower arrangers or very occasionally the rector's secretary. I never incidentally forgot a parishioner of mine in Chatham, when he heard I was to be a bishop, saying at once: 'I know why this has happened, vicar, it is because you have a good secretary, and furthermore know how to use her'; an interesting exaggeration from a man who ran a large business very successfully. Hardly any parish priests had secretaries then.

How best to meet the key lay men and women up and down Somerset was a harder nut to crack than, as a priest, being a good visitor into people's homes in one parish. Some better bishops than I manage to remember the names of all their churchwardens, but with more than a thousand of them at any one time I only carried a very few in my head, and anyhow they were always changing; but it was certainly satisfying to be able to say, every so often, to one of these stalwarts: 'Bill, how super to see you again.' After Tim Gregson had become my (totally voluntary) Lay Assistant, he

helped me organize Bishop's Evenings twice a year, when we invited a hundred lay people to an evening in the Conference Room
of the Palace, with a speaker that was likely to attract them. We had
politicians and art connoisseurs and the Poet Laureate, no less, over
the years, all well-known people, and we asked mostly non-churchgoers to join us, generally but not invariably from among men and
women I had met on my rounds. Almost everyone used to accept,
and many told us afterwards that it was the first time they had set
foot inside the Palace, and they never expected they ever would. It
seems to Rosemary and me, having been able to use it for twelve
amazing years, that this ancient building and the large grounds are
an asset to the whole church; we never thought of it as just our
home; it was also the diocese's, the county's and indeed the
country's.

   For example one June Saturday Piers and Julian had a party for
about a hundred of their friends in our part of the house and over-
flowing on to the bit of lawn that was more or less private to us outside the drawing-room window; at the same time in the conference
room all day there were sixty or so in an orchestra from Southmead
Hospital Bristol, who every year made music in the Palace with their
friends for the pleasure of it; the Diocesan Committee of the
Mother's Union was using the chapel for a couple of hours over
lunch; while out on the main lawns all afternoon three hundred
uniformed small girls were having their annual Brownie Revels. In
other words the best part of five hundred people, from four
different organisations belonging or not belonging to the Church,
were able that day to enjoy a lived-in house and garden, which has
been the Bishop's home since Jocelin, appointed by the Pope in
1209 to be Bishop of Bath (there was no Bath & Wells until 1244),
got permission 'to build a house, enclose a park' (still in the church's
property, a lovely lung for townspeople to walk their dogs in), 'and
stock it with deer'. No deer, but we did once have six hundred and
fifty people in three marquees in the floodlit grounds, for a ball in
aid of the West Front Appeal; undoubtedly the fact of the event
being held within those fourteenth century curtain walls was a considerable draw, and it netted £4000 before dawn broke.

   The Bach Choir all had supper with us one night after their cathedral concert; Sir David Willcocks, their charismatic conductor
then, never forgot it ('a hundred and twenty to a hot meal, how did

you manage it so effortlessly, it has never happened in any other bishop's house', he used to delight in telling Rosemary); the Chapter-General of the Order of St John, of which I was a sub-prelate from 1977 onwards, came one year for the annual service in one or other of the cathedrals of England, with a big reception for tea afterwards in the palace. At tea we invited the six or seven members whom I particularly knew on Chapter-General to come round later on for a whisky, a simple thing they dined out on for years (they were with us from 9.0 p.m to midnight); a hundred and fifty naval officers from Bath joined us for their first-ever garden party at the palace; twice that number of mentally-handicapped adults and children and their wonderful helpers, belonging to the ecumenical 'Faith & Light' organisation, came over with me from the cathedral for a boisterous picnic lunch. There was certainly never a dull moment in the uses of this stupendous 'plant.'

The thirteen-acre grounds were extremely important to us. Rosemary and I arrived with very little idea as to how a large garden like this should be managed. The head gardener we inherited was knowledgeable, but idle, and sadly, after his lunch break every day in the nearest pub, he was generally drunk and incapable. In between times he was delightful, and took quite a shine to Rosemary, which suited us well, as nothing she asked was too much trouble. After some argument he had with a visitor (needless to say it was after his alcoholic lunch break), I was about to gear myself to sack him at the instigation of the Church Commissioners (one could see their point, as they paid him), when the very shaken under-gardener came rushing in one evening, when I was out, to tell Rosemary that his colleague had not turned up at the potting-shed at the end of the working day, and he had eventually found him unconscious in the vegetable garden, out of sight among three-foot high Brussels sprouts. They got him to hospital but he died that night of liver failure. We missed him in a strange way. His number two, Harold Carter, had to retire shortly afterwards with bad arthritis, but still gets around in his electric buggy; he is someone we always enjoy looking up, and the Wells friend after whom the young ask most keenly.

Advising us in the garden all our time in Wells was the Vice Lieutenant of Somerset, David Tudway Quilter, who years before had planted an arboretum and has a superb garden just on the edge of

Wells; he is a top-class gardener and was the perfect person to whom to turn on all things horticultural. After a failure of an appointment to be our new head man, we were lucky enough to engage a Scottish couple, Bob and Marguerite Caldwell; Bob had been trained in the Edinburgh Botanical Gardens, and was a very good plantsman. He had unaccountable 'grumps' every so often, which neither of us liked at all and used to tell him so; Rosemary would not talk to him at all when he was grumpy, and that generally shook him clear of them, as he was very fond of her; we both came to love him and Marguerite. They retired shortly after we left, whereupon, doing some voluntary gardening in the railway station flower beds at Bradford-on-Avon where they had gone to live, he died of a heart attack with a trowel in his hand. An eating apple he gave us for Beckfords flourishes, and is a good reminder of him.

But it was David TQ who was the moving spirit behind our establishing an arboretum in three unused acres of the walled garden, on which the city was casting envious eyes for an extra car park. 'How about your planting up that rough area, to mark the Queen's Jubilee?', suggested David, 'that will scupper any car park idea'. Rosemary and I jumped at it at once, the Church Commissioners gave permission, and David invited Mr (later Sir Harold) Hillier to come over from Romsey to plan the layout with us all. That in itself was a fascinating experience, to watch this renowned expert stride around with a fistful of canes, declaring as he thrust another one in 'We'll have an *Acer saccharinum* here, with a *Paulownia tomentosa*' (he paces on) 'here', and he did that thirty-five times over until our space was filled.

By the spring of 1982 we judged that this part of the garden was looking sufficiently like an Arboretum to be open to visitors, and we asked Julian's brand-new father-in-law Sir Dennis Paterson (Julian had asked him that morning if he could marry his eldest daughter Cecily, and been told he could) to declare the Jubilee Arboretum open. Cecily's parents had just flown in from Australia, where Julian had met his wife-to-be when they were both teaching at Timbertop in Victoria, so we were pleased for her parents on two counts, namely the honour to Australia of doing this for the Queen, and the delight of their daughter's engagement. Over the following five years Rosemary kept open with the ride-on mower the grass paths between the trees, and with everything properly labelled it all

looked quite professional by the time we left. Despite some miscreant climbing the eight foot high wall from Tor Street in the week
before Christmas one year, and sawing out the top of our *Abies
cephalonica* for his family's Christmas tree, DTQ's brilliant idea was
definitely beginning to come to fruition.

In the rest of the walled garden there were a dozen or so allot-
ments managed by the city council, with the smallest section re-
tained for our gardeners to have a greenhouse, and also to grow all
our vegetables and soft fruit, and very well on the whole successive
gardeners did it, partly because they had the time, through the
lawn-mowing being let out to contract. Below the Tor Street wall we
put two beehives quite early on. My beekeeping came about because
one of the gardeners picked up an old box against our wall one
May, only to discover that it was full of bees in a tight mass. A local
schoolmaster friend, whom I knew was a bee man, identified it at
once as a cast, in other words a small swarm. 'I think I can find a
spare hive', he said, 'how about your starting? These bees belong to
you now'. So we did, collecting second-hand gear easily enough,
and quickly mastering the basics, enabling us soon to acquire and
fill a second hive.

In good years we were spinning the combs twice, and totting up
maybe seventy-five pounds of fine quality honey. In fact in our
second year we won the novices class in the local show, on the
strength of which I was invited to the Horticultural Halls in Vincent
Square to speak and give away the prizes at the National Show.
Never can the VIP have been there under false pretences than I
was; indeed I knew I must confess to the assembled company that if
it were not for my schoolmaster-guru helping me with the changing
of queens, I would not have been capable of seeing round the
beekeeping year. That did not seem to worry the pundits, who were
more than a little chuffed to have a tame bishop on the premises for
their big day, and I went home to Wells with plenty of complimentary pots of the delicious stuff.

Rosemary and I mainly looked after the rockery, and the four
beds we created for the fifty roses we were given as a leaving present
from Liverpool, together with the flower borders round the main
lawns. We did this by giving a lot of time to the garden on my day
off; and I was also generally there with Rosemary for a couple of
hours on Sunday afternoons, between morning and evening en-

gagements round the diocese. I had a lot of fun laying false trails for Sunday visitors, who unprompted would come out with: 'So the old so-and-so makes you work on Sundays, does he?', or more frequently 'What's the bishop like, then?'. Every so often my sub-terfuges would catch up with me a year or two later when the same visitor to whom I had been 'economical with the truth' was drawn to Wells again, and made a point of having a cheerful go at me for fooling them. So we would go into the Undercroft for a cup of tea and a laugh together. I loved being around on open days, as again and again they gave me worth-while contacts with strangers.

Meanwhile we began to make some changes in the part of the palace which was used for functions, and had been worked up ex-tensively by Jock and Hester Henderson. I persuaded the Commiss-ioners to change the name of the 'centre block', the boring term which I had inherited, to 'Henderson Rooms', in order to mark their innovative work there. The local trustees, formed under a deed drawn up by Bishop Jock, agreed to fund our first resident Warden, a retired soldier named Major Alan Blair, and he soon became a familiar figure around the place. A bluff and friendly widower, he lived in the top flat, and looked after the fifty or more voluntary stewards who came in from the parishes and gave their time to be on duty in house and grounds during open afternoons. We re-organised the portraits (most of them not of a high quality, if the truth be told) into some kind of chronological order; and we commissioned two fine tapestries for the Undercroft by a Swedish woman, Marie Cecille-Major, which greatly enhanced, with better lighting, that 13th century survival of Bishop Jocelyn's first build-ing.

Furthermore, helped occasionally by our young, we pickled at least thirteen layers of white paint off the glossy white Tudor stair-case. It was very hard work and took us a year or so, at odd times, generally late at night. From what used to be the bishop's study before the 1947 reordering (when William Bradfield[37] and all his family moved out into the north wing only), we gave to the Blue School the largely empty deal shelves which had been against all the walls. We moved some of the better books into my study, and the Commissioners disposed of the rest, which were uncatalogued and undistinguished. We were in consequence able to uncover and pre-

---

37. Bishop of Bath & Wells 1946–1960

serve *in situ* under glass a few sections of green Victorian wall paper, and more importantly reveal some much earlier wall painting, in the process discovering two blocked-up windows, which against some expert opposition we and the Commissioners' architect decided to leave exposed; they had been sealed up for more than a hundred years. Finally we could then paint those original study walls, and hang some of the best portraits there, to create a much more interesting room for visitors, and also for my own staff use, or for the diocese or county to hold small meetings.

Beyond the ruined Banqueting Hall we established a sporting grass tennis court which did our family and friends well for ten summers or more. For the big front lawn we were approached in our first spring by croquet players in the city: 'Would we consider allowing some local enthusiasts to play there, if we keep it neatly marked out; and we would promise to look tidy ourselves, as we should be so prominent to people leaning over the gate?' The charmingly-worded request was irresistible, and so was born the Palace Croquet Club, its members always immaculate, the women in whites, and the men in blazers and white trousers. They actually became an added attraction to the general scene of peace and time-less tranquillity, however brutal the dispatching of opponents' 'woods' to distant corners. We also continued what must have hap-pened often over the years, namely outdoor theatre on the Banqueting Hall lawn itself; after a notable *Twelfth Night* once there was a large hole for weeks in the *Choisya ternata* where Sir Toby Belch had decided to eavesdrop on Malvolio.

'What a place for geese and duck, as well as your swans', com-mented a Wildfowl Trust staff friend who called one day early in our time there. By then Rosemary had started the small shop in the Undercroft, partly to use surplus garden produce; so the Commiss-ioners allowed us to keep any profits to purchase birds from Slim-bridge, and a knowledgeable master at Monkton Combe School became 'wildfowl adviser to the Palace'. Within three years of buy-ing both native and exotic birds, we had fourteen breeds of duck or goose on the moat, excluding the mallard and the swans. Our bantams even managed to bring off successfully some clutches of pintail and carolina eggs, after we had discovered the hard way that they were very bad mothers themselves. We lost occasional birds to foxes, but a regular fifty to sixty waterfowl on the moat became a considerable draw to local people, and several schoolteachers brought their pupils down in the lunch hour to study the less common varieties. One year we had twenty-five tufted duck alone; they were a particular joy to watch, as the ducklings dive within an hour or two of hatching, and it was delightful to see dozens of these balls of black fluff hurtling along below the clear water.

We had three Tenants' Dinners in the august surroundings of the Long Gallery during our twelve years; these were the men, with their wives, who rent Church Commissioners farms in the west of England. Long-service awards were given out in a convivial atmosphere by the First Estates Commissioner, then Sir Ronald Harris; he was a keen tree man, so at the height of the Dutch Elm disease which removed so sadly the magnificent English elm (for ever?) from our countryside he and I planted in the park on the morning after one of the dinners a *Sapporo* elm, which is resistant to the disease; it was a small conservation effort which pleased us both greatly.

Those farmers' evenings were a real joy; many of them churchwardens, all of them 'backbone of England' men, thoroughly enjoying themselves in an unfamiliar setting. We also once had a smaller dinner for twenty-five or so Somerset peers and MPs, who told us in their thank-you letters that it was the first time they had ever got together. After dinner Peter Nott, the new Bishop of Taunton, rather than I, led a discussion on current issues before Parliament; as a newcomer to the red benches (this was in 1981) I decided that a bishop not yet in Parliament would do this better, and very well Peter tackled it In 1985 he was made Bishop of Norwich, and I appointed to Taunton Nigel McCulloch, who was still in office there when I retired, but later had ten years as Bishop of Wakefield and in 2003 became Bishop of Manchester. Peter and Nigel were both much-loved and very effective bishops in the diocese, and I could not have asked for finer colleagues.

For a short time we had the pleasure of an episcopal 'extra' in the person of Bishop Jack Cunningham, who had resigned his see in Zambia in order to make room for a particular indigenous priest; he simply knew in his bones that he would be excellent in the post, and was proved to be perfectly right. Jack was keen to be an incumbent in the west of England, and having met him and been much drawn to him I was glad to be able to offer him the living of Mells. He began to do sterling work both in parish and diocese, but only eighteen months after he joined us sadly had a series of heart attacks and died. In his memory we launched the Zambia and Wells link, which twenty-five years on has become significantly valuable from both viewpoints.

I was very fortunate in my archdeacons: Peter Haynes was in office at Wells when I arrived, as was John Burgess in Bath, and I appointed Len Olyott to Taunton. I invited Ted Thomas to come to Wells when Peter left to be Dean of Hereford. In and through all the work that relentlessly came before us, we went on enjoying each other's company, and I went on valuing tremendously all they did as my eyes and ears. We were a staff meeting twelve or so strong, with the very able diocesan secretary, Michael Draper who was there most of my years, and the chairman of the diocesan board of finance, of whom I had two in succession. I inherited the long-esatablished John Hayward, and on his retirement I appointed Derek Satow; Crewkerne business man and retired admiral respectively; these two very different men gave themselves selflessly to hundreds of hours of voluntary work for the common weal.

'Bath and Wells, Bath and Wells? Beautiful diocese,' mused David Edwards, then Provost of Southwark, as I bumped into him one day in Victoria Street when I had come up from Somerset for Westminster meetings, 'really beautiful, and I bet you get some really beautiful problems'. He was right of course. I had learnt in Liverpool that a bishop's problems, as in many walks of life, never come singly; they were generally in threes, so much so that many times I found myself reflecting that there were two very tough ones to tackle and where was the third? It generally obliged. These teasers ranged from the vicar who could not keep away from the bottle and whose wife was at the end of her tether, via the churchwarden who had fallen in love with his fellow churchwarden's wife, to the fine parish priest whose male partner had just moved into the rectory to the consternation of the chairman of the PCC, to the incumbent who had wrecked everything by eloping with the daughter of the man who kept the village store, to the long-standing scandal of the rector's mistress living only three doors away from the vicarage; all these were actual crises we had. Quite rightly the buck stopped with the diocesan bishop, however much he might in certain instances share the burden with one or more members of staff.

Bishop Stuart Blanch, never a man to give overmuch time to worrying (he was far too full of faith for that), used to keep an 'Impossible' file, and it was widely rumoured that individual problems stuck there would be quietly thrown away every six months. I never quite reached that sense of detachment, or rather, because Stuart was such a gifted man pastorally, with an amazing ability to turn a problem into an opportunity. That was what again and again he did, getting his driver (he never learnt how to drive; 'my feet invariably landed up on the wrong pedal') to take him to the home where trouble was seething under the surface or sometimes in furious eruption. There (and more than once this was rehearsed to me by grateful people at the receiving end) he would sit down in the vicarage kitchen over a coffee, smile that unforgettable smile, and ask: 'Well what does the Good Lord say we should be doing about this one?' I tried to emulate him, and could quote instances myself of where an answer to that question did come through. All I can say is that these problem-priests and problem-parishes were in the tiny minority, and that I grew to love and admire the clergy up and down both dioceses as a result of my sometimes very close personal knowledge of them and their families. They were the first demand upon my time.

There was one major commitment which I did not have until 1981, when I became far enough up the seniority list to enter the House of Lords. This exceptionally long wait, due to fewer bishops than usual retiring during my first six years, suited me admirably, as it meant that for that first half of my Wells time I did not have the demands of the Lords taking me away from the local scene. Not that I ever felt when I got into the London train, always with a load of work to do on it before meetings and engagements there, that I was abandoning the parishes. In fact rather to the contrary, in that the wider scene undoubtedly rubbed off on my thinking and my 'doing', and I hope I did the nearer work better because of whatever I had to turn my mind to elsewhere, after I had driven to the station in Castle Cary or Bath *en route* for the big city.

There had been, as I have mentioned, concerns which took me to London regularly before we even arrived in Liverpool, let alone in Wells. In the mid-sixties I was elected to MECCA, not the holy city of Islam but at that time the acronym for the Missionary and Ecumenical Council of the Church Assembly; it was my membership of that body which had eventually taken me to Africa in 1975. After the General Synod started in 1970, MECCA became the BMU, the Board of Mission and Unity, and I joined it. MECCA and BMU's thrust was an important one. Its ponderously-named but significant late-sixties paper entitled Mutual Responsibility and Interdependence in the Body of Christ, or MRI for short, had a perceptible effect on the way the dioceses and gradually the parishes began changing their inherited approach in missionary concerns of 'us to them'.

As I had written, and have quoted above in the *Rochester Diocesan News*, 'Missions' were at last becoming 'Mission', whereby both 'we here' and 'they out there' are all engaged on it for Christ. It was not an easy change for the old school of missionary, or for missionary organisations generally; and of course we did not all become fully 'interdependent' partners overnight, except in the important area of prayer for each other; in that area giving and receiving could and did quickly become, really for the first time, a mutual 'responsibility'. Monetary gifts were, and still remain a generation or more on, a different matter, because of the obvious disparity of income between the west and the developing world. '10% of PCC income for the wider church' began to be taught about then, and hundreds of parishes up and down England have practised that level of 'away-giving' ever since.

The whole concept of the proper stewardship of money in church affairs was slowly beginning to filter across the Atlantic during those years, and like many junior members of the hierarchy I attended a number of conferences about it. There was fire in the belly of the leading advocates of this new idea, revolutionary to English anglicans, who from time immemorial had been used to putting small change into the collecting bag; I can clearly remember in Oxford days tussling in my conscience, God forgive me, over whether to give a respectable half-crown, or would a florin do? In country parishes everyone knew that the squire would cover any shortfall at the end of the financial year. The 'new' teaching of proper stewardship sought to do away with that kind of thinking for ever, and a very slow struggle it has been these thirty or forty years since the idea of proper stewardship began to spread. With Hurst Green's fairly major campaign, which we called *Extending our Church*, behind me as an incumbent, and now finding that Bath & Wells, rural old England at its strongest, was much too relaxed about giving, I got a group of clergy and laity interested in a plan which we called *The Standard*.

A first-rate priest who was Vicar of North Petherton, Brian Whiting, a disciplined no-nonsense catholic, made himself totally familiar with the scheme I was hoping to get across, and ran it enthusiastically from his parish base. Before long we were able to share it with several other dioceses, some of them becoming more successful than we were in going for a standard of '5% of your net income after you had paid your taxes and kept a roof over your head'. This was naturally inadequate in the opinion of those who practised tithing, but the view taken by the committee was that it was a start. Our logo was an apple, with one 'pig' (which was roughly a twentieth of the whole apple) cut out to indicate that you gave that pig to the church before you began consuming the rest of it, and this proved quite an eye-catcher. Doing it this way meant that parishioners were more kindly disposed towards a new standard involving a major increase in their giving practice, than if we had gone for unequivocal teaching of the Old Testament tithe, as a minority of anglicans gallantly do. Maybe we were wrong, but we certainly cut ice with more people because of this approach.

Brian was indefatigable in travelling round the diocese on 'Standard' business; the apple lent itself to lots of amusing 'variations on a theme', Adam and Eve and all, but Brian presented it so attractively, and relieved me of a great deal of work over the whole project. So it was distressing to many of us that, shortly before one Christmas Midnight Mass, Brian was attacked in his church porch by a drunk who could not be restrained until the vicar himself (Brian was previously an SAS officer) landed him a punch on the nose. In the process Brian cut his knuckle slightly on the man's front teeth, causing untreatable poisoning to set in from some of the intruder's blood getting into Brian's hand and so into his blood stream. The hospital told me after he had died that in fact what killed him was called AIDS, the terrible killer of which no one had then heard; the man he punched was in an advanced stage of this illness newly on the world scene, and Brian became ill very quickly. With increasing sadness I visited him several times in his vicarage and finally in hospital, and I shall never forget this weak and dying priest insisting to the ward staff that he got out of bed and dressed in his best clerical suit to receive his bishop, who felt about two inches high as we prayed together for the last time, a night or two before he went to his Maker.

Possibly because of *The Standard*, on top of *Extending our Church* years earlier, having got into the church press, I was elected by the Bench of Bishops to represent them on the Central Board of Finance. 'You may be on to something important on Stewardship, Johnnie,' said Ted with brotherly frankness, 'but have you really got much of a clue about money?' He was absolutely right, of course, but maybe I brought some parochial earthiness into the high finance. When some years later the CBF chairman had resigned (on age grounds) and I being by then vice-chairman had to present the annual accounts to a full chamber in Church House, Ted and a good many others were as amazed as I was that I managed it; mercifully there were no awkward questions for which answers had not been prepared by the staff, and I came through unscathed.

On top of the BMU and CBF taking me more to London, there was the growing amount of work from the RSCM and the BRF, the chairmanship of each of which involved up to five or six visits to town every year. The Bible Reading Fellowship had rather dingy offices in the Parish House of St Michael's Eaton Square, off Buckingham Palace Road, and perhaps because of their unprepossessing surroundings the morale of the organisation had become very low; sales of the daily *Bible Reading Notes* we had produced year after year, since Canon Mannering started the Fellowship for his Bristol parish just after WWI, were going steadily down, and our originally flourishing publications' department had also badly lost its way. Our secretary was due to retire shortly before I was going to leave Wells, so I asked Archdeacon Michael Turnbull,[38] whom I had recently invited to chair the executive committee, to see if it could come up with some radical proposals.

They began by recommending to the council the appointment of a young man named Richard Fisher, an ordinand with a year or so to fill in before going to theological college, to be the secretary for as long as he could spare, and see if he could get us turned round towards a fresh enthusiasm and more promising finances. He did that quite brilliantly, rescuing BRF from its faintly fuddy-duddy

38. Later Bishop of Rochester 1988-94 and then Bishop of Durham 1994-2003.

image, moving out of London to new offices in Oxford, widening the range of BRF publications; and now, more than fifteen years on, Richard has a big staff, and rightly see this work as the full-time ministry for the church to which God has called him.

The success story of BRF since my rather uninspired twelve years' chairing of it means a great deal to me. Father and mother had introduced me to bible reading after my confirmation in 1935, so I read the BRF passage and the notes at boarding school every night, often under some chaffing in various dormitories (not bullying; I never met bullying in five years at Rugby), and then in the army for nearly six more, including using them, to my batman's astonishment, in many different holes in the ground in Normandy after the invasion of France, and later in the heat of Central India, where the wartime paper they were printed on tended to go limp and tear easily. After that, keeping up the practice in my bedroom at Christ Church was easy. From going to theological college onwards I decided to maintain my use of the Notes, as well as taking up the practice, quite new to me as an ordinand, of saying the daily offices. The result is that I have now been an active BRF member for nearly seventy years, and I find more than ever that the rôle which the Fellowship sees for itself, namely 'to help people to grow in their Christian discipleship through regular bible reading and prayer, resourcing them for their spiritual journey', continues to be very much what Rosemary and I experience from using what BRF faithfully continues to offer us.

My work with the Royal School of Church Music was quite different, even though it too involved the regular chairing of a Council in London. I met Dr Gerald Knight in Canterbury in the 1940s when he was the Cathedral organist there and later Director of RSCM; Gerald was a friend of Uncle Julian of course (KJFB had joined the cathedral staff in 1942), and it was the two of them together, I am sure, who were responsible for my joining this increasingly influential body, and being elected to the school's council while I was still a young vicar. Because our founder Sir Sidney Nicholson had been the organist of Westminster Abbey, we were allowed to meet where he began it all in 1927, in the abbey's little-known Jerusalem Chamber, an historic setting which RSCM has been very fortunate to be able to use ever since. Lionel Dakers took over from Gerald, and when he knew that he would need a new chairman before long he gave me a good lunch at the Garrick and twisted my arm. Inheriting the Council in 1977 from a fine musician in the person of Ted Roberts, then Bishop of Ely, I relied from the start on the behind-the-scenes help of Rosemary to stop me making too many musical gaffes. Actually, once the Council and other leading RSCM lights had heard her play Schubert *Impromptus* on the Concert Grand in the great hall of Addington Palace, Croydon (which was then our gracious headquarters), my personal credentials as chairman, even though I could not play a note of anything, were safely established.

The amusing and indefatigable Lionel was Director for all my eleven years in the chair, and we thoroughly enjoyed each other's company, sparking one another off in a satisfying way, although of course it was always LD who went on to do the work which we had mulled over together. He was a truly gifted leader in what he loved doing, which was the cheerful promotion throughout the Anglican Communion of the responsibility and sheer joy of making the best possible music for God in our worship. To see and hear him in action with sixty or seventy choir members from a rural deanery, practising for an evensong and then taking them through a service in which they were amazed at what they were capable of, was unforgettable, for them as well as me. But this versatile musician was equally at home in the Albert Hall, conducting a massed choir of eight hundred voices.

Our 1987 Diamond Jubilee Festival Service in the presence of our patron the Queen, in that incomparable setting, was almost the last act of my chairmanship. We had Archbishop Robert Runcie and Cardinal Basil Hume and the Reverend John Johansenberg, the leading Free Churchman of the day, there too, and just before the service six or seven of us foregathered in the Albert Hall Manager's office, where I introduced Rosemary and Janie to Her Majesty. We were able to thank the Queen personally for the privilege of the family often using the Royal Box when the Royal Family did not want it. Janie looked stunning in a suit of green Thai silk she had just brought back from one of her and Jonathan's visits there; she had finished making it specially the night before. She was 26, married two years earlier by me in Wells Cathedral with the full choir, so the Albert Hall was memorable for us all to share in the vastly extended torrent of sound that LD drew out of the combined choirs from scores of parish churches and some cathedrals, including our own. Lionel began the *National Anthem* with that stirring David Willcocks' introduction, as we all processed in, myself at the rear and on the steps leading down to the arena, where we all stopped and turned, bursting with pride in RSCM and our royal patron, to face the Queen in the Royal Box.

I suppose that bishops go in and out of cathedrals and parish churches more than most ordinary mortals, and I have loved experiencing music-making in both. There is plenty of encouragement there for the future; interestingly of course the music groups which are the norm now in evangelical churches hark back in many respects to the balcony music-making of Thomas Hardy's day, and (as then presumably) the best of them can and do encourage fine singing by the congregation. To join in a really good 'song' (and there are plenty, in among many banal ditties) in one of Piers' churches, or in St Nicholas Durham where Janie and her family worship, in both cases with strong groups providing the music, is now for me every bit as inspirational as being part of a big service in Salisbury Cathedral, with a thunderous noise from the organ reverberating round the building.

It is ordinations which particularly link the bishop and cathedral people with parish church congregations and non-churchgoers. There are firstly the candidates themselves, who after much preparation have reached this immensely significant moment in their lives; each of them probably bring twenty or more family and friends, among whom there will be a few keen Christians, but the majority will be men and women who have no link whatever with the church, but wanted to come and see in these secular days their relation or friend taking this extraordinary step of ordination, so had been glad to accept the family's invitation to witness it. On top of all of them the regular cathedral congregation turns out in force; but so also do members of the churches where the ordinand is either already a deacon now being ordained priest, or is being welcomed by them to join the staff of their church as a brand new deacon. Add again, particularly if it is high summer and the tourist season is in full swing, a small smattering of people on holiday who thought they were only going to look round the cathedral ('so nice to find this place is open on Sundays'), and are fascinated to come upon hundreds of people queuing to get in, so 'why don't we join them to see what goes on?'. The Church of England is therefore very much on show at ordinations, and they are great opportunities in consequence.

I must have ordained about two hundred and fifty men and women during seventeen years as a serving bishop. Mervyn Stockwood kept a meticulous list of all his ordinands, during twenty-one years in the teeming diocese of Southwark, where many more were ordained each year than we had in Bath & Wells; and he remembered them, to their intense delight, with a card and a prayer at special anniversaries like Jubilees. Much less creditably I simply rejoice every now and then if a priest comes up to me, or sends me a line about some other matter, and says 'you ordained me in 1975' or whenever. At my last ordination in September 1987 I had the satisfaction of making eight women deacon; but the admission of women to the priesthood was not agreed until the summer of 1992, when I was thrilled as a retired bishop to be invited to Wells for its historic 'first' that autumn; and a little later I was asked to preach in a Somerset church where one of our best 1987 women deacons was celebrating the eucharist for the first time since her priesting a day or two earlier.

To many of my friends' surprise at the time I had voted against the ordination of women at the General Synod's initial run at the new idea early in the '80s. I did not then believe that a rural diocese like Bath & Wells could have taken it; in other words, I acted (not for the first time or the last) as a representative, not a delegate. Many would say that I was too timid, and should have joined my bolder brothers in giving a lead in this controversial issue; and probably they would be right. Six years later, and after much more talk about it in the press and in the parishes, with a great deal of feedback to me, and explanation by the staff up and down the diocese, and not least after a lot of personal soul-searching, I had no hesitation in going into the Ayes lobby. What strength now is being brought by women, with their different outlook and sensitivities and skills, into the ministry of the Church of England, and the logical extension of this major change in how our church operates will lead eventually to the consecration of some of them as bishops.

If ordinations are in my book very much part of the wider church, reaching out as they do in their influence far beyond diocesan boundaries, so to a lesser degree are confirmations. I probably took about five hundred of them in the two dioceses, often for thirty or more at a time, so it is small wonder that again and again in unlikely situations round the globe men and women, often a very long way from their roots, remind me of my having confirmed them. As at an ordination there is a not-dissimilar mix of congregation, whether the service is in a great cathedral setting, or more often in a packed parish church: in other words there are some regular churchgoers belonging to that particular building, with apprehensive candidates to be put at their ease, proud parents, siblings, and slightly bemused godparents and other friends of the parents who may have little or no connection with a church anywhere. So getting the mood right was a constant challenge, which was one of the reasons why, after I had retired, I never really warmed to taking confirmations to help the Bishops of Bristol or of Salisbury, in churches which were totally new to me, and where inevitably I had no idea of the 'feel' of the parish, nor knew the parson and his people. This did not apply to confirmations in public school chapels which are quite different anyway from cathedral or parish church ones. While I never failed to enjoy the public school ambience, and the welcome to a scene that I was at ease with, the problem is that the bishop has got to try to lift the confirmation out of the school atmosphere, and link it to the boys' and girls' home churches, and to the world they live in; I know I frequently failed to do so.

These ordinations and confirmations I always saw as belonging to that part of a bishop's job which has effects far beyond his own geographical area. But on top of them, of course, are the many occasions when a bishop is asked to speak or preach at events which actually are outside his diocese. Obviously they are of varying importance, and he has to weigh up the value of these invitations and watch carefully the frequency of them, taking him as they do away from the area which he has been specially called to serve. One regular request was not difficult to accept: the Bishop of Bath & Wells is the Visitor of Wadham College, Oxford, and it never took me long to decide that letters of invitation from the dreaming spires, and specially from Wadham, should, other things being equal, be agreed to by return. Rosemary and I stayed several times in the college, and had some gorgeous occasions there, particularly in Sir

Claus (later Lord) Moser's time as Warden. His wide knowledge of music made for an immediate bond with Rosemary.

Often there were equally attractive one-offs: to address the Royal Agricultural Society at the eve-of-show service on the Stoneleigh Showground, an extremely impressive occasion with a band and choir in the arena and the main stand comfortably full, then walk all round the feverishly-working rural scene as hundreds of men and women put finishing touches into the small hours to their displays, before going on with Rosemary to a big dinner, and a night with one of the show officials; or to spend thirty-six hours in HMS *Ark Royal* as a guest of the captain, in order to gain an idea of the naval chaplain's job, and if possible recruit one or two 'really good priests' for the senior service. For this I was picked up by helicopter from the Fleet Air Arm Station at Yeovilton and dropped on to the flight deck of this huge new ship as she sailed down channel off the Sussex coast, *en route* for trials in the Mediterranean. It was a winter's night with half a gale blowing, and sadly I did not feel well enough to have what would have been a delicious dinner with the captain in his sea cabin. Better by the morning, I enjoyed taking the first-ever confirmation in the new ship's chapel. The chaplain presented three candidates to me, a rating, a petty officer and a young lieutenant; it was still quite rough so that I had consciously, with the great vessel's movement, to guide my hands on to their heads. We then had an exhaustive tour of most of the ship, followed by a happy lunch in the ward room, before I was slung overboard in a sort of breeches buoy contraption from one of the boat's davits. This dropped me down the towering side of *Ark Royal* (with not too hard a bump) on to the deck of a tug from Falmouth which was bouncing up and own alongside to collect me, amid rousing cheers from some of the ship's company lining the rails to see this great sight. We bucketed back to Cornwall, while the giant ship as she disappeared towards the horizon gave a whisk of her tail and set course for Gibraltar, saying goodbye with a loud hoot on her PA system. I did manage to recruit one of my clergy to the senior service a few months later, and he had twenty-two years of fulfilling service as a naval chaplain.

Several invitations came my way, as they do to all bishops, from the City of London of which I had become a Freeman in order to be chaplain to the Gunmakers' Company. One year I preached the

Spital (derived from 'hospital') Sermon in St Lawrence Jewry, and that invitation carries with it a night in the Mansion House for the preacher and his wife; the huge mahogany twin beds had their own bell ropes, labelled His and Hers. Sir Christopher Leaver was then Lord Mayor, the youngest at the age of 44 in living memory; he and Helen had toddlers, and they made sure that they all spent two or three nights a week in their own home, so that the little girls did not get delusions of grandeur through being handed their Ribena by liveried footmen off silver trays. We were back there for another night, equally agreeably, a few years later after I had preached at the Guilds Service in St Paul's Cathedral. For this all the gowned guildsmen from the Livery Companies entirely fill that enormous nave; quite a frightening responsibility I found it. Another year I preached for Trinity House in St Olave's Hart Street, to which I walked in procession with Prince Philip who is the Master; we were followed by twenty or more 'elders' in their admiral-like frock-coated uniforms. Lunch afterwards saw the men in the handsome conference room, while the wives were all, by ancient and I thought rather reprehensible custom, banished into a different dining-room, where they actually had a super time. Furthermore when we went to 'collect' them, they must, judging from their cheerful state, have had just as good food and drink as ours was.

So this kind of outside engagement, the lot of every bishop in some form or other, is great fun, provided, as I say, that he and his secretary are careful about rationing them. The London ones of course were easier to handle because one could generally fit in other things that needed to be done there. But I went to quite a few cathedrals for various occasions: my beloved Canterbury, to preach at The Buffs' annual service back in the 60s, before the regiment had had its second dose of amalgamation (we had already become the Queen's Own Buffs); the Friends' annual service in Hereford, where we stayed in the Deanery when Robert Willis, formerly a Rector of Tisbury, was dean before his promotion to the top dean's job in the Anglican Communion at Canterbury; Guildford, for the Gordon Boys School Commemoration, on the strength of my very modest Sudanese links; Winchester, to preach on the Creation theme at a special Harvest Festival; Exeter, because of my great grandfather's fifteen years as bishop there (I had been asked for a Hymn Festival, although he actually wrote *Peace perfect peace* while he was still Vicar of Christ Church Hampstead); Salisbury, the first time for the funeral of Archbishop Campbell MacInnes, formerly of Jerusalem, and a great friend of our family (his mother had been my godmother and I was a page at Campbell and Joy's wedding), and the second time for the final service of Wells and Salisbury Theological College in May 1976. Ted pushed father to that in his wheeled chair, as it happened only two months before his death. I also preached in Westminster Abbey, at the civic service for a new Lord Mayor of Westminster, who was a personal friend. For the sermon I worked on the theme of 'Render unto Caesar!' (Matthew 22.21) which I also used in St Paul's for the Guilds' Service.

A number of headmasters risked inviting me to preach in their school chapels: I went several times to Marlborough, where I was on the Council for thirteen years, and to many more, mostly schools with which I or the family had some link. My span of public school preaching, over thirty years or so, covered the transition period from compulsory to voluntary chapel, and by the time I retired very few of these schools any longer had one big service on Sunday attended by everyone, let alone the universal fifteen-minutes' daily service of my youth. One public schoolboy parent told me recently that the senior boy who cares admirably for a batch of juniors in her son's house said most sincerely to his charges at the beginning of term: 'I should certainly go for confirmation; it's real cool, and you get super presents'. *Plus ca change* . . .

In far and away the most important aspect of worship in church, my half-century in Holy Orders has seen major change over how the Church of England says its prayers: the ways in which clergy and laymen put together and conduct church services have obviously been so much my bread and butter these fifty odd years that it would be unnatural not to expand a little on this large subject here; if 'autobiography' means that the 'self' is 'writing' about his or her 'life', then I must certainly do so, as without question a priest spends a huge amount of his life preparing for and conducting worship in church.

I was brought up on the 1662 *Book of Common Prayer* of course, but '1928' as it came to be called was in wide use by the time I was conscious of such things. This post-first-war Church of England effort at revising the time-honoured Prayer Book words, passed by the

House of Lords but rejected by the Commons so never presented for the Royal Assent, nevertheless appeared in print with the enigmatic comment in the preamble: 'the publication of this Book does not directly or indirectly imply that it can be regarded as authorised for use in churches'. That seemed to be the signal for parts of the book to be adopted up and down the country, and the hundreds of congregations that began valuing it had no idea that the service was illegal. It quickly became popular in hundreds of churches which had got impatient with the straitjacket of the 1662 *Book of Common Prayer*.

For instance father, never a great one for innovation, used parts of it regularly when he was Rector of St Mary's Chiddingstone before the second war; and so did the school chaplains at Rugby, again hardly a hive of the *avant-garde*. In particular I remember how familiar became the revised 'Prayer for the whole state of Christ's Church' (with 'militant here in earth' no longer added); and there was the totally new and beautifully-fashioned:

> And here we give thee most high praise and hearty thanks for all thy saints, who have been the chosen vessels of thy grace, and lights of the world in their several generations; and we pray that rejoicing in their fellowship and following their good examples we may be partakers with them of thy heavenly kingdom.

Those cadences struck home to me wonderfully after mother's death during my Rugby years, and later on I used really to love saying out loud as a priest words that had woken me up in the School Chapel to the reality of the Communion of Saints. I generally reinstated the 'militant' phrase, which had been omitted in 1928, and added 'and triumphant in heaven', which had come into vogue and seemed to me to include both worlds felicitously.

So that was how things were for me liturgically through the fifteen years after confirmation, until I got to Bristol as a deacon in 1950. There in St Matthew Moorfields, as I have explained, I was introduced to a whole new way of doing things in church. Wells Theological College had indeed taught me that the old 'Sung Eucharist', rather suspect to a family like ours as 'too high church', really should take the established place of Matins, which was the main morning service in the vast majority of parishes, particularly perhaps country ones such as father's in West Kent. At that prime church-going hour it was, I was beginning to realize, Holy Communion, the one act of Christian fellowship started by Our Lord, which should be there, instead of simply being held at eight o'clock in the morning, attended by the keenest Christians, while most middle-class churchgoers went to Matins. Only 'the village' went to Evensong. How dreadful that statement of fact looks, set out on the printed page, but that was exactly how things were in the rural hierarchy of pre-WWII Britain, where the servants could not possibly get away from the big house on Sunday mornings, as they were busy getting lunch ready for the family's return from church. In the evening, however, 'the staff' were given free time specially to enable them to go, and they met their friends from the many other houses that were big enough to support even one maid. They would have felt uncomfortable at the morning service; at night they met their friends and relaxed.

None of this applied in the East End of a large city like Bristol. From his anglo-catholic background of All Saints Clifton, which he loved (and where his colourful funeral was eventually to be), Mervyn Stockwood had come to the conclusion during his curacy days in St Matthew's that the old-fashioned Sung Eucharist he had inherited there seemed totally irrelevant to everyone but its small band of devotees. Now that he was the vicar, he knew that he must change the style, the name and the words. It says a great deal for the bishop that he gave his enthusiastic endorsement to this controversial young man doing those three things, and over the third one without any doubt breaking the law of the land.

It was in that autumn of 1950, five or six years only into Mervyn's incumbency, that I began to get caught up in the refreshing spirit of the St Matthew's Parish Communion; he had written a booklet for the service, bound in a light green folder; no one had prayerbooks open, something that was quite new to me. Mervyn's service had the 1662 and 1928 words, considerably altered and simplified by the vicar, on the right hand-side of the page, and a lively commentary, in italics, on the left. For the next three and a half years that service became the centre-point of my life in the parish, exactly as my imaginative vicar was visualizing for every soul who came to that altar. There I saw for the very first time the true etymological meaning of the word 'liturgy': 'the people's work', expressed by the offering of bread and wine as representing both the labours and the recreation

of men, which Christ himself had chosen to be his supreme memorial. For the first time too I was appreciating the three-fold nature of
the eucharist: the taking, the blessing, the sharing. My learning
curve from Matins as the main morning service for Anglicans to
Communion (as the Mass has always been of course for Roman
Catholics) was a steep one, and a mind-changing experience for the
new priest that I was.

During those nineteen-fifties (and on into the early sixties) the
Church Assembly's Liturgical Commission was tackling the replacement of '1928' by an entirely new Prayer Book, rather than a revised
'1662' again, amid the growing realization that many lively parishes
up and down the land (most certainly not just St Matthew Moorfields) were taking the law into their own hands and experimenting
with new services which might or might not be receiving the sanc-
tion of their diocesan bishop. It is important for the nostalgic lovers
of 1662 to grasp that the creation of a new prayer book during the
mid-20th century was not the result of a few enterprising, still less
maverick, clergy during those post-WWII years spoiling for ever
'our priceless heritage' by indulging in change for change's sake;
the liturgical boys were hard at it for some years sorting out a mess
which had striking similarities to the total liturgical chaos there had
been in England before the 1549 Prayer Book (1662's precursor),
when the churches of the 'new regime' (i.e. the Reformation) were
all doing their own thing.

More than four hundred years later, therefore, while a Liturgical
Commission was again working away behind the scenes, I left the
excitement of St Matthew's worship for a parish of my own. I certainly missed the sheer enthusiasm of those services as I began to
make modest changes at St John's Hurst Green, which I knew perfectly well was a very different social mix from down-town Bristol; I
realized that in commuter-belt Surrey I would not get away with
what Mervyn had apparently so effortlessly achieved in a working-
class parish. So I judged that the best I could do was: a) to introduce
a fortnightly Parish Communion as the main morning service
rather than Matins, which was then reigning for three Sundays a
month, and b) to begin, before it, a Family Service, which rapidly
grew from scratch to being a hundred or more strong, using a booklet produced some years earlier by the same Bishop Woodward of
Bristol who had been, as Bishop George Cockin after him, such an

encouragement to Mervyn. The young families took to the simple Woodward service at once. It was not all that good, and needed to be played around with to make it eucharistic, but it served to bring in people whom I guessed would not have crossed the church's threshold if I had offered them the *Book of Common Prayer* or even 1928, whose status was anyway waning by then. As a result of that fairly major change, there were vibrant St John's congregations when we left in 1962, and my successor was strongly placed for introducing a weekly Parish Communion, and then using a few years later the first tentative efforts of the Liturgical Commission.

In Chatham I inherited an equally lively crowd which already had a weekly Parish Communion as a result of David Halsey's pioneering work, and they were using Series 1, which was the Commission's first venture (it was virtually 1928). Series 2, when it came out in 1964 or 5 was however very novel, much more akin to what Mervyn had been doing for fifteen years. I sounded out the Parochial Church Council on it, and had no difficulty over their agreeing to 'give it a go'. People liked it from the start, as they did in a steadily growing number of parishes all over England, and the little light blue booklets soon got dog-eared through use in thousands of congregations, albeit mostly urban or suburban ones. Series 3 was more radical still, and met with a lot of opposition because the whole shape and language of the service was markedly different, but again we had begun using it by the time I left St Stephen's in 1970, although with a higher proportion of grumblers than there had been over the start of Series 2.

During the nineteen-seventies the drafts of the Church of England's proposed prayerbook, based on the booklets which had been used by so many of us for the best part of fifteen years, followed in seemingly slow motion year after year for our debating in the General Synod chamber at Church House, until the long-awaited day came when the *Alternative Service Book* 1980 was published. It drew wisely and extensively on the liturgies of other churches, as well as making use of modern scholarship. Never intended to be the last word in liturgical revision, nor to supersede the *Book of Common Prayer*, I and the great majority of the clergy loved it from the start. The fine preface, an apologia for the *ASB*'s whole production, was written by John Habgood[39]; it is magisterial, and I wish that his

---

39. Bishop of Durham 1973-83, then Archbishop of York 1983–95

name had appeared under it, but perhaps rightly it was anonymous, as Cranmer's had been in 1549.

Particularly good in the new book, for example, was a stirring and stylish introduction to the Marriage Service; and a totally fresh approach to Baptism, including some excellent prayers. All this material began to commend itself to the clergy very widely, worthy as it was of Tyndale or Cranmer at their best. Congregations too, very naturally more conservative than their priests, really did make their own such innovations as 'Yours Lord is the greatness!' for the offerings of the people in the communion service; or the acclamations in the eucharistic prayer itself: 'Christ has died, Christ is risen!'; or the breaking of the bread with the words 'to share in the body of Christ', and the response 'though we are many, we are one body, because we all share in one bread'. The first 'After Communion' prayer, too, was becoming immensely liked: 'Father of all, we give you thanks and praise that when we were still far off, you met us in your son and brought us home.'; it was written by the New Zealand theologian member of the Liturgical Commission, Dr David Frost, who brought it (I was told) to a drafting meeting expecting the usual crop of emendations, but all round the table it was approved; and there it is now intact in the *ASB's* permanent successor, *Common Worship*.

Contributions of that quality made the *ASB* as a whole into a different book altogether from the far less congregational and more priestly 1662 approach; I defy anyone to make a serious case for writing off all the language of the *ASB* as trivial. The best argument against that charge is that many of the new words and phrases and their significance began, as I have mentioned, to find their way into the hidden life and liturgical 'feel' of thousands of men and women in the pews, and thankfully remain enshrined in *Common Worship*. This latter was the year 2000's final effort to revise our liturgy, promised by the Liturgical Commission after thirty-five years of work. Good as *CW* is, it is proving to be not so much a prayer book for the pews as a very useful resource book, together with its supplements, for those leading worship; and what we have now will be how the Church of England, officially anyway, orders its services for a long time to come.

My personal contribution to the final revision of the *ASB* (that is thirteen years before *CW*) was at the General Synod in York in July

1987, when I had put down a motion for the retention of the traditional *Lord's Prayer* alongside and as an alternative to the new one. My chief argument in making this proposal (and I would make it still) was that the *Lord's Prayer* in its traditional form was now the one prayer that the great majority of the population knew. Not to have it available at funerals and weddings, the only church services which 90% of non-churchgoers attend, was, I suggested, a recipe for still further alienation. The cheerful and stimulating debate which followed my speech included plenty of good arguing on either side, and everyone was inordinately kind to me, while at the same time pulling no punches; they realized it was my last public appearance before I retired.

The most amusing time came when after an hour or so the Dean of Carlisle rose to his feet. Everyone knew what he was going to say, because whenever this senior priest felt he had had enough of any debate he always said it: 'Madam Chairman, I beg to move the closure of this debate'. Standing Orders say that the chairman then asks the mover of the original motion before the house whether he or she supports the closure or not. I replied that I thought this would be a pity, as there were more people who wanted to speak from the floor, and also that everyone seemed to be enjoying themselves. For some reason that last throw-away remark brought the house down; and when the laughter abated and the chairman put the closure motion there was nothing like the quorum required for it. So we carried on, with a wise amendment brought forward by John Habgood, which only marginally affected the main motion. After a short further debate, the chairman put the amended motion which was comfortably carried. So the old Lord's Prayer stood, and stands still in *Common Worship*. Immediately after the vote, which was the last item in front of Synod that night, Archbishop Runcie, my friend since Oxford days, said his official goodbye to me, official but as always with Bob on such occasions lightly and charmingly phrased, on behalf of the Church of England. It was quite a moment.

Another major responsibility for a diocesan bishop outside his diocese is of course the House of Lords. On 26 November 1981 the Bishop of Gloucester, then John Yates, and I together got to the top of the waiting list and took our seats among the twenty-six bishops.

In the archaic ceremony (which included three times, or was it nine, doffing my mortar board to the Lord Chancellor) I was 'introduced' by David Say of Rochester (it had to be him) and David Halsey of Carlisle, my predecessor in St Stephen's Chatham. Several of our young were in the public gallery, fascinated by the proceedings, and trying not to laugh at their dressed-up father making his debut. At the end of the carefully-rehearsed mediaeval movements for every new member, the Lord Chancellor, remaining seated on the Woolsack, reaches out to shake the hand of the newly-introduced peer on the latter's way out, as he walks past to hand over the letters of credence. Their Lordships offer a low rumble of 'Hear Hear's, by way of a welcome; rather strangely, it sounds a very warm one. We had a family lunch in the dining-room beforehand, which I should have enjoyed more if I had by then had my ordeal.

Thereafter I ate frequently in the Lords, sometimes with guests; if you are on your own there is the admirable custom that you sit at the long table, taking the empty place next to the last peer or peeress who has sat down there, saying who you are as you sit down. I have had some enthralling meals beside well-known people because of that sensible arrangement. In retirement, bishops can sit on the steps of the throne to listen to a debate (i.e. not on the benches, and not uttering), and can use the library and dining-room and bar, which is more of a privilege than it was because, in rather petty fashion, the ousted hereditary peers can only do this on a limited number of days a year.

My maiden speech was on child care in the public sector. I built it up round a brief because the church needed to 'say something', and I was the duty bishop, so had to be there. Every diocesan bishop I have known has a conscience about not contributing more frequently to the deliberations of the Upper House. Their Lordships very much like the bishops being there, and indeed often comment to the one or two on parade how few of us there are present. But it is not because we do not enjoy being there, we do enormously; it is simply because of full diaries at home or elsewhere. The duty bishop is expected, as well as saying prayers every sitting day, to be in the chamber for part at least of the week's business. Without checking *Hansard*, my recollection is that I put down three or four questions, and made three or four speeches in my six years. On one matter not remotely of international importance I got quite involved, and that was through being a countryman: it was straw-burning.

As recently as the early eighties, the surplus straw from thousands of acres of arable land was torched after harvest. Farmers could not be bothered to go to the expense of baling so much more than they needed themselves or could easily sell. So from mid-July, depending on the season, all the rural acres of England, indeed of the British Isles, were smothered by billowing smoke, often dangerously drifting across roads. Great columns of the stuff rose into the clean summer air, depositing smuts over thousands of cottage gardens, on to people's washing lines and (the many fewer there were then) private swimming pools; and in the process, up into the stratosphere, went tons of carbon dioxide. The stubble was disfigured by blackened lines of ash, and millions of insects and small mammals died in the flames. The wonder was, looking back on it, that there were no major conflagrations, especially in dry summers, and that the outcry against straw-burning was so slow in coming, and even then was as muted as it was, being left to a private member's bill in our House. This was the only occasion that I gave time to working at the details of a bill. We were finally successful in banning the practice, in a very thinly-attended chamber late one night; so much so that when 'House Up' was called around 12.15 a.m. and I caught a taxi outside the Lords' Entrance for my club, the cabbie was so surprised to see this handful of peers coming out two hours later than usual that he asked if war had been declared or 'something equally nasty'.

There cannot be a Church of England diocesan bishop alive who has not appreciated the privilege of taking part in the affairs of state as we do in the Upper House. The whole experience is epitomized in my thinking by the prayers he takes every day before business begins. Never less than twenty to twenty-five peers and peeresses make a point of sharing in them, humbly kneeling down and turning round to pray at their red benches, and the Lord Chancellor doing the same on the Woolsack. He is a yard or two only from the bishop, who stands throughout. The latter can vary the psalms, of which there are three or four to choose from in the special folder he is handed by the doorkeeper; but the prayers themselves, from the *BCP* of course, plus a fine one for Parliament, are immutable. After prayers have been said, the television screens in the passages say as much, and for good measure the doorkeepers move along them calling out 'Prayers have been said'.

At my final Prayers before the summer recess of 1987, which I knew would be also my last appearance on the bishops' benches before resigning from the see and therefore losing my seat, I ventured to break this long-standing rule, with which I was perfectly familiar, that there should be no variation in the prayers. On that final afternoon, however, I decided to put a bidding in before the Grace, to the effect that we might all be blessed with refreshing holidays and be ready to return after them with a new determination to serve church and state in the next session; or words to that effect. When I had said both my bidding and the Grace, which indicated that I had finished, The Lord Chancellor, then Lord Havers in his rather brief reign, (he made no secret of not liking the post), got laboriously up from his knees, smiled and murmured to me before bowing to Their Lordships: 'I did like that extra prayer, where did you get it?' Within half an hour the Clerk of Parliament had rung Lambeth Palace to say that the bishop on duty had infringed regulations, and would the archbishop please make sure he was reprimanded and that it did not happen again. Bob Runcie ran me to earth late that night in Wells: 'So you have been a naughty boy, John; how very enterprising of you. I have told the clerk that that was your last appearance, and you would not therefore be making a practice of it; so there won't be a summons to the Tower. Sleep well'. The rule obviously makes some sense, as it stops over-enthusiastic politically-minded prelates loading prayers so as hopefully to influence voting; one can imagine for instance: 'Lord we pray for very wise consideration of the bill banning hunting before us this afternoon, and ask you to help us be tolerant of minorities.' But a bidding prayer for happy holidays, well really . . .

There were however few irritations like that. I always enjoyed how the particular could find a place among major national items, specially at Question Time. For instance I once gave notice of a question to the Secretary of State for Health as to what provision was going to be made for the long-term patients at Mendip Hospital (outside Wells) who were unlikely to be found homes in the community when the entire Victorian plant of this mental institution was shortly to be closed. It was a matter on which the local health authority could not make up their minds and into the bargain was being absurdly uncommunicative; in fact the Mayor and Council of the City of Wells had come to the conclusion that there was no proper plan at all. It seemed exactly the sort of thing I could raise in Parliament, so I put down my question and was as usual told approximately when it would be coming up, in order that I could make sure I was there. Having been called by the clerk, I stood to say the accustomed words: 'My Lords, I beg to ask the question standing in my name on the order paper'. A civil servant had got a good answer for the government front bench spokesman to give me by way of a reply, and I did not need to ask the supplementary which the questioner is allowed to put. In the corridors afterwards Lord Denning stopped to thank me for putting a purely local question; it had been followed by one on the reduction of the armed forces, far more important obviously in the national scheme of things. 'Local issues keep these chaps on their toes', he said to me encouragingly. He was quite right in this particular case: after my 'question', there was immediate evidence of a much better attitude towards these unfortunate people.

I had memorable dealings with Tom Denning over the misuse of byways by joy-riding four-wheeled drive monsters churning up these ancient tracks. Unfortunately it was legal because of a 1617 Act which allowed 'vehicular traffic' on them. Tom sensibly argued that vehicles then were farm carts. Only now, more than twenty years later, with so much damage being caused by this 'sport', does the anomaly begin to look like being dealt with, after our attempts then in the Wiltshire Wildlife Trust, despite Tom's great knowledge of country laws, had failed. He also agreed with alacrity one year to my request that he should unveil for our family the refurbished bust, then in the foyer of the Public Record Office, of our forebear Lord Langdale, 'my illustrious predecessor', says Tom, 'as Master of the Rolls'. Henry Bickersteth was the Master who had organized the building on Rolls land of the PRO in 1869 in Chancery Lane, and was in consequence something of a hero to this humble and immensely distinguished judge. He made a delightful speech after Ted had asked him to do the honours in a brief ceremony in the foyer of the PRO, where the bust was at that time. He then bore off our twelve-strong family party to a very good lunch in Lincoln's Inn, at which I remember Lord Hailsham looked in, wondering what the old man was up to. Tom was immensely popular and had time for everyone. He was a devout Christian; so I was rather sad a few years afterwards, when he died at the age of a hundred, to be the only robed bishop at his funeral in Westminster Abbey.

Among the few other senior peers I got to know quite well was the octogenarian Roman Catholic Lord Longford, *paterfamilias* of the large Pakenham clan; he lived to be 94. He came up to me one day having seen a snippet about Wells in *The Times*; it read: 'Bishop shoots tyrannical goose on his own moat'. I had indeed shot with much regret a fine (home-bred) barnacle goose one afternoon, because it had taken a liking to our carefully-reared exotic duck-lings and was busy drowning them all. Caspar, the best gundog we ever had, plunged straight in as springers unhesitatingly do, swam fast to the other side where the goose was dead, gathered up this heavy bird with some difficulty and paddled laboriously back, accompanied by the 'O my' of a passing American tourist. He was clearly so surprised to see a bishop doing such a thing that he went off to the *Wells Journal* and told them all, so I had a merry interview with the local reporter, who was a good friend, and a countryman to boot, and of course I had to agree to him using his piece; he enjoyed cashing in with a minor scoop to London.

Frank Longford, deep in a book about Anglican and Roman Catholic bishops, raised the goose story over lunch at the long table one day, and I felt we clicked. Perhaps his Church of England roots were saying things to him. We got to know each other, and I began to admire his ceaseless concern for the underdog, particularly for the prison population, and he eventually asked if he could include me as a chapter in his *The Bishops: A study of Church Leaders today* (Sidgwick and Jackson 1986), so we had several sessions over his notebook in the Lords' interviewing rooms for us to talk. I must have let him have the script of a recent presidential address I had given at our April 1983 diocesan synod, and he printed in the book the headings of it in his seven or eight pages about me. Reading them again twenty years after I made the speech, I remember it was not very well received because in an area like Somerset there was immense distrust of anything even vaguely pink in politics; indeed a retired major-general once walked out of a sermon I was preaching in a village church about loving your enemies. It must have been when I was chairing the newly-constituted (and long-since defunct) Peace Forum of the British Council of Churches. We had recently had Douglas Hurd (now Lord Hurd of Westwell, then a minister at the Foreign Office) staying with us after speaking at one of our Bishop's Evenings, and hearing in our drawing-room that I was chairing this Peace Forum he had kindly invited me to join a think-tank of his. At one of those FCO meetings I had voiced in a rather diffident way that maybe HMG should be thinking now how we should relate to Russia after the Soviets had vanished into history; this was some years before the Berlin Wall came down. Douglas, understandably in his position, allowed me (without saying very much himself) to be given very short shrift from the other ten or twelve people sitting round the table. 'It's all too far into the dim and distant future, Bishop', sums up Douglas, 'I think that is what our colleagues are saying'. All this is relevant to what Lord Longford wrote about me in his book (*op.cit.* p 98):

> In the bishop's speech he expressed his convictions under the headings summarized below:
> i. Pacifism is an honourable Christian way forward, but today it must remain an ideal. Nuclear war is in a different category from all other wars.
> ii. Nuclear weapons cannot be disinvented.
> iii. The unilateralist hope is a non-starter; there is real mileage in a nuclear freeze and in banning all nuclear tests.
> iv. All people of goodwill in the west must back the idea of negotiating with the Soviets.
> v. All inflammatory remarks about evil Soviet intentions are unacceptable.
> vi. Churchmen should give time to going to peace meetings.
> vii. CND has become too labelled politically as left-wing; its leaders should consider disbanding it and joining the struggling World Development Campaign.
> viii. We must all learn to be pro-active rather than simply re-active.
> ix. Have we not a major opportunity as a Church to unite our country in peace-making?'

I was rather disappointed that not a single comment, rude or otherwise, reached me by letter or phone after Frank's book was published; several of my points were anything but typical of bishops' views, Roman or Anglican; and it was another three years before the Berlin Wall came down.

Incidentally, whereas Frank had labelled the ten Anglican bishops fairly correctly as being Evangelical, Liberal or whatever, and the ten RCs simply as Archbishop or Bishop of this or that see, Frank described me (without prior consultation, I may say) as 'Bishop of Bath & Wells, bishop by tradition'. He was such a delightful man that I never held the sobriquet against him. Maybe he had a point anyway; it fitted to some extent with the teasing comment of the Archbishop of Canterbury in his farewell to me in York: 'Of course the bishop comes from a long clerical line, and no doubt the Bickersteth blood has turned a delicate shade of purple over the years'. Moreover while Frank introduced his Bath & Wells chapter in the book by calling me 'energetically serene or if the phrasing is preferred serenely energetic', Bob Runcie ended that same speech of his with: 'in the Bickersteth family every day is Stir-up Sunday'. Ah well!

Lord Longford was in fact only writing two or three years after Tim Heald in his *Networks* (Hodder & Stoughton 1983) had worked me in to his 'Happy Families' chapter, in which he engagingly expands on the way in which tradition seems to operate in some clans, quoting several service families, and for the church the Temples, Burrowses and Bickersteths. He says of the three bishops he cites: 'All three seem to have had a strong vocation which was initially over-ruled or at least threatened by the weight of the past'. In my case he refers to my strong feeling on leaving school that I wanted to spend my life in some aspect of rural work, a hunch I found being overtaken by the six years in the army, during which, as I have described, the idea of priesthood took hold.

Easily the peer I have come to know best as a result of being in the Upper House is Lord Sandford. It was actually John's wife Catherine whom I met first, because of our belonging together to the Church Army's housing committee in the early eighties, when I first got my seat. John is a few months older than I am, and had had fifteen years in the Navy during which he was twice wounded, and won a DSC. He retired in order to be ordained from Westcott House Cambridge, and had began his ministry in the St Alban's diocese as bishop's chaplain and ecumenical officer when he inherited the title on his father's death, and decided to go into politics full-time. Soon making his mark among leading Conservatives, he

became Under-Secretary of State in the Department of the Environment and founded there the Sandford Award for excellence in
heritage education. I used to love seeing him bounding up the
gangway between the red benches to take his accustomed seat in the
second or third row, unless he was answering questions or representing the Minister on the government front bench. I well remember staying with them in their house in Smith Square during the
Falklands War in 1982, when both of them were glued to the television screen.

Not long after that conflict he had an incapacitating stroke, and
has been confined to a wheeled-chair ever since. He cannot con-
verse, being only able to say the first word or two of any sentence he
begins; it then peters out, frustratingly for him, and he gesticulates
in the hope that you will grasp what he wanted to say. Wonderfully,
there is almost always laughter as you guess away, eventually leading to triumphant 'Yes, Yes'. For several years John came regularly
with me to Nobody's Friends, Catherine took him to the House every
Wednesday, where he joined other disabled peers and peeresses at
the bar of the chamber; and early on they often went off to friends
at week-ends. For their Golden Wedding in St Stephen's Rochester
Row seven bishops took part in a service for the renewal of their
marriage vows, and it fell to me to read with John and Catherine at
the chancel step the vows themselves, which of course John could
not repeat, and I was almost too moved to say his for him, just
before Catherine said hers. With the ousting of most of the hereditary peers, John lost his seat in the Upper House, to his great sadness, but Catherine reads the papers to him, they watch TV, his
mind is alert, and these two heroes are both very much *au fait* with
what is going on in the world, which they now see from such a
different, and (who is to deny?) a more sensitive and thoughtful
perspective. Along with many others, I love and admire them both
more than I could ever adequately describe; someone should write
a book about them.

Lord Hailsham, whose father had held the Great Seal before him,
became Lord Chancellor during my time. Much the most effective
bishop on the bench then was Gerald Ellison, the Bishop of London. Of course he had a huge advantage over practically all of us in
living so close, and therefore over his years as Bishop of Chester
and then of London he had acquired a very good working know-

ledge of how the House did its business. So I was rather thrilled to be asked to accompany him and one or two other bishops to discuss the possibility of a small change on the bishops' benches. Gerald made his case: 'Could not, in view of the exceptional contribution by one or two bishops in each generation of us, the bishops themselves elect one of their number to retain his seat for three or five years after relinquishing his see? To make room for him, the serving diocesans would be reduced by one, and younger bishops in the queue for entry would willingly have their entry postponed, so that the House would go on having the presence of a wise retired bishop who would suddenly have much more time to attend the chamber'. The Lord Chancellor heard Gerald out patiently. Then he uttered: 'Thank you my Lords for this most interesting suggestion, and for putting it so cogently this evening'. Gerald had set out our idea really well; and at that moment we felt, we agreed afterwards, rather encouraged. 'But the House of Lords' went on the great man, 'is a funny old place in my experience, and if you start tinkering with it, the whole institution could very easily all fall down. I'm very sorry to disappoint you. Good evening!' or words to that effect, so we left with our tails somewhat between our legs.

But there was another British institution which began to take a large amount of my time and energy for ten years from 1979, and this was the Crown. On 1st December that year, to the barely-disguised amusement of my family and friends, mixed indeed with a modicum of disbelief that such an office existed, I was appointed Clerk of the Closet to the Queen. As the sovereign does not leave Sandringham until some weeks after Christmas, I was not granted an audience so that Her Majesty could talk to me about the job until 12th February 1980. That day saw the start of a privileged decade for me in the Royal Household; and thankfully Rosemary also came in for much of its interest and excitement.

THE CROWN

During the early part of 1980 the news began to filter round the diocese of Bath & Wells that their bishop had an extra job. 'Is there really such a position in the late twentieth century?' was a common reaction as people reached for their copies of Gilbert and Sullivan. After I had resigned from it ten years later, Dr Robert Dunning, the Victoria County Historian of Somerset, and I wrote *Clerks of the*

Closet in the Royal Household (Alan Sutton 1992). Being the historian and friend he was and is, he had challenged me with the idea of writing it within a month of my appointment, but as he expected I put him off until there was more time. So it was not until 1988 that we met to plan things, and decided to split the necessary research down the middle; at his suggestion (for which I was very grateful) I took the easier later period from the Restoration onwards, while he tackled much the harder early part from, as he discovered, about the 1430s. I was probably the 55th clerk in those 550 years.

'The Clerk of Closette kepith the stuf of the Closet. He preparith all things for the stuf of the aultrez to be redy'.

So ran the regulations set down for the Household of King Edward IV in 1478. In other words the closet was the little oratory where the Sovereign could hear Mass; but in the field (sovereigns being so often on the move) the clerk still had to prepare the 'aultrez'. Probably the best-known surviving royal place to pray is in St George's Chapel Windsor, built one story up, so to speak, above the level of the sanctuary, so that the grieving Queen Victoria after Prince Albert's death could watch the service privately. As the centuries passed, the clerk often became the most intimate clerical friend the monarch had, and some very distinguished men held it, including four who went on to be Archbishops of Canterbury and four to York. In modern times the relationship of Randall Davidson, the clerk who was Dean of Windsor, then Bishop of Rochester, and finally Archbishop of Canterbury was a close one to the aging Queen. I happen to have been the first Bishop of Bath & Wells to have been made the Clerk.

Rosemary and I had seen for the first time the inside of two of the great 'official residences' of London, the Mansion House and Buckingham Palace, during our Liverpool days. In Sir Ian Bowater's year as Lord Mayor we were invited to his and Lady Bowater's 'dinner to meet the Archbishops and Bishops' in July 1970, when I had only been consecrated three months; and no small thrill it was to us both for me to get into my purple frock coat and all that goes with it. Rosemary looked gorgeous in a blue and green dress she had made (a favourite of hers and mine for many years), as we walked up the Mansion House's grand staircase lined by the Honourable Artillery Company gunners in their 17th century uniforms. Among them I spotted, with difficulty because of the anonymity of uniform, Mike Gilbert-Lodge, with whom I had been a fellow subaltern in The Buffs; he had joined the HAC after the war and was a keen territorial. Sure enough there he was, halfway up the stairs, (helmet, cuirass and all), standing stiffly at ease with his magnificently-accoutred comrades-in-arms, staring impassively, eyes front, except that he permitted himself a wink as Rosemary and I walked slowly up in the queue.

Our first Buckingham Palace Garden Party was in 1971; suffragan bishops in those days, perhaps still, are only invited every other year. It was very moving, I found, to hear the band stop playing and everyone falling silent as the Queen and the royal party come out of the building to the top of the steps for the National Anthem, while the entire company of six thousand or so guests, in a memorable two or three minutes, stands stock still, looking towards her from wherever they are on the lawns. Most years we would find there twenty to thirty friends or acquaintances with whom we were glad of the chance for a catching-up talk, but again you can engage well-known people you have never met before in a tea-tent conversation or while strolling about, as at any garden party. As soon as Janie was seventeen we took her with us (in continuous rain unfortunately); and in another we were invited to a special one, hosted by Queen Elizabeth the Queen Mother in the absence of the Queen in Canada, for four hundred and fifty bishops of the Anglican Communion and our wives. The scores of overseas ones were here for the once-every-ten-years Lambeth Conference of 1978, of which I was a member; we were meeting (for the first time since these conferences were begun in 1858) not at Lambeth Palace but at the University of Kent in Canterbury; a special train brought us all up to London for a great service in Westminster Abbey and for the Buckingham Palace Garden Party.

But my first visit there for an audience, as I have briefly mentioned earlier, was recorded as follows in the Court Circular of 12th December 1975:

> The Queen received the Bishop of Bath & Wells (The Right Reverend John Bickersteth) who was introduced into Her Majesty's presence by the Right Hon Roy Jenkins, MP (Secretary of State for the Home Department) and did homage upon his appointment.

The Secretary of State for the Home Department administered the Oath.

The Right Reverend W.G. Fallows (Clerk of the Closet to the Queen) and the Gentlemen of the Household in Waiting were in attendance.

The occasion itself is in the main as formal as that account of it in *The Times* next morning, although both before and after it the various members of the Household who look after you could not be more informal with the new boy. Lt Colonel Blair Stewart-Wilson, Scots Guards, was the equerry on duty; he met me at the Grand Entrance and took me into a waiting-room to connect with the Clerk of the Closet, Gordon Fallows, Bishop of Sheffield, who had arrived just before me, and it was most encouraging to see a familiar face. The two of us bishops donned convocation robes there, with Gordon and the Colonel telling me between them what was about to happen. As soon as Gordon and I were with the Queen in the 1844 Room after a few minutes standing with Household members in front of a roaring fire in the Bow Room, Her Majesty shook us both by the hand and motioned me to kneel at the faldstool, where I knelt before her once she had sat down. The Clerk stood beside me, holding a cushion with the open Bible on it. The Queen put her hands together, and held them up for me to clasp them, whereupon the Home Secretary in his morning coat, standing beside the sovereign, began to recite the Oath of Allegiance, line by line, with me repeating each phrase or grouping of words after him, thus:

> I, John Monier Bickersteth
> Lately Bishop of Warrington
> Having been elected Bishop of Bath and Wells
> Do hereby declare
> That Your Majesty is the only Supreme Governor
>   of this your realm
> In spiritual and ecclesiastical things
> As well as in temporal
> And that no foreign prelate or potentate
> Has any jurisdiction within this realm
> And I acknowledge that I hold the said bishopric
> As well the spiritualities as the temporalities thereof
> Only of Your Majesty
> And for the same temporalities

I do my homage presently to Your Majesty
So help me God
God save Queen Elizabeth

The Clerk pushed the open Bible in front of my nose, as soon as I had taken away my hands from the Queen's, and I kissed it. The formalities over, the Queen got up and walked back a few steps to where she had been in the middle of the room when we first saw her, and I got up from the faldstool and followed her there.

The Home Secretary and the Clerk, still holding the Bible, moved across too, so that we formed a quartet to stand and talk, the conversation begun of course by the Queen. Her Majesty asked whether we had arrived down from Liverpool yet, the Clerk made some comment about how very strange Somerset would feel for me after Merseyside, and the Home Secretary remarked that the crime rate might be rather different. So there was immediate informality, with some laughter thrown in, for several minutes until the Queen proffered her hand and says: 'Well I hope you and your family will be very happy in your new home and work', which was the signal for me to go. The Clerk and I turned, walked towards the door, stopped short of it, turned and bowed, turned back and walked out of the 1844 Room, for a final turn and bow to the Queen from just inside the Bow Room, before the footman closed the double doors. The Home Secretary stayed with the sovereign for a few moments more, then he too emerged. Our ten or twelve minutes with the Queen were over, and with homage done my confirmation as Bishop of Bath & Wells was complete. Every detail of Homage is crystal clear to me, twenty-five years on from my own, because of my sharing in it as Clerk so often in my Household years. That first time mine was the last audience before lunch, Roy Jenkins rushed off back to Westminster, while the Deputy Master, after his two bishops had disrobed, bore us both off to the mess, where we met several other members of the Household for a very welcome drink. We all relaxed, I reflecting on the exhilarating mixture of the archaic (that Tudor oath against the Pope), the religious and the secular ('spiritualities and temporalities', kissing the Bible), the formal (but somehow never pompous) Crown ritual, and the *sotto voce* fireplace conversations. I loved it.

Eighteen months later I had a letter from the then Rector of Sandringham, Canon Alan Glendining, inviting me to preach in the

Parish Church there on the third Sunday in January 1978. That was followed up, once I had accepted, with a further invitation, this time from Prince Philip, conveyed by Blair Stewart-Wilson, to come on the Friday rather than the Saturday so as to shoot next day. Years later a bishop who had been told that he was about to be invited for one of those January week-ends, (there is only one invitation, always in January, to a diocesan bishop each year, other that is than to the Bishop of Norwich, in whose see the Sandringham Group of villages lie; he goes quite often), rang me to say he did not know one end of a shotgun from the other, and would it be all right to refuse the shooting side of things? I was able to inform him to his considerable relief that the Palace homework would have been much too good for the invitation in his case to have included shooting. In fact I have never met another bishop who did shoot there, except for Robin Woods, Dean of Windsor and later Bishop of Worcester. He knew the Royal Family very well indeed, and used to answer cheerfully to his fellow-bishops' tease of 'Royal Robin'; I would guess that he shot many times at both Sandringham and Windsor, whereas I only went once to each.

'You must have asked to shoot that week-end', said Prince Charles to me with a rather reproachful smile one day when, some years later, we were on our own during a visit of his to Wells in connection with the West Front Appeal, of which he was the tireless patron. 'Not directly, sir,' I replied perfectly honestly, but I went on to explain that I already knew the Queen's private secretary, Philip Moore, because we were both Governors of SPCK and had become friends, so I am fairly sure that I said to Philip, after hearing from the Rector of Sandringham, that it would have been fun to shoot as well as preach. What is quite certain is that the Duke of Edinburgh who runs the shoot would have had no means whatever of knowing that I enjoyed a day unless he had been told, so my uninformed guess is that Philip Moore was the messenger. The Prince of Wales seemed happy with the explanation; I certainly have no regrets about the hint I must have dropped with the right person.

So it was that on the evening of 20th January 1978, (not with Rosemary, no wives are included in this preaching invitation to bishops) I was met at King's Lynn station by a royal second chauffeur ('first chauffeurs drive the Queen', he told me), and whisked for twenty minutes through the snow-covered countryside, to swing in past Sandringham House's lamp-lit gates, the chauffeur flicking on the interior light of his car as he slowed down to show the policeman who we were. He drove us past clipped yew hedges to the porch; a footman opened my door as soon as the car stopped, and I got out to glance up at the Royal Standard, with a great beam of light on to it in the inky black sky. Blair Stewart Wilson, to my great delight, was waiting to welcome me.

Thus began the most memorable country-house week-end of my life. I kept a careful record as it went along, in a small exercise book which is full of conversations and impressions. In addition to HM the Queen and Prince Philip, there were also staying in Sandringham House Queen Elizabeth the Queen Mother, then a very sprightly 77-year-old, the Prince of Wales, Princess Margaret, the King and Queen of Spain, Lord and Lady Tryon and Lady Jane Wellesley; and the Kents must have been in a house on the estate, as the Duke headed up the six of us guns next morning. The Prince of Wales went hunting, but Prince Philip (not shooting that day) came out with the guns, introducing me before the first drive to Montague Christopher, the charming aristocratic headkeeper. No pheasants are reared on the estate; they are wild, large and fast. All the royal family who were around, as well as their guests, equerries and ladies in waiting, joined us for the sit-down shooting lunch at Wood Farm, where incidentally Prince John had mostly lived for his short life early in the twentieth century. The lunch was the greatest fun: footmen, in the royal livery of red and blue, kept us unobtrusively supplied with food and drink, and I could not help feeling, as the wine and cheerful talk flowed, that although the footmen made it grander the whole thing was gorgeously similar to so many other shooting lunches I have been lucky enough to share in. I see from the card that Mr Christopher gave me afterwards that we shot 85 head of game, and I must have done adequately enough for him to approach me in the brake going back to the house and ask if I would like to go out goose-flighting with him on the Wolferton Marshes on Monday morning before I caught my train; so of course I said 'Yes', but I was not sure if I had the right-size shot. 'Don't worry,' he said, 'I'll look after all that'. So that was fixed, for a gun-room gathering at 6.15 a.m. on Monday.

On Sunday I celebrated Holy Communion early, in Sandringham Church; the rector was elsewhere in the group, so I was on my own.

Queen Elizabeth and Princess Margaret were there. It was *Book of Common Prayer* of course, and through lack of practice (we were fifteen years or more into 'Series' 2 or 3) I missed out the Prayer for the Queen, but mercifully realized it in time to put in a special prayer for 'The Queen's most excellent majesty' in a place of honour just before the blessing. Susan Hussey told me afterwards that it would certainly have been remarked upon if I had not made amends handsomely, as I did. After breakfast back at the House I was driven to the Rectory, arriving just as Canon Glendining swept in from two services in other churches. We walked over to church together, meeting in the vestry the choir of ten or twelve, mostly children, and after processing in we had one verse of the *National Anthem* before Matins started on its stately way, psalm, three canticles and all. A choir girl read a lesson from Proverbs quite beautifully, the Duke of Kent the second, which was the Parable of the Sower, equally well. I preached on John 1.42, 'Come and see', which had been the Gospel two Sundays earlier, and I had prepared and used it in two village churches in the diocese. The Bishop of Norwich (then Maurice Wood) had written a kind letter of welcome to his diocese, in which he said: 'Just think of being in a normal small church, and you'll be fine.' As 'Come and see' had gone rather well in two Somerset villages, and it was still the Epiphany season, I decided to adapt it, and in fact have done so many times since, the last actually in our own St John the Baptist's Church Tisbury in 1998. Generous noises were made back at the House after the Sandringham use of it, and it seems to have been appreciated wherever I have preached it over the twenty years of adaptations ever since.

This is my exercise-book record of the following morning's venture:

> The sergeant of police woke me just before six, and a Range Rover full of guns (Blair Stewart Wilson and Philip Moore were also shooting), keepers and dogs was soon bumping out over the frosty stubble fields, alive with pheasants whirring away into the woods. Ten minutes later I was placed on my own in a deep ditch, just at very first light. I could hear the geese, and partridges too. A gorgeous red sky was growing in intensity every minute. A small skein came in from the sea, too high I decided, and a bit dark to see them properly. I lent against the steep-sided bank, gun well up and still entirely hidden below the

level of the field. More music from a further lot of birds, and then I saw them, much lower these ones. I fired at the leading goose and saw it crumple up ahead of me with the first barrel; fired again and then lost them over the edge of the bank behind me. But one anyhow, and that was rather pleasing, my first goose ever (there had only been one other opportunity, from Liverpool). No time to think about it, as the sky was suddenly full of them, scores and scores, all in full-throated cry, perhaps a thousand pink-feet visible to my limited vision alone, across the gold and apricot sky, and a wonderful torrent of sound they were making too. Mostly a bit high by now, but I fired twice more, without being able to see how successfully. I heard other shots, and after ten minutes, without any more birds coming in against the stiff cold wind (from which I was well-shielded, eight feet below ground level), a keeper appeared in the growing light, to climb down into the ditch beside me. A belated skein flew over, but I was not concentrating, and my shot went astray as one of my feet slipped in the mud at the crucial moment. Just after eight, the keeper felt we should go, and we found the rest of the party at a prearranged RV; neither of the others had had any luck; I am sure I had been kindly put into the best place.

But Mr Christopher was ecstatic: 'Three geese, sir, well done; it would be a privilege if you would accept my scarf in memory of such a superb effort'. I was quite overcome, because he obviously was too. Back at the House we three guns came in to the dining-room, ravenous for a quick breakfast. Prince Philip looked up from his *Times*: "Rather successful, bishop, I hear", he said with a cheerful smile. Within half-an-hour I was saying my goodbyes at the front door. My suitcases and gun, and a brace of boxed pheasants (have I ever gone home from shooting, before or since, with pheasants in a box?) were there before me. I said goodbye at the car to the valet, the chief steward, the equerry and the lady-in-waiting (having taken my leave of the Queen last night), and in a flash I was on the branch line from Sandringham Station to King's Lynn, in good time for the London train.

I think I wrote six thank-you letters. Not of course expecting any myself, I did receive one, from the rector, thanking me for my sermon, and he went on: 'You left Sandringham in a blaze of glory, and I think your three geese is a bag which has given more pleasure than many a pheasant *battue* to the Royals and certainly to the game department'. But what really thrilled me was a melting letter a fortnight later from the headkeeper, 'Mont' Christopher saying: 'now that the season is at an end, and I have time to catch up with thoughts and things, thought it would be nice to send you a game card of your expedition on the Wolferton Marsh. It comes to you with my wife's best handwriting, and our sincere wishes for your happiness. Every one was happy to see and hear you at Sandringham. "Come and see" again'. So he had picked up on my sermon, and I felt very small. For some reason William Cowper, son of an eighteenth century country rector, letter-writer, poet, described in the *Oxford Companion to English Literature* as 'having a simple, gentle and humane personality' swam into my ken as I read his letter:

> God moves in a mysterious way
> His wonders to perform.

There was a very great deal to tell Rosemary when I homed in on the Palace in Wells.

The sequence of all that was that, not long after Gordon Fallows had died of cancer while still under sixty, I heard from Philip Moore in the autumn of 1979 that the Queen 'had it in mind' that I should succeed the bishop as Clerk of the Closet. I suspect that the idea was actually Philip's, but that is the sort of question to which I shall never know the answer. It may also have been partly Lord Maclean's doing, as we had got to know each other well during holidays on Mull; Chips' family seat of Duart Castle on the Sound of Mull was where he retreated when he was not on duty as Lord Chamberlain. Whatever the unfathomable processes, I was invited to that private audience with the Sovereign in early February the following year, having been gazetted Clerk two months before.

Again Blair Stewart Wilson was the equerry on duty, which made for calmness; I had not seen him before in his black square-cut frock coat, the Scots Guards' full dress uniform, and very resplendent he looked as he took me upstairs to Her Majesty's sitting-room and showed me in. HM motioned me to a chair beside her and began by thanking me very much 'for taking on this job; I hope you will rather enjoy it.' We had ten minutes talk, and I had the opportunity to ask if Rosemary and I could give a party in Wells for the Chaplains later in the year: 'Yes indeed, that would be fine, we had one in Jubilee Year'. HM getting up was clearly the signal for me to go, and Blair was waiting in the passage to bear me off to the Equerries' Room; the difference from my own homage two and a half years ago was that I was now in the Household, rather than a visitor, and I really felt the family atmosphere.

The morning after all those introductions I was crossing Buckingham Palace forecourt again, to go in by the Privy Purse entrance as I did unchallenged for the next ten years; this first unescorted visit was for the Homage of the new Bishop of Sheffield. It was General Synod week, so I was in London anyway. Willie Whitelaw as Home Secretary administered the oath; I fell for him as everyone did. But I discovered after two or three homages that he invariably found the formal wording of the oath too much of a tongue-twister, and tended to add a superfluous 'as' after 'as well' in the line: 'as well the spiritualities as the temporalities thereof'; an extra 'as' just before 'spiritualities' invariably threw the new bishop who was repeating the words after him; it made the sentence more unintelligible than it was anyway. When I got to know WW a bit, I pointed his regular mistake out to him: 'Absolutely right', he agreed at once, 'I must think about what I'm doing more, and I'm going to write it all out in capital letters, with bar lines to help me break up the phrases properly.'. He had done precisely that by the next homage, and showed me with pride what his secretary had set out for him, and there were no problems from then on. I remember him once arriving a little late at the Grand Entrance, where I always waited for the Home Secretary; he was clearly flustered, and with some reason, as it was the morning that the Woman Police Constable Yvonne Fletcher, had been shot dead in St James' Square, during a demonstration outside the Libyan Embassy. 'Terrible, terrible', he said, 'I've told the Ambassador and his staff they must all be out of the country within two days'. It was the lowest point of Britain's relations with Colonel Gadaffi.

For the whole of my tenure of office as Clerk of the Closet the Conservatives were in power, but of course there was a variety of Home Secretaries: Peter Walker, then Minister of Agriculture, stood in once for WW, having asked the latter if he could, because Philip Goodrich was doing homage on appointment to Worcester, and that was Peter Walker's constituency; Cecil Parkinson, then Minister of Trade, deputized for Leon Brittan, as the latter being a Jew felt it inappropriate to administer a Christian oath; Michael

Heseltine before, I think, he had picked up the mace and brandished it against someone or other (he was very lucky not to be suspended from the House for that one); and Douglas Hurd, whom I got to know best of all the Home Secretaries with whom I did homages.

I attended for thirty of them, including both the primates and several bishops on their being moved from one diocese to another. Bob Runcie had been Bishop of St Alban's, John Habgood of Durham; but they both had to make fresh subscriptions to the oath, following their appointments to Canterbury and York respectively. In that farewell speech to me I have referred to at the July 1987 Synod in York, Bob commented on my Clerkship: 'He introduces to the Queen all, rather nervous, bishops when they arrive at Buckingham Palace for the ceremony of homage, and his particular blend of "brace up and calm down" has been appreciated by us all'. Be that as it may, what I know they and their wives really did appreciate was lunch in the House of Lords after homage. For some bishops, as for example the two new archbishops, or men translated from one see to another, there was nothing particularly exciting about walking past Richard Coeur de Lion's statue and in through the Peers' Entrance for the first time, so I made a different plan for them; but for the others it was lunch in the Lords that was mentioned every time in the thank-you letters. They also all wanted to know what scripture passage I had chosen for them when they kissed the Bible immediately after the oath; the answer was that I varied them, Joshua 1.6 being a favourite: 'Be strong and of a good courage'.

The actual Bible put out for me to use I altered during my time, from a rather worn undistinguished Victorian one to the new copy, now kept at Lambeth Palace, but actually delivered to HM by Bishop Herbert of Norwich, then Clerk of the Closet, during the Coronation Service. This suggestion of mine was warmly approved as a good bit of history, but that coronation Bible (twenty-five were printed, I discovered) is very heavy, and my successor sensibly soon gave up the idea, partly because getting it from Lambeth each time was an extra chore no one was keen about. I did however achieve the clerk being able to put the Bible down after use on a newly-provided table, which I suggested as a way of my avoiding having to stand with it on its cushion all through the post-homage conversation. This was a miniscule innovation but it necessitated quite a bit of organising, not of course with HM, but with the Lord Chamberlain's office. Any kind of change is stoutly resisted, I very soon discovered. I got nowhere with an attempt to reconsider the almost vicious anti-papist thrust of the oath, being firmly told that this was all part of the history of England, which of course I could not deny.

By the same token I was presented on appointment with the chaplains' badge of office which they wear on their black scarves. A bishop, however, is generally the celebrant at the eucharist, whether in his cathedral or out and about in the parish churches, and so he is not often in convocation robes, which include the scarf. So I asked HM in that first audience whether it was in order for me to wear the badge on my cassock, where I had boldly ventured to put it, pinned just below my dog collar, and I explained why. 'Yes, I noticed it was there' said the Queen, 'what a good idea'. Months went by, until I was next in Chips Maclean's office in St James' Palace: 'Oh, by the way, John, I was wondering why you are wearing the chaplain's badge below your dog collar like that', he commented a little crossly, 'it's not where it's meant to go'. I said my spiel about otherwise hardly ever being able to use something I was very proud of, how I had pointed out my dilemma to the sovereign, and how she had readily agreed to my suggestion. That of course, rather unfairly on my part, silenced the criticism, but I got: 'You should really have asked me first'. I resisted capping that with: 'But you would have said no, Chips'.

That mild enough exchange was positively the only difference I ever had with a Lord Chamberlain who was universally loved; Chips and Elizabeth became firm friends of ours, and we often stayed in St James Palace with them, either for agreeable dinner parties with all kinds of interesting people, or simply for a bed after some City or West End occasion, to which the Macleans might or might not have been going. Furthermore when he was Lord High Commissioner for the General Assembly of the Church of Scotland one year, and resident in Holyrood Palace for three weeks in the early summer, we were invited to spend three never-to-be-forgotten days there.

We drove north to stay first with friends who live near Perth, Alan and Liz Seaward, so Alan kindly delivered us to the door of the palace around tea time. The factor, 'agent' in English terminology, was waiting for us at the door and most welcoming. He took us upstairs to the long passage of main guest rooms. 'Here's your room, milord', he said as he flung open the door of what was clearly a dressing-room, and put my bag down there; 'and I'll take your wife along to hers', as Rosemary disappeared down the corridor, I noting which door she went through, before discreetly shutting my own behind me until the factor had gone downstairs. We quickly consulted, and decided to bite the bullet right away over an informal cup of tea to which he had suggested we came straight down. I asked if I could move in to join Rosemary; it seemed crazy to go to the subterfuge of simply ruffling the bedclothes in my dressing room and creeping along clandestinely to the second of the two gorgeous-looking made-up beds in Rosemary's palatial room. The factor was immediately smiling broadly: 'Of course, milord; who am I to stop a bishop sleeping with his wife'. That lovely lilting-Scots 'Who am I?' became quite a classic in the family.

The house party was ten or twelve strong, including a Church of Scotland duty-chaplain, who took prayers, a parade of course, with an address every morning before breakfast in an ante-room, and said grace at lunch and dinner. After the last duty at which I heard him in action I thanked him warmly for all he had contributed to our memorable stay: 'That's very kind of you indeed, bishop, and would you please go on praying hard for me because I've to do all this for another three weeks'. The Macleans were due to have a steady flow of short house parties like ours, but we rather gathered that our early one was about the best, because it included the Keys Ceremony, whereby the Lord Provost of Edinburgh hands over the keys of the Castle to the High Commissioner, as the latter takes precedence for the duration of his stay in representing the Queen. That was most impressive, as also was the opening address by Chips to the Assembly; for this all the former Moderators turn up, and sit arrayed in the finery of their former office in a special enclosure, irreverently dubbed the Play Pen.

In 'the pen' I spotted among those seven or eight veterans of the Kirk the 90 year-old Dr George Macleod, Founder of the Iona Community, who was a great friend of Mervyn Stockwood, and often came to St Matthew Moorfields in my Bristol days; so it was good to have a word when the official part of the proceedings were over. The whole experience, complete with two magnificent black tie dinners, Elizabeth having local guests on top of the house party, was amazing; and we said our very inadequate goodbyes in quite a haze, as the faithful Alan Seaward picked us up at the end of our visit, to return from all the pomp and splendour to the peace and quiet of their lovely highland home.

We attended three Diplomatic Parties in Buckingham Palace during our Household years. For our first in November 1980 there was a terrorist scare (have these really been going on for twenty-five years now?), and as soon as I had parked my car in the inner courtyard after depositing Rosemary at the Grand Entrance a policeman asked me if I would open my boot, and into it leapt a handsome yellow Labrador to smell round everywhere for explosives. Upstairs in the Ball Room the assembled company stands around for an hour or so over drinks, and then non-diplomatic guests sit on the tiered sofas round the walls while the embassies get their contingents organised into a couple of rows standing on the floor in front of us, facing inwards, ready for the Queen to welcome them all. Each country has maybe four or five staff present, or up to twenty for the bigger ones, the ambassador introducing all his or her people for HM to shake hands with them in the hour or so after the Royal Party has come in; I notice that Prince Philip, in breeches and silk stockings as I am (the only bishop there), is wearing his Garter, the first time I have ever seen it in place on anyone. The Grenadier Guards Band is in the Gallery, and it is an animated international scene below us, ending at 11.30 p.m. or so, after the Queen has talked with all the embassy groups. We then all surge into several other rooms for an excellent buffet supper, with hot and cold food and more champagne for another hour, which whizzes by until the band strikes up the *National Anthem*, which is the signal for us all to go home. Thirteen hundred people had accepted invitations for that evening, I gather, of whom only three hundred were British. We linger a few moments among the last twenty cars in the courtyard, before driving dreamily down the Mall to our room in the Royal Commonwealth Society, and there is even a parking space outside the front door of the club.

The most time-consuming and interesting part of the Clerk's job is to do with HM's College of Chaplains. But first briefly to the least demanding, which is 'safeguarding HM's theological reading,' or at least any official part of it. Since the Sovereign promises in the Coronation Service, as Defender of the Faith, to uphold the laws and customs of the Church of England, the careful creators of the Elizabethan Settlement clearly wanted to make sure that no 'erroneous doctrines' crossed his or her path if they could help it. So the Clerk has been charged since the Reformation with vetting any theological book which HM may be officially offered. I had only two: the first was a massive German tome on Christology in three volumes, which a Lutheran Professor in Hamburg was very keen the Queen should have. I sent one volume off to a German don I knew in Oxford, asking him to glance through it, for a fee that to my household colleagues' huge amusement I guessed at and succeeded in getting out of Sir Rennie Maudsley, the Keeper of the Privy Purse. 'Would anything in this learned treatise', I asked my don friend, 'be a serious threat to Her Majesty's anglican orthodoxy, should a scholarly enthusiast insist that she had sight of an English translation, and HM on some whim eagerly devoured its contents?' He was able solemnly to assure me, I am sure with only reading the minimal, that there was no immediate or foreseeable danger within its eight hundred pages. So those three volumes are no doubt on the royal library shelves in the Keep at Windsor Castle, my Oxford accomplice having composed a suitable thank-you letter for HM to send to the donor.

The other 'theological books' call on the Clerk's time was much nearer home, in that the Palace asked me to 'go through with Her Majesty' the *Alternative Service Book 1980*, shortly before a specially-bound copy was to be presented to her at General Synod that summer. I therefore had another private audience, for which I had marked two or three places in the book which I felt might interest the Queen. HM listened graciously, as one would expect, asked one or two questions, but predictably gave no hostages to fortune by making any significant comment to me. When shortly afterwards Archbishop Stuart Blanch officially handed to the Sovereign the presentation copy at the opening session of Synod, he brought the house down, without a hint of *lesé majeste*, by remarking in that lovely throw-away style of his: 'We did seriously think, Your Majesty, of having two books specially bound, this new 1980 one, and the other 1662; but we eventually decided that Your Majesty probably had several copies of *The Book of Common Prayer*'.

The chaplains, however, were a major responsibility. Numbers have been kept at thirty-six priests since King Edward VII reordered the college in 1909, the Clerk having the responsibility of keeping up the strength to thirty-five; the reason for this, as HM explained to me, is that she likes to have one vacancy up her sleeve, in case there is not one available when she might want to appoint some priest at short notice. With virtually no guidance, because of my predecessor having died in harness, I gradually set about this unusual assignment of recommending suitable people for a royal honour. Lord Stamfordham, in the Edwardian period the King's private secretary, had put the criteria like this to Hubert Burge, Bishop of Southwark, Clerk at the time: 'I do trust that you will continue to recommend to the King men who are likely to move on to higher places, thus keeping up the healthy flow of new blood which has been secured during the last ten years'. I added to that the nomination of particularly fine men who were giving outstanding service to church and state, but might never 'move on to higher places'.

As it was for me to keep my ear to the ground, I consulted with bishops, got second and third opinions on likely men, and bore in mind which diocese had not got any chaplains at all. The processes involved (and these included my consulting Buckingham Palace, of course, when I had any proposals) took up quite a lot of time, and I enjoyed doing it because I soon realized what immense pleasure the appointments brought, both to the recipients and to their wives. I started regular gatherings of the college, rather than the occasional ones they had known before. An initial lunch and cathedral evensong in Wells in 1980 for Rosemary and me to meet them all was followed by a memorable Windsor meeting, which began with a service in the Parish Church in the Queen's presence, where she had not worshipped for twenty years, before a reception and photograph in the castle. We had one at Hatfield House with the Marquis of Salisbury, and my last was a first-ever joint event with HM's Medical Household in both Buckingham and St James' Palaces. My successors as Clerk, I am glad to say, have been able despite budget restrictions to keep up these triennial gatherings. They are immensely appreciated, and there is no doubt that this fairly disparate group of men began to develop a feeling of belonging together to honour Her Majesty and the Crown generally; this was all the more noticeable in a decade that saw the Royal Family in considerable disarray.

Because the Clerk is in no way part of the inner circle of the Household, I never had any kind of inside information on the troubles within the three royal marriages, nor was there the remotest hint given to me that I might be able to help pastorally. If that had been wanted, I would have been asked; I remained perfectly clear throughout all the ten years of behind-the-scenes turmoil in the Royal Family that it was not up to me to offer help. There are domestic chaplains, quite apart from the Archbishop himself. I was as sad as everyone else, not least of course because Rosemary and I had been to the wedding of the Prince and Princess of Wales in St Paul's Cathedral, coming specially down in the night train from our Scottish holiday for it; and full of joyful hope that stirring event was for us as for millions. I simply hoped that there were priests and counsellors caringly involved, in a way indeed that Clerks who had in an earlier age been very close to the Sovereign would certainly have been.

There was an amusing extra meeting for chaplains one year, when a national newspaper decided to run a feature on the Clerk of the Closet and his doings, largely because they were so intrigued by the title, still more that there was a body of chaplains for whom the Clerk was responsible to the sovereign. 'Could you not call an extraordinary meeting?', they said. 'Yes if you pay for it' was my reply; this of course they did, and we had a cheerful reception which the Dean kindly held in his historic home in Little Cloister, off Dean's Yard Westminster. There had to be photographs of course, and we were generously allowed to face the camera immediately in front of the Abbey High Altar after the doors had been closed to the public. It happened that the particular photographer laid on by the paper preferred his subjects to achieve smiling faces by saying 'whisky' rather than 'cheese'; and furthermore we had to declaim the two syllables as loudly as possible. I must say I was very glad that no one was about; or rather I had hoped there was not, until the head verger told me with a dead-pan face, as we adjourned afterwards for a superb meal at the paper's expense: 'The Roman Catholics have been saying Mass this evening in the King Henry VII Chapel immediately behind the High Altar screen'. Well, if there had to be someone who overheard us declaiming 'whisky' in full voice . . .

Most of the time, of course, the chaplains are out and about in their home and work situations. I put up the first black priest for the Queen's consideration, and immensely thrilled he was on his appointment. So the scarlet cassock has remained, I dare to think, a sign of quiet distinction up and down the country. Certainly the Sovereign regards it as such, in that on one occasion the Queen was in a cathedral where all the clergy were in scarlet, a situation HM immediately observed and later raised with her private secretary. I was accordingly asked next day to enquire why, only to get the answer that the last dean but one had thought the colour went well with his gothic building. There was an explosive reaction in the Palace, and I was instructed to find out the overall picture from forty-three cathedrals. Four admitted unauthorized use, and mercifully none were willing to go to the stake for the retention of their 'nice colour'. It was suggested that they moved to 'Windsor Red', which in itself was a thoughtful gesture by the crown, made all the more so by the Privy Purse footing the bill for the Dean and his canons to buy their new cassocks. The Lord Chamberlain and I decided to admit defeat before even joining battle on the widespread use of scarlet by choirs.

My loyal and efficient Deputy Clerk, Canon Anthony Caesar, looked after the Rota of Waits, which is the quaint description of the list compiled every year for all the chaplains to preach at Matins (generally) in the Chapels Royal at St James' Palace. He kindly let me choose my Sunday before he began the chore of writing around; I went in spring or autumn, which meant preaching in the Queen's Chapel one year and in the Chapel Royal the other. It is used in winter, the Queen's Chapel over the road in summer, when visitors to London enjoy seeing the choristers in their Tudor uniforms and the gentlemen of this well-known choir crossing the road to Marlborough House while the traffic is held up. I like both buildings, which each have their historical interest, the latter of course considerably newer, in that King Charles II had it built for his Roman Catholic wife to have a priest to say Mass there. Queen Victoria stopped going to church in public after Prince Albert died, so had the chapel in Buckingham Palace built in 1843, after which no sovereign has worshipped other than very occasionally in either of the two chapels at St James' Palace, and I had to explain to new chaplains that they would never be preaching to the Queen. They and their wives are all introduced to HM at their first Garden Party, on the Buckingham Palace terrace when the Royal Family emerge from the house *en route* for the lawns. Rosemary and I much enjoyed our annual preaching visits to those chapels; the congregation of sixty or so has very bright people in it, who sometimes bore us off to lunch in their homes. Moreover the choir remains one of the best in London, Mr Popplewell being the organist and choir master all my time, in the steps of great musicians like Byrd and Gibbons.

I resigned the Clerkship two years after leaving Wells. Inevitably, once I had retired, I was beginning to lose touch with the bishops and leading laymen up and down the country who helped me recommend suitable men to fill vacancies, and so it seemed much fairer to hand on to some other lucky bishop this fascinating extra to my episcopal life. I can be confident that no other Clerk can quite match my most moving royal experience of the decade, which was the Windsor celebration of HM's 60th birthday on 26th April 1986. Before it, after the rehearsal a week earlier for the service in St George's Chapel, Johnnie Johnston had handed me a handsome presentation case, saying 'The Queen would like you to have this'. It was the first-ever Clerk's Badge, the royal cypher above a scroll in blue and gold, saying 'Clerk of the Closet', hanging from a scarlet collar ribbon. Although I never inquired, this was clearly the very positive outcome of my mild brush with the Lord Chamberlain seven years earlier. Furthermore in that intervening period David Say, the Bishop of Rochester, who had been Lord High Almoner (yet another Gilbertian-sounding post) for two decades, had been presented with his first-ever badge too. So the palace evidently felt a badge would be appropriate for both office-holders, and I was glad to wear mine for another three years.

Before the birthday service, the Dean, Bishop Michael Mann, and I welcomed all the Royal Family at the Galilee Porch ('feels just like Sunday', giggled Princess Margaret as she shook my hand), and Michael and I were soon moving down the North Quire aisle behind the choir and the Yeomen to the Great West door, past a sea of faces known throughout Britain. I saw Alec Hume and David Owen and Quintin Hogg in the front row. After a fanfare outside for the Queen and Prince Philip, we turned and went right up into the sanctuary, having halted first to bow HM and the Duke into their stalls. All the Garter Knights in their stalls were wearing the star of the order on their morning coats, Rosemary was in front of them with Jill Mann, sitting opposite the Runcies and Habgoods;

the two archbishops were not taking part because someone had decided this was a Second XI occasion, with Michael and me in seats just inside the altar rails. There were prayers, the Vaughan Williams *Te Deum* and I Cor. XIII read by Prince Charles. Then I went to the sanctuary step, and prayed the Prayer for the Queen and the Royal Family before turning to give the royal couple the blessing they had asked for from the 1928 Marriage Service, altered in the last sentence so that it read:

> God the Father, God the Son and God the Holy Spirit bless, preserve and keep you; the Lord mercifully with his favour look upon you; and upon all the people of the nation and commonwealth whose lives are dedicated to the service of others, may God bestow his blessing of faithfulness and peace.

We processed down the quire aisle as far as the screen, and turned east again for the General Thanksgiving, the Dean's blessing and two verses of the *National Anthem*. I suddenly realized that singing his head off a couple of yards to my left was the Lord Chancellor, his voice rising to a crescendo as he, the senior lawyer in the UK, bellowed: 'May she defend our laws!' Looking back many times at this tremendous occasion, I know that that was the moment when I felt most emotional. Then we were out into the rain as the Queen stepped into the state coach, the Windsor Greys in the traces, and a Sovereign's escort of the Blues and Royals behind. We shook hands again all round: 'What a fine service', said the Duchess of Kent, 'so much better without a sermon if you know what I mean'. Michael and I walked up the fast emptying nave into the Quire where Mrs Thatcher and Denis were standing by themselves, looking around, absorbed by the Garter Banners and Helms, the fan tracery roof of that incomparable building, and so on. 'I've never been in this part before ', said the Prime Minister rather surprisingly, so the Dean expounded briefly. After unrobing, Rosemary and I connected, and we walked up to the Deanery for drinks and a buffet lunch; after which we went across to the Henry VIII Tower for coffee in Henrietta Ryan's home, where Tim Gregson who had come with us from Wells had watched the service. Henrietta then gave us a super tour of the Print Rooms where she was the No.2; it is an amazing collection, begun like so much else by Prince Albert who had the whole lot brought down from London 'in artillery wagons'. We drove home in time to see on television part of the Covent Garden Royal Performance, at which the Queen and Prince Philip were present. Before that and after Windsor, she had been in Buckingham Palace to watch 6000 schoolchildren do a forecourt dance in her honour waving 12,000 daffodils; and the sun shone for it.

A friend's daughter walking home down the Mall at 11.50 p.m. that night saw the lit-up royal Rolls Royce glide in through the palace gates. What amazing stamina Her Majesty has, reminding me of the Chinese diplomat who said in a confidential aside to me at a dinner once: 'Of course we think of her as the Queen of every country beyond our borders'. 'No wonder', I wrote in my exercise book after the 60th birthday party, 'that our monarchy wins such international admiration. It's been good to have been caught up in the celebrations'. Euphoric stuff maybe, jotted down while those events were fresh in my mind. But those two short sentences will do as an epitaph on my privileged ten years in the Royal Household. The Clerk soon realizes that he is only on the periphery of things royal, and quite naturally so in that he is very much part-time; but the scores of full-timers, some of whom I got to know well, took trouble over making me feel I belonged. My considered reaction is that despite the Queen's *annus horribilis* and all that went with it for much longer than twelve months, the nation is most wonderfully served by the monarchy, and in particular of course by our rightly-admired sovereign herself. The passing years may properly see the abandonment of some of the flummery that goes with the Crown, but I have yet to hear a convincing argument from anywhere in favour of some viable alternative to what we have, and under which, through political comings and goings for so many hundreds of years, there has been a stability which is the envy of the world.

I was not seriously out of pocket through resigning from the clerkship. For ten years I had received the annual salary of £7 out of the Privy Purse, which (after tax deductions) had been paid into my bank in quarterly instalments. Fun, that; it kept things in proper proportions.

OVERSEAS JOURNEYS

I have no idea whether I was used for overseas trips more or less than other bishops on the bench in the 1980s. I owe my own first assignment to Robert Runcie knowing his bishops well, and he must have tucked away in his mind the fact that we had two sons working in Australia and another in Sri Lanka. Bob had two 1984 invitations to be answered, one to keep a diocesan centenary in New South Wales, and the second to consecrate a new bishop for Kurunegala, one of the two Sri Lankan dioceses, which was vacant through the early death of Lakshman Wickremesinghe. 'Might it appeal, John,' asks Bob one day at a Bishops' Meeting in the previous autumn, 'to carry out these two engagements for me?' Needless to say it did, greatly. So it was that in mid-April that year, with Peter Nott well-established as Bishop of Taunton and fully capable of taking over the diocese for a month, Tim Gregson now properly in harness as my lay assistant, and Mary Masters my excellent secretary between them looking after things in the palace, Rosemary and I were driven to Gatwick by Janie for the overnight flight to Colombo. Sam was reassuringly at the airport to meet us, after his 5 o'clock start from up-country Kurunagala.

Sam was in Sri Lanka because six months earlier he had gone straight from his last year at Oxford to be secretary to the visionary and gifted Bishop Lakshman. The bishop was not very well, from diabetes, an illness to which Sri Lankans in general and the Wick-remesinghe family in particular are prone. But Sam was captivated, as everyone was with whom Lakshman came in contact, and he was revelling in this totally strange and exceptional opportunity to ex-plore a new country, and serve under a truly remarkable man.

Very soon, however, after his arrival it became only too clear to Sam as well as to people on the spot, his family and the diocese, that their beloved bishop's health had taken a turn for the worse. In Wells, we just thought how disappointing it was for Sam not to have a boss to whom he was warming every week able to work at full stretch; so it was a great shock to hear him on the phone one morn-ing to tell us that the bishop had died in the night. 'But don't worry, Dad, I'm perfectly all right. Everyone is being helpful, there is a lot to get on with, and I am quite sure I must stay on and do what I can here'. He had obviously done a very great deal by the time Rose-mary and I arrived four months later for a week's reconnaissance before returning from Australia for the consecration of Lakshman's successor. 'Sam really runs the diocese' we were told without hesita-tion by several different people; and we were not long in discover-ing that that was more or less true. 'He must have got the hang of things from you' was what priest and layman alike were disarmingly and quite seriously saying to us.

It was splendid to travel about for a few days from our Kurunagala base, meet some of the key people who would be involved in the consecration, and get a tiny impression of the country and its people. Fr Andrew, the bishop-designate, was out in the diocese, but we met his successor Fr Neil who had just moved in next to the cathedral as the new vicar of Kurunagala parish; two or three Sisters, whose mother-house was in far-away East Grinstead, were already ensconced, having looked after Bishop Lakshman. Between them, with Sam, they showed us round the cathedral which nestles below the giant Elephant Rock. It had been imaginatively designed in the 1960s by Bishop Lakdhasa de Mel, to be in keeping with Singalese architecture. I remembered Lakdhasa from when he was working in England for a spell; he married a British officer's widow, a union which had been much frowned upon by the church in Sri Lanka. But his wife had carried it all off superbly and became greatly loved in the diocese, lived on in the town after her husband's death, and indeed entertained us very kindly, full of chat about mutual acquaintances in the London scene.

Sam also took us to meet the Christian Wickremesinghe family in Colombo, notably its materfamilias, Lakshman's mother. Her daughter Mukta, was married to Sam Wijesinghe, a Buddhist and the government Ombudsman to boot, and both of them had been a tremendous help to Sam when Lakshman died; on our first night in the bishop's house she came in to measure curtains for Fr Andrew, a bachelor, and a man apparently quite unconcerned about domestic arrangements of any kind. He always slept on the floor, and ate beautifully with this fingers. Mukta (who has, sadly for her family and her country, died recently) was a very bright Oxford graduate and head of Sri Lanka's Girl Guides; she blew in cheerfully with another brother who was about to take over the British Council in Colombo. It was interesting to connect with a number of Sam's friends at that sort of level, such a contrast to most of his contacts who were much less westernized.

As well as meeting people, we also went with Sam to places. Fr Udeni, who had become Sam's closest friend among the clergy, took us to the diocesan farm called Christodya, where the community gave us a great welcome, and we toured the orphanage and the farm buildings and workshops where youngsters are trained for various trades. Flowering trees and lotus flowers were everywhere; and ripening mulberries outside our window attracted the bulbuls and barbets. Rain tipped down as regular as clockwork at 3.45 p.m. every day for two hours, but it did not stop us doing things. One day we drove out to Hewadiwala with Banda, the bishop's driver, temporarily of course Sam's, to meet another young Englishman, Richard Worssam; he was working in a community school there for the Church Missionary Society (whereas Sam had come out under the label of United Society for the Propagation of the Gospel).

It was the village sports day for the Buddhist New Year, and everyone was there, maybe three hundred laughing people, indulging in slippery pole, blindfold pillow-fights astride bars, and so on. Not only because of the sports day but always there seemed to be walkers along the side of the roads in single file, mile after mile of them. In the town I preached on Palm Sunday morning to some two hundred in the cathedral, the service partly in English and partly in Sinhala, the mixture seemed to flow along all right; and later in the packed village church of Meetanwala in deep country; Fr Udeni interpreted for me, and as it got dark Tilley lamps were lit, reminding me of the one I used constantly in Normandy during the war. The devout and attentive congregation sat on wooden benches; I could hardly see their dark faces, and it was much more the real Sri Lanka, I felt.

Similarly the Sigiriya day was one to remember; first paddy, then forest (including teak) and villages in the clearings for a further hour, and so to this 1400 year-old archaeological site, 'discovered' by an Englishman only in the 1880s. It was built as a rock fortress, with a moat, water gardens as a nice balance to the defensive purpose of it all, and then brick steps leading hundreds of feet up towering rock to a perilous path, where the famous frescoes, the colours still vibrant after five hundred years, were painted on the plastered cliff-face. We decided it was too hot for us to go to the top, so contented ourselves with looking up to the giant lions' paws another hundred feet above us in the same huge rock. The massive scale of the whole construction reminded me very much of the Abu Simbal Temple on the Nile which I had seen in the 50s.

After drinking gallons of water when we had got down, we had renewed energy to drive on for two hours to Polonnaruwa, another great archaeological site dating from a mere 1100 AD. It is a ruined city of red brick, overgrown and crumbling, right out in the bush, with scores of monkeys scrambling all over the guard stones and elaborately-moulded arches and bulging buddhas carved out of solid rock. But what particularly appealed to us were the birds, no doubt in such large numbers because of it being deserted and miles from anywhere. We saw, as Sam had got rather well up in Sri Lankan birds, scarlet-backed woodpeckers, hawk eagle, bare-tailed bee-eater, hoopoe, white-breasted kingfisher, red-wattled lapwing and many more, all mixed up with large butterflies by the thousand. It was far-and-away our best wild-life afternoon of the whole month abroad. Three hours and more back to Kurunagala, and an excellent supper of (guess) curry, but curd and treacle to follow, a local delicacy and quite delicious. So to bed under our nets, the frustrated mosquitoes buzzing outside them, and the geckos tut-tutting on our bedroom walls.

Kandy was an interesting day too, not only for the Temple of the Tooth (our bare feet scalding on the pavement), but also for the couple of hours in Mowbrays (the CMS Girls School), in poor fettle because its normal complement of 300 Tamils was down to only 190 because of the 'Troubles'. I tried to emulate the kind of encouraging words I was sure our archbishop, whom they knew I was representing, would have offered to the plucky headmaster and his wife. From there we three went on, still with Banda driving, to spend the night with the Rajiahs in their planters' hill-top bungalow, with the luxury of a hot bath, fine silver on the dinner table, and fireflies dancing above the lawn as we went to bed.

We woke to stunning views of the tea-covered hills all round us, and reflected over our first English-style breakfast, served by softly-padding servants, how superbly the British had sited their comfortable homes from home. 'When we were children', said our Tamil host sadly, 'we never really knew under the Brits who were Sinhala and who were Tamils. It has all blown up since Independence. When I take you down to the factory you will see the burnt-out shops, the outcome of tempers flaring up, and the jostling crowds in the market suddenly dividing on racial grounds to start burning and looting.' The sadness in his voice was palpable. We ended up in Colombo for the night before our flight in the large colonial-style home of Mrs Wickremesinghe; it was a treat to stay with one of the old Ceylon families, their house filled with heavy furniture, the walls covered in brown frames of faded group photographs of solar-topeed grandees. The 'Wicks' had very much taken Sam under their wing, which greatly pleased his parents; and certainly the old lady could not have been more welcoming.

Having been met by one son in Sri Lanka, there were two more waiting for us in Sydney. That week in Kurunagala had given us an introduction to the island and its people, which undoubtedly would make for more intelligent conversation when we were back for the consecration in a fortnight's time. In Australia we needed no such preliminary taste of the country, as we had been there for Julian's wedding two years before. So we stayed briefly in his and Piers' homes a mile or so from each other, explored some 'seascapes' that were new to us (Gary Beach and Pitt Water); saw where they both worked; had a gorgeous joint day's sailing in a borrowed yacht in the harbour; went to a very good performance of *Messiah* in the Cathedral, where the Dean rather embarrassingly gave us both a public welcome (maybe someone had tipped him the wink that I was in Australia on behalf of the Archbishop of Canterbury); at-tended Easter Communion there next day with Julian and Cecily, and was able to greet the excellent choir in the vestry beforehand, wearing my hat as Chairman of the Royal School of Church Music, to which St Andrew's Cathedral is affiliated; went that evening with Piers and Carolyn to the university church of St Matthias, very evangelical and bursting with life and obviously greatly appealing to them both; bathed at Palm Beach in the breakers rolling in from the Pacific; gave a talk on the Church of England to thirty-five or so parishioners in the rectory of St Peter's Cremorne; and left early on Anzac Day, unfortunately missing all the parades, but kindly seen off by our four on to the small *Fokker* aircraft, for the hour and a half's run to Griffith airport. It was a very happy and packed four days.

The Bishop of Riverina greeted us warmly in the airport room, with his wife and daughter, and the bachelor Archdeacon Law-rence. We all had a picnic lunch together, before walking out on to the tarmac for three of the six of us to climb in to the bishop's per-sonal plane. Appointed to the diocese when he was just still young enough to train for a pilot's licence, Bishop Hunter had persuaded his Board of Finance that this was the way he could best do his pastoral work; so he duly learnt to fly, and was presented with the *Cessna* for his use as long as he was bishop. It was Rosemary's first trip in a light aircraft; rather disappointingly for her, she was always asked to sit behind the bishop and me, so that he and I could talk more easily about the people we were to see when we landed. This first time we went up through a hole in the clouds to 6500 ft, but were soon circling round to spot and then land at the airstrip at Ivanhoe, where we bumped over the recently-graded dirt to where there was the owner of an old Ford waiting for us. There were no buildings and not another soul in sight, as the Bishop simply locked up his plane, and we swept off to meet over tea the twenty-strong congregation of the corrugated-iron church of St Peter's. I was asked to introduce myself, so for the first time gave the church a message from Bob Runcie and his autographed portrait, a centenary booklet (which I had put together with the help of friends) about the life of the Church of England as we saw it in 1984, and an engraved glass paper-weight; I had brought a supply of all three for each Riverina church I was going to visit.

We were away in the fading light to make landfall before the sudden Australian dark, over mile upon mile of sheep country; twelve acres to the sheep we were told was the going rate in this apparently barren scrub. Into view quite soon, after fifty miles, came White Cliffs, bare brown earth and low cliffs dotted with what looked like white shell holes, but in fact the spots where the 1850-80 settlers had dug for opal, and were now to our amazement the caves where the inhabitants live. Clive and Jean George, in their 70s and ex-Cornwall fifty years earlier, met us; with them were twin 70-year-old sisters, Eve and Tot; Tot was a war widow, and we were proudly told how they had marched side by side, alone, past the little Anzac War Memorial earlier that day, one sister with the Australian and the other with the Union flags. We all drove to the George's home, a seven feet high cave with a central column left standing to hold up the rooms round it.

Lit by electric light from the town generator which supplies most of the two hundred citizens, we sat having tea in this unreal set-up, admiring their opal collection, keenly produced in answer to my question as to whether there were any still to be found, before moving to the cave of another member of the congregation, where I robed for evensong in their little church next door. 'Now thank we all our God' was played lustily by Clive George on the harmonium ('I used to be the organist in our village church fifty years ago'), the bishop took the service and I preached at five minutes notice, just as if everything was as normal as a village church in Somerset. The entire party of fifteen then adjourned for supper to the only café, ('The White Cliffs Hilton'), and at the bishop's request I talked again, this time about being Bishop of Bath & Wells. Out past midnight under the myriad stars (including the Southern Cross, quite magical), and a few yards to flop into bed next door to the church. Our host had no electricity in his cave, so in candlelight (after admiring our second lot of personally-found opals) we settled down to sleep with the bare rock all round us, and even two bedside tables of rock left specially for the purpose. It was hard to believe this was really us.

We were up before six, as it was just getting light, for me to celebrate Communion in church, followed by a huge breakfast for everyone in the biggest cave-house, and then off to see the most prized find of all, the fossilized-in-opal ten-million-year-old plesiosaurus, six feet long, and carefully extracted (only a rib had first been visible) a mere three years earlier by a young prospector. After that the bishop unlocked his Cessna, and we sailed up into the blue sky, looking down with new eyes on the brown, white-pockmarked earth, able now to visualize this tiny survival of the opal-rush of a hundred years earlier, and its warm-hearted inhabitants.

Broken Hill was an hour and a half on, a town of 30,000 people, an astonishing contrast to White Cliffs. Here the 'air strip' had become a concrete runway of course, and we were driven to see both the headquarters of the Flying Doctor service, and also the School of the Air in session. The delightful headmaster explained to us that the furthest child we would be talking to lived 320 miles away; the school's hundred and fifty children are all of primary age, flying in after they reach eleven or twelve to their secondary education in Broken Hill itself. They tend then, he said, to have severe behavioural problems because 'school' has not meant to them doing things with other children. When secondary age hits them, they suddenly realize that this 'school' means having a fellow pupil at a desk a yard away who may want to 'crib' your work, and knock a ball about in the playground without your getting steamed up if you keep on having it pinched from under your nose. Rosemary and I had great fun taking it in turns to talk on the phone with various pupils.

Then we had prayers with thirty-odd parishioners, an impressive number on a weekday, in the very catholic-looking church, followed by lunch in the Archdeacon's house, which was a bit of a rush because the bishop knew he had only just enough daylight to get us home. It was a three hour flight, mostly over dried-up bush again, but nearer civilization the Murrumbidgee irrigation scheme below us quite suddenly changed everything into green fields and thousands of acres of farmland for the last quarter of the journey. We touched down just in time at Narrandera, taxi-ing into the bishop's hangar with three minutes to spare before all light aircraft have to be out of the sky. We got a warm welcome at Barry Hunter's home, and a cheerful supper with Dorothy and their daughters before early bed in their garden annexe. Peacocks strutted about in the gloaming on their lawn; and not so pleasantly screeched us awake early next morning, when we drove for half an hour to Griffith for the first of all the receptions and TV interviews and speeches and dinners and big services we had come for. We had the following day off at a huge fruit farm; for the benefit of the photographers we were both air-lifted on to our host's fruit-picking machine above a large orange grove. At night there was very well-attended ecumenical service, at which I preached on the rainbow, and was enthusiastically thanked right away, much to my embarrassment, by an RC Sister of Mercy for 'my inspiring homily'. We went straight on to the main dinner of the visit, three hundred sitting down, more speeches, toasts and all, after another full and exhilarating day.

The biggest of the centenary events was on the following morning, with two thousand chairs set out on Griffith Racecourse for an open-air eucharist celebrated by the bishop. I read out the messages I had brought from the Queen and from Robert Runcie, and preached under the baking hot sun, rather far away from the awnings. But it was a memorable occasion, with a large-scale picnic immediately afterwards, and the opportunity to talk to many of the people who had come vast distances to take part. The furthest communicant I chatted with had travelled for 420 miles; I privately compared the reluctance of English churchgoers to worship in the next village. The Bishop and I drove reflectively home; I think from what he said as we pottered into Narrandera in the evening light, the autumn reds of the *liquidambar* foliage glowing in the sun, and galahs in their pink and grey plumage rioting about among the gums by the riverside that he was happy about the long and carefully-planned day. We said an evensong of thanksgiving together in his chapel.

We were in the air early next morning for the last part of the visiting; while the bishop taxis along any airstrip he crosses himself, with a reassuring: 'In the name of the Father and the Son and the Holy Ghost', as we take to the air. We landed three hours to the west in a cloud of locusts, learning how to brush them out of the way as we stumbled towards the inevitable veteran Ford. Barry flew on further west to bring in Wentworth on the centenary events, while we visited a remote homestead called Windamingle, where we stayed with knowledgable ornithologists. They took us a wonderful drive round their nearby 8000-acre lake, and kept up a running commentary on what we were seeing. Back at the property ('farmhouse' in English-speak), we had a long interview with a freelance photographer who had come more than a hundred miles to do a feature on this visiting bishop and his wife. She quizzed us interestingly on Church and State in the United Kingdom, continuing the discussion over a hilarious dinner party in the room where they have a monthly service; the last arrival, we were told, has to read the OT lesson,('we always hope the passage is full of impossible names if he's really late'). We sat up chatting, and Rosemary and I were barely in bed when there was a knock on the door, and there was our hostess in her nightie, saying 'Joey's here'. Joey turned out to be a kangaroo they had reared after her mother had been killed on the road, and as she was growing up they were trying to get her to go back to the wild. But late at night she still liked to come 'home' for bread and milk on the verandah; it was quite an experience, right out in this isolated place, to watch mother and new just-out-of-pouch, completely wild, baby hanging on to domesticity for what the mother remembered it offered.

The twice-a-week postman came to breakfast during his 600 km round, and the bishop arrived to fly us all on to Hay, where within five minutes and with my ears still popping from the flight I was celebrating the Holy Mysteries and preaching; the archdeacon read the Gospel and the bishop served me at a weekday lunchtime service which drew a good congregation of twenty-five people for St

Philip & St James' Day. Afterwards we had a merry Q & A session with them all, before our last flight back to Narrandera; we had felt splendidly safe under his piloting for 1650 air miles.

After a quick turn-round we were driving to the final event of the week: a broadcast civic service, for which I preached, after the bishop, rather to my surprise, had emulated the English custom of knocking three times on the west door for admission. I initiated clapping Barry at the end of my address, which was a bit of a gamble, but they all cottoned on at once, and thanked me profusely afterwards over champagne on the church lawn in the dark, when everyone had streamed out of their newly-consecrated cathedral. Their hard-working bishop had certainly achieved an imaginative programme to celebrate the first hundred years of the diocese. His people, together with Barry himself, were embarrassingly appreciative of what little we had both done during the week, and we felt strangely bereft of so many devout Christians we knew we would never see again in this life, as we went north to Sydney next morning by an Ansett flight.

We had only two days this time in Australia with the elder boys, but fitted in going to the weekly Healing Service in St. Andrew's Cathedral with them, where again although we thought we were *incognito* we were welcomed in a full nave, the entire congregation rising to their feet to sing us a greeting to the tune of *Edelweiss*. That regular service must be about the best piece of outreach achieved by a cathedral anywhere, most of the men and women in church that night, said the canon in charge of it, not belonging to a church anywhere. On the only other evening of this much more 'flying' visit than ten days earlier, we had a farewell meal with our Australian four, Piers and Carolyn and Julian and Cecily, and then we were away to our next duty of consecrating a new bishop; or rather helping to do so (I was to be one of the three consecrating bishops) in Sri Lanka. Sam and the faithful Banda met us at the airport for the bumpy hour and a half drive to Kurunagala; we were reliably told that not even the main roads had been touched since the British left.

Sam had had a difficult fortnight as he had feared he might, with people not doing what they had promised to do, an endless badgering for tickets, and the 76-year-old archdeacon losing his temper once with him. 'But I think everything is pretty well ready', says this

twenty-two-year-old son of ours, organizing, surprise surprise, his
first-ever consecration. Apparently Fr Andrew had found the time
which I had spent with him talking generally about 'being a bishop'
helpful, whereas I had come away from it feeling I had been quite
useless, having known the local culture for only four days. We were
to stay this time with Mrs de Mel. She told us that she thinks the
quiet and holy Fr Andrew will be a very good contrast to the outgo-
ing and innovative Lakshman.

Next morning there was the rehearsal (two hundred and fifty
people at least in the nave for it, just watching), and then the legalities presided over by Bishop Swithun of Colombo. The maidan outside the building was a hive of activity, with lorry-loads of chairs rolling in, and corrugated iron sheeting against the rain being erected
for the overflow, above the nine hundred who would have tickets.
Sam moved efficiently around, greeting everyone; all the priests
knew him of course, but so did dozens of others. Through Lakshman's pioneering work with the Buddhists there was the extra complication of where their priests were to sit without upsetting the
faithful who might have been expected to be in their quite prominent places. By 7 o'clock the following day a Kandyan band in
bright orange and red uniforms struck up thrilling music in the
compound which was already packed with people, many with TV
sets which they had brought along with them so as to tune in to the
CCTV. We heard afterwards that eleven hundred souls had crammed into the cathedral, and nearly four thousand were in the
grounds watching and singing and sharing in the festivities. 'You
are probably used to happenings like this in the UK, but this is our
first ever in Kurunagala', said one of the clergy, 'the earlier bishops
were all consecrated in Colombo, so we are making the most of it as
you can see', commented the archdeacon.

Two retired Sri Lankan bishops, as well as we three consecrating
ones (my companions were from Malaysia and India), together with
three RC bishops brought up the rear of the long procession of
clergy; and seven Buddhist monks in their saffron robes had prominent places in the nave. Scores of Buddhist boys and girls danced
up the aisle scattering *frangipani* petals ahead of our processions.
The service itself, despite all of us being so crowded in, was deeply
spiritual, and certainly I found the actual moment of consecration
when we three bishops laid our hands together on this composed

kneeling figure, immensely moving. Even the administration of communion to scores of surging upturned black faces (none of the orderly queueing of home) seemed to remain by the grace of God focused on what we were about, and utterly reverent. The Buddhist monks all left after two hours, because they have to eat before noon; but they returned to be in the compound among the seething throng, and came up in turn to greet the new bishop as he sat on a raised platform outside, after the service was over. Bishop Andrew had an hour or more of that on top of the strain of the three hour service, receiving notables from government and the locality; Bishop Swithun had read out loud my message from the Queen, 'Head of the Commonwealth', right at the beginning of the service. An orchestra accompanied most of the singing which quite properly was mostly eastern, and included the hauntingly beautiful song in praise of Sri Lanka, a sort of *Land of Hope and Glory* equivalent, and not specially 'religious', which lifted the roof off. Rosemary and I picked it up quickly, as Sam had said we would.

The crowds gradually melted away in the afternoon heat, and we were suddenly on our way back to England, Banda driving us to the airport hair-raisingly badly, as he kept almost going to sleep after working most of the previous night; we were very glad that Sam was going to do the driving back north. So we climbed skywards leaving our three boys to their work, all of them 'east of Suez',[10] and our pangs of sadness much tempered by being able now to imagine them in their varied occupations.

Moscow the following year was quite different. The Archbishop was invited by the Russian Orthodox Church to send a senior bishop to what was grandly called 'An International Round Table Conference of Religious Leaders and Experts on "New Dangers to the Sacred Gift of Life: Our Task".' Robert and I both smelt all kind of rats from the start. Clearly it was in part to be a Communist propaganda stunt, with the very state-dominated Orthodox only ostensibly in charge. But as archbishop he was quite clear that we should accept; and because he knew I had been to Uppsala in the 60s for the 4th Assembly of the World Council of Churches, and had also been fairly vocal recently against the Campaign for Nuclear Disarmament, he felt I might fill the bill. So off I went by myself for

40. From *Mandalay* by Rudyard Kipling v.6 l.1

five days in mid-February, with the Moscow temperature at 24 degrees below. Rosemary was understandably, in view of Anglo-Soviet relations at the time, not too keen about my going.

Delegates were put up at a bleak 'Stalin-era', but adequate, hotel, after I had been encouragingly met, from the two hours going through customs, by a girl on the British Embassy staff, 'just to make sure you were all right, and here is Alexander from the patriarchate who will look after you'. Being very English I tried that night to open the bedroom window, but thankfully failed and barely kept warm enough in bed, after a midnight look-down from the seventh floor on to the poorly-lit snowy square, with fur-hatted figures still scurrying about.

Next morning I shared a mini-bus with a Zimbabwean Methodist minister, a French-speaking Madagascan RC priest, a Muslim Imam from the edge of the Caspian Sea and a Buddhist monk from Viet Nam; and the fifty of us from all over the world were soon in session in a modern church centre, which we were proudly told had been paid for by the church on a site provided by the state. The communists were constantly at pains, it became easy to grasp, to show the world that they wanted to be friends with their church, despite all the repressions that went on behind the scenes. Metropolitan Philaret of Moscow welcomed the delegates to Russia, and then handed over to Metropolitan Gregorios of the Syrian Orthodox, a delightful man whom I had got to know a bit at Uppsala, so we fell gladly on each other's necks. He told me in the first coffee break that I was the only Englishman, so although some of the business would be in English I would have to rely a good deal on the simultaneous translators in their booths behind us; and very efficient they proved to be.

In fact one of them came up as we were beginning work again to say that Philaret would like me to dine with him that night, and I would be picked up at 6.30 p.m., which I duly was, wondering where on earth I would land up in the dark streets. It turned out (a great honour, I gathered) that I was the only guest; there was his lay secretary, and an interpreter who got very little dinner, as we talked hard for two hours around our eating. Philaret was full of questions, for example: 'Why is it always thought by the Right in your country that peace talk is a Left-wing activity?' It proved a very hard-working meal, as I really had to think fast during mouthfuls. Once or twice he steered us away from what I had asked him: the Polish question was one instance (the shipyard unrest bravely initiated by Lec Walesa was at its height); it was anyway near the end of the evening and he simply got up with 'end of discussion' noises, which I recognized from the way, back in England, the Queen finishes interviews. As I was being driven back to the hotel, I reflected that his often guarded replies were probably because he knew his room was bugged.

For those few days we visitors from the free world constantly recognized when the Orthodox were clamming up. I got to know one priest better than the rest because he had good English, and I asked him at one stage about the religious prisoners. 'They are in prison because they break the laws of this country', he said; 'haven't I been reading about some of the Greenham Common women being taken off to gaol?. 'Absolutely' I replied 'but they will get a fair trial quickly and maybe a fine or a short sentence. Your Christian friends seem to go off to the gulags indefinitely'. He changed the subject with a nice smile. I told the British ambassador that story when several of us were invited to lunch with him in our superb Embassy on the banks of the Moscow river; there were icebreakers at their laborious work, as we piled out of a couple of taxis to a stunning view of the Kremlin the other side of the massive ice floes. 'Yes', mused Sir Iain Sutherland, 'the Soviets leave the central hierarchy alone for the most part; they do this for appearance sake, just as this conference you are all at is for the shop window too. But out in the sticks and underneath the official jargon you are being subjected to, you are quite right, there is relentless persecution, and there are some brave young Russian Christians.'

Next day we saw some evidence of that last comment, when we came in for the end of the Liturgy at Church headquarters; twenty or more men and women from the various offices had attended. As they went off back to work down the corridors, I saw that they were almost all young. This was in stark contrast to the congregation I experienced that afternoon on a remarkable visit at my request to the only Baptist church allowed to function in Moscow, where my interpreter and I got a great welcome as we shared in evening prayers and bible reading for maybe five hundred people; practically without exception they were black-shawled old women. Over tea and biscuits (shades of home) in the church office afterwards, I presented the minister with a dozen Bibles and a concordance all in Russian, which I had brought from the UK, with Soviet permission incidentally because I was Bob Runcie's representative. They were overjoyed, as they were clearly very short of Christian reading matter. 'We shall almost certainly cut up these Bibles into their various books, e.g. Isaiah or St John's Gospel, so that more people can have sight of them', he said as if it was the most natural thing in the world to do. Once again I felt about two inches high.

Equally old, but interestingly with a smattering of soldiers in uniform, were the congregations in the Zagorsk monasteries to which we had an outing by coach one morning. Founded by St Sergei in 1309, the breathtaking domes and red and blue and gold and white walls of this fortress were unbelievably striking. Zagorsk was full of life, with seminarians and an academy, housing in the whole complex nearly a thousand souls. Our Austrian bishop asked the guide whether their priests were trained to visit people's homes in these vast housing estates we had driven past on our sixty-five mile motorway run.

'There is no need', came the reply, 'our churches are full anyway'.

'But you only have fifty-five churches open in the whole of Moscow,' countered the Austrian.

Our nice guide Theodore could not cope with that beyond a shrug of the shoulders; he was really proud of his country's achievements, and rather like thousands of Germans not realizing what was happening in Nazi Germany, he knew nothing of the Stalinist reign of terror. 'You don't realize how vast the Soviet Union is', he said, 'how much there is to do here and how hard everyone works. There is no unemployment, there is enough for everyone to do.'

Judging by the spotless Moscow Underground constantly swept by women, I could believe him. 'How do you see the orthodox Church to-day, archbishop?' asked a Canadian Presbyterian. 'That is very difficult', replied the archbishop quietly, 'I am encouraged that so many men are coming forward for ordination, we have four hundred and sixty of them in the seminary; and we were not meant by the Saviour to have it easy, we follow the Way of the Cross. It is our millennium in 1988, and preparing for it now in 1985 helps us to remember that many things can happen in the secular world between now and then, while the Church goes on'.

Those were courageous words, of which the commissar who was no doubt in our company could make what he liked; it was in fact to be after their millennium by only a year that the Berlin Wall came down.

It was a relief to get away from the feeling of being watched all the time by spending a free afternoon with my cousin Gerard McBurney, in Moscow for a year at the Music Conservatoire; he took me to *Swan Lake* at the Bolshoi, which was wonderful. He said:

> But Moscow is a strange grey place, absolutely everything is sub-ject to control. They love their homes more passionately than ever, because only there is there no control. Ah, there goes a woman into a shop for the ruling class. Did you see her getting out into the snow from that posh car? She is probably arranging a 4th class, the highest, wedding for her daughter; that grade will allow for the best photographs, top quality food and clothes, but the couple will not be able to have their honeymoon abroad un-less it is to a Warsaw Pact country. The result is that all these thousands of people you see around you have no idea whatever what the West is like, as they see no foreign papers or films; and nothing in our papers here can carry any sort of criticism what-ever of the Soviet Union. There is a saying that there is no news in *Izvestia*, which means News, and no truth in *Pravda*, which means Truth. They hate foreigners whom they are convinced are all determined to do them down. They will none of them talk politics for fear of informers.

I thought of what he had said when my personal student guide Alexander said to me on our last day: 'I hear you know the Queen? For me she sums up all that is best in your country. Kings and Queens are very rare to-day, and they must be preserved. We must never fight each other'. Sadly he came back to that comment at the airport where we bade each other rather a moving goodbye: 'Don't let anyone in England let it get back here what I said about the Queen', he said earnestly, with tears in his eyes. There was the tragedy of our world, the great hindrance to global peace that there was before the 1989 demise of the Soviet bloc. 'I thought you would like to know', said the captain of our BA flight when we had been airborne a couple of hours, 'that we are now out of Russian air space'. Yes, it was quite a relief.

I told the Archbishop in my report, roughed out in the plane coming home, that my first 'real' sharing in the Orthodox liturgy ('real' by contrast with several I had experienced in the UK) would be my most lasting and hopeful memory. The communiqué we produced from the 'Peace Conference' meant very little. It needed the usual burning of the midnight oil to get the nuances and balance right, and it had to make all the appropriate noises of gratitude to both the state and the church for making us so welcome; for instance we had even been each given the equivalent of £150 pocket money to spend, in shops where there was hardly anything worth buying; we mostly gave it when we were leaving to our student guides. As so often in conferences, but perhaps very specially at this one, it was the 'out-of-school' times of conversation and encounter which were so valuable.

For me too, as I say, it was above all the worship which have remained in my mind: the candles in the darkness, the glinting ikons, the haunting music, the deep reverence, the motionless old women standing still for a couple of hours or more, while we only slipped in and out of various services for ten minutes or so. Even those brief glimpses had their lighter moments as when in one church two of us bishops, the Austrian RC and I, because we were priests were ushered through the *ikonastasis*[41] to meet some of the officiants, and got engaged behind the not very sound-proof screen in a loud discussion, with plenty of laughter, about the Church of England and the Pope But the worship itself did indeed again and again convey to me the hope there was locked up in this fairly time-serving organization; and to be time-serving is probably the only way the church could survive in a hostile regime. At Eastertime a few weeks after I got home, I found that I could echo the Orthodox Churches' 'Christ is Risen', more utterly from the heart than ever before with the faithful's thunderous reply 'He is risen indeed'.

My last two overseas assignments as a serving bishop were in May 1987. As they were only six months before I was going to retire, I was more than a little unhappy about the timing, but my staff were understanding, and I was clear that I could not say no in either instance. The first was to Japan, not because I was Bishop of Bath & Wells, but because I was Bishop Bickersteth. The fact was that with-

---

41. This is the solid screen in every Orthodox church separating priest from people.

out being rude to another province of the Anglican Communion, I could do no other than accept, because the Japanese bishops, most of whom I had met at Lambeth 1978, were almost childishly insistent that because of Bishop Edward Bickersteth, my great uncle, I must be at the centenary of the NSKK. That is the Japanese acronym for the Holy Catholic Church of Japan, for which Uncle Edward, then Bishop of South Tokyo, had drawn up the constitution a hundred years before. Bob Runcie knew that the Church Commissioners would not finance my expenses as well as his, so he lit upon the plan of twisting the arm of USPG and CMS, both of which missionary societies had been involved in the birth pangs of Japanese Anglicanism, and were still on the ground there, to pay my fare. The two societies generously said yes without demur; they knew better than most how much store the Japanese set by heredity, not to say in pre-Christian terms ancestor-worship.

On a mid-May evening I left Heath Row independently of the rest of the Church of England party who were reaching Japan from somewhere else. I was going to have a night in Hong Kong on the way, as a guest of Janie's father-in-law Nigel Rigg, an old Hong Kong hand of thirty years or more. He kindly met me after the plane had swept in to Kowloon airport, where every aircraft seems bound to run into the high-rise buildings which are cheek by jowl with the airport perimeter. Nigel took me on a quick tour of the New Territories, including a drive down Buffs Avenue; I remembered that my cousin Raymond Grace, when serving with the regiment after he had come out of prisoner-of-war camp, had done a Hong Kong tour. I was glad of the chance of this lightning visit, and there could not have been a better person to give me an idea of it all: we drove up to the Peak at midnight to look out over the sea of lights in every direction, and lunched next morning in his golf club, set in beautiful Scottish-looking countryside.

My fleeting first impression of Japan as we dropped down to the runway on a grey evening next day was of thousands of paddy fields, with tiny houses scattered among them; and then in a flash we had managed by a whisker not to land in the sea. Susan Ladenberg[12] met me at the barrier, and it was a delight to stay with them. By way of a thank-you for the trouble they took over me, I was able later on to wangle them into the delegation's prestigious reception

---

42. I had married her to Michael in 1985; he was working there for Schroeders.

and very posh dinner (twenty-eight of us sitting down, after there had been a hundred and fifty at the reception), both given for Bob Runcie at the Embassy. In its large grounds this must be one of the finest British ambassador's residencies anywhere in the world.

Early next morning a Japanese priest drove me to the Bishop of Yokohama's house where three other clergy who had a little English came into coffee; this was served by the bishop's wife who did not join us but hovered obsequiously in the background, which was indeed what all wives still did, I soon discovered. They took me into the cathedral to show me, laughingly and not at all embarrassed, the memorial plaque to the wrong Bishop Bickersteth, namely my great-grandfather Edward Henry of Exeter, instead of his son, their 'founder', Edward of South Tokyo. The two brass plaques near each other in the north quire aisle of Exeter Cathedral are not dissimilar, and I imagine that the local photographer was simply instructed to secure a copy of 'the bishop's plaque', and by bad luck took the wrong one. 'That'll be really interesting in a hundred years' time', I said, and they enjoyed that. Two of them took me down to Yoko-hama Docks, got going again after the war damage when General MacArthur was the powerful American Military Governor running the country, whom of course they only knew by name, but they realized I would remember him. 'How shall we value the yen?', they told me he was asked by the vanquished after their surrender. 'Right', he said, 'there are 360 degrees in the compass. Let us say 360 yen to the dollar'; and so, unquestioned, it was.

In the docks we called on the Missions to Seamen chaplaincy, of which I knew because father had been Chairman of the Mission Council, something he did 'very well', I have often been told, for twenty years. I knew he had always taken a particular interest in the Yokohama centre because of Bishop Edward. A Free Church Danish pastor, and a Japanese RC priest share the work with our chaplain, and I was most impressed by it all. Later I was shown round the cathedral, and addressed the students at the NSKK Theological College, capping that the next day with a visit to the strangely-called Koran School which Edward had founded in 1888. I took their Daily Service, standing with the headmistress of these 1100 girls on the platform of their school hall. I then addressed the entire school, with the interpreter's help, though I began and ended with Japanese greetings which I had written down and carefully practiced; it drew deafening applause. After a break for very unpleasant green tea, during which I was introduced to a former member of staff who had begun teaching there sixty-five years earlier, I set off round seven classes, having to address them all in turn, including one class who were having their teeth checked by five dentists, another whose teacher had been on Eileen Bickersteth's staff at Bedgebury[43] in the 60s, a third who were all in white overalls learning how to write their own names in huge black characters, and another who were doing PE, but stopped in order to sing me in English the entire *Hallelujah* chorus which they had learnt by heart in my honour. It was all very humbling, particularly as only a handful of the children are Christians, but every girl takes part in prayers, voluntarily, six days a week, because they are so proud of their founding by an anglican bishop, whose real live great nephew, also a bishop, was standing in front of them that morning.

That night Archbishop Browning, then the Presiding Bishop of the Episcopal Church in America, preached in a packed cathedral, using words from Bishop Edward's *Life*, which meant he had done his homework, and I thanked him as I read out the messages of congratulation from the Church of England General Synod and the two missionary societies, all of which I was representing. I went too fast for the interpreter, and another one who obviously had better English had to replace him; as the first one looked rather crestfallen due to my inconsiderate speed I led a round of applause for him, which they all thought was quite hilarious. After the service we changed quickly, and twelve of us expatriates, including the two archbishops, American and English, had an excellent restaurant meal of *shabu- shabu*, which is rather like *fondu* in that you dip every conceivable delicacy into a boiling hot sauce, sizzling away in a dish over a flame in a hole in the middle of the table.

Next day I was taken by air to Nagasaki by a charming ex-soldier of the Japanese army, exactly my age, not with very good English; but the significance of what we were doing together was lost on neither of us. He took me to the Hypocentre Museum, a four-storey building dedicated to the story of the atom bomb. There were several school parties being taken round, and I gathered that visits there by the young were very much part of the curriculum; they

43. Eileen, a grand-daughter of Bishop EHB, was Headmistress of Bedgebury School for Girls, 1932-64.

were led in prayer, presumably by a Shinto or Buddhist priest, and they all added prayer papers to the thousands fluttering in the cold rain. Scores of artefacts were on display to emphasize the horror of it all on that August day in 1945. 'Never again, never again', my old soldier guide, my contemporary, kept on saying. But it was interesting that the oldest Japanese teacher in Koran School the previous day had told me she thought the dropping of the bomb had been the right thing to end the war.

Back in Osaka, I was very nearly late for the main Centenary Service, for which we had been lent the RC cathedral because it was bigger than ours. Owing to the taxi driver not knowing accurately enough where we were bound for, I had an anxious drive, but swept in to this huge 1960s building just in time to robe, with a 'close-run thing' murmur from Bob Runcie as we moved off in procession. I was impressed by the eleven dioceses of NSKK producing fifteen to twenty priests each for this major occasion, and they all looked so young. I commented on this afterwards to Pam Cooper, a missionary teacher of long experience who agreed that there was a good supply of young ordinands; but she also told me that most Japanese over forty dye their hair black, which indeed accounts for the way I hardly saw any grey-haired men about anywhere, in or out of church.

There were no teenagers at the service, but I reflected that nor would there have been any in England. The Cathedral was packed, including the galleries; I gathered there were 2700 people in all. Bob preached on Peace; I had preached at the anglican Cathedral evensong two nights earlier on Unity. 'Pleasantly complementary, our two sermons', observed Bob when I thanked him afterwards, as we all posed for photographs among the great crowd in the hot sunshine outside. It was easy to forget in that milling throng that Christians of all traditions amount to less than 1% of the population; this after Bishop Bickersteth a hundred years ago, in that high Victorian confidence of the time, had written:

> 'If we can get missionaries flowing in strongly, there is every possibility of Japan becoming a Christian country in the lifetime of many who are alive now.'

The reality in 1987 could not have been more different than he had hopefully envisaged; but of the enthusiasm of the Christians that I met there could be no doubt.

So after a final reception, and much present-giving and speech-making and bowing and hand-shaking, the Church of England delegation was on its way, coming by the top-of-the-world route via Alaska. I shaved at Anchorage in comfort, three hours after leaving the VIP departure lounge in Japan. Only three of the twenty-three-hours journey was in darkness. The long haul to London from the mountains and larchwoods of Alaska was almost entirely over hundreds of miles of frozen sea north of Canada, until we hit the North Atlantic and began to curve down right-handed for the UK. The wide drafty corridors at the palace in Wells seemed huge that night, as I shared news with Rosemary and mentioned the discomforts of the small Japanese homes, even of well-to-do people, where the corridors are so narrow that you have to squeeze against the wall to let someone pass. 'I've come to the conclusion', Michael Ladenberg had said, 'that the places where they live are quite unimportant to Japanese people. Work, unremitting work, is what matters, so they don't waste money on homes, still less on the width of the passages in them.' But I have a lasting memory of the warmth and generosity of our hosts, and of the steady courage of their Christian witness in maybe the most materialistic society in the world.

Before the end of that month of May, I was in the air again, bound for Sri Lanka again, this time for the consecration of the new Bishop of Colombo, Jabez Gnanapragasam, to succeed Swithun Fernando who had just retired, and so once more Bob Runcie needed to organize three bishops for the task. Having accepted this second request from Bob, I bethought myself of course of Sam, by now working for Overseas Development with the Foreign Office in Khartoum. I rang him up in January: 'any chance of your getting a spot of leave to come across to Sri Lanka in May do you think?' I asked hopefully. 'I can't see why not, Dad' was his immediate response. So by the consecration date on Ascension Day, we were together again on Sri Lankan soil, which was marvellous, though this time sadly without Rosemary.

This service of course was in Colombo's colonial-style cathedral, not in Bishop Lakdhasa de Mel's striking but smaller creation in Kurunegala. But it was good to meet so many friends from three years before, and much more so to revel in seeing Sam being fêted back. The service was very similar, with if anything even more Buddhist involvement beforehand by way of marching bands and gaily-coloured Kandyan dancers, with their musical instruments going full blast at various points in the service. I very nearly had an accident with a full chalice which I was carrying up to the altar in my bare feet, a practice Christians there adopted long ago from the Buddhists; I missed a step and stubbed my big toe agonizingly on the hard polished floor. I just managed not to pass out, pulling myself together to bow to the Prime Minister in his prominent seat. The cathedral authorities were very pleased incidentally that he came, leaving before Communion indeed, but not until after we had brought the roof down with the 'National Anthem', as it was described on the order paper, though in fact it is a thorough-going Christian hymn, which I remember had thrilled me last time, with its really exciting tune, but where I have described it earlier I had not grasped its significance as a 'national' anthem, even though it includes phrases like:

> O Father, Thou hast promised to all who follow Thee
> In loyal and lowly service let each from other learn,
> The guardian and the guarded, till Christ Himself return,

Not to speak of the intensely moving:

> O consummation glorious which now by faith we sing,
> Come cast we up the highway, which brings us back the King.

I spotted Sam in the congregation and caught his eye as we smiled happily; he had sung it many more times than I had. No one seemed surprised when I enthused about it afterwards, hinting how intrigued I was at singing about our Christian faith in the 'National Anthem' of a Buddhist country; but I remain none at all the wiser as to how that had happily, and no doubt many years earlier, come about.

Sam and I stayed together in Joan de Mel's hospitable home, from which after the consecration we took a day off to get up to Kandy, so that Sam's Kurunegala friends could come down to see him on a much shorter trek than Colombo; we rang Rosemary from the rather decrepit Queen's Hotel, colonial relic that it is and looking as much, both inside and out. On the fourth and last morning of our brief visit we went south to Galle, the old Dutch fortress town, where we decided on a swim in the large L-shaped private pool of a very upmarket hotel, almost empty because of visitors having been scared away by the Troubles; in fact we thought we must be the only users of the pool until we swam towards the point of the L, and were slightly surprised to find the elephant, which belonged to the hotel as a tourist attraction, taking the opportunity to have a dip himself in the other bit of the L. All good things come to an end, and that night we were both in the air going our separate ways to Khartoum and Heath Row. My report to Bob Runcie was based on a little more knowledge of that lovely country and its fascinating people than I had had three years earlier; 'we think you ought to stick around, Bishop,' said the retired Bishop Swithun, 'we could between us do quite a lot to help these two fairly new members of the episcopate'.

Those occasions (Sri Lanka twice, Australia, Russia and Japan), on top of the one to Central Africa in 1974 as a representative of the Board of Mission and Unity, were the six official visits abroad which I was asked to fulfil as a bishop on behalf of the Church of England. But there was one other while I was still in harness, and that was because I was a member of the House of Lords, where I had come to know quite well a Labour life peer named Derek Whaddon; we had connected through a mutual interest in countryside matters, in particular over the then Council for Rural Industries. He twisted my arm in the autumn of 1985 to join him in a goodwill trip by representatives of both Houses of Parliament to Rumania, all of us to be sponsored by a clothing firm of which he was chairman; the idea of it was, I decided, a joint one of his, Parliament's and the firm's Managing Director, who undoubtedly had an eye for the main chance with regard to his business.

I had a very full diary as usual, and demurred, but made the mistake of saying I might consider it if I could bring my Lay Assistant, a condition which I was quite certain would end the matter, as the firm was already paying the expenses of four peers and four MPs. In fact that suggestion of my bringing more or less a chaplain-not-in-a-dog-collar (as Tim Gregson became to the company) seemed to appeal all the more to this lavish firm, and the four days behind the Iron Curtain were suddenly on. We were driven by private cars to the firm's private aeroplane, standing ready on a private runway at

Heath Row, after drinks in a private lounge, and quite unnecessary presentations to us all of cut glass, very unsuitably as we were just about to take to the air for a week. Over lunch on board Tim and I looked around at our new companions: the peers included Lord Wilson of Rievaulx, not long over a fairly damaging stroke, and the staunch Tory Jock Bruce Gardyne. Among the MPs was Harold Walker, a Deputy Speaker. Possibly my friend Paul Dean, another Deputy Speaker and Derek Whaddon were behind my being asked to go; the firm was keen to have a bishop for respectability's sake in a country where the Church, as throughout the Soviet bloc, was used shamelessly to promote government aims. That very morning the centre page article in *The Times* by Bernard Levin had detailed some of the horrors and unaccountable stupidities of the repressive regime for which we were heading on a 'goodwill' visit: 'typewriters have this last week been confiscated by the authorities from all foreign journalists' we read, as we dropped down rather doubtfully on Bucharest.

After being met by cars to whisk us to our comfortable hotel, we were driven to the British Embassy for a most interesting two hours' discussion, no Rumanians, and no members of the firm present, just us eight Parliamentarians. The ambassador talked about the condition of the country, about the importance of our being there as long as we took everything we were shown with a pinch of salt; he spoke quietly and earnestly, the former because this room is almost certainly bugged, and 'if we all talk quietly the speakers will have a job to pick up much', and it was tantalizing to have to leave in order to move on through poorly-lit streets to a restaurant dinner where the food was plentiful but boring. Harold Wilson, in boisterous form, embarrassed us all by singing *On Ilkley Moor baht'at*, but thankfully he wanted to do it solo.

Next morning the Counsellor at our embassy, Maureen Macglashan who was churchwarden of the English Church, picked up Tim and me in her car for a communion service. The American priest had just us three in his congregation, and we agreed afterwards that it was good to be reminded like that of how difficult it must be to be Christian in a communist country. Later in the morning the whole party was taken to be shown the moving of the two-hundred-and-fifty-year-old Antim Monastery, which was being bodily shifted fifty yards by the government to make room for a road; they had dug under the footings somehow, in order to insert rails on which to ease it inch by inch to its new position; we would not have believed it if we had not seen the marks where it had been the day before. Our wide-eyed query: 'Why not lay out the new road a little differently?' seemed too simple.

The delegation then split up, and Tim and I found ourselves in a seminary, where I spoke to nearly four hundred students in their college hall, a cheerful fat monk interpreting for me. He told me that Mervyn Stockwood, whom I knew loved Rumania, had once called him an old glutton, which he had obviously dined out on with great delight ever since. From there Maureen, our First Secretary friend, took us for an audience with Justin, the Patriarch, who was giving us ten minutes.

To Maureen's amazement, she told us afterwards, we were still hard at it an hour later, 'clearly because the patriarch wanted to talk'. Certainly conversation ranged far and wide: being a Christian in a socialist state (he was giving nothing away), Christians in prison ('all ours here have committed some crime against the state'), Bishop Tutu's stand against apartheid in South Africa (the patriarch had not heard of him), the ordination of women ('it can't be right when the Church has not done it in 2000 years'), and many more subjects too in one of the most remarkable hours of my life, which only came to an end when our helpful diplomat had to go off on another engagement; I asked the patriarch to give us his blessing before we left.

Next morning we were all back together for a tour at breakneck speed into Moldavia by coach in order to see some of the famous painted churches, among them Moldovita, with the great Last Judgment entirely covering the outside of the west wall; and Sucevita with its painted two-feet-square panels for every day of the year, so that each child in the village could know his or her name-day and feel that that bit of the building always belonged to them. I then suggested to the delegation that as it was St Luke's Day it would be good to pray together. Lord Wilson at once agreed (he could be charming when he was lucid), and the interpreter got the request across to the parish priest, who gladly gave me a lectern in front of the *ikonostasis*. I read from the Bible, expounding briefly on the passage in Acts about the coming of the Holy Spirit, and 'everyone hearing them in their own tongue', prayed some collects, and led the Lord's Prayer, which our hosts recognized and joined in in Rumanian which was just what I had hoped for. We stood throughout the twenty minutes or so, which of course is Orthodox practice anyway.

The Scots MP in the party was the first to break the silence after the service: 'That was wonderful, Bishop; thank you very very much'. I purred quietly, as one does at such kindly-meant remarks that often come the way of clergy. 'And I'll tell you why it was so guid', went on our Scot, 'because I was brought up on hour-long sermons from a Wee Free minister, so yours is the shortest service I've ever been to'. It would not have worked trying to explain to our hosts why we were all convulsed with laughter.

On the way back to town we passed a village church from which a wedding couple was just emerging to clapping and photographs. 'Stop', calls Harold to the coach driver, 'we must go and greet the happy couple'. So we obediently pile out and make for the villagers. 'I was Prime Minister of Britain', says Harold, brazenly interrupting a private occasion, and saying through our interpreter to this astonished bride and bridegroom: 'and this is the Bishop of Bath and Wells who is going to give you a blessing'. I was wearing a cassock and purple cloak (as I did every day), so maybe the couple realized vaguely what was happening. All of us rather distinctly shaken by what the incipient altzheimers former PM had done, we quickly embussed again, to be given much more than we deserved in loud applause from the bemused villagers as we went on our way.

Mercifully he was less bullish that evening when we had our audience with President Caucescu in his huge ugly new palace. I am not at all proud of that. We sat round a large table, and Harold asked me to read out the message from the archbishop, after which he bowed to me graciously in acknowledgement. Then the President began to talk quietly about the problems facing his country, blaming the shortage of rain for the power shortages (we were very conscious of 40 watt bulbs everywhere), outlining their need of hard currency, and then listening intently to the business talk that followed. We were there an hour or more. The ambassador told me privately afterwards (he was there for the whole audience) that the fact of this particular firm being fêted by the President would make things awkward for him, as other British companies would start expecting the same VIP treatment, 'and this man is so unpredictable

as head of state that I shall not find it easy to pacify other delega-
tions. Clearly your MD knows how to pull strings'. But I heard the
bottom line to the whole venture soon after Tim and I had written
our thank-you letters, genuine ones as we learnt a great deal, and
were superbly looked after by the firm as well as by our own
diplomats, and the Orthodox Church; this was that the firm concerned, who had paid for the entire enterprise in such lavish style,
was in serious financial trouble. The very bottom line of all was, of
course, the people's execution of the President and his wife on the
balcony of that very same grandiose palace four years later, when
the Soviet bloc was collapsing, and the victims of all that villainy
against the people of Rumania, and of the vandalism of historic
places like the middle of Bucharest were exacting their revenge.

After retirement I had a few more expeditions abroad because of
being a bishop. The first arose from being invited in 1988 to be the
C of E bishop on the British Atlantic Committee. This had been set
up soon after the momentous founding of NATO itself with the
object of helping ordinary people, in as many strands of UK life as
possible, to believe in and support NATO's work; and through their
various networks to encourage others up and down the land to do
the same. The committee met two or three times a year in comfortable rooms at the English-Speaking Union in King Charles Street,
and we were chaired for all three and a half years by the impressive
and immensely knowledgeable Sir John Killick, a career diplomat
who had been Ambassador to the USSR and also to NATO. I was
the only priest or bishop on the committee, and partly because of
my visits to Soviet countries I thoroughly enjoyed serving under
John's brilliant guidance; only when I read his obituary fifteen years
later did I realize what a very distinguished man he was, and certainly at every committee meeting we learnt something new about
the amazing phenomenon that Stalinist Russia was. I was asked
three years running to assemble and take parties of clerics to NATO
HQ in Brussels.

To put together a thirty-strong ecumenical team I had to write
round the secretaries at the London office of all the main members
of the British Council of Churches, explaining the aims of this
three-day conference hosted by NATO every year for the Church in
Britain. I asked for senior men and women, lay or ordained to

represent their particular denomination. The Committee did precisely the same for lawyers and medics and business men and trades-unionists and so on; there must have been twenty similar conferences to ours every year. Once I had mustered my team, I handed over the ticket-buying and all the arrangements to the BAC office, and then simply showed up at Stansted Airport to meet and lead the party, 'receiving' them as it were from the secretary of BAC, the efficient Major-General Popham. Whereas some members of the BAC were very right-wing indeed, the general was much more neutral as between the West and the Soviets, and his administration was impeccable.

From our Brussels hotel onwards, NATO people were in charge. I met some interesting fellow delegates on my three trips, but oddly seem to have made no special notes on any of them. I did however, through the accident of my three year stint being on either side of the collapse of communism, come in for a fascinating turn-around in the international scene, and one which I am bound to say so shook NATO that most of the staff I encountered, or sat under in briefings and lectures and in discussion groups, were frankly baffled by it. For example the chief lecturer on East-West confrontation 'across the great divide' made such small alterations to his presentation to us as between pre- and post- the demolition of the Berlin Wall that in my report to the BAC later I expressed the disquiet we churchmen felt.

There seemed to be so much distrust of everything Russian still, their motives, their intentions, their continuing hostility to the West and so on, that my members were thoroughly disquieted, getting the impression that Brussels wanted to convey to us a 'business as usual' approach. It was gratifying to have an abject, but grateful letter from some very high officer (was it SACEUR[44] himself, I think it might have been?) to Sir John Killick, copy to me, saying that many lessons had been learnt from that clerical delegation's visit, and they apologized for the unsatisfactory element which we had 'rightly challenged'.

Looking back on the incident, and the very altered mood of the final conference I was involved in, I have sometimes reflected that those who had been so closely involved in every aspect of countering the Soviet regime must have found it harder than the rest of us

44. Supreme Allied Commander Europe.

to come to terms with the sea-change in world affairs that happened in that early summer of 1989.

My very last overseas visit with the Church was in Holy Week 1996, a few months short of my 75th birthday; and it was particularly good that Rosemary received an invitation too. I was asked through being a chaplain and sub-prelate of the Order of St John of Jerusalem, the 'venerable order' to which I had been admitted as long before as 1977, when Bishop Cuthbert Bardsley of Coventry, a giant of a man if ever there was one, and I were sworn in together at Priory HQ in St John's Gate at Clerkenwell. In the years since then, I had tried to attend Chapter-General there whenever I could, and in the course of time I got to know most of the leading personalities, notably Sir Maurice Dorman, our much-loved Lord Prior. But it was a complete surprise to be asked in the autumn of 1995 whether I would come on a St John pilgrimage to the Holy Land as the chaplain, Rosemary accompanying me, and both of us as guests of St John.

It was almost too good to be true, especially as although I had been there many years earlier, it would be all new to Rosemary. Of course we said yes to the person who proposed the whole idea, and would be our very experienced leader, Sir Godfrey Milton Thompson. He had been the senior medical officer in the RN, and latterly Hospitaller of St John, which meant that he had overall responsibility for the Order's Eye Hospital in Jerusalem. To our delight Frances Bickersteth, Uncle Ralph's lively widow, joined the contingent, as there were a few spare places. It proved to be an unforgettable ten days.

We flew, twenty-five of us, to Amman, because of beginning our tour at Petra, new to almost everyone. We all took the tourists' horse-ride down through the narrow cliffs to the 'rose-red city', emerging to face the great structure itself carved out of the solid rock between 50 BC and 50 AD, which was every bit as wonderful as I had expected it to be. We bussed on to Jericho, saw Jerash and Acre on a day spent visiting Crusader castles; and then I had the moving experience of celebrating Communion for the whole party right on the shore of Lake Galilee. In Jerusalem itself we sang 'There is a green hill' very early one morning outside the Church of the Holy Sepulchre until the Orthodox guardians rushed out to stop us, but not before we had completed one verse; we joined in the Palm

Sunday processions down the Mount of Olives; we sat in the Shepherds' Fields outside Bethlehem, and in the ruins of Caesarea Philippi, probably on the site of that famous question to St Peter: 'Who do you say that I am?', and I took prayers and bible-readings and meditations in or near a dozen or more of the most sacred places in Christendom. The members of the party were very congenial, the planning by Godfrey impeccable, and we had lots of merry meals together, many of them out-of -doors in the not-too-hot sunshine. The political situation was infinitely less tense than it is today, though it was already restricting the work of the hospital; so, as the Palestinians could only get there with difficulty, the hospital was just beginning going out to them in minibuses fitted up as mobile eye clinics. We all felt proud and humble to be associated through St John with such sterling ministry in the name of Christ the Healer.

But that Holy Land visit was a long time after our Wells goodbyes (in 1987). There was my last tenants' dinner in the Henderson Rooms that summer; we hosted a family re-union for our 187 relations because Rosemary and I suddenly realized that big enough venues in a family home for this kind of occasion were rare these days and we had a now-or-never opportunity; we had a farewell staff lunch in the Star for Tim and Dr. Elizabeth Gregson, as Tim was retiring when I did; Rosemary and I sailed up from our lawn in a balloon for a hour's flight on a peerless autumn evening as a present from my staff, to be met when we landed further along the Mendips on a rather bumpy meadow, by the voice of my invisible registrar Martin Cavender through the hedge, with: 'As soon as I can penetrate this so-and-so hedge we'll crack a bottle of champagne', and he did the first, so we all did the second.

We had a £600 charity sale in the garage yard for bits and pieces of ours which we knew we would no longer have room for, a great party except that we somehow sold a motor mower which we had borrowed and it was quite tricky getting it back; the diocesan staff gave us a lunch in their Old Deanery headquarters, with the additional kindness of the secretary telling us that a room there was to be a *Bickersteth Room* in the building, and could we please find a photo for it; we went to Bath City Hall for a lunch and presentation from the Mayor and Corporation.

To sum up all the goodbyes we had two farewell services in the cathedral. The first was an evening eucharist on St Matthew's Day, the date of my ordination thirty-seven years earlier in Bristol Cathedral. The clergy robed; we had an altar half-way down the nave against the south wall, the congregation facing it in a great arc, and it worked rather well. Nigel McCulloch, the suffragan whom I appointed in January 1986, knowing (both of us of course) that we would only have eighteen months together, and the three archdeacons concelebrated with me, and the Wells Cathedral School orchestra shared music-making with the organist and choir. Both Rosemary and I loved our close association with Anthony Crossland in that important hot seat of his; in his quiet way he contributed a very great deal to the sum of Wells music in our time. On that St Matthew's night we ended with one of Charles Wesley's great hymns, to the Orlando Gibbons tune, 'Forth in thy name O Lord I go', the choir processing out towards the Lady Chapel once we reached the last two verses, singing by themselves the first as they moved east, but the choristers only (on arrival there) singing:

> For thee delightfully employ
> Whate'er thy bounteous grace hath given
> And run my course with even joy
> And closely walk with thee to heaven.

There was an awe-inspiring silence as the sound died away.

The second service a month later, just before we left, was non-eucharistic and ecumenical. We called it 'Pilgrims'. We cleared the nave of chairs, collected enough carpeting to cover the floor to make the stones a bit less cold to sit on; and the 'weakest went to the wall', where there were cushions for a less tough generation than our forefathers'. The Bath Abbey Choir joined the Wells Cathedral one and RSCM members throughout the diocese to sing 'The heavens are telling' from Haydn's *Creation*. John Roberts, the Abbot of Downside, read 'Christ is alive' from Michel Quoist. We had 'Love Divine' to *Blaenwern*, and 'O for a thousand tongues to sing' to *Lyngham*. We had the Blue School brass, St John's Band from St Audries School Quantoxhead, the Abbey Five Dance group, Taizé chants with the East Harptree choir, and 'Majesty' and 'Our God Reigns' led by the Holy Trinity Nailsea band In a break, everyone got up to ease cramped limbs and go to 'stations' all over the cathedral to talk, and have bread and 'wine' by deaneries.

I simply wore my cassock, taking some of the service from the pulpit, but mostly I moved about greeting people. Janie was at home, which was lovely for Rosemary and me, reminding us how much pleasure all the family had had in our home and the city, the cathedral and the county. Rosemary and I were the last people out of the building. As we walked across Palace Green together in the darkness, I saw a figure on the drawbridge; there was not another soul in sight, the crowds had all gone home. It was my secretary Mary Masters, who had been in to collect something from her office, and there could have been no one better for our last good-byes. We hugged for the first time.

Two mornings later the furniture vans arrived, the Wells chapter of our lives was over, and the seventy-fourth bishop since Edward the Elder founded the see in 909 was on his way; 1975-1987 were indeed years when, by some divine inadvertence as I have often thought, 'the lot had fallen unto me', if Psalm 16.7 may be slightly misappropriated, 'in a fair ground: yea I had a goodly heritage.'

Robert Runcie at Wells for the Cathedral's
800th anniversary celebrations, 1982

Opening the joint Anglican and Roman Catholic Secondary School of
St Augustine of Canterbury, with Mervyn Alexander, Bishop of Clifton, 1982

H.M. The Queen and Prince Philip leave Windsor Parish Church
with her Chaplains

. . . and Her Majesty entertains the College in Windsor Castle, 1983

At a sunny Glastonbury Pop Festival, 1983

. . . and with the Youth Chaplain, Bob Fyffe, at a wet one in 1985

Prince Charles on his fourth visit as Patron of the Wells Cathedral
West Front Appeal. Bishop Nigel McCulloch in the centre, 1987

Leaving the Palace to make
the first Women Deacons,
my last ordination
27 September, 1987

Forum for the Future

Reaching forth unto those things that are before,
I press towards the mark of the high calling of God in Christ Jesus.
Philippians 3.13

And I heard as it were the voice of a great multitude
and the voice of many waters, saying Alleluia,
for the Lord God omnipotent reigneth.
Revelation 19. 6

WHEN All Saints' Day 1987 dawned on Rosemary and me, we woke up in our first own house and jumped out of bed to enjoy the view of deep countryside from the bedroom window. We had had many carefree country holidays (in which Rosemary agrees I was fairly good at switching off), but they always had an annoying habit of coming to an end. That autumn, however, our permanent holy days began; and the lovely thing is that so much of what I turn my hand to in this continuing holiday of ours, 'non-churchy' as most of it is, proves to be somehow a logical development of my priestly life.

Going to church our first Sunday told us at once that we would be happy in the hundred-strong congregation. St John the Baptist Tisbury, two miles down the road from Beckfords, was going to be a good church for us. What is more the rector grasped immediately that I wanted to be in the pews, only helping out when he was stuck at six o'clock on a Saturday night for a celebrant next day; and his successors have been kind enough to get the message, mercifully without giving me a bad conscience, as there seems to be a steady supply of retired clergy who are pleased to assist in one or other of the Tisbury Team's many parishes.

In fact the most ecclesiastical activity in which I got immersed right away was through being county chaplain of St John Ambulance. I enjoyed those five years of St John Council meetings at our Devizes Headquarters. They often led to my having to find my way around rambling Wiltshire lanes in order perhaps to bless a new ambulance for the local St John unit; and I planned and led their annual carol service. I found myself developing a huge regard for the men and women and cadets who give so much of their time to this 'venerable' charity.

So with no other priestly responsibilities I was free to move in other directions. There was for example the early letter from my friend the County Historian of Somerset, the scholarly and gifted Dr Robert Dunning: 'You've no excuse now, you know', he wrote, and so it was that *Clerks of the Closet in the Royal Household* came to be written over the next three years by us both. 'For a start you must get a Reader's Ticket at the Public Record Offce', says Robert, so I did, and soon learnt how to call up the archival material I needed for working away in that magnificent Round Reading Room. Sometimes if the manuscripts were very old and precious I had to don gloves, and sit at a special desk under the eagle eye of the staff member on duty.

We each pressed on with our own halves of the project, I sending him my work every so often for editing, and when we reached the stage of putting everything together made the welcome discovery that our styles were similar enough for the 'join' to be invisible; in the end we were quite pleased with the result. Evidently Buckingham Palace was too, as we were given the honour of a private audience with the Queen in 1991, at which Robert and I presented HM with a leather-bound copy for the Royal Library at Windsor. Furthermore the Privy Purse was instructed to pay for a book launch, which through the chaplain there I arranged to hold in the large foyer of the Queen's Chapel of the Savoy. The occasion was most kindly graced (among twenty or more family and friends of Robert and me) by several members of the Household; and then Rosemary and I gave a lunch party in the fine panelled dining-room of old Royal Commonwealth Society building.

The book, avowedly on such an abstruse subject, sold badly, but it will probably stand for some years as the definitive history of an ancient office, the ten year holding of which brought me, and often Rosemary as well, some wonderful experiences, and at the end of it the Queen's gift of a knighthood in the Royal Victorian Order. 'You'll get a CVO for sure', Ted had commented to me in his pleased brotherly way some months before I resigned. But when it happened: 'It's a K, Johnnie, well done indeed', came the excited voice down the 'phone when he opened his *Times* on the morning the honour was gazetted. I had long felt that Ted would have got to the top, with a decoration or two, if the end of the Political Service because of Sudanese independence had not caused his early retirement in 1956 at the age of only forty-one; it was typically unselfish of him to be so genuinely thrilled for me, over thirty years later.

As a result of that award I am included in the gathering at Windsor, every four years, of the Order's members. There is a service first in St George's Chapel, the entire building packed; seven or eight of us who are KCVO bishops or deans sit in the sanctuary. We then all troop up the hill for a buffet lunch in the Castle. Everyone present has served The Crown, so there is always a good cross-section of past or present Household members: my last two conversations at the 2003 occasion were first with an estate carpenter (an M in the Order) who had worked on the restoration after the fire damage to St George's Hall where we were standing, and second with the Princess Royal (who is a G).

But the great thing is that Rosemary and I can do almost everything together. From that first Sunday in church (there is no better way of starting from scratch in a new place), we have made a widening circle of friends, and got to know an area which we like more and more. It is hard to remind ourselves now that when Humbert's advertising leaflet about the house appeared among the Palace mail on the day we bought it in May 1984, we had to go to the map to see where Tisbury was. The exploring of our new county for the work with St John began to be paralleled by the travelling Rosemary and I were increasingly doing on Wiltshire Trust for Nature Conservation concerns. By 1989 I was on the WTNC Council as well as that of St John, the two HQs being conveniently only a hundred yards apart in Devizes. Long before I had finished my St John chaplaincy, I was beginning to give far more time, indeed many hundreds of hours a year, to WTNC affairs. We had begun by simply going to the meetings, noting, as we had to drive some distance to them, that there was not much going on in our south west corner, hard against the Dorset border.

Someone else was well aware of that gap in the organization too, none other than General Robin Brockbank, who in those late 80's really 'was' the Trust. He asked if he could come over for a chat, the consequence of which was that he invited Rosemary and me to form and lead a group, to add to the seven or eight he already had covering the rest of the county. Robin said they had known for some time on the council that the best part of twenty villages hereabouts did not see themselves as belonging to any group: would we therefore create a South West Wilts one? Who could ever resist the charm of this very special cavalry general?

The group was very soon up to more than three hundred members, with fifty to sixty at monthly meetings, and were all of us enjoying ourselves. I was put up for the Council the following year, and completed a satisfying term of office six years later. Rosemary and I offered to go to other county Trusts to see what they were doing. We only managed two, not far from each other in the Midlands, where we stayed with unknown people, one of them a fine ornithologist who gave us a day in the hides round Rutland Water. I also did some farm visiting in our area, the most quirky being one owned by two brothers and a sister, who had inherited their time-warp property from their father when he died in 1947.

They were still using only his methods of running the farm. In particular this meant thousands of wild flowers in the meadows, and the farm buildings untouched in forty years, so the sash windows were propped up with broken broom handles. Five large lambs, perfectly healthy as far as I could see, shared the front room with the television and the three of them who watched the racing while talking to me. I was there to encourage them, because of that wonderful unsprayed grassland, to think of the Trust in their wills, and they had been quite interested in what I was saying. But Glorious Goodwood defeated me that time, and by the next the one-toothed old sister, who ran the brothers, had remembered some great nieces who knew nothing about farming or conservation, and alas 'would probably want the money' from selling the farm to the highest bidder.

I did in fact spend a lot of time on legacies, which is commonplace for charities now but was very new then, other than for the big names like Dr Barnardo's. I offered at a Council meeting to visit solicitors' firms up and down the county with Trust leaflets, to invite them to suggest to any clients who might ask for help in drawing up their wills that they might include the Trust. Over a six months period I went to eighty Wiltshire law firms, but (pleasantly received as I was) absolutely nothing happened. No one died for eight years or so, and we later heard from the RSPB, who were pioneers in this kind of effort, that that is about the time it takes for a legacy drive to have any effect.

At Council meetings in the summer of 1989, I was starting to pick up literature about Creation Festivals. There was one in Coventry to which we could not go, but the ever-present lure for me of Canterbury took us to one at Christ Church College there before the end of the year. The idea of the church using its wonderful 'plant' to stage such a festival seemed to me to have a lot going for it, and with rather guarded support from the council but the enthusiastic backing of Robin Brockbank himself, I was knocking on the Dean of Salisbury's door around New Year's Day 1990: 'Could we mount a Creation Festival in the Cathedral and Close over the May Bank Holiday?'

Once the Chapter had agreed, we realized that there was no time to lose, but with several new committees handling different aspects of what proved a big enterprise, and a recently-retired warrant officer from the Blues and Royals in charge of the seventy organizations taking part, we were more or less ready in time, and it made quite an impact. Prince Philip, wearing his hat as President of the World-Wide Fund for Nature and Chris Patten, then Secretary of State for the Environment contributed excellent pieces for the programme and Jonathon Porritt was among the very good speakers we invited to emphasize the fragility of our planet. We lost money over it, because it is not possible to charge anyone for coming into Salisbury Close; but various kind well-wishers, who saw the importance of it all at a time when not many did, kindly baled us out, and we just managed to cover our £45,000 expenses.

A small panel of Portland stone, carved on the site during the week-end, with (picked out in red) 'Creation Festival 1990', and our logo of the sun's golden rays, was accepted by the Dean as a permanent record of the event, and the master mason himself let it in to the cloister floor, near the Chapter House entrance. I glance gratefully at this lasting memorial several times a year, privileged as all of us at the sharp end felt to have been responsible for what is still much the most ambitious visual attempt yet by the Church of England to highlight the wonders of the natural world, evolving as it all has under God these millions of years, but only in the last century or so terribly threatened by mankind.

Another of the lecturers at the Festival was Eve Dennis, then of the Nature Conservancy Council and developing Church and Conservation ideas at Stoneleigh.[45] One of her passions was the opportunities that churchyards offered for the saving of wild flowers; because of being on chalk there could be as many as a hundred different species in each. After her lecture in Salisbury, Rosemary and I felt that we must take up her challenge, and try to persuade clergy and churchwardens in the county not to mow everything in sight in the interests of tidiness. The result was the establishment of the *Living Churchyard* project, for which we had training days and competitions in various parts of the county, and a lively committee recruiting tactful naturalists, who were ready to undertake the rather uphill task of getting the enthusiastic retired brigadier mowers on to our side. After some years the scheme has become well-established, and a good many of our six hundred or more churchyards now belong to it; what is more they sold the idea to the Dorset Wildlife Trust, the neighbouring county, which is of course part of the Salisbury diocese.

Another more indirect outcome of the Festival was the Wiltshire Wildlife Trust's[46] buying of Oysters Coppice Semley, three miles or so from Beckfords. For some years our Trust had managed for its owners this eighteen-acre oak and ash and hazel woodland as a Nature Reserve, and as it was the closest reserve to our SW Group a number of us in the group began working there, keeping open the path round the wood, cutting and laying hedges, clearing 'coups' among the trees to encourage butterflies and so on. Turning up there, however, one morning we saw a 'For Sale' sign on the gate; a quick 'phone call revealed that indeed the owners had decided to sell, without restrictive covenants, and had not had the courtesy to let us know:

'As a matter of fact we have already had two offers above the asking price', I was told rather ashamedly down the telephone. We think the sale idea may have been activated by the considerable publicity there was about the Creation Festival, including a photograph in *The Times*. Two of us drove straight to Wimborne, persuaded the rather embarrassed owners to put the offers they had had on hold for a fortnight, and undertook there and then to raise the asked-for £11000. With twenty-four hours to spare we got the

---

45. Headquarters of the Royal Agricultural Society.
46. As the Wiltshire Trust for Nature Conservation had by then become.

money together for the Trust to buy the wood; and thankfully the people who responded so generously to my urgent appeal are still friends.

Successive working parties keep up our activities there, but now with an owner's concern; we do not 'tidy' much, but we and many visiting walkers can continue to delight in the riot of bluebells every May, the deer, the badgers, and the birds, including the quite rare Lesser Spotted Woodpecker. The working party enjoys itself there once a month; we sit round the barbecue in all weathers for our midday break, and put the world to rights.

Without any doubt the Creation Festival also rubbed off on our gardening enthusiasms. We began to see, as so many do increasingly, that caring for one's own garden is a tiny thing we can tackle ourselves within the huge picture of the need to care for the whole natural world. For instance we dug a pond that year, all of eight feet long, but big enough to add something extra to the garden, to which we rejoice in belonging, rather than it to us. We sit in it to read or to eat at some moment every possible day from March to November, and we labour in it, thankfully still able to do everything except the hedge-cutting. Ours is not a classy garden, but it is certainly a very great deal more interesting than it was when we bought Beckfords.[47]

We can claim to have helped nature make it so, by many hundreds of hours of activity, far far more than we ever had time to give to our four earlier gardens. When we have put it all to bed for the winter, with plenty of leaf mould and compost heaps maturing, the cross-cut saw comes out; it was a wedding present, and whereas most of these saws now hang as ornaments in the bars of country pubs we get warm twice over from sawing up, and in due course burning, the beech and ash cordwood we buy from the local woodman, a good friend who is also head server in St John's.

What is more we have a 'fruitful vine', which was given us as a leaving present by Bob Caldwell. Deciding, after advice, to grow on his little 'whip' in our greenhouse, we planted it just outside, where it gets the dews of heaven, but we could and did let the 'rods' develop inside, and more than ten years on it gives us a hundred or more bunches of *Black Hamburgs* every year. As we have a dozen

---

47. We named our 1799 cottage after the man who built it, William Beckford 1760-1844, art collector and creator of Fonthill Abbey two miles up the road from us.

other varieties of fruit as well, our little half-acre patch is encouragingly prolific.

Meanwhile, to add yet further to the pleasure of our Beckfords
lives I was lucky enough to be offered a rod in the Abbey syndicate,
which has the privilege of fishing for rainbow trout on the private
and very beautiful Bitham Lake, half a mile from our front door.
Any fisherman worth the name will aver that to enjoy lake fishing as
I do is very much second best to using one's skill on a river, and I
know from experience that that is right. Bitham is only ten minutes
away and the setting is superb. We catch fish; Rosemary gallantly
rows (as there is no bank fishing), and the accessibility means that
she does not become a fishing widow. Every so often too I am kindly
offered a day on the Test or the Avon or the Wylye, all not far from
home; the Wylye days each year are with Malcolm Fraser who first
taught me to fish in the 1970s, and we two friends have met to fish
somewhere every year since.

In the mid-nineties my pen was getting itchy again; I needed a
new writing project, having had one kind or another of them for
ever: school in the 1930s had meant essays; as a soldier I had edited
regimental magazines at home and abroad on and off for five years
or more ('ask Bick; he'll have a go'); at Oxford and Wells, like every
student that ever was, I wrote and wrote for four more years; and
then after being ordained in 1950 I was into sermons for the next
nearly half-century, not to speak of a steady stream of articles, of
drafts for reports, of reports themselves, of hundreds of letters and
endless speeches for this or that occasion, grave or gay (the latter in
its unadulterated sense). As is the way, therefore, with very many
clergymen I am actually a compulsive writer, as you yourself will
have discovered if you have got thus far in this rather discursive
book. On that particular morning in the downstairs lavatory at
Beckfords I felt I might have lit upon a fascinating subject for my
pen (I was no typist then, not that I am much of a one now): it was
conveniently to hand as I was sitting there. 'It' was the eighteen-
volume three-feet-length of *The Bickersteth Family War Diary*.

We had housed the *Diary* for Ted ever since Burgon's death in
1979, simply because we had tended to have bigger houses than his
and Elspeth's. 'Is there a book in all these pages?', I said to Rosemary when I had emerged? I rang Ted at once; he saw that I was

not prepared to take no for an answer and agreed to my suggestion that I chose some good excerpts for us to show together to a *Nobody's* friend of mine, in the shape of John Murray of Albemarle Street. So I left a volume with him on a London visit, and made a date for the three of us to talk the idea through in his wonderful old Dickensian office, where his grandfather, his father, he and then his son (all John Murrays) had their famous publishing business. John was immediately supportive: 'this is superlative stuff', he told Ted and me as we sat there goggle-eyed, 'we will test the waters with the editor of the *Spectator*', he said. So I did, the following week, and the editor rang back enthusiastically, to say he would like to put in the piece I sent him (it was the account of Julian ministering all night to the soldier who was to be shot at dawn) in a two-page spread, and would I be happy with £75?

This was all very euphoric, and still more so when several publishing houses wrote on seeing the article that if I was considering a book they would like to hear from me. I simply acknowledged their kind enquiries, knowing all too well that I was still a very long way away from any possible book. But I made a start, deciding to tackle the Great War only (eleven volumes), and furthermore mainly to use only the letters home of those two inseparable bachelors, 'the uncles' whom I had known and loved for ever, Julian then a padre, and Burgon a cavalryman. So Rosemary and I began, in the most Heath Robinson method imaginable: I simply chose the pages I felt we wanted to include, and took them down one volume at a time to our Tisbury photocopying service. Then with scissors and paste I glued short typed slips to link the diary passages, and took the 'joined up' typing to a lively eighty-year-old retired university don from Canada, Dr Norah Moorhead, who had come (about the time we arrived in Beckfords) to live in an apartment at Pyt House, the gracious eighteenth century mansion then used by elderly people a mile away.

She retyped beautifully the whole of what I gave her; and it was a bonus that she keen on it, because of the Canadian link. As the months went by, it became quite exciting to view this growing pile of A4 pages, which I knew would now be presentable enough for me to offer a publisher when the time came. Few books which have gone into a third edition can have been born in a more amateurish fashion.

After three years' work I was ready to take up the publishers' invitations at the time when the *Spectator* article had appeared. After some disappointing 'nice No's', (a phrase I had learnt from the Household: 'I suggest you write him a nice No', when I had brought along to my immediate boss in the Palace some impossible request from an unknown chap), the military publishers 'Pen & Sword' agreed to receive the script. I caught the train to Waterloo with a large plastic bag containing more than three hundred typed pages, edited from three thousand, and climbed the rickety stairs to Leo Cooper's rather scruffy office off Shaftesbury Avenue to present my text. A month later I heard from him: 'I like it very much indeed', he said, 'we will publish it.'

Donald Coggan, an old friend of the family, especially of Burgon, gave us a Foreword; John Terraine, well-known in military history circles, wrote an Introduction; Humphrey Stone, from our village, designed the book, and by Christmas 1995 we were ready to launch *The Bickersteth Diaries 1914-1918*. We did it in an ideal family venue, namely King's School, Canterbury, Canon Anthony Phillips, then the headmaster, doing the honours very well indeed for a merry party of sixty or more family and friends, together with local notables. Most bought signed copies to set the ball rolling. Then we just waited, publisher and editor alike, to see what the reviewers were going to say. It was a real advantage that the First World War, indeed both Great Wars, were just beginning to acquire the fascination they still have (but had never previously had) with the general public.

The reviews were slow in coming, but we need not have worried. Four months after publication day in January 1996 it suddenly all started, with Frank Field writing the first, a very good one in *The Financial Times*; the biographer Tim Heald, a neighbour of ours in the Donheads wrote an equally glowing review in the *Daily Telegraph*; and we were away. Further ecstatic ones came tumbling out, some in unlikely periodicals such as the *Tablet* and *Country Life*; by the end of the year there were fifty or so of them. We were much helped by Ted offering to fly over to Canada, where we hatched a launch at Hart House in Toronto University, which drew an appreciative crowd although it was fifty years since Burgon had retired; and in Australia we had another one mounted by Julian in Sydney. This huge interest resulted in the 1st edition being sold out within months of publication, and the publishers produced a reprint in paperback in time for Remembrance Sunday that same year. That was followed eighteen months later, for the 80th anniversary of the Armistice (1998) at the end of WWI, by a third edition, this time in hard cover again. Everywhere the story was the same: 'This is the best book I have ever read about how one family came through the Great War', or 'How could those brothers write such arresting English with a stub of pencil from a muddy trench' or 'You deprived me of sleep last night; I finally put the book down at three o'clock this morning', together with every variety of similar comments. It was frankly very exciting to glow in the success of a book I had not written.

I often wish that grandmother and the uncles were still around to contemplate what has eventually happened to those letters home which describe so graphically the terrible times through which they were passing. We would laugh and cry together, I am quite sure; and Burgon might well remember that it all began because of what he wrote in August 1914 (I quote it on p.xix of my Prologue in *The Diaries*), urging his mother 'to share with Julian, stuck out in Australia, those momentous happenings which are affecting all of us'. She must have agreed, and began to collect the letters from France, and to cut out material from the papers (how the Victorians loved newspaper cuttings). It was Burgon too who in 1916 told the distinguished war correspondent Sir Philip Gibbs what his mother was so painstakingly doing; and Gibbs, who was a friend of the family, had written to her (p.69 op. cit.):

> I am sure that what you are doing is immensely worth while, especially if you are not afraid of putting in the little details of everyday life. The big things belong to history and will be familiar enough, but afterwards the next generation will search for the intimate records, and the psychology of the men who served'.

Because that remarkable lady had done just that, 'putting in the little details', had kept on at it through thick and thin, and had not given the whole thing up when one of her sons was killed, the fact is that eighty years on what she had done was received with such widespread acclaim: 'The entire book' said the *Daily Telegraph* review, 'deserves to become a classic in the literature of war'.

All this time Rosemary and I were getting more and more fond of living 'out in the sticks' as our friends tend to describe Beckfords. 'Every time I come and stay, Dad', commented Janie once, 'you take me on a different walk'. There and then we totted up fifteen without difficulty; and they all start from our front door, because of the land for our row of cottages having been chopped out of a field. We have no motorway noise and no light pollution; we put in solar panels in the year of the Creation Festival to use every bit of warmth in the sun, there is a field over the hedge for the dogs to run in when the sheep are not there, and the view is stunning; we constantly talk about our good fortune. So it almost seems indecent to mention holidays when life is one long one. But the fact is that in nearly eighteen years we have been lucky enough to have some wonderful experiences in far-away places.

Only one of our ten Australian trips has been on duty, and that was before we left Wells; they have all have added something of interest to our love of the continent. One year in those parts we went on to look up friends in the south island of New Zealand where we saw an *Echidna* in some rain forest off the Harz Pass, shortly before standing at the foot of the (retreating) Fox glacier; on another we saw the dry-looking bush of the noble Stirling Ranges in Western Australia burst alive with wild flowers in an October spring; we have driven the Great Ocean Road from Adelaide to Melbourne, built by German prisoners in the first world war; we have stayed by ourselves at the Patersons' property in the Maclaren Vale vineyards of South Australia; and we have watched from ten feet away the blue bower bird making his nest of blue objects in one of the very small remaining pockets of rain forest in Queensland.

In other parts of the world we have been on a week's walking holiday among the wild flowers in the Pyrenees; we have trodden Nepali mountain tracks from Pokhara in the foothills of the Annapurna, and lurched memorably on elephant howdahs (five beasts in line astern through the mist of early dawn) to look unsuccessfully for leopard; we have glided down the Zambesi at dusk to watch eighty African elephants walking sedately to water; we have walked on the walls of Dubrovnik, to drop down on to that matchless *stradum* and slip into a Franciscan church just off it for an evening of chamber music; we have attended a Provencal wake when staying with friends in a sixteenth-century *maas* in the Petit Luberon; In Venice we got blessed by a priest at the *Salute* because of getting mixed up in a crowd of gondoliers about to start a race on the Grand Canal; we have revelled in *Fidelio* in Vienna's State Opera House and in *Madam Butterfly* in the Opera House on Sydney Harbour; we have seen the Impressionists in the Quai d'Orsay, Rembrandt's *Night Watch* in the Rijkmuseum, and Michelangelo's *David* in the Uffizi; we have stayed in the rented house Jonathan and Janie took in Chengmai; we have strode along the *levadas* of Madeira, where the gradient is so gradual that you suddenly find you have climbed a mountain; we have spent a night in a shanty town just outside Port Elizabeth with the intrepid black priest and his wife; we have gazed up at the splendours of the Rocky Mountains from the observation car of the overnight train from Banff. Wherever we have been we have met wonderful kindness from complete strangers, and rejoiced at the limitless variety of God's Creation; and we have homed in on Beckfords more thankfully than ever.

But meanwhile that fountain pen of mine was poised once more; or rather I had acquired my first computer, the family having been so horrified that we had mounted the entire *Diaries* enterprise without one, that they gave us an old model. I discovered later that 'old' in computer circles meant that it had been around for all of three years; this one was more than adequate for us both to get the rough hang of how it worked. 'Rough' is still the right word, albeit our understanding of this particular modern miracle is a good deal better than it was.

The choice of what to do turned out to be a very simple one, as I woke up one July morning in 1996 saying to Rosemary: 'I think I'll have a go at the Open University'.

'Excellent idea', she said at once. I duly registered that same week, having discovered that July 31 was the cut-off date for the next academic year, and got my application in for the following February with two days to spare.

'As a matter of interest', I asked at the area office, 'how many have registered this summer for a course in the OU in 1997?'.

'I can tell you in a moment', she helpfully replied, 'Yes. World-wide there seem to be including you 225, 310. It looks like being quite a good year'.

That this was the astonishing figure for the number of under-graduates in one year alone is some indication of the success story that the OU is; and it is also incredibly efficient.

I knew it was History that I must go for, having moved as long ago as 1936 to read only Ancient History because it is part of classical studies. Now was the chance for which I had been waiting, and it was sheer delight to plunge right away into the subject of my first choice which was 'The Age of Enlightenment'. I later read 'Culture and Belief in Europe 1450-1600'; 'Princes and Peoples: France and the British Isles 1620-1714'; and finally 'State Economy and Nation in Nineteenth Century Europe'. We undergraduates were a motley bunch, with me the oldest in I think only two of the years. The age range was huge, the motivation as varied; I specially admired the thirty or forty-year-old students who had enrolled with a view to im-proving their qualifications; most had to get up early and stay up late to do the TMA preparation before or after their day's work. By contrast I settled down to a pattern of only about six hours a week; not enough really, and when every four or five weeks it came to actually putting together a 1400-word essay ('Tutor Marked As-signment' in OU jargon) I had to step that up, as I also did, much more so, when in September I was revising for the exam. I dis-covered I could just about maintain that amount of OU activity across the academic year, though of course there were weeks when any study went almost overboard.

For the tutorials I had to drive early on Saturday mornings to Basingstoke or Reading or Southampton, so that I could sit with a dozen or so other students for a couple of hours under successive tutors, most of whom were very good. Considering the complexity of the subjects I chose, and that I was starting without much know-ledge of them beyond what I had picked up in general reading over the years, I was pleased to do quite presentably overall; the OU does not have Finals, which was a blessing as I had to interrupt studies twice because of Rosemary being ill, so I took five years altogether instead of three. I cannot speak highly enough of the Open University; I thoroughly enjoyed it all as one of the best ele-ments of these exhilarating years since we left Wells.

It was great that Rosemary and the family were as thrilled as I was that I joined the OU; it has actually been quite a natural progress-ion from *Clerks of the Closet* (1988–91), to *The Bickersteth Diaries*

(1992-6) to the Open University (1997-2002), and now to these reflections on my life; and in these it is high time that I gave space to that same family which took such an interest in what their pater-familias was doing in his late seventies.

It is true, of course, that for rising fifty years, each and all of Rosemary herself, our four children, and later their spouses and now our fourteen grandchildren have never been far away from all my thinking and doing. Indeed it seems to me that for a happily married man to call a book written by himself an 'autobiography' can be misleading if every page is to do only with the book's subject; to present a true picture of the *autos*, the 'self', he must include a good deal about his personal life, and I have tried to do this earlier for instance by including my two love affairs in the 1940s. Since then, however, I have deliberately chosen in these pages not to insert personal and family happenings in their chronological order, because I found early on (two years ago, to be precise) that they tended to break the sequence rather awkwardly. What follows, however, will I hope constitute some attempt to explain how profoundly my whole life has been influenced by my replying as I did to the Bishop of Salisbury's question in St John's Hurst Green on 20th April 1955. His question of course was none other than: 'Wilt thou have this woman to thy wedded wife?', and I replied, deeply conscious of the enormity of what I was saying (and I recall the moment with crystal clarity): 'I will'. Rosemary and I walked out of church later in a gorgeous haze, which has continued (as with every happily-married couple, despite all the odds against it) ever since.

My professional wife carried on teaching in that preparatory school for the summer term after we were married. Thereafter she either taught in pupils' own homes round about, or had them to the Parsonage. I even tried to learn the basics myself on her fine upright (the Steinway Grand did not come to us until we moved to Chatham in 1962), but over a month or two and despite patient encouragement from my beloved, I was still stuck on middle C and scales, and the call of the garden became too strong for my limited spare time. But Rosemary's teaching has showed no sign of stopping; the highlights of her skills since we were married were undoubtedly most in evidence during the nineteen years she taught at Wells Cathedral School, eleven of them while we lived in the

Palace, and the last eight from here which meant a fifty-mile round trip from Tisbury. Every so often, therefore, to match 'you confirmed my son at Taunton in 1980' to me come the equally welcome to her 'you taught me in the cathedral school'.

We had four children in six years, so to put it mildly home life in Hurst Green was pretty busy. The house and garden were just right for a young family and for visiting mums and babies from the parish, so this was a built-in catchment area for bringing that age range into the life of the church. Rosemary must have had sixty or more at its zenith in the Young Mums' group she formed; and her involvement with the parish was never more helpful and memorable (as I have described) than when she was the continuo for *Noye's Fludde* in the spring of 1962; she had remained at the piano for rehearsals until the day before Sam was born, and was back on that stool to hugely-justified acclaim when he was only a fortnight old.

By then Piers was at the local Primary School, but once we had moved to the Medway Towns that autumn he began at the Chestnuts in Rochester, where the redoubtable Miss Snowden-Smith had run a splendidly old-fashioned dame school for pre-preparatory boys for years and years. The well-authenticated rumour was that in the war, when she had had to take in girls to keep the school going, she only had them if they wore shorts and played football. There was good teaching and good discipline, and we were glad to get Julian in there too when he was six. By then we had some help with the children, Roma Durnford from Gillingham first, then Elizabeth Luthi from Switzerland, Tineke Bal from Holland and finally Renate Schart from Germany; they each in their turn became good friends of us all, and contributed much to the smooth running of our quite large household. Later when our four were a bit older we switched to taking in as paying guests overseas students studying locally, and again we had a succession of charming men, mainly Nigerians (both Ibo and Yoruba, significant enough in itself), and also Solomon Balas, an Israeli with whom we kept up for some years. So horizons were widening all the time for the young.

Janie, and later Sam we got into a first-rate school in Rainham, twenty minutes away, and the school bus ran from our church drive. The unconventional headmistress (she interviewed us in mid-summer wearing a thick overcoat and snowboots), was herself a fine teacher, and had attracted an able staff. The next step for the older boys was boarding school, which was made possible for us financially by the Trust Fund we set up after Uncle Julian had made me his residuary legatee before he died in 1962; and Uncle Burgon added to it fairly steadily over the next seventeen years, with an extra lump sum after his death in 1979. That fund only ran out in the 1980s just before Sam left Oxford. It is true to say that neither Rosemary nor I really questioned the ethos of those days whereby middle-class people like us began boarding their children at the age of eight. I know that when we had said goodbye to Piers on his first day, and he had put on a wonderfully brave face on our departing, we pulled straight into a layby for me to cry, and Rosemary nearly succumbed too. The kind phone call that evening from the second master's wife that Piers had gone to bed happily, and further reassuring ones over the next week, were no doubt standard practice, but they certainly helped us.

The school he very quickly settled into was Hildersham House Broadstairs, to which we were rather more drawn than two or three others we saw nearby. Hubert Snowden, the third generation owner, of whom I had heard through my Rugby links (he was an enthusiastic OR all his life) was very much the traditional prep. school headmaster, a golf-mad bachelor; and if no one had actually heard him bellow at his football team from the touch-line at a school match: 'Now come on you lot, no jam for tea if you don't get a goal very quickly', he was the kind of man who might have. Both we and the boys in due course developed a real affection for him, which seemed to have been mutual. When Piers eventually captained the school cricket side in his last term, Hubert said to him in our hearing: 'Well Piers you must be the worst cricketer in definitely the worst school side I have ever had, but I'm very glad indeed that I made you captain, as you've been tip-top at it.'

Julian did well there too, and became Hubert's last head boy. Hildersham was a private business, as most prep schools were then, and the combination of parents increasingly wanting schools near home so that their boys need not board, secondly of Hildersham and the other Broadstairs schools being too far into that south-east corner of England, and thirdly of the rest of his family wanting to realize their considerable assets tied up in the school plant, meant that Hubert decided to close down. Sam had only four terms there before the school finished, and this suited us admirably, as by then we were in Liverpool, and we easily got him into a similar establishment, Holmwood, in Formby, one station up the line from Crosby, where he too became head boy four years later.

Merchant Taylors', the excellent Direct Grant school in our village on the edge of Liverpool, was the obvious choice for Janie, and she did her GCSEs there quite young. The buildings were only ten minutes walk from Martinsfield, and I often thought when I went with her of father walking me to Gibbs's in the 1920s, three times further from home as it was. For her Sixth Form years she followed Piers and Julian in boarding at Marlborough, finding the art teachers there specially gifted; without question they took her natural talent forward a great deal, to help her achieve later a very good degree from the Central[48]in London to round off her formal education.

Once Sam in his turn had left Marlborough I became a member of the Council, and it was a thrill for Rosemary and me to hear many times during my Council years how each of our four in their differing ways had contributed to the school's life. We had had no hesitation in choosing Marlborough, partly because of its very good reputation, partly because it lies in such lovely country, (when 'home' for our children was in the nature of my work much more likely to be in towns), partly because I had many links with the school through the Jelf side of the family, and partly because, although Rugby might well have helped with some kind of bursary for the offspring of Old Rugbeians, we benefited at Marlborough much more extensively through their 'Sons (and by then Daughters) of the Clergy' Fund.

Piers had that year's farming with the Colmans after he left school, and was then successful in applying for the Royal Agricultural College outside Cirencester, emerging in due course, after playing Rugby Football for the college and making many friends, to finish his exams for the Associateship of the Royal Institute of Chartered Surveyors during his first job, which was with Savills' in their Wimborne office. There we bravely bought a house for him, and he learned the ropes on the agricultural side of the firm, acquiring skills and interests which will be with him all his days. That was immensely satisfying for me, as I looked back at my own

48. The Central College of Art and Design, later merged wih St. Martin's nearby.

rather unformed wish to go in for some form of agricultural work after university, a wish which only gradually faded after my six years' soldiering and the first stirrings of a call to the ordained ministry.

Julian and Sam both got into Christ Church, to the joy of Rosemary and me because of both our families' House links. Julian got a Half Blue for rowing in the Lightweights; Rosemary and I watched them at Henley in the pouring rain, going down to an honourable defeat by a stronger Cambridge crew. Sam distinguished himself in his Finals, and came back to Oxford after those memorable eighteen months in Sri Lanka to have a year at Linacre College, which he collected a B.Sc. needed for work. Needless to say it was wonderful for both Rosemary and me to have such a good excuse for several years to drive to Oxford. Piers had bought a house there when he got back from Australia, to be his home while studying at Wycliffe, so we often had days with one or other of the boys, returning therefore to the dreaming spires far more often than if I had only had the fun of occasional Gaudies.

Julian was the first to get married. He had gone out to Australia soon after coming down from Oxford, having successfully applied for a year's teaching at Timbertop, the outward-bound-style element of Geelong Grammar School, up northwest of Melbourne in the foothills of the Great Dividing Range. It was an adventurous time for him in more ways than one, in that halfway through his contract a mathematics graduate, fresh from Adelaide University, joined the staff, and she within two years became our daughter-in-law. We flew out to Julian's marriage to Cecily Paterson in St Peter's School Chapel Adelaide, very nearly late for the whole purpose of our journey, because the Philippines Airlines plane broke down in Manila.

In those days passengers were never flown on to their destination in another plane; we just had to wait, for three whole days, and only made it with twenty-four hours in hand. We had already met Cecily of course because she had flown to England after they had both left Timbertop, but everyone and everything else was new to us; and how struck we were by the Australian light; we still are, every time we get out from the plane on arrival there. We were made wonderfully welcome. As I looked down the aisle from the altar of the

---

49. He was Headmaster of St Peter's 1919–33.

school chapel, which had been so much at the heart of Uncle Julian's headmastership,[49] boys were kicking a football about outside his old house; and I was able to rejoice over this remarkable pattern of events whereby his great-nephew was in the very same chapel nearly fifty years later to marry the daughter of a distinguished 'Saints' old boy.

Piers had decided to resign from Savills after four years with them in order to come out to Australia for Julian's wedding, and try for a job there. Three days after the wedding he was taken on by Jones, Lang, Wootton in Sydney, whence he came home temporarily a year later in order to marry Carolyn Longhurst, whom he had met in his Wimborne days. I married them in Carolyn's church at Angmering, a year and a day after Julian's wedding in Adelaide. They returned to Sydney for six more years, coming home for good in 1989, for Piers to enter Wycliffe Hall in North Oxford. That call to change direction so drastically, and go to a theological college, led to a curacy in the Wirral and the start of full-time ministry in the Church of England, the sixth generation of our name to become Anglican clergy. But neither my father (who began working as an accountant), nor I, nor Piers had left school with that intention.

Two years later we had yet another August wedding. Janie began to realize that I might leave Wells for good before she and Jonathan Rigg (whom she had met at Marlborough) got round to being married; they had remained firm friends from those days. Jonathan had got his degree, and was by then working for a doctorate while teaching at the School of Oriental and African Studies, where he was steadily becoming the considerable expert he is in South-East Asia geography. So Rosemary and I had the excitement, for our only daughter, of a service in the Cathedral, with the choir in full voice, the bells crashing out on cue, and a Palace reception afterwards, for which the sun shone after a drizzly start, enabling us and our guests to spill out on to the lawns, and sit on the grass if champagne legs demanded it. The photographer had a field day for fine shots in such a unique setting. Jonathan and Janie stayed on in London in their married state, so at least we did not lose a third offspring to the far corners of the earth.

Sam meanwhile was well into overseas postings, without much consecutive time in England for courting. It was another eight years before he managed it, when he was in Khartoum, his second job (after Pakistan) in what was then the Overseas Development Agency,[50] of the Foreign Office. Hannah Parks was also in the Sudan as a VSO studying traditional medicine in an anthropological institute. She came home, about when he did, to start the seven-year training to become a doctor, and as they were both getting older she was married before qualifying, triumphantly vindicating her late decision to follow her well-known father into medicine by passing her last exam. some time after the wedding. For this, in the spring of 1993, we all went to Hannah's home in Dunwich; not quite 'all' because Cecily, very understandably in view of two young to care for, did not fly home with Julian. But we did have several grandchildren with us, a splendid extra dimension for Rosemary and me. I shall never forget Joshua, aged four and very smart in bright red trousers and matching braces, gazing enthralled at Sam and Hannah driving away from church in a horse and cart, probably the first such he had ever seen; or of George, all of three years old, in the marquee on the lawn at Whitefriars, and being offered cherries still on their stalks by his father, but (again it might have been a first) not at all sure whether they were all right to eat.

Sixteen Bickersteths and Riggs were gallantly put up in a house we were lent by kind neighbours of Hannah's; they even got out their canteen of silver for us to have a proper dinner party the night before the wedding, as the owner of the house (who had moved out to accommodate us) discovered it was Carolyn's birthday. As the Patersons had found us a house in Adelaide, and the Longhursts one near Angmering, we really were done very proud by all three of our sons' in-laws in 1982, 1983 and 1993, and when it had been our turn in 1985 Rosemary and I, for Janie's wedding, put up lots of Riggs in The Rib, a mediaeval house at the top of our garden belonging to the bishop; I had let it to the cathedral school headmaster, but the wedding was conveniently in the summer holidays, and the HM gladly let us borrow the house.

That memorable 'sample' of grandchildren at Sam's wedding was only the start towards our final tally of fourteen of them, reached with Timothy's birth to Sam and Hannah in 2002. Piers and Carolyn have three; they live near Reading, where Piers is Rector of Arborfield with Barkham, and a considerable figure among evangelicals

---

50. ODA became DFID, the Department for International Development, no longer part of the FCO, in 1997.

in the Oxford diocese and beyond. Julian and Cecily have four; they have just enlarged their home in Wahroonga, in North Sydney. Julian, a trained conservator of furniture, founded (in 1993) and runs International Conservation Services, which tackles conservation of a wide range of artefacts belonging to individuals and national bodies both in Australia and further afield; he is vice-chairman of the council of the National Trust of New South Wales. The family belongs to Christ Church, St Ives, where his older children now help to teach some of the crowd of youngsters who flock there.

Jonathan and Janie, with four children, live in Durham, where Jonathan is a geography professor on the university staff, and Janie (co-author with Jonathan of many travel books) is an artist; they worship in St Nicholas in the City. Sam and Hannah have three, have just completed three years in La Paz, and shortly begin in Mozambique to which Sam has transferred, still in the Department for International Development, and Dr Hannah, after a three months' course on tropical diseases, is again using her medical skills; the family links up with their local interdenominational church wherever they are stationed. It is deeply satisfying to Rosemary and me that all fourteen of our grandchildren are growing up to love and serve God. I often gratefully think of them living their lives very much according to the precepts of the Order of St John: 'Pro Deo et pro utilitate hominum'.

So they are a vital part, these eight adults and fourteen grandchildren, of my 'Forum for the Future', inextricably and wonderfully bound up as they are in my Christian believing. But I also want for the first time in my life to try and set down in writing other contributory factors to the faith I live by. I have read several bishops' autobiographies and often biographies too, outstanding men of the calibre of Michael Ramsey, and also of the generation before mine like William Temple. But little if any space seems to be given to their motivating force, that is their personal faith. These books are full of what they did. 'But what did they believe in?', I have frequently found myself asking. So what do I, someone nowhere near their league in celebrity or scholarship or competence in theology, actually believe in? What, in fact, makes me tick? I think I ought to make as sure as I reasonably can that when, or more probably if, my descendants pick up these pages in fifty years' time, they can glean some kind of picture not only of the people and places and experiences which have made me what I am, but also of the developing faith that went with, or rather very often arose from, what was happening to me, from my mistakes and sadnesses, my pleasures and joys, and from new insights along the way, as I have learnt lessons from family, friends and strangers during these six decades or so of my 'peregrinations':

(i) Without question I must begin with mother's death in 1936. Not least due to wise handling by father, and the amazingly perceptive love by a sister still only eighteen years old, I never had a traumatic period of bereavement. As I have tried to explain much earlier, somehow or other I did not feel 'bereft.' Rather did I sense, in no sort of spooky fashion, that mother was still very much around in spirit; we 'encountered' each other every Sunday in the Communion service. Furthermore, exaggerated as it sounds, but I am glad to repeat it because it is true, I felt we belonged to each other still through the Communion of Saints, and I was beginning to know Christ.

This was not least owing to a letter which I had had from grandfather on my confirmation day eighteen months earlier. In it he suggested that, after I had received the consecrated bread and wine, I put (while still at the altar rail) the fingers of one hand into those of the other ('no one will notice your doing it' was his understanding footnote to a self-conscious schoolboy), and say quietly, looking at the thumb and four fingers of one hand, five words: 'We have with the Father'; and for the other, spell out five letters: 'J e s u s'. This I began to do every Sunday after mother died, having till then mislaid somewhere grandfather's six-page epistle, which had bored me at the time and I had put it away hardly read. The simple action which he suggested started to give me, yes, a worthwhile line to Christ himself: Jesus is there, on ahead with mother as well as being here behind the forms of bread and wine. My clasped hands gradually became my ABC in theology; I loved it. I do it still.

(ii) Fifteen years on there was the revolutionary experience of St Matthew Moorfields, from 1950 to 1953. There I was not throwing away, far from it, my memories of trying to follow Christ before arriving in Bristol, or of abandoning as no good the faith of my forefathers. But I was realizing in the course of that one curacy the limitations of the only public expressions of believing which I knew.

I was able to add to them the sheer excitement of a crowd of people 'taking and blessing and sharing'; and living out the meaning of Acts 2.42: 'they continued steadfastly in the apostles' teaching and fellowship, in the breaking of bread and the prayers'. Christian faith and practice, in other words, stopped being the mainly personal activity I had always reckoned it was, and became what 'the body of Christ' did to renew itself.

I found it immensely attractive. It convinced me that I had done the right thing in being ordained, so that I could pass on at least some of this vital faith to others. I saw under Mervyn's influence that 'the faith once delivered to the saints' encompassed the whole of one's being; of concern for the welfare of others and for the needs of the nations; of a Christian approach to politics and economics; indeed of one's total attitude to life. Every part of it could be brought to the Lord's Table on the Lord's Day, so that one could go out inspired for the superhuman task of trying with God's help to change for the better the world we live in.

(iii) My growing-in-the-faith extended enormously with the World Council of Churches Fourth Assembly at Uppsala in 1968. I was a parish priest getting more and more involved with Christian Aid, through which I was discovering the desparate state of so many of the world's poor. In Sweden that summer I was also grasping for the first time that the very future of our delicately-balanced earth, threatened now as never before in its millions of years of existence, must be a profound concern for the whole of mankind, and certainly not only for us Christians meeting comfortably on a university campus. 'No man comes to the Father except through me' said Jesus (John 14.6), but I have never taken that to prevent, in some way we cannot yet see, the followers of other religions coming after their deaths through Our Lord to the Father's Judgment Seat. Uppsala was the catalyst where I learnt that 'ecumenism' was the encouraging new fact of our time, whereby the churches were discovering how better to operate together for Christ. It is our duty to open the world's eyes so that we may care for the very planet itself; after all *oikoumene* means the whole inhabited earth.

This really hit me in that conference. Twenty-two years on, the Creation Festival which the Wiltshire Wildlife Trust very deliberately mounted under the vault of heaven and in the shadow of Salisbury Cathedral, was also a profoundly Christ-centred occasion;

and in it we were again and again implicitly saying the same thing as Uppsala had, namely that our God is much too small if we ever allow ourselves to arrogate only to baptized Christians the steward-ship of the one earth.

(iv) If my mother's death, St Matthew Moorfields, and Uppsala and the Creation Festival have all been major factors in my faith journey, so also, as I have just described (at some length, unrepent-antly), must the fourth be my marriage and all that has flowed from it in the birth and upbringing of our children, seeing them carve out their own interesting lives, making good marriages and produ-cing such a fascinating crop of grandchildren for Rosemary and me.

(v) Lastly, for the fifth factor, I jump right back to the day of my birth, in that I am what nowadays seems to be called a 'cradle Chris-tian'. Perhaps I have missed the phrase all these years; be that as it may, I am glad to own up to it. Father and mother taught me to pray, they read bible stories to me before snuggling me down in bed, and they always took me to church. I have memories of being cross sometimes over all three, rebelling while my parents pers-evered.

When I went to boarding school, mother wrote me out a small collection of prayers for each day of the week (I still have the note-book, and used some of them for my own children forty years later); and as father knelt beside me for my prayers on the last night before my first term began (when I was eight), he put his hand on my head and said a prayer and a blessing, a practice he kept up long after I had begun praying by myself. I knew that he would slip into my room and do the same thing before big moments, like join-ing the army, or at the end of embarkation leave, or going up to Oxford, or beginning at theological college, or indeed for the last time on the night before I got married. I valued this action of his more and more as the years went by, looking forward to it even. So my parents took infinite trouble about bringing me up as a believer, hoping and praying, I am sure, that gradually other factors would come in to the equation, as they did, to help me make their faith into one of my own. So I gratefully reiterate the five: i) My mother's death, ii) My curacy, iii) Marriage and parenthood, iv) The World Council of Churches Assembly in Sweden and later the Creation Festival, and where it all began, v) Being a cradle Christian. Thank God for the effect on me of those five things.

I must add one more thing about the faith I inherited. Father had suggested before I went back to school a few days after her death that I copy two prayers into that book which mother had begun for me when I had gone to Lambrook. The first was the Collect for All Saints' Day:

> Almighty God who has knit together thine elect in one communion and fellowship in the mystical body of thy son our Christ our Lord, grant us grace so to follow thy blessed saints in all virtuous and godly living that we may come to those unspeakable joys which thou has prepared for all them that unfeignedly love thee, through Jesus Christ our Lord

And the other was the third verse from Bright's communion hymn:

> And then for those our dearest and our best,
> By This prevailing presence we appeal,
> O fold them closer to thy mercy's breast,
> O do thine utmost for their souls' true weal;
> From tainting mischief keep them white and clear,
> And crown thy gifts with strength to persevere.

Using both these regularly, father tentatively suggested, would help keep us all together as a family. He was perfectly right. They also helped to give me the first tentative idea of what the church was: it was people who believed in 'the fellowship' on the one hand and found it real (that collect), and it was also people whose families went on loving each other and belonging together, whether they were in this world or the next (that hymn).

I quickly learnt the lines by heart, and they became so much a part of me that particularly at the altar in the Rugby Memorial Chapel, where Uncle Morris's name was on the Roll of Honour (I mentally added my mother's to it too), both those prayers made 'I believe in the Resurrection of the Dead' true for me from that moment on. Father helped again by writing in the book which he gave me as a Christmas present that year, less than a month after mother died, 'with love from father and mother'; it was a John Buchan, and he did the same with successive books for the next forty years. So I started feeling as a young schoolboy that I already belonged to 'all the whole company of heaven', about which we rejoice in the eucharistic prayer. My mother belonged to it, and so did I; that was on the one hand a huge comfort, but there was also an exhilaration about it, which brought the act of Communion alive, as I have tried to explain in context, earlier in these pages.

All this, though I was quite unaware of it at the time, paved the way for me, as a churchman of the kind who had gone to Matins as his regular service every Sunday at 11 o'clock (with 'early service' as special every now and then), to be more receptive to the big changes of the Parish Communion movement when it reached the Church of England in the 1940s-50s. I was that much more ready because I had come for myself to value, more (I dare to say) than most middle-of-the-road anglicans I knew, the way that the Lord's Supper alongside the Bible (in other words Word and Sacrament together), was opening up for me the 'many-splendoured thing' that is the Christian Faith. Later on, that early confirming of my faith was further formed in countless ways, as a countryman, a soldier in wartime, as a priest and then a bishop, and as a blessedly-happy family man delighting in children and grandchildren.

All this time I have kept on believing in the Church of England. 'I should think so too' the reader may exclaim, 'you have been an ordained minister of it since 1950'. Quite so, but many of my contemporaries, both lay and ordained, have (some with a flourish of trumpets, most just by voting with their feet), lost patience with 'the dear old C of E' for its 'woollyness', its 'anything goes' approach, its refusal to take an immovable line on many issues of doctrine and practice. But for me the four hundred-year-old Elizabethan Settlement, crafted in days like our own of great turmoil in both national and international affairs, has stood the test of time. We have remained a church that knows it must be *semper reformanda*. Undeniable as it is that many (by no means all) pews are emptying at an alarming rate, I do not see signs of God giving up on the Church of England and producing a totally new alternative to what we have, warts and all.

The 2004 paperback *A Mission-shaped Church*, warmly commended by Archbishop Rowan, is every bit as revolutionary, in a very different way, as was John Robinson's (1962) *Honest to God*, which was denounced at first by Michael Ramsey, the archbishop at the time. But being the saint he was he was gracious enough to say publicly later that my childhood friend and theological college tutor had made many Christians think. Out of today's upheavals, God will show their successors in the *Christian Churches Together* what is the way we should go to win souls for him in the 21st century.

I have for some years regarded 'The Grace' (2 Corinthians 13, 14) as encapsulating my believing:

The grace of our Lord Jesus Christ' is supremely seen in the Cross. 'By grace you are saved through faith', says St Paul (Romans 5 passim). 'He died that we might be forgiven', says the hymn-writer, and another puts it: 'May the grace of Christ our Saviour', and 'In the cross of Christ I glory, Towering o'er the wrecks of time'. Christ's grace reaches us in a myriad ways, from Bible and sacrament, through an unexpected kindness from friend or stranger, through someone or something of surprising charm or beauty. The grace of the Risen Christ is 'new every morning'.

'The love of God' for and in his creation opens the way to our learning to love 'whatsoever things are true' (Phil.4.8 et seq.) We reflect God's love in the way we love our families and friends, the way we care for people in need both on our doorstep and across the world. We see it in the wonders of nature and the skills of men and women in thousands of fields. Because of God's creative love I can marvel at a Chopin who could compose his *Preludes*, even as I listen to Rosemary's talent in playing one of them; 'It's Him again' is a prayer of gratitude and praise for God's love which I often use.

'The fellowship of the Holy Spirit' links the church triumphant in heaven with us in the church militant here on earth; Jesus founded the Church to spread his Good News of salvation in the world he came to save, where we see too all round us the Spirit at work in adherents of other religions and none. 'When he the Spirit of Truth is come, he will lead you into all the truth', said Jesus (John 16.13); the Spirit continually 'unpacks' more about Christ. But there is also the echo of that in God 'making all things new' (Rev. 21.5), where 'all' must include the whole of mankind.

Among its priceless treasures, I find that The Grace, (*Amazing Grace*, John Newton) quietly reminds me every time I use it that I am a forgiven sinner, in much the same way that a prayer of Mervyn Stockwood's does, which I have never seen in print. Maybe he wrote it himself; stupidly I never asked him. In those heady 1950s Bristol days, I began to assimilate it and make it my own. It runs:

'O Christ the Master Carpenter, who at the last through wood and nails didst purchase man's whole salvation, wield well thy tools in the workshop of this world, so that we who come rough-hewn to thy bench may be fashioned to a truer beauty by thy hand, through the same Jesus Christ our Lord'.

That is among the best 'non-churchy' prayers I know, and not many weeks pass without my coming back to it. It centres on the person of Christ Himself. It brings in Jesus' humanity, his country upbringing, his hands-on style, his having to do with beautiful things, as well as centring on the crucifixion, out of the pain and agony of which came the opportunity of renewal for every human soul. It worries me not one whit that in this world of space and time we still have to be agnostic about so much; more and more of the origins both of planet earth and of man are being ever more wonderfully revealed to us, but I like the fact that when it comes to God himself we so far only 'see through a glass darkly' (1 Cor.13.12). Everything, one could say, is still to play for; Bible and sacrament, sustaining as they are, constitute just the foretaste of the promised party. As the post-communion collect for All Saints Day in *Common Worship* has it:

'God, the source of all holiness and giver of all good things, may we who have shared at this table as strangers and pilgrims here on earth be welcomed with all your saints to the heavenly feast on the day of your kingdom, through Jesus Christ our Lord.'

'What a lot of fun we had together' came the quiet voice from the bed. It was that of the deeply-spiritual, bible-loving Stuart Blanch, whom I had gone to see in the hospital where he was dying of cancer in 1994. A sister told me when I emerged that it was a long time since she had heard such gales of laughter coming through the door of that side ward where we were praying together. Driving back to Wiltshire, I reflected on how right Stuart was about the fun of serving God, of peregrinating with the Church. The first words of the *Shorter Catechism of the Westminster Assembly* (1647), long a favourite Q and A of mine, leapt into my head:

Q. What is the chief end of man?
A. Man's chief end is to glorify God and enjoy him for ever.

I immensely enjoy God, as I thank him 'for my creation, preservation and all the blessings of this life, but above all for his inestimable love in the redemption of the world by our Lord Jesus Christ, for the means of grace and for the hope of glory.' (From the General Thanksgiving, surely one of *The Book of Common Prayer's* finest gifts to the English-speaking world). Those magnificent words sum up everything that I try to live by in my 'landscape of faith', and they are also my Forum for the Future.

What then of the 'glorify' part in the Church of Scotland's sonorous reply to its own pretty basic question? Our Master praised 'fruits' as doing the best glorifying; James his disciple called them 'deeds'. They, the Bible reminds us, 'glorify God', when 'words' on their own signally fail the test; Christian Aid, you could say, is an essential aspect of worship. But that is not to render 'words' unimportant; if you love someone, you want to express it. For words of love and delight in God, Father, Son and Holy Spirit, I go again and again to the pen of my holiest predecessor in the diocese of Bath & Wells:

> Praise God from whom all blessings flow,
> Praise Him all creatures here below,
> Praise him above, ye heavenly host,
> Praise Father, Son and Holy Ghost. Amen

Thomas Ken 1637-1710

Amen

Index

Cappella Archive provides a mastering service
for the written word. The typeset book
file is stored in a digital archive
and copies are individually
printed to order.